Fabulous Yesterday

Fabulous Yesterday

CORONET'S 25TH ANNIVERSARY ALBUM

EDITED BY LEWIS W. GILLENSON

DESIGNED BY MARTIN ROSENZWEIG

HARPER & BROTHERS   PUBLISHERS   NEW YORK

FABULOUS YESTERDAY

"Diary Of A Wound" from *Thank You, Mr. President* by A. Merriman Smith; copyright
1946 by A. Merriman Smith. Reprinted by permission of Harper & Brothers.

"Backstage With A Martyr", copyright 1940 by Eleanor Copenhaver Anderson.

"Kingdom Of The Night" from *The Last Woods* by Edwin Way Teale, published by
Dodd, Mead & Company; copyright 1945 by Edwin Way Teale.

"Virginia Country Squires" copyright 1938 by Eleanor Copenhaver Anderson.

"Our Changing Premarital Morals" from *Premarital Sexual Standards In America* by
Ira L. Reiss, copyright © 1960 by The Free Press, A Corporation.

"The Invisible Divorce In Every Marriage", © 1959 by Herbert Gold.

"I Remember Fiorello" from *Life With Fiorello* by Ernest Cuneo, copyright 1955 by
Ernest Cuneo.

PHOTO CREDITS
Page xiii, Bob Willoughby from Lee Gross; 29, Sybil Shelton from Monkmeyer; 30-31, Takahiro Ono; 32-33, 35,
36-37, Burt Glinn, Werner Bischof, Ernst Haas from Magnum; 34, Erwin Blumenfeld; 38, Balogh from
European; 39, Martin Iger; 40-41, Charles Trieschmann; 42, Steven Wilson; 43, UPI Photos; 44, Ergy Landau
from Rapho-Guillumette; 45, Camara; 46, Hermann Eisenbeiss; 47, Eberhard Seeliger; 48-49, James Abbe, Sr.;
50, Weegee; 51, Dorothea Lange from Magnum (FSA); 52-53, Kathryn Abbe; 53, right, Herbert Bayer; 54,
U.S. Army Photo; 57, The Bettmann Archive; 74, Andrew St. George; 75, UPI Photos; 79, Wide World; 80,
Wide World, Frank Zagarino, Allyn Baum, Gene Pyle; 89, Orville Andrews from Alpha; 95, Martin Iger;
102, 108, top left, Culver Pictures; 103-107, Carroll Seghers, II; 108, right, Wide World; 109, Wide World; 111,
Peter Bent Brigham Hospital; 121, left, Wide World; 121, right, Farabola from Pictorial Parade; 133,
Wide World; 143, Cornell Capa from Magnum; 164, Princeton University; 197, Karsh from Pix; 203, Larry
Barbier from Globe; 209, P. E. Guerrero; 213, Wide World; 219, Arnold Genthe; 223, Frank Howat from Black
Star; 226-227, Sam Shaw; 229, Sanford Roth from Rapho-Guillumette; 231, NBC-TV; 234, 236-237, Pictorial
Parade; 235, European; 239, L'Europa from Pix; 240, Eve Arnold from Magnum; 241, Jacques Lowe; 242,
Bob Willoughby from Lee Gross; 243, Globe Photos; 244, Patellani from Pix; 245, Eve Arnold from Magnum.

CONTENTS

War and peace

Survival of the spirit

Manners and morals

The cult of personality

Foreword

IN NOVEMBER, 1936, THE PUBLISHERS OF ESQUIRE launched *Coronet* magazine; in October, 1961, they announced that this issue would be its last, thus rounding out exactly 25 years of publication.

Since *Coronet* had a record circulation of 3,200,-000 readers, it is obvious that economics, not lack of popularity, was responsible for this decision. It is obvious, too, that this fact gives us a unique opportunity to cover the complete life of a national magazine from its birth to its last issue in a magnificent, profusely illustrated album worthy of *Coronet*'s quarter century of publishing.

Though its presses grind no more, a magazine, like any mature human being, dies hard. Although its appearance may be suspended, its character, molded by the times in which it functioned, may remain very much alive.

And what a time for publishing was this 25 years—a period of ferment, of change, of endless novelty, all good food for the growing body of any publication. Even a cursory look back tells us that this had to be America's generation of greatest contrast. When did we sink to such economic depression and rise to such affluence when we finally ground our way out of it? When did we suffer such a terrible war and build, via the UN, such a cathedral structure for universal peace? Could we ever have imagined such tyranny as exemplified by the revulsion which the name Hitler connotes? And did we ever really expect to see in our time such an eruptive demand for human sovereignty as we now witness in Africa, where "have not" peoples are finally realizing their destiny?

As we shuffle through the pages of 300 separate issues we observe, with nostalgia and some pardonable pride, that our writers, artists and photographers flew into the turmoil of the generation like pilots flying into the eye of the hurricane to assay its turbulence and chart its course. And when the observer invested his report with the flavor of his personality he rose in stature from artisan to artist.

This kind of journalism was the objective of David Smart, the founder of *Coronet*. He gave the magazine a regal title and subtitled it "Infinite Riches in a Little Room." Until it happened along, no one believed that 5½ by 7⅜ inches of magazine could succeed in doing justice to fine paintings and photographs and in projecting original ideas in words of provocative quality and disciplined quantity. This the little book succeeded in doing. Sinclair Lewis, André Maurois, Bertrand Russell, Arthur Davison Ficke, Richard Tregaskis, Manuel Komroff, Erwin Blumenfeld, Peter De Vries, Margaret Bourke White, and later John Steinbeck, Adlai Stevenson, John F. Kennedy, Robert Frost, Joyce Cary, Meyer Levin, Leon Uris, Jean Kerr and so many, many, more made *Coronet* their forum and their gallery where they mounted ideas which would reach as many as ten million readers every month.

From its inception until its latter days, the magazine kept to a pattern of change. A magazine devoted to the precept that it should lead and not cater to taste, its audience at first was modest. But as our population developed a new sophistication and became emboldened with awareness of its cultural potential, the magazine of "Infinite Riches in a Little Room" provided felicitous accommodation. In its last half-dozen years its editors plunged into areas of hitherto assumed taboos, and gave out strong opinions on such matters as segregation, education, nuclear testing, capital punishment, health insurance, birth control, the Israel-Arab conflict, Castro vs. Batista.

Though these views might have irritated those committed to opposite opinion, it stands as a testimonial to the maturity of the audience, even more than the editors, that the letters to the editor seldom were censorious.

The generation has gone; the magazine has gone with it. But history teaches us that the dynamic events of one day must certainly influence the events of another day, as a stone dropped in the water sends out ripples which reach shores however distant. And the ideas fused into this one magazine will certainly find expression in some form, altered or intact, in another journalistic venture. So it is with this, as with all magazines. Living things they are, and as living things they must die. But if life has a continuity of purpose and the grave is not the final end, then the spirit of this magazine must survive.

We hope this volume will help to keep alive the *Coronet* image. It was not really designed as an anthology in the formal sense. Much of the best which appeared in the magazine appears here. But much also which was superior was regretfully pre-empted when it did not fall into the theme of the volume: a reflection of our Fabulous Yesterday, an exciting generation of contrast.

We hope that our selections and commentary blend the image of the period with the image of the magazine. In editing the volume we found it almost impossible to separate one from the other. If you feel similarly as you peruse it, then we will have chosen well and will have some satisfaction in knowing that we contributed a small artifact to the archives of the years 1936–1961.

LEWIS W. GILLENSON, editor of *Coronet*, 1955-1961

A postscript

Four talented and dedicated people helped to prepare this volume: editors Donald Allan and Richard Kaplan, picture editor Philip Doyle and art director Martin Rosenzweig. Without them it could not have evolved as it now is, if indeed it could have been possible at all. My deepest thanks to them.
LWG

The
art
of
living

This was a period when men ventured tentatively into remote caves of mystery and emerged with more answers than they knew what to do with. Science uncovered new ways to control nature—ostensibly for human betterment. Genius was channeled into better and bigger laboratories; electronic microscopes and huge telescopes insinuated themselves into the hitherto unseeable to give answers and postulate new questions for still bigger answers.

A new breed of scientists shot rockets into the air which circled the earth in minutes, and perfected devices which would convert outer space into earth's limitless back yard. Astronauts prepared for life in space, just as the first "fish with legs" eons ago painfully crawled from the primeval seas onto the untested land. Research biologists hovered on the brink of an electrochemical discovery of manufacturing life itself. From the laboratories came automation, longer life, undreamed-of comforts and unexpected problems.

Yet, sadly, even this wonder generation could not produce the genius who could develop a microscope to search the soul of man, a telescope to clarify his views of the future, or a laboratory to unlock the secrets of his fears, torments and insecurities. The flowering of our new science only served to bring our human failings into sharper focus.

We searched for balance and, at moments, found it, as in ages past, in the collective experience of those whom life has made wise: a witty P. G. Wodehouse who refuses to permit outside circumstance to dampen his light heart; a caustic Sinclair Lewis who poked a finger into the potbelly of bathos; a realistic Mary Ellen Chase who, early in life, learned the meaning of common sense and never lost the lesson. They saw, in different ways, what scientist-novelist C. P. Snow calls the tragic gap of language, concept and purpose between the world of scientific creation and the world of spiritual fulfillment. And, from their understanding, they wrote the words which might help others to understand better—and to make living an art.

In the midst of events and crises which demand the loftiest of purposes and creativity, society will always play generous host to the manufacturer of a better mouse trap.
The quiet, keyhole good sense of Martin Panzer made his article one of the most quoted of 1953 and beyond.

The Best Way to Spend $100

BY MARTIN PANZER

THE WORLD SEEMS TO BE FULL OF MEN AND WOMEN who go through life in a state of almost constant annoyance at trivial things and happenings. Somehow, they feel that life is conspiring against them by throwing in their path little obstacles that rob the day, and often the night, of joy, happiness and peace of mind.

What kinds of obstacles? Well, take the case of Larry Stevens, a typical American husband, who undergoes an endless series of irritating ordeals because of a weakness in his plan for living. Let's start with him on a Monday morning and follow him through a day of self-inflicted annoyances.

From his first conscious moment on arising, he is aware that something unpleasant looms ahead. It is his daily shave, and it is going to be an unhappy chore because he likes to get as many shaves as possible out of each blade. Today will be the ninth shave for this particular blade. Which means that his skin will be chafed and nicked—an harassment that will stay with him all day long.

After his shave, Larry experiences another irritation. His shoelace snaps and he doesn't have an extra pair in the house. Since he has neglected to have his other shoes shined, he solves the problem inadequately by tying a knot in the broken lace. The chances are that he will be self-conscious about this, too, for the rest of the day.

He manages to get to the office on time, but some-how he doesn't feel happy about it—or about anything else, for that matter. The irritations of the early morning are carrying over.

By lunchtime, however, he feels a little more cheerful. He is hungry and looks forward to the pleasure of a good, relaxing meal. Unfortunately it is raining, and because he doesn't want to get his suit wet and wrinkled, he stands under a store awning downstairs, waiting for the rain to let up.

By the time he feels safe to venture out, there are only fifteen minutes of the lunch period left. By this time he is so nervous and upset that he is no longer hungry. He races to the drugstore, grabs a sandwich, swallows it in chunks, and gulps his coffee. By three o'clock, he will have heartburn.

Now oddly enough, while Larry was gulping his coffee, his wife Gladys was taking an aspirin to alleviate a splitting headache, resulting from the fact that nothing had gone right that morning. Larry had squeezed the last bit of toothpaste out of the tube. Her last pair of nylons had been spoiled by a run when she put them on.

When she started the toaster for lunch, the fuse blew and she didn't have another on hand. Either she would have to run out and buy one, or they would be without lights that evening. Meanwhile, food in the refrigerator would spoil.

Why do people make themselves so unhappy so often, and for such trivial reasons? Because it has never occurred to them that for a trifling sum—say, $100 a year—they can change their whole mode of living. They have never stopped to think that for a few cents a day, they can find more contentment and peace in life than are enjoyed by those who spend fortunes on traditional forms of luxury.

If Larry Stevens had planned his life properly, how different that Monday might have been for him and his wife! He knew that he could count on two perfect shaves in his favorite double-edged blade—the first one on each edge. At a cost of about 2½ cents a day, or only $9 a year, Larry could have had a smooth and painless shave every morning.

The annoyance caused by the snapped shoelace might also have been avoided. For a dollar, Larry could have bought enough shoelaces to last him for several years and put them in his bureau drawer. Instead of being unpleasantly upset, he would have derived a sense of gratification from his foresight, and his whole day would have been more enjoyable.

For a few dollars, Larry could have had an extra umbrella to keep at the office. Pro-rated over four years (the average life of an umbrella), it would have cost about a dollar a year for the extra protection. But suppose it might happen that on occasion, both umbrellas would be left at home?

Why not walk calmly out into the rain without an umbrella? Perhaps the rain *would* wrinkle his suit and make it necessary for him to get an extra pressing at a cost of about forty cents. If it happened ten times a year, it would cost him four dollars extra. But how much annoyance he would be spared, how much anxiety he might avoid!

As for Gladys, what would it have cost to have a pleasant morning instead of one that ended with a headache? Practically nothing. She had to buy stockings and toothpaste and fuses, anyhow. Instead of buying these necessities one at a time, she could buy them five at a time. Five tubes of toothpaste meant an investment of about two dollars; five pairs of stockings, about seven dollars; five fuses, thirty cents.

For this modest expenditure, she would experience a sense of luxury and satisfaction every time she needed one of these items. What is more important, there would be an indirect improvement in her relationship with Larry. No matter how hard she tried to be objective, she was bound to feel some slight resentment against Larry when she found that he had used the last of the toothpaste. This and other annoyances might very well carry over into her subconscious, and make her greeting less cordial on his return from the office.

There cannot, of course, be any definitive statistics on happiness and unhappiness. It is probably safe to say, though, that bereavements, illnesses, financial reverses, disappointments in love and other such major misfortunes account for the deepest unhappiness, while endless little annoyances and frustrations account for the most frequent unhappiness.

Petty annoyances are like drops of water: they can wear away anything they touch—the hardest rocks or the toughest nerves. If you cut by half the number of drops that fall on a stone, you double the time required to wear away the stone. By the same token, if you cut by half the number of petty annoyances in your life, you save and spare by that much your mind and your body.

Why not, then, start today to reduce the number of little nuisances in your life, especially since the cost is so low? For about $100 a year, you can use a brighter bulb for reading and have extra bulbs handy when old ones burn out; you can have enough shirts so that you won't always be racing between the laundry and your last clean shirt; you can have a dozen extra bars of soap and a dozen extra packs of tissue always handy; you can have twenty-five four-cent stamps available so you won't be stuck when you have to get your letter out in a hurry; you can install a telephone extension in another room or even on another floor so you won't always have to run to answer the telephone or to have privacy for conversations when you desire it; you can have three clocks in the house instead of one; you can have an extra pen and a dozen pencils and a dozen blotters available for the moments they are needed; you can have a carton of fifty match books in a drawer so you'll have a light when you want it.

You can also have a hundred bobby pins, a dozen needles, a thousand pins, a dozen spools of thread, a hundred buttons, three bottle openers, an extra ice-cube container, two spare pocket combs, extra iodine, bandage, cotton and other first-aid items; you can have a hammer and a pair of pliers and a screw driver and some nails and tacks and picture wire, so you can do odd jobs around the house with-out calling in a carpenter; you can have enough hangers in your guest closet so you won't be annoyed every time you have a few more guests than usual; you can have spare cuff links so you won't be late to the office because you have to look for your only pair, which has been mislaid.

Why not try this new idea for happy living? Add to the list if you want—and think how each little item will insure more serenity and comfort, and how all of them together will revolutionize your life —make you a better, less tense, more tolerant and happier person. It may even give you so much more zest for living and doing that it will pay dividends in actual cash.

When you feel good, you do everything better. And when you do everything better, you naturally make more money. It might even happen that $100 spent to eliminate petty annoyances from your life will bring a cash profit greater than any you have ever made before.

Isn't the investment small enough to make the risk well worth taking?

♛ March, 1953.

In 1937 author Manuel Komroff predicted for America a postwar cultural renaissance. The war ended and the predicted rebirth arrived. But like all movements, it went to extremes, inundating us with babies, split-level houses and the deadly conformity of suburbia. Here, the writer of the best-selling book, **The Crack in the Picture Window** examined these new phenomena, and delivered a satirical broadside against their excesses.

Anyone for Elegance?

BY JOHN KEATS

IN SUBURBIA, WHERE SO MANY AMERICANS LIVE THESE days, "modern, casual living" is stone cold dead. No longer must you be sloppy. The new way to show that you're really moving with the time is to become an inconspicuous consumer of elegance—for elegance is the momentary word in suburban fashion, food, household furnishings, entertainment and recreation.

To see just what's going on, let's visit people we'll call Fran and Nick Baxter. They live with their three kids in a brick rambler on Apple Drive in one of Virginia's sprawling housing developments across the Potomac from Washington.

Nick and Fran have always been taste-setters. They have never been quite the first to try the new. Yet they have always been among those who first carry any taste to its best example, thus inspiring everyone else to further efforts. They came to Apple Drive from Illinois, together with a load of somewhat gloomy furniture of no particular description. Fran was rather nowhere herself, with hair severely parted on one side, then curled up around her ears. She wore cotton house dresses; Nick drove a matter-of-fact Chevrolet. The kids wore cotton shirts and corduroy trousers. In short, the family came right out of a Norman Rockwell-type painting of happy home life in a Midwestern town.

During their first year on Apple Drive—1949—Fran paid close attention to her new surroundings. Everywhere, she saw women wearing blue jeans and shirts to clean house and go to market. She saw the Picasso prints on the walls, the sling and bucket chairs, the low coffee tables made of old doors, the cute window drapes made of mattress ticking, the bookshelves of bricks and blond wood planks.

Husbands "did-it-themselves"; families cooked out in back yards and engaged in block parties. When people entertained indoors, everyone enjoyed casseroles set out buffet-style (because the parties were always large and there are no dining rooms in Apple Drive ramblers) and the hostesses wore fancied-up tight trousers and sat on the solid-color rugs. Brain-numbing Martinis were served by the gallon. Modern, casual living was the style, so Fran opened her first charge accounts and got with it.

Out went the nondescript furniture. In came the Hardoy, Saarinen, Eames and Herman Miller chairs. Fran paid $250 for her Saarinen. Picasso's blue period went up over the fireplace. Fran hacked off her hair, curling what was left of it *under* her ears; tossed out the house dresses and went in for Ship 'n' Shore blouses and blue jeans. The kids wore cotton shirts, sweaters and jeans. Nick bought

the second station wagon to appear on Apple Drive, and Fran gave him a swatch of power tools for Christmas. Nick made a coffee table out of the cellar door of a deserted 18th-century farmhouse.

Fran's bookcase was built of *glass* bricks and *bleached-oak* planks; hers were the third driftwood lamps in the neighborhood, but hers were the *first* wall-to-wall single color rugs. The Baxters' Martinis became drier than anybody's, and in no time at all, the first metamorphosis was complete.

The Baxters did not, however, look like all their neighbors in all things. They looked—in George Orwell's words—"more equal" than anybody, because they brought casual living to its fullest bloom. Best of all, the modern things looked just right in Fran's new house.

Today, you'd never know Apple Drive. Another transformation is taking place, and the Baxters are doing a little better at the job than their neighbors.

Gone is Fran's white Arzberg china, replaced by an English pattern. Her flat silver is no longer Scandinavian stainless steel but traditional Chantilly in sterling. Picasso has given way to a classical still life. The driftwood lamps have vanished; tall, rococo table lamps with big, tubular shades, ruffled at the edges, have taken their places.

Nick doesn't "do-it-himself" any more, and the ashes in the outdoor fireplace are cold and dead. Fran's hair is long again, this time with a gentle wave to her shoulders. She wears a housecoat for breakfast and to clean house; sweater and skirt in the yard; a suit to the supermarket, and a long dress at dinner. The children dress in Viyella shirts and Ivy-cut khakis.

The Baxters no longer pitch big buffets, but small supper parties featuring wines and roasts, ending with cheese and brandy. The white walls and the raspberry ceilings have been done over into off-white ceilings and a kind of folksy, homey wallpaper featuring early Americana. Despite the still-brisk sale of car coats, Fran's coat is long.

Foreign cars being the vogue, Nick's station wagon has been replaced—not by a Volkswagen, but by a Volvo or Simca. A chandelier now hangs from the living-room ceiling, and that expensive Saarinen chair has been disposed of, along with all the other slings, baskets and buckets.

Long, single-color drapes replace the sequined mattress ticking that once looked so clever. Floor-to-ceiling bookcases have been built; the new furniture is all Italian and French Provincial; the wall-to-wall rugs are gone and dark-stained floors now show around the edges of the bright Orientals.

Perhaps the most dramatic change—to one who knew the Baxters when—is that the Martini has disappeared from their lives as though it had finally dried up altogether. The Baxters now serve Vermouth Cassis. Indeed, the only thing Nick and Fran have carried over from their days of "casual living" has been their habit of buying everything on time.

Finally, the Baxters are planning to move—but not to a split-level. They're looking for an older house in the city; will settle for a two-story colonial

in one of the closer-in, longer-established suburbs.

As with the Baxters, so with their neighbors. One wonders why.

Unfortunately, the Baxters aren't the kind of people who could, or would tell you why, but their next-door neighbors, whom we'll call the Howards, were glad to explain.

"Well," Sarah Howard said, stubbing out a king-size filter cigarette and picking up *her* Vermouth Cassis, "I guess we just got tired of being slobs."

"But you never really looked like slobs."

"We got to feeling we were," Mrs. Howard murmured. "Anyway, I guess we all thought it was time we grew up. We're all making more money."

(Apple Drive families in 1949 earned between $4,000 and $5,500; today, between $6,200 and $8,500. Most American suburbanites earn between $4,000 and $7,500. Apple Drive is a fairly fancy, but not very fancy development.)

"All the kids are in school now; they're not only out of the house most of the day, but they're big enough to know not to put their feet on the couch. Let's just say we got to feeling it was more ladylike to wear a housecoat in the morning than to go around in blue jeans with our shirt tails hanging out."

But the neighborhood parties? Why did they vanish from Apple Drive?

"Look," Sarah Howard said. "Let's not kid ourselves. Block parties were *boring*. Besides, the neighborhood is changing. You don't know all the people on the block any more, so you aren't buddy-buddy with them as we were in the beginning when we were all politicking like crazy to get storm drains put in."

Growing up, as Sarah put it, might be one explanation; perhaps the best. For instance, as recently as last year, *The Nation* was able to report that people spent time, money and effort quite uselessly in the pleasurable business of inflating their egos— they spent simply to show that they could.

Apple Drive was guilty of this to some extent, buying high-fidelity recordings of the voices of frogs in a New York State swamp in order to ooh and aah over woofers and tweeters—as though the machine was a good thing in itself, a proof of affluence and discrimination.

This is no longer the case; for despite Apple Drive's heavy spending, the thrust toward elegance is characterized by a search for value. If the hi-fi set is encased in Italian Provincial, it at least produces Wanda Landowska's harpsichord instead of the mating calls of up-state batrachians, and nobody chatters knowingly about woofers.

Perhaps nothing better illustrates the trend toward elegance than a recent party:

Fran Baxter and her neighbor, Sarah Howard, are still friends with a former Apple Driver who moved to a large, older house in Washington. The three ladies decided to pitch a party in this house. It would be black-tie—Apple Drive is not yet in the white-tie class. Everyone was to bring his own bottle—of champagne! A butler (hired by the three hostesses for the evening) iced the bottles and served

them. A maid (hired for the evening) took the coats and tidied up. A four-piece orchestra (also doing a one-night stand) provided the waltzes. And Apple Drivers past and present danced the night away and sipped champagne in evening clothes!

This many-sided change in taste has brought about a change in manners. In 1949 there was much back-slapping and double hand-shaking; ladies were always swirling in and out of one another's houses for coffee breaks—uninvited but hardly unexpected. In 1956, everyone was a little older, and given, now, to kissing each other when meeting socially. In 1959, however, everyone seems more grown up than in 1956; a gentle embrace replaces the kiss; we hear the dulcet accents of the soft sell. The consumption is deliberately inconspicuous.

Department store buyers confirm the trend to elegance. I have no intention of burdening you with dull statistics, but let me cite one numerical example. It is just as revealing of changing purchasing patterns as the bring-your-own-champagne party is revealing of changing taste in casual entertainment.

An electrical-appliance store in Apple Drive's nearest shopping center has sold one thousand cut-glass chandeliers so far this year. Two years ago, it sold *none*.

No matter what you think of Apple Drive's neighbors changing their lives much as a woman might change hats, no matter what reasons you may wish to discover for the phenomenon, the fact is that a trend toward elegance *is* underway on Apple Drive.

It probably won't last. In fact, Apple Drive is nearly ready for yet another change. For it is historically true that the final realization of an art form is the end of it; when people like Fran and Nick—never the leaders, but always the exponents—take up Vermouth Cassis drinking, someone else is already bored and is hitting out for undiscovered territory. (For instance, Apple Drive's drinking habits eventually filter down to Apple Drive from Madison Avenue; and up and down Madison Avenue, people are already saying, "Never mind the Cassis bit, let's just have the Vermouth." Next year, Nick and Fran will be saying this too.)

Meanwhile, if you live on one of America's Apple Drives, and/or would like to join in the current gaiety, here follows a rough reference guide.

You're Elegant if you:

• Have small rugs that permit you to show off the wood of your floors; these rugs may be beige, or Oriental—real or domestic.

• Use candles to light your living room at party time. Best are scented, dripless candles.

• Read *The Affluent Society*. It is considered even more elegant to be able to understand it.

• Follow Fran's changes of clothes. Subdued colors, please—high fashion is NOT Elegant, but garish. For men, Ivy is still in, but not too poisonous an Ivy. Some men need shoulder padding, slightly more hat brim. Clothes should look "sensible."

• Use patterned china. English rose is Elegant.

• Change to French and Italian Provincial chairs, furnishings. Both styles are comfortable, traditional. French Provincial has warmth of curves; Italian consists of graceful rectilinear lines. It is Most Elegant to have two or more Elegant styles in the same room.

• Put valences across your picture window. Drapes must pull together by means of draw strings: reach the floor; may be ruffled. Plain colors. A favorite is electric blue.

• Say that modernistic houses and furnishings are "cold." An even More Elegant epithet is "sterile." (Only a clod says they are "uncomfortable" even if this is the most accurate description.)

• Go to the concert instead of the movies.

• Entertain in tiny groups. Most Elegant are black-tie suppers for four. At such times, caviar with sour cream and chopped onion is Elegant. But it's More Elegant to serve salmon eggs with the same dressing, because this shows you (a) know the taste is just as good, if not better and (b) that it costs far less to achieve the same value, and thus shows thoughtful discrimination, lack of fear of conformity, etc.

• Drive a foreign car, even if you have ten kids and need a station wagon. (Everyone knows you can afford a station wagon, but station wagons aren't Elegant any more. A foreign car implies you have a sense of values; it suggests you're not spending much for transportation because you're sinking the dough on a trip to Europe or a summer place.)

• Say that you're antisocial, that there's no real reason to have "to get along with everyone."

• Discover "good" American wines and cheeses.

- Hang old gold watches on dark green walls. (Severe, dark etchings and tiny landscapes in three shades of dark brown are also quite Elegant. They're so bad that everyone supposes they're originals by some famous artist.)
- Join an amateur theatrical group.

On the other hand, you're Dead if you:

- Serve clam dip with Martinis. (You're also Dead if you serve Bloody Marys, Screwdrivers—and Very Dead if you serve Bull Shots. All that was *last* year's last gasp.)
- Ladies, wear blue jeans, fancy pants, open-toed or gimmicky shoes, sacks, chemises. Men are Dead if they still wear duffel coats. Rigor mortis is setting in if you still buy suburban coats. ALL coats are *long*, if they're Elegant.
- Drive a big, overchromed car. (So it's comfortable, but is it Elegant?)
- Have wall-to-wall carpets. (This means your floor is a splintery mess.)
- Still have brick-and-plank bookcases. (Grow up, chum, we're out of Bohemia now.)
- Smoke "real" cigarettes.
- Go to square dances. (They may be fun, but they're for squares. They're surely not Elegant.)
- Say "that's for sure."
- Do-it-yourself. (It is Elegant to understand, at last, that almost anyone else can do it better, and in many cases, cheaper. At any rate, it's Elegant to be able to say somebody did it for you.)
- Serve barbecued chicken at your outdoor fireplace, meanwhile wearing a funny apron and claiming to have made the sauce yourself. (1952 was so long ago.)
- These lists of the Elegant and the Dead are by no means complete, but they do illustrate ways in which Apple Drive currently separates the chic from the gauche. Anything you can do or acquire which trends in the general direction of the life and manners of the Hapsburg Empire is welcome on Apple Drive today, and you are cordially invited to use your imagination to take it (or leave it) from here. At the moment, we have Elegance.

A Vermouth Cassis, anyone?

I mean, while it lasts?

♛ March, 1959.

A man whose name is synonymous with Anglo-Saxon humor, P. G. Wodehouse proved that even forced confinement within occupied France during the war could shake neither his wit nor his gaiety. In the early Twenties he wrote a score of musical comedies and the lyrics of one of the tenderest songs ever written, "My Bill." The following piece might indicate why the Old Party is constitutionally incapable of dullness—a welcome tonic for a generation never without need of the lift of laughter.

Over Seventy

BY P. G. WODEHOUSE

A LETTER HAS JUST REACHED MY DESK FROM THE DESK of Mr. J. P. Winkler. He writes:

Dear Mr. Wodehouse:
For some time we have been presenting in newspapers and on radio a feature entitled "Over Seventy," which includes expressions on living by those who have passed their seventieth year. You have been doing much these last fifty years, perhaps you can tell us something about it. . . .

That piques me a little, that "fifty years." What do you think I was doing before then, Winkler? Loafing? Gad, sir, I was the talk of London when I was in my early twenties.

Those were the days when, if you had not seen me in my frock coat, top hat, varnished boots and spats setting out to pay what were termed morning calls, it was pretty generally admitted that you had not seen anything. And I used to ride down the Strand on my bicycle to the offices of the *Globe* newspaper, where I was at that time employed, frequently using no hands. Long before fifty years ago I was leaving footprints on the sands of time, and good large footprints, too.

However, I get the idea, J. P. You want to start the old gaffer yarning away at the fireside in the hope that something will emerge which you can use in newspapers and on radio without any of that sordid business of paying for it. Right ho! Let's see what we can dig up.

What changes, you ask, do I notice principally in my daily life now? Well, for one thing, I find that the attitude of taxi drivers toward me has altered. Where before, after nearly running me down, they

used to lean out sideways and shout, "You silly fool," they now say, "You silly old fool." Shows the passage of time, that, Winkler.

For another thing, I find myself getting more and more out of touch with modern novels. Their authors seem to have such extraordinary ideas about age. "He was a man not far from fifty, but still erect and able to walk across the room under his own steam," they write. Or: "Old though the Colonel was, his forty-seven years sat lightly upon him." I have reached the stage nowadays that, when picking up a novel and seeing that a new character the author has introduced is sixty-eight, I say to myself, "Ah, the young love interest."

In real life, I must confess, I tend to become a little impatient with these kids of sixty-eight—noisy young brutes with their space helmets and their toy atom-ray pistols rushing about all over the place yelling at one another. Want their backsides smacked, if you ask me.

But probably you are referring to physical changes, J. P. Some of these are very marked. I still do my daily dozen before breakfast, but it is an open secret that I can no longer touch my toes. And, as the years go by, I find that I tend to become bulkier. I do not look like Jackie Gleason, but I have lost that streamlined slenderness which once used to make so many people come up to me on the street and ask for my autograph, thinking I was Fred Astaire.

It is one of the mysteries of life (Ah, Sweet Mystery of Life—Victor Herbert) that foods one could eat pounds of in one's youth without any spreading of the waistline cause the old codger—as I was referred to in a review of my latest book (*America, I Like You*—Simon and Schuster—at all bookstores)—to bulge in every direction. Unless, of course, he is a corpse in a detective story.

I think that if I had my life to live over again I would be a corpse in a detective story, for they always seem to do themselves so extraordinarily well without ever putting on extra weight. "I have concluded my autopsy," says the medical examiner, "and the contents of Sir Reginald's stomach are as follows: Caviar Frais, Consommé aux Pommes d'Amour, Sylphides à la crème Ecrevisses, Points d'asperges à la Tallulah Bankhead, Suprême de Fois Gras au Champagne, Délices Strasbourg, Friandises, Diablotins, Corbeille de Fruits Exotiques," and, of course, about half a pound of cyanide.

And in Chapter One, Sir Reginald is described as a stern, gaunt old man with the slender lines and the lean, race horse slimness of the Witherington-Delancys. It looks as though it were the

cyanide that did the trick.

As a result of this bulk, and a certain stiffness in the joints, I am finding it more and more difficult to catch the cat at night. This cat is a stray who clocked in one evening and insisted on being added to the household. We let her out at about ten o'clock for a breath of air, and once out she hears the call of the old wild life and decides to make a night of it. This means that, unless caught and returned to store, she will hit the high spots till five in the morning, when she will come and mew at one's bedroom window, murdering sleep.

When you are in the middle seventies you have passed your peak as a cat-catcher. There was a time—say between 1904 and 1910—when it would have been child's play to outstrip the fleetest cat, but now, as I say, the joints have stiffened somewhat and the old footwork has gone back on me. The thing usually ends in a bitter, "All right, *stay* out," from me and a quiet smile from the cat as she glides into the bushes. And then the reproachful mew outside my window with the clock striking five. There seems no way of beating the game.

Still, life is not all catching cats and, anyway, things have brightened a good deal lately owing to our cat having been bitten in the foot by another cat—no doubt in some night-club brawl—and being able to operate only on three legs. One more such episode and the thing, as I see it, will be in the bag. I may not be the sprinter I once was, but I feel confident of being able to outsmart a cat walking on only two legs.

Do I have a regimen for keeping fit? Why, yes. As I say, I catch cats, or, at any rate, try to catch cats, which gives me all the exercise I need in order to remain in good fettle. And apart from the running, there is the falling. Owing to the hurricanes of the year before last most of the trees on the estate are shored up with wires and there is, as any doctor will tell you, nothing better for the liver than to trip over one of these when going all out. It amuses the cat, too.

We septuagenarians have to watch our health like hawks, and in pursuance of this aim I make a practice of smoking all day and far into the night. Smoking toughens and fortifies the system. Tolstoy said it didn't, and where is Tolstoy now?

I think that about cleans the thing up, J. P., does it not? What you were trying to say in that letter of yours, I imagine, was, "Hello there, Wodehouse, how *are* you?" My reply is that I am fine. All the same, a letter like yours does rather make one realize that one is not the bright-eyed youngster one has been considering oneself. A rude awakening, you might call it, and one that must have come to my house-master at school (who recently died at the age of ninety-six) when he said to a new boy on the first day of the term: "Wapshott? Wapshott? That name seems familiar. Wasn't your father in my class?"

"Yes, sir," replied the stripling. "*And* my grandfather."

W January, 1957.

The art of gamesmanship developed its vogue after the last war with the famed books by Stephen Potter. Yet back in 1937, CORONET had launched a series on how to talk horses, politics, gourmet lingo and the like. One of the most delightful, Frank Schoonmaker's advice on wine chatter, is as timely now as it was then; read carefully and with a verbal swipe you'll plonk your adversary.

How to Talk Wines

BY FRANK SCHOONMAKER

THE BEST WAY TO TALK ABOUT A SUBJECT, PARticularly an unfamiliar subject, is to ask questions. I mean, let me add, the right questions.

It is fairly safe to assume that a wine expert sitting next to you at dinner knows more about wine than you do. And please remember that there are, along the wine trail, a thousand pitfalls lying in wait for the unwary. Even G. B. Stern, whose *Bouquet* is one of the best books on wine ever written by a woman, pulled a classic boner by mentioning Chateau Cheval Blanc as a white Bordeaux ("Blanc" means white all right, but "Chateau White Horse" is a red wine). You, who probably know a lot less about wine than G. B. Stern, have a better than even chance of putting your foot in it if you decide to put your best foot forward. The most you can hope for is to make the connoisseur sitting beside you realize that you are intelligent, that you know something about wine, that you would like to know more, that you appreciate the fact that he knows more than you do.

Avoid, above all, the dogmatic statement. If you say that you prefer Sparkling Burgundy to champagne, your neighbor is likely to counter with a highly embarrassing "Why?" And if you mention the fact that you don't like Rhine wines because they are too sour, it's at least possible that you will get, in return, "Then I suppose you have never tasted a *Trockenbeerenauslese* from the Rheinpfalz?" —and what you will answer, I'm sure I don't know, for the *Trockenbeerenauslese* from the Rheinpfalz are among the sweetest natural wines in the world.

Try to make the wine expert feel that you take advantage of every chance you have. Say, for example, "Isn't it too bad that it's so hard to get decent-size wineglasses, I mean eight-ounce wine glasses, in this country? A beginner can't get any bouquet out of these thimbles."

Or "Why must everyone wrap up wine bottles in napkins? I suppose you can always tell just what you're drinking (he can't, but he would just as soon you thought he could), but how about the rest of us? I'd like to see the label, and know."

Ask, whenever possible, questions that provoke a couple of minutes of monologue.

"Do you think the wines we're getting from California are as good as the ones they made before the war?"

"Do you really think that one cocktail—naturally I don't mean four—makes it impossible to appreciate wine with dinner?"

Say as little as possible about wines you have never tasted. Don't depend on secondhand information, on the fact that a friend told you that the "vin du pays" in the village near Tours where he spent a month in 1917 was better than Chateau d'Yquem and cost fifty centimes a liter drawn from the cask, or on the fact that you read somewhere that no Chateauneuf-du-Pape was fit to drink until it was ten years old.

When you are on familiar ground and perfectly sure of your footing, be frank about what you like, even if you know you're not supposed to like it. Say, "Well, I'm a heathen, I admit. I just don't like claret." Or, "You know, I *like* a sweet white wine with turkey. Of course one's not supposed to, but what can you expect of a person brought up on cranberry jelly?"

The foregoing is, obviously, pretty elementary. And with only this at your disposal you will, beyond any question, run out of ammunition if you have to hold up your end against a wine expert for more than a quarter of an hour. If the conversation gets more abstruse, here are a few things that you shouldn't say:

1. Don't say that wine doesn't agree with you because it is too acid, and that you are forced, in general, to stick to Scotch and soda for that reason. There are at least a hundred million healthy, happy, normal people in the world who drink wine twice a day, and if you happen to have an eccentric digestion, there is no use being forthright about it.

2. Don't say you like sauternes. It will brand you inevitably as a beginner. Say, if you will, "I sometimes wonder why we ate melons during Prohibition; a glass of sauternes with a cantaloupe makes *such* a difference." The remark "I like sauternes" is, in other words, about as impressive to the expert as the statement "I like tomato ketchup."

3. Don't say you like Liebfraumilch. According to German law, any blend of Rhine wines can be called Liebfraumilch, and the blend may be good, bad, or indifferent.

4. Don't say you like Sparkling Burgundy. That,

today, is the mark of the country cousin.

5. Don't say you like champagne cocktails. It is extremely chic to drink a glass of champagne instead of a cocktail, but champagne cocktails are not chic. If the wine is good, you have no business putting sugar and bitters in it; if the wine is bad, you don't drink it or offer it to your guests.

6. Don't insist that you like only very dry wines unless you do, and unless you have the knowledge to back it up. Such a statement is generally the hallmark of a snob, and your true wine expert, although he may vastly prefer dry wines to sweet, will always speak of the fine sweet wines of the world with a certain deference. It is quite in order to say that you don't like sweet Sherry before a meal, or any sweet wine served straight through a dinner. If you go farther, you are on dangerous ground.

7. When Burgundy is mentioned, don't, for heaven's sake, talk about Pommard or even Chambertin, unless you mention a specific Pommard (or Chambertin) of a given year. The Pommards, Chambertins and Chablis are the Joneses, Browns and Smiths of the Burgundy family. There are eminent individuals of that name, but everyone knows some Mr. Jones or other.

8. Don't turn up your nose at domestic wines. It is unquestionably true that a lot of domestic wines, these days, are bad, but your true wine lover expects to live to see the day when the wines of California and New York and Ohio will be far and away the best buys on a wine merchant's shelves. If you want to make the connoisseur sitting next to you come out with his pencil and notebook, mention a brand of domestic wine that you have found consistently good for a year or eighteen months.

9. Don't sneer at homemade wines. The people who made wine at home during Prohibition were the real wine lovers—the people who wanted wine and were unwilling to do without it. If you ever tried to make wine yourself, mention the fact—your wine may have been undrinkable, but watch the expert's eyes light up when you say you tried.

10. Don't say you have no use for any wine except the best. A real connoisseur has just as much respect for an unpretentious, decent, honest table wine, as he has for a rare vintage claret. An honest workman is, when all is said and done, just as worthy of praise as a great aristocrat, and doubly so if the aristocrat is not all he might be.

So far, you will probably say, so good. By avoiding such obvious pitfalls you will make no errors, but "no hits, no runs, no errors" never won a ball game nor made a friend. You can keep out of trouble, sitting beside a wine expert, by talking about archaeology or detective stories. But you will get nowhere on wine. So here are a few things you may say you like, remembering always that any such remark, if you don't know what you're talking about, may leave you out on a limb.

Say that you like dry sherry, really dry sherry, and like it *chilled*. Don't please mention "Dry Sack" as a dry sherry, for it is a fairly sweet Amoroso.

Be careful of the word Amontillado, which is rather loosely used in English-speaking countries. "Manzanilla, *chilled*," is an Open Sesame.

Say that you prefer, in a great many cases, young wines to old. There has been far too much talk since Repeal of antediluvian vintages. A great many wines, particularly less expensive wines, such as most of us drink on most occasions, are at their best when under five years old. Real wine drinkers know this, and only snobs are afraid to admit it.

Say, if you insist on talking about vintages, that you prefer the 1929 red Burgundies to the '28's and the '26's, that you have never tasted a bad 1923 except one or two of doubtful authenticity, that you have been disappointed in most 1919's, that you hear the '34's will be very fine, that you have found the white Burgundies of 1928 superlatively good. Say that you think the 1929 clarets (or Red Bordeaux) are by far the best now available, and that the 1933 sauternes, while less good than the '29's, are more to your taste, being lighter and less sweet. Say that you think the '28's are the best champagnes you have ever tasted, that you are inclined to believe that 1934 was as good a wine year in Germany as 1921, that you think the 1929 Rhine wines are beginning to go off, that you wonder whether the 1926 clarets will come round, that you understand that 1936 was one of the worst vintages on record, that you believe the 1920 Rhine wines will outlast the 1921's. But if you start rambling along this way, watch your step.

If you want to give your wine expert a few uneasy moments, there are one or two highly embarrassing questions that you can ask.

"Has it ever occurred to you that most of the wines that people say won't travel are produced in exceptionally beautiful parts of Europe?" This is a poser and no mistake. Vouvray is said not to travel, though it will, and Vouvray is produced in the chateau country; it seems less good in St. Louis than in Blois, but you rarely drink it in St. Louis on a vine-covered terrace beside a river, with the gray walls of an old castle rising out of the sheer green of plane trees. Frascati "won't travel," in the opinion of couples who spent their honeymoon in Rome, and the same thing holds for the wines of Capri. Unfortunately, it is also true that the wonderful little street orchestra which played so divinely for you in that charming restaurant in Venice ten years ago would sound a good deal like a hurdy-gurdy in Chicago or New York. Such is disillusionment, but the wine expert will hate like the devil to admit that he is disillusioned.

But the expert's worst moment comes when you ask, in all honesty, "Isn't there a place for those of us who can't remember the names of the crus classes, who don't know Clos de Beze from Clos de Vougeot, but who just like wine?" Your connoisseur, at this, may stall or change the subject; if he is an honest man, as a good wine drinker should be, he will simply say, "My friend, you are the salt of the earth; you are right. When all is said and done, a wine is good when it tastes good."

᎒ August, 1937.

Were one to attempt to characterize this generation by its most prominent habit, there could be little argument that it would be smoking. Sooner or later it was foredoomed that the scientists of the mind would be psychoanalyzing smokers. One of them, Dr. Ernest Dichter, made such evaluation his life's work. This lively piece gives indication as to why he is one of the busiest social scientists in the land—and why Madison Avenue keeps him so fully engaged.

Why
People
Smoke

BY ERNEST DICHTER

DO YOU THINK WHEN YOU LIGHT A CIGARETTE THAT you are indulging in a purely physical luxury? Sorry, you're wrong.

When you are having a smoke after meals, or in a conference, or at a party, you are seeking, in part, a psychological release. Study your smoking habits and see how this analysis fits you. Psychologically, smoking is chiefly a substitute or a conditioned reflex.

Smoking is fun. We are inclined to look back at the carefree enjoyment we had in childhood. Smoking, for many, is a substitute for our early habit of following the whim of the moment. It gives us a legitimate excuse for interrupting work and snatching a moment of pleasure. An accountant said: "When I drop work and sit back for the length of a cigarette I feel much fresher. I wouldn't think of just relaxing without a cigarette."

Smoking is self-reward. Most of us are hungry for rewards. A cigarette is a reward you can promise yourself as often as you wish. You can say to yourself, "When I have finished this piece of work I'll have a cigarette." The first and last cigarette of a day are important as such rewards. The first, after breakfast, is an anticipated reward. You ease yourself pleasantly into the day. The last cigarette is definitely a "closing of the door" on the day.

Smoking is a substitute activity. A waiting period, as for someone who is late, stimulates almost automatically the desire for a smoke. It seems to make time pass faster. It permits you do something. Being restrained in activity while compelled to wait

is a very unpleasant experience. The cigarette thus has a useful effect. This is one reason why prisoners of war or soldiers awaiting the signal to attack sometimes crave a cigarette more than food.

Smoking is also a playful creative activity. The smoke is manufactured by the smoker. Watching the smoke is fascinating to some smokers. This brings into the picture the psychological affinity of the human being to smoke and fire—especially in moments of contemplation and at night.

Smoking is often a conditioned reflex. Certain situations, such as coming out of a place where you can't smoke, beginning and ending work, voluntary and involuntary interruptions of work, hunger feeling, or reading, cause an automatic reaching for a smoke. A frequent reflex is that of taking out a cigarette when you see someone else do so, even though at the moment you had no desire to smoke.

Fun, reward and conditioned reflex all apply to smoking as an accompaniment to other pleasures. Smoking introduces the holiday feeling. After a meal, a cigarette is like another course. It is an expected completion of other forms of enjoyment.

Physically, smoking is an oral pleasure. The physical pleasure of smoking cannot be explained by taste sensation alone. We must consider the powerful sensitivity of the oral zone. Reactions of the oral area stem from earliest childhood. There is a direct connection between thumb-sucking and smoking.

"In school I always chewed a pencil or pen," a journalist told me. "You should have seen the collec-

13

tion I had. Whenever I try to stop smoking for a while I get something to chew on, like an empty pipe. Also I chew a lot of gum."

Various methods of making definite use of smoking also are psychological and carry with them pleasures of power and control.

"Smoking helps me think" is a common expression. Concentration is facilitated when all outside stimuli are excluded. Smoking provides in its way a "smoke screen" blurring out the outside world. In the same way smoking provides a screen and a covering occupation in embarrassing or tense moments. Besides providing companionship, and perhaps consolation in solitude, smoking promotes sociability and friendship. People doing the same thing have at least one point of agreement. Life and literature are full of stories of situations smoothed out and people brought together by smoking.

One of the most frequent uses of smoking is for aid in relaxation.

I might interpolate here some results of a study of smokers reported by Dr. Emil Bogen in *The Journal of the American Medical Association*. In this report 50 per cent of 600 smokers questioned said they did it for relaxation. Other responses were: for sociability, 65 per cent; for the fragrance, 60 per cent; for stimulation, 50 per cent; to steady the nerves, 45 per cent; to quiet hunger, 30 per cent; visual pleasure in the sight of the smoke, 25 per cent; feel of the lips (oral pleasure), 25 per cent; feel of the hands, 10 per cent; taste, 5 per cent.

The matter of inhaling or not inhaling the smoke is incidental to the present inquiry but it may be noted that research by a leading manufacturer of cigarettes showed a high percentage of inhaling. Of 201 smokers queried—164 men and 37 women— 86 per cent of the men and 92 per cent of the women inhaled.

Mannerisms of smokers are psychologically revealing. Some smokers twirl the cigarette in their fingers, revealing that they have a sensuous pleasure in the handling of it. Holding the cigarette with the thumb and forefinger, the fire end inside toward the palm, is an indication of toughness or of the desire to simulate that quality. Stinginess or fear of poverty is shown by smoking the cigarette down to the last possible puff. Waste and lavishness are revealed by the opposite type who throws away a cigarette half or a quarter smoked. One who scatters ashes in a room may be a loose thinker or one who is contemptuous of the rights of others. A very cautious person taps the cigarette continually, never allowing a crumb of ash to accumulate. A show-off type may smoke a long ash which ends in dropping on his clothes or on the floor.

Almost every person has his own way of smoking, just as he has a specific handwriting. People will assume a way of smoking because they have found that it fits what they think is their personality. One "glamour girl" smoked with a long dark holder. She said: "I studied that very carefully. Don't you think I'm the Latin type?" The long holder is like a big hat, it's alluring and yet it warns, "Don't you dare come close," at the same time.

In this study of hundreds of smokers there was one point on which all had the same reaction. Every responder, even among those who were not excessive smokers, was worried about the quantity he smoked. Nearly every person had tried at one time or another to cut down smoking. One said characteristically: "I give up smoking one month every year. I wish to prove that I can do without it."

This periodic worry or abstemiousness points to an underlying guilt feeling that many smokers have. The buried feeling is that smoking is not only harmful physically but also has the taint of immorality.

Most of the smokers questioned, who are now of mature age, said that in their adolescence smoking was a forbidden and sinful thing.

An elderly man said, "We were a bunch of boys on our way to a football game. I had trouble in lighting a cigarette, my first. A man passing yelled to me, 'Throw that thing down, you little rascal!' I was shocked and frightened. Yes, I certainly remember my first cigarette."

In sum, the advantages and pleasures that the cigarette has to offer are such that their power is difficult to defeat by warning or preachment. It is a safe bet that the cigarette is here to stay. The writer is a nonsmoker. But the analysis left me with the feeling that I might be missing something.

♛ August, 1944.

In the Fifties the ubiquitous television box dismayed the social observers who inveighed against its threatened destruction of the conversational arts. Almost forgotten were the campaigns of the Thirties, after the fearful advent of the radio. In this piece Arthur Davison Ficke, one of America's best poets, warned against the sins to shun and the virtues to cultivate.

The Art of Conversation

BY ARTHUR DAVISON FICKE

TO LEARN HOW ONE SHOULD NOT TALK IS EASY enough. Terrible examples abound on all sides of one. Here are four, transcribed without the slightest exaggeration from real life.

1. A very learned but not very agreeable man of my acquaintance rarely emerges from his habitual silence except to interrupt a conversation by saying: "What's your evidence for that statement?" When you have adduced your evidence—supposing that you chance to be lucky enough to have any—he purses up his lips scornfully and retires again into his silence.

2. Recently at a large dinner I was placed next to a lady whom I had never met before. She told me at once that she had just returned from such an interesting visit to New York. She said that the first night there she went to the theater, she said it was a splendid production and she proceeded to recount to me in detail the exciting plot of the play. The play was *Hamlet*. By the time the dinner was over, she had got almost to the end of the fourth act. I never did learn how the play came out.

3. I have a cousin who is a nice fellow—but he is hipped on a theory of his own invention which he calls "The Dogma of Rhythmic Dynamic Balance." According to him, if a thing is "on balance," it is good; if it is "off balance," it is no good. No matter what subject you mention to him—whether it be Hitler or the New York Yankee team or the weather, he will immediately account for its good or bad qualities by showing you how it fits into his theory.

4. One day last summer four of the most brilliant talkers of our time happened to be gathered together as guests in my living room. There was a Nobel Prize winner, a novelist, an editor and a poet. It was one of those perfect conversations in which each man present takes his due part—presenting without insistence or rancor his own views on some of the most debatable aspects of our modern world, and listening attentively to what everybody else has to say. Nobody was oratorical, nobody was impatient, nobody tried to hold the floor all the time, nobody was bored. The air was electric with the amiable clash of five different and highly individual minds. We were ready to go on all afternoon and perhaps half the night.

Then a lady whom I know only slightly drove up—and I had to bring her in. She sat down, and for more than fifty minutes poured out an uninterrupted stream of minor autobiography.

Finally the Nobel Prize winner, who has red hair and a quick temper, gave me a look of indignant anguish. I nodded to him; yes, I knew only too well that it was my responsibility as the host to take some action. So the next time the lady paused for breath, I turned swiftly to my redheaded friend and said: "You know, there are certain resemblances between what this lady has been telling us and some of the things you were telling us of Russia!" "Yes!" he said—and instantaneously began to speak; the other three men aroused themselves from the dozes into which they had fallen—and before the intruder knew what had happened, the conversation that she had murdered was alive and on its feet again. We gave her no further opportunity to open her mouth; but I am sure that she was unaware of the plot against her, for when she went away she said she thanked us all so much—and wouldn't I please telephone her to come over any time that this interesting group was gathered at my house again. We stared at one another in wonder, poured ourselves some more beer, and then we continued our talking.

These four examples of horror that I have mentioned are enough of horrors. Let us now consider not the improper but the good way of talking—

1. The first essential of good talking is that one should have something to say. Everyone has something interesting to say—but it will not be a thing that he memorized last night out of one of those remarkable books that tell you how to be a social success and speak French in twelve lessons. It will be something real, native to his character, derived from what he has seen and felt and thought. Conversation cannot be copied or learned by heart. It is neither a diamond set in one's front teeth to be flashed in momentary glory, not is it a wooden leg which one has bought in the hope that it will be mistaken for a real leg. Good talk is as much a part of oneself as one's lifeblood.

We need not be afraid to speak of the subjects we know best. It is not true that "shoptalk" bores other people. On the contrary, "shoptalk" is a wonderful kind of talk if it is presented not in technical terms but in words of wide human comprehensibility. All of us are eager to have a glimpse into the special fields where other men are working; and we are wholly sympathetic when they speak to us of their established facts, their present hopes and their great future ideals. The conversation of such a man will enchant us. I know a naturalist whose accurate information and gnomish fancy enable him, when he talks of skunks, to disclose in these humble and grievously misunderstood creatures a charm and mystery which theologians have in vain tried to attribute to angels.

2. The second essential of good talking is not to dwell too long on one's personal prejudices. If you hate Mr. Roosevelt or if you admire Mr. Roosevelt, your simple statement of that fact is about all that we your listeners care to hear. We know now where you stand on this controversial matter. We have already heard every possible argument on both sides. You must do us the honor of assuming that we too read the papers; we are not ignorant of the reports of unemployment and graft and high taxes and all the rest of the truths and lies that have been disseminated; and we doubt whether your reading of the press has put at your disposal any information that is not at our disposal also. And so we beg you to refrain, as an act of grace and mercy, from explaining the whole matter to us all over again.

3. The third point worthy of attention is the desirability of ending what one has to say in a manner that gives easy and attractive opportunity for the other person to take up the discussion and to develop the topic further as he expresses his own views. To do this requires no more mysterious mental equipment than a genuine interest in learning what are the thoughts of the other man. Some people do not have this interest; all they want is to blurt out their own opinions and then stop, with a kind of "And that's that!" manner. Good manners, propriety, consideration, lack of egotism are essentials of good conversation. One should never end a statement with a dead wall of allegation for the other man to butt up against; one should always slide a door open for his entry—as by saying: "But perhaps you know more of this matter than I do. What are your views?"

4. A conversation should not be an attempt to prove something or to defeat the other fellow in an argument. It should be half-playful, half-serious; it should be an attempt to hold up an object to the sun, to view it from many angles, to enjoy its form and color and to try to discover a little more of its significance than one knew at the beginning. It is a joint exploration, not a battle.

In one way, conversation is like a game of tennis; in other ways it is like a dance. In certain respects you are playing against an opponent whose swiftly delivered ball you must return with strategic skill if the game is to be kept going; but in other respects, you are not confronting an opponent but are co-operating with a partner to whose movements you must respond harmoniously if the dance is not to become a grotesque burble-bumble. A good conversation is likely to shift momentarily back and forth between these two states: at one moment it will be a fencing match, at the next moment a necking party. But it ought not to get stuck permanently in either of these situations. Half of the fun and adventure of a conversation is that you never know exactly what kind of an encounter this really is. If it weren't a little dangerous, it would be dull; if it were steadily hostile or steadily acquiescent, it would be a waste of time.

5. Yet, as a fifth point, it should be noted that experienced talkers are wary to avoid a certain type of subject. It is folly to discuss Catholicism or Communism or Atheism or Capitalism with a person whose views are diametrically the opposite of your own. When one gets into these regions, where the emotions are deeply involved and where perhaps inherited prejudices overrule all other considerations, it is wiser to shift to some other subject. Sooner or later, what ought to be a pleasant and thoughtful interchange of ideas will degenerate into a slugging-match, and what fun is that?

6. As a sixth note on this subject, may I record a curious personal impression? It seems to me that many of the best conversations I have ever listened to were spiced with considerable intervals of meditative silence. If I am right about this, then it would seem to follow that one need not be in a hurry to express one's views. Probably they are not very wise views, anyway; but such as they are, it may be well to produce them in ripened, orderly fashion. There is no hurry; there is no hurry at all. This is not motoring; we are not trying to rush from one uninteresting place to another uninteresting place; we are strolling through a countryside, for our refreshment and instruction, and examining the landscape as we pass.

7. And lastly—one should attempt in talking to be severely accurate in his choice of words and to employ the full range of his vocabulary. It gives the speaker distinct pleasure to try to use the precise word that expresses just what he means, and it brings an equal pleasure to the listener. The habitual use of such adjectives as "nifty" and "rotten" and "swell" to describe everything from chocolate ice cream to the philosophy of George Santayana is the mark of an unreflective and undernourished mind. We should try to speak richly, not meagerly; specifically, not vaguely: we should define and color our thought like an autumn maple branch against a blue sky, not lose it in obscurity.

But perhaps you, sir, know more of this matter than I do. What are your views?

♛ February, 1939.

The rapidity of changes during the generation sometimes caused us to look away from first causes and tried experience. It was a generation of warriors and statesmen and of scientists with astronomical visions which staggered even their intellects—particularly when their theorems became realities and exploded about them. It was an age of senseless anxiety, one which too frequently separated from their common sense those who should have known better. A talented author and a veteran educator, Mary Ellen Chase demonstrates in this article why she is capable of keeping her own.

What Has Happened to Common Sense?

BY MARY ELLEN CHASE

WHENEVER I RETURN TO THE ISOLATED VILLAGE ON the coast of Maine where I now spend every year from early June until late October, I am pleasantly impressed by the way in which my neighbors there hold on to certain old words and terms, now too rarely heard.

One of these is *grit*, with its companion, *gumption;* another is *get up and get*, which in Maine means to depend on oneself; and yet another is *common*, or *horse sense*. My neighbors, who are all fishermen, and their wives need these words to describe the human qualities which they extoll above all others. For fishing, whether for lobsters or herring, is a hard and precarious calling. It demands gumption and horse sense, or, in more polite terms, the spirit of adventure, self-reliance, the power of decision and the determination not to

be downed by adverse circumstances.

In other words, one has to *get up and get* in order to wrest a living from the sea and to preserve one's self-respect as well as the decent opinion of one's fellow men.

My neighbors are frankly suspicious of anyone who seemingly lacks these old American virtues, and they are not slow in the expression of their skepticism. Last summer, they voiced their common ·judgment of a newcomer to the village who, arriving in search of better fishing grounds, had lost most of his lobster traps in a northeast gale and had been bewailing his fate with too little reserve. In doing so, they employed other homely yet apt phrases still current among them.

"Why don't he shut his mouth and pick up his feet?" they said. "He's bound to *run aground* no matter what he does. You can't sail straight by takin' time out to bawl about bad luck."

Since they and I stem from the same coastal and rural background, I realize that we were brought up on the same plain yet wholesome fare. In the country school of my childhood, we were faced daily by precepts written on the blackboard each Monday morning by our "old-fashioned" teachers who knew it to be their duty to instill iron in our souls as well as common fractions in our minds.

Precepts, I gather from modern notions of education, have quite gone out of date; and yet those which we were obliged to memorize each week have not only somehow stayed with me through many years, but have also proved salutary in many moments of indecision and anxiety.

Usually our weekly precept was in terse prose: *It takes a live fish to swim upstream, but any old log can float down.* Or, *Don't expect others to bear your troubles. They have their own.* Or, *Life isn't all you want, but it's all you have, so have it.*

Nor did country schools alone dispense such robust aphorisms. Most American parents fifty years ago dealt them out liberally, sometimes even sternly, in the upbringing of children. My own home and parents were typical of the general run. I was taught early both by precept and example that *a job once undertaken has to be completed whatever the cost*, that *no one but the maker of them ought to be expected to pay for mistakes* and that *it is always best to keep one's head a safe distance from one's heels.*

I realized early the first of these relentless truths when at ten years old, I undertook the job of driving our family cow to pasture every morning and fetching her at night from May to October for the payment of five dollars. In spite of her name, which was Constancy, she was the most unpredictable, not to say ornery, of cows.

Whimsical by nature and agile of movement, she was given to hiding in thickets and swamps at the close of day, and bounding away once I had discovered her. I shall never forget the exasperations and furies of that interminable summer, the terrors which lurked in gathering darkness over the pasture, the mosquitoes and the black flies, and the countless tears shed in secret. But no one came to my rescue or even to my assistance. The job was mine alone, as was the hard-earned five-dollar bill in October.

The old words, *grit, gumption* and *common* or *horse sense,* the old sayings of school and home, are passing out of our speech, except in rural areas, and with such passing there is surely the suggestion of our apparent lack of need for them and for what they counsel as to our conduct as individuals and, therefore, as a people.

In their places we use today a growing number of new words and terms to describe our states of mind and our meeting of those difficulties and questions which will always beset us. We are now *insecure,* or *ill-adjusted,* or *frustrated,* or made ineffective by a *sense of inferiority.* We suffer from *emotional blocks,* or *phobias,* or *psychoses;* or we are *self-destructive* from some obscure cause.

An examination of these new words, moreover, makes one uncomfortably aware that they lack the affirmation and the optimism of the old. There is implicit in them the notion that we are surrounded by foes difficult to defeat.

This new vocabulary comes into use early with our concern over our children. We now hesitate to look upon them as simply ill-mannered, or undisciplined, or spoiled. We fear that they are *problem* children, who need expert care and utmost caution lest they become *neurotics* or *uncontributive members* of our human society. Anxious parents study them with the help of books and, as a last resort, turn to guidance clinics or to specialists in child welfare and nurture.

The children are too seldom encouraged, as were their parents and grandparents, to face problems by themselves, to make their own decisions, and to pay the consequences of their own mistakes.

Nor are adults free from the waves of anxiety which seem in these latter days to be engulfing us concerning our potentialities as human beings. Too many of us are looking about for some panacea which will ease the burdens of our past and present errors in judgment and lighten our fears of the future. We are sadly conscious that life is slipping by and that we are neither contributing to it as we might or getting from it what it offers.

Something, we feel, is wrong somewhere, and, without making any stout attempt on our own to discover what it is, we turn to wiser friends, or, if we can afford it, to professional advice, or to any number of books which have lately flooded the market and which guarantee to show us how to understand ourselves, or to advance professionally, or to gain self-confidence by influencing others, or to help us "stop worrying and start living."

It is the number and popularity of these books which suggest too potently the restlessness and anxiety of far too many among us. Yet even a cursory reading of them reveals only what we used to call plain old common sense: their authors are telling us nothing which we have not always known.

They, one and all, urge upon us what common sense has always urged: a calm and objective weighing of ourselves; a frank and even merciless recognition of our weaknesses and failures; a determination to oust at any cost oversensitiveness, which is but a form of self-indulgence; a new attitude toward our families and our communities; a sense of personal responsibility for the well-being and relative happiness of both; a fresh start; a game played with patience, resilience and humor—in short, a reliance upon our own powers of self-discipline.

No one in his senses would, of course, suggest that such books are not often helpful to the anxious mind. Nor, more importantly, would one deny that modern psychiatry has contributed untold help to our civilization. There are many sick minds among us which demand expert diagnosis and treatment. And yet, the assumption that most if not all of us have somehow acquired mental and emotional conflicts which we cannot cope with by ourselves surely has its dangers.

As Americans we are, or at least we *were,* adventurers, and our history is the story of a game played against tremendous odds and gloriously won. Why not recall that fact and the tough moral fiber which made the winning possible, and start games on our own—contests against lethargy and discouragement, bewilderment and laziness, irritations and ill-tempers? Against frustrations (who isn't frustrated in one way or another?), against those nagging notions that we have problems different from those of others, or that we are neither wanted nor needed by our children, or that we have nothing to give to our own time and place?

Life may not be all we want, but it's all we have, as my old school precept said, and it's high time that we *have* it. We shall not find its secrets or its possible riches in the advice of others, however wise, or in books, however revealing, unless we complete (or better *substitute*) that counsel and revelation with our own American heritage of grit, gumption and common sense.

These homely virtues have never been lost or actually dispised. They or their opposites have only been dressed up in a variety of ways and handed out to us under other names. It would be an act of patriotism as well as of wisdom to haul off their modern disguises, return their old, wholesome names, and start at once to put them into practice.

ᛟ May, 1954.

The art of living in this generation, as in any other, is evidenced best by successful relationships among all people—friends, neighbors, a husband and wife, and by this touching story of a father's relationship with a son.

"Let Go of My Hand, Son"

by Admiral X, as told to Jack Lincke

AS ONE LOOKS BACK OVER THE INCIDENTS IN REARING children, it is surprising how things we considered little at the time assume such large proportions later on.

A series of these began when my little boy was brand-new. Like most neophyte fathers, I was not completely aware of the implications of having a son. For quite a while we simply sized up each other while I stretched my Navy flight pay far enough to cover the appropriations he was always voting for himself.

One morning when I went in to kiss the Skipper, as we called him, he wore a welcoming smile that seemed to say he had accepted me. While I was holding him, he discovered my thumb and began chewing it.

I was scheduled for an early flight and had to get under way, so I pulled my thumb loose. He set up a wail. I gave him back my thumb and he was happy for a little while.

This was repeated several times, until finally I said: "The whole squadron is waiting for me. I have to shove off. Let go of my hand, son."

I went out the front door feeling like a heel, with his complaining cries filling the house.

For several months, this hand business occurred almost daily. It seemed that I was always trying to get him to let go so I could leave for work. Then came his first attempts to stand. This consisted of the usual comical efforts that ended with a gear-up landing.

I soon discovered that every time he wanted to try his sea legs, he would hold out his hands and give me to understand that he wanted to hang on to one of mine.

I used to say: "Look, fellow. Hanging on to my hand won't help. Come on now. Get going!" I'd always end up saying: "Do it yourself this time. Let go of my hand."

He had just learned to walk when I gave him his first pony ride. He had no use for that horse, and as he sat there yelling to be taken down and stretching his arms pleadingly toward me, I wondered if I had a softy for a son.

Finally, I got the pony moving and walked alongside with that boy of mine hanging on to my hand like it was the rip cord of a parachute and his main tanks were blazing. He never once stopped yelling.

We didn't go there to the riding place again until one day as we were driving past, the Skipper shouted the equivalent of "Horsie." We gave another try, and still he wouldn't let go.

This was repeated on several more occasions. Then, finally, I said: "You know quite a bit about this by now. Sooner or later you'll have to do it alone, so let go of my hand."

I swatted the pony and stood still. The Skipper cried for one or two rounds, then settled down happily. Within a week he had the pony at a full run.

The Skipper was around five when I began giving him swimming lessons. One day I told him it was time to try it by himself.

"Dad, I'll sink!" he protested, grabbing my hand and hanging on for all he was worth.

"I'll be right beside you, and I won't let you go under," I told him. "Come, let go of my hand."

He let go and managed to swim to where he could touch bottom. On the way home neither of us spoke for several blocks and then he reached over and took hold of my right hand resting on the car seat. "Dad," he said proudly, "you never let anything bad happen to me, do you?"

The Skipper next went through roller skates, then came the bicycle. I rode it home from the shop with only minor inconvenience to traffic, a few tiffs with mutts and a slight lack of oxygen.

The Skipper climbed on and I helped him balance while we went around the block. Finally, I stopped and said: "My engine is overheating. Try your own power."

He was sitting on the saddle and balancing by holding on to my hand. "Do you think I'll be able to make it?" he asked.

"I don't know," I told him, "but there's one darn sure way of finding out."

Before I had even missed the passing years, the Skipper was in prep school and "we" were going out for football. When my flight duties permitted, I would leave the air station early and get over to the field to watch scrimmage. Once in a while, we'd punt a few and try some passes.

One day the Skipper got clobbered. He started off tackle with his head down and met not just a tackle but also a guard and a halfback. My man lost.

They carried him off the field and the coach applied various restorative measures. In a moment, the Skipper opened his eyes, rolled them a few times and sat up. He shook his head a bit and grinned sheepishly.

Then his grin slackened; he looked down and, slightly embarrassed, said softly, "Dad, let go of my hand."

I believe this was the real point of no return. As the Skipper started back onto the field, many things beat through my head. He could swim, shoot, ride a horse, whip about 40 per cent of the kids on the boxing team. This was no longer the little guy who used to turn to me whenever things got thick.

When the Skipper passed his entrance exams for the Naval Academy, I was stationed at San Diego. Before I realized it, the day had arrived for him to leave and we were at the airport waiting for his plane. I was trying to remember whether or not during the past year I had told him all that he ought to know.

This would be the first time the Skipper had been away from home for more than a week. Since his mother's death, we had been together constantly.

Then the dispatcher called "all aboard," we were shaking hands and I was conscious of the strong grip that was just a little too darn strong. Then our fingers relaxed. Life had told us both to let go.

The Skipper was within a few months of graduation when the Japs attacked at Pearl Harbor. I was at sea aboard my carrier most of the time until after Guadalcanal. It was rough, rugged going.

On many a strike, I'd glance suddenly over the planes in my group, looking for the Skipper. I knew subconsciously that some day he would be up there —not in my group, certainly, but in someone's.

Then there would be only one hand, the hand that we hoped was outstretched to all of us, The Big Hand. In the sky, in a scramble, there was only you, your teammates, the flak and the enemy—and The Big Hand we hoped would hold all of us up there, and bring us through.

Two years later, I was in the hospital at Pearl Harbor. A Jap shell had exploded in the cockpit with me and, from the hips down, I was loaded. In fact, the only difference between me and a junk yard was that the junk yard couldn't swear.

I had just graduated to a wheelchair when my world almost cracked up. The Skipper was flown in with other casualties. His carrier had taken a Jap bomb right after he had landed and his plane, with him aboard, had been blown over the side. He was painfully but not seriously wounded.

The Senior Medical Officer had me wheeled over to the wing where the Skipper was. When I saw him, he had just come out of the operating room.

After thirty-one minutes and three seconds, he opened his eyes. It took some time for him to focus on me and still more for recognition to penetrate the anesthetic.

When things were oriented, he grinned slightly and I heard him whisper, "Hi, Dad. Glad to have you aboard." Subconsciously, I took his hand to say, "Hello," as two men would, meeting on the street. He grinned again and said, "Air's sort of rough. Hang on, will you, while I try to pick up a little air speed."

The time passed so quickly that we were hardly conscious of having healed up or of being on the convalescent list. Just as quickly, it was time for us to return to duty.

One morning we decided to take a lunch up to Sacred Falls. We both felt fit and it was a beautiful day. I called to the Skipper a couple of times to find out why he was in such a helluva rush. Forty-eight years and that Jap shell had slowed me down more than I had realized.

Just before we got to the falls there was a steep climb. My wind had petered out and I stood at the bottom blowing. The Skipper turned around, smiled and stuck out his arm.

"Take hold, I'll give you a tow."

He gave me a yank and almost lifted me to the top. From this point we could see the falls. Yet my thoughts were not on the falls, but on the chap beside me who was no longer the thumb-chewing little guy I'd spent so much time pulling my hand away from.

Two weeks later we were standing at the head of the runway at Pearl Harbor where his squadron's planes were lined up, engines idling, preparatory to taking off for their carrier. A short distance away was my own newly assigned Air Group, waiting for me to lead them out to ours.

I didn't have to look at his two full gold stripes, the ribbons on his chest, his gold wings or the Navy Cross to recognize that this was a man. But we didn't know that it was to be for the last time —as we let go of each other's hand.

Ⱳ April, 1955.

The social bite of Peter De Vries' current writing has made him one of the country's most successful authors. In the earliest issues of CORONET, he reflected the magazine's style, his period and his own talent in his frequent contribution of quick verse.

Language Study

BY PETER DE VRIES

Chuck Enslow worked in a factory
He threw tools all over the place in fits and they
   said Chuck is hotheaded
Once a box fell from a pile and just missed his head
If it had hit him he'd have been killed

But it didn't and he wasn't and he went on working
He saved some money and started a business
The business prospered and he became very wealthy
   and retired
Now he threw Sèvres vases and bridge cards around
   and they said Mr. Enslow is temperamental

Wealth made a lot of differences
He used to eat now he dined
He used to tire now he wearied
He used to be goofy now he was eccentric
He used to be a glutton now he was an epicure
One day he died of heart disease
If the box had hit him they'd have said he kicked
   the bucket
Now they said he suffered an untimely demise
What a horrid word worms is

                     ♛ August, 1938.

In 1941, when Sinclair Lewis, our country's first literary Nobel Prize winner, was very much alive and kicking, he wrote his own obituary for CORONET. He called himself a "cheerful pathologist" who exposed the clichés and sentimentalities of his day. Before his death in 1951, Lewis could have boasted that, even if he didn't needle the Babbitts out of existence, he made them easier to lampoon and thus made it tougher for them to get away with it.

The Death of Arrowsmith

BY SINCLAIR LEWIS

SINCLAIR LEWIS, WHO DIED PEACEFULLY IN HIS SLEEP yesterday afternoon, at his small country place in northwestern Connecticut, has, at the age of eighty-six, been rather generally forgotten. For the past ten or fifteen years he has indulged in so secluded a life, devoting himself, apparently, only to his cats, his gardens, and brief essays on such little-read novelists as Mark Twain, that to many persons it may have been a surprise to find that he was still living. Yet at one time he was a figure of considerable notoriety, because of his jeering yet essentially kindly shafts at the pomposity and inefficiency of politicians and industrialists.

Although now they are almost unread, a few of his novels, particularly *Main Street, Arrowsmith, Babbitt, Elmer Gantry* and the ponderous four-volume chronicle of an American family, *The Tintayres*, which Mr. Lewis began in 1944 and completed in 1950, are familiar to all sociologists and literary historians for their picture of the priggish and naïve half of this century. That this picture was well rounded or unprejudiced, no one will maintain.

Mr. Lewis seems essentially to have been a cheerful pathologist, exposing the clichés and sentimentalities of his day—the hearty falseness of Senators and what were once known as "business boosters," the smirking attitudes toward women in his times,

the personal ambitiousness of the clergy, the artists and the professional men, and the brazen mawkishness of patriotism.

To the discerning reader of later years, it is evident that Mr. Lewis smote—or tried to smite—sentimentality because he knew himself to be, at heart, a sentimentalist to whom green hills and barricade-jumping soldiers and smiling girls and winter storms were as childishly exciting as they were to any popular female novelist. It also was evident that he mocked the cruder manifestations of Yankee imperialism because he was, at heart, a fanatic American, who never really liked the condescensions of the English people among whom he often lived—including two solid years in Derbyshire in 1951-2.

The "style" of Mr. Lewis' rather long-winded pictures of Americana seems, on recent study, to indicate a descent from extraordinarily discrepant literary ancestors. From a perusal of his books, together with his own admissions, one may find him astonishingly deriving from both Dickens and Swinburne, H. G. Wells and A. E. Housman, Thomas Hardy and H. L. Mencken and Hamlin Garland. On the other hand, he seems to have left no literary descendants. Unlike his celebrated contemporaries, Theodore Dreiser (1871-1952) and Colonel Ernest Hemingway, who was so dramatically killed while leading his mixed Filipino and Chinese troops in the storming of Tokyo in 1949, Mr. Lewis seems to have affected but little the work of younger writers of fiction. Whether this is a basic criticism of his pretensions to power and originality, or whether, like another contemporary, Miss Willa Cather, he was an inevitably lone and insulated figure, we have not as yet the perspective to see.

For a good many years, Mr. Lewis was an extensive and, it would almost seem, a foolishly experimental wanderer. He began his work with years on newspapers and in magazine and publishing offices; he traveled through every state in the union; he knew most of Europe and, after the end of World War II, in 1944, most of Asia. He even —possibly in unconscious imitation of his idol, Dickens—dabbled with acting, over three or four years, appearing in various professional companies, with no especial credit or discredit either.

But on his return from England in 1952, he settled immovably in the rural Connecticut to which he had many ties. Though Mr. Lewis himself was born (in 1885) in a Minnesota prairie hamlet, where his father was a typical country physician, that father and his ancestors for eight or nine generations were born in Connecticut, along the Housatonic River, near which Mr. Lewis himself has lived these past twenty years. He attended Yale, and did his first newspaper work on the New Haven *Journal and Courier*. It was natural then that he should have settled in Connecticut, being weary of travel and of what he himself once called (in his brief travel book, *Tea for One-and-one-half*, Random House, 1945), "the chronic wanderer's discovery that he is everywhere such an Outsider that no one will listen to him even when he kicks about the taxes and the beer."

Lewis was tall, lean, awkward, with a rough complexion and, in his later years, a skull completely bald, save for a fringe of still rusty hair. Had he sported a tousled wig and a chin whisker, he would almost comically have been taken for an impersonation of Uncle Sam, and a large share of the yearly dwindling number of interviewers and librarians who made a pilgrimage to his home (a pilgrimage invariably ruined by the old man's derisive frivolity about all artistic poses) have noted that with advancing years he became more and more the Last Surviving Connecticut Yankee. Even his voice assumed a Yankee twang, now forgotten save in bad plays.

His neighbors tell, as their liveliest recollection of him, that when Dr. Sir Wilfred Willoughby Westfrisket, Eisenbein Professor of American Literature at Oxford, waited for him at his home one entire afternoon, Mr. Lewis was at a local garage, playing pinochle with the village constable.

Although Lewis seems to have had no "school" of imitators whatever, it is to be surmised that his influence on our literature has been healthful in his derision of dullness and formalism. His use of American lingo and humorous exaggeration intermingled with the more nearly scholastic manner that was an inheritance from his college days, is at least the equal in dignity and romantic charm of any prince, any labor leader with ten million followers— or any novelist!

His only surviving near relatives are his elder son, Wells, who was, it will be remembered, a captain in the A.E.F. of 1942, and who is probably a more distinguished, certainly a far more subtle and fastidious novelist than his father; his younger son, Michael, president of the Afro-China Airways; and his nephew Freeman Lewis, the publisher.

The funeral, which was at the Millerton Cremation Sanctuary, was, by Mr. Lewis' dying request, attended only by the three servants (or, as he eccentrically called them, the "helpers") on his estate, together with the venerable Dr. Carl Van Doren, president emeritus of Columbia University and formerly ambassador to France. The only music was the playing of Beethoven's *Seventh Symphony*, on records, and the only oratory, Dr. Van Doren's sole observation, "This was a good workman and a good friend, who could still laugh in days when the world had almost worried itself out of the power of laughter."

☙ July, 1941.

In any age man judges himself by devising his own self-tests. In this strangely candid document, Homer McCoy, a prolific writer, reveals his inner moment of truth when, poised on death's edge, he accelerated his life instead of braking it—and thus proved his conquest of fear.

"My Long Road Back"

BY HOMER McCOY

I WAS SUPPOSED TO BE LONG DEAD, BUT I'D NEVER FELT better as I pressed the accelerator and passed the aged jalopy I'd been timidly trailing since the last town. Why, there was nothing to it—and I must have been doing almost fifty. I wished the doctors could have seen me.

The doctors, half a continent away back in California, would have been shocked if they'd known what I was up to. I should have been following their orders, resting and recovering from the series of operations they'd performed on me. Instead, I'd run away; and everything I'd done since was a medical and an economic mistake. Like the plane trip from the Coast. Like buying this new station wagon back in the city.

Yet I wasn't really running away, least of all not from my trouble. I was facing it. During this recess the doctors could do nothing for me. But I could—I could give myself a real test that would tell how I was, and how I was going to be, much better than the specialists with their blood samples and their biopsies.

Long hospitalization can reduce you to an irresolute, inefficient and soggy mass of meat. A slob. You are banana-fingered when you dress yourself. You have to learn to do many things all over again.

I figured I was relearning pretty good. For I'd stumbled along well enough to get up into the northern brush country of Minnesota, my home state. I gave the gas pedal another jolt.

Having made and acted upon the weighty decision of passing the jalopy, I thought I'd earned a rest. It was overdue, anyway. The doctor had told me not to sit too long at a stretch, but to lie down and elevate my feet. All right, doctor. My legs, encased in elastic stockings, were starting to pulse and pain.

I got out of the car, went around to the rear, opened the tail gate and began blowing up my air mattress. I blew until I got dizzy and had to slow down.

This was to be expected. I no longer had my old lung capacity. There'd been a blood clot following one of my operations. It had made it through the heart and lodged in a lung. This pulmonary embolism had killed off part of the lung.

By the time I'd injected enough air into my mattress, I was tired. I crawled over the tail gate and placed a pillow at one end for my head, another for propping up my feet, and lay down. With my legs raised, the throbbing and hurt in them began to ease. I could almost feel the blood seeking and finding detours in its return passage to the heart. The blood's freeway had been blocked because the doctors had ligated, or tied off, the iliac veins to lessen the chances of more blood clots. The elastic stockings were a further preventive.

I remembered the encouragement given me by one of the doctors, a wit. "After all," he'd told me, "there's nothing unusual about your condition, except that it is seldom encountered in a man who is still living."

Well, I was living, and good. I got behind the wheel and started off, driving a little faster.

The highway now ran wide, straight and purposefully through the pine-covered hills where years ago it had meandered in a lingering fashion. It no longer skirted the big bay on Lake Shamineau, but from the top of a grade I could see the shining water. Basically, however, the country had scarcely changed during the quarter of a century since I had been there last. This gave me a feeling of security—a sense of everything being just as it had been, with me and with the world in that wonderful, carefree period B.C.—Before Cancer, that is.

The little town that was so near my destination was in its familiar state of arrested deterioration, I saw, as I drove slowly down the main street. What used to be the bank was now a bar.

The sight of it gave me an inspiration, followed swiftly by resolve. I would saunter into the bar like anybody else, climb onto a stool, look the bartender in the eye and order a bourbon and soda, exactly the way I used to. Never mind the doctors and their orders.

I made a U-turn and parked before the place, excited and happy. I was making fast decisions and carrying them out.

I walked inside slowly and carefully to hide my limp, and attempted a jaunty swing up onto a stool. My left leg played its familiar trick, buckling and sending me lurching against the bar.

Embarrassed, I held on and eased myself onto the stool, then looked furtively about. No one had paid any attention. Why should they? Here was one place where lurching was a common and accepted routine.

I drank cautiously, for I was out of training, and got through my first drink so well I had another. "This is fine therapy," I muttered to my glass. "I'll probably become a lush and drink myself to death, for therapeutic reasons."

I finished my second bourbon-and-soda, left, got into the station wagon, executed another U-turn and drove on.

Two miles from the village I turned onto a country road and inched along, searching for the old abandoned logging trail that would take me where I wanted to go. I couldn't find it, and I felt sick and hollow. To come this far, and fail—perhaps—perhaps I'd expected too much.

Then I drove around a bend and saw it. It would still accept a car, although I could see no signs that cars used it any more.

I went slowly in low gear, and at length emerged into the clearing which was road's end.

The spot was just as I remembered it. Once it had been the site of a sawmill, but the buildings had rotted away and the piles of sawdust had long since disappeared. Along one edge of the clearing ran the stream—spring-fed, small, chattering.

I was hungry, but I didn't eat. I was too tired. Anyway, I wanted to make a lot of room for the whopping breakfast I would have in the morning. I was anticipating that meal.

I undressed all the way, even taking off the elastic stockings. The doctors would have frowned on this, but it was worth the risk.

By the time I crawled into my sleeping bag, twilight was yielding gracefully to darkness. I smoked and watched the tree trunks melt away to become part of night's curtain. I doused my cigarette and listened, feeling safe and secure, for the wilderness music to begin. I could hear the stream, its voice blending with the soft soughing of wind in the pine trees to make a background theme for the soloists.

The first performer was a whippoorwill, its musical signature a timid fanfare that opened the nocturne. Far off a brush wolf yodeled. A tiny creature, probably a white-footed mouse, scurried through the pine needles near me. Then came a dominant, compelling voice—the hollow booming of a great horned owl. And immediately after, the shriek of a snowshoe hare as the owl's piercing talons squeezed out its life.

The cry of the hare jerked me to a sitting position, sweating and afraid. Death had struck swiftly and unexpectedly in the forest. It could strike again. Me, maybe. What was I doing out here alone, so far from help? What if I had another embolism? Maybe I hadn't been so smart after all.

During the silence following the sound of tragedy, the forest held its breath. It was a vast arena of terror and I was panicky. But gradually the wild things began stirring and talking, going about their business as if nothing had happened.

I began to relax. Okay, the owl had killed the rabbit. It had to be. The owl was a controlling agent through which Mother Nature maintained her delicate balance. I must have a place on her scales, alive and as I was. If not, I should have died months before.

I snuggled back into my sleeping bag with a sense of peace and satisfaction. I was getting along fine. I had overcome the obstacles of civilization and now I was coping with the wilderness. I slipped into a light but untroubled sleep.

I woke up at dawn, unzipped the sleeping bag and dressed, leaving off the elastic stockings. I brought out my gas stove and got the burners going. Next I unpacked food and utensils.

Then I opened a large can of syrup, took it to the stream and emptied the contents into the current. I had no use for the syrup. I merely wanted the container for making coffee. I could have brought a regulation coffee pot with me, but the best outdoors-style coffee is brewed in a syrup can.

I rinsed the can of its sticky residue, filled it with brook water and put it on the stove, measuring enough coffee into it for a strong compound. Afterward, I slung in another large handful. That last extra load always did the trick.

A visitor dropped in on me—a Canadian jay. I'd almost forgotten how neighborly they were in attaching themselves to campers. The jay perched on the station wagon and watched me fix breakfast.

As I remembered, male and female Canadian jays looked alike. I hoped the bird was a female, and proceeded on the assumption that it was. Now I had a date. I hadn't had a date in ever so long.

"How do you do, Madame," I told the jay.

While I scrambled the eggs with sausages I kept talking to the jay.

Seated on my camp stool and using the tail gate of the station wagon for a table, I ate. The hospital with its correct but tasteless diets seemed long ago and far away. I luxuriated over the potent coffee and a cigarette, recalling a quotation from somewhere: "Fate cannot harm me, for I have dined today."

When I had cleaned my dishes I put together my casting rod. I had only two lures—basic models that hadn't been altered since I was a kid. They were red and white spoons, each with a trailing treble hook. These I had removed, replacing them with single barbless hooks.

With rod over shoulder, I set out along the path through the woods, slowly and gropingly, testing my legs for this, the most sustained work they had been asked to do since leaving the hospital. They were adequate, they would hold out if I took it easy. There was no reason for haste.

E. Karlin

I emerged from the path onto a meadow bordering the river. I had forgotten that when I left the meadow I must climb a steep, pine-covered hill.

When I got about one-third of the way up the hill, trouble overtook me. The needle-carpeted path was slippery, and my legs began to ache, then throb, and sharp pains geysered up them. They quit on me, buckling, and I fell and rolled down against the trunk of a tree.

I tried to get up, but couldn't make it, and lay still with waves of pain rolling over me, thinking they must be blood clots rushing toward the heart and that I'd been an idiot to leave the elastic stockings behind. I must have rushed things too much, I concluded, and passed out.

I came to feeling good, lying head downward on the hill, my feet above me correctly elevated. The doctors would have approved the way I had fallen. I looked around and saw that my rod was undamaged. So was I. I could have made it back to the car easily, but there was no turning back now, with my objective so close. I could make the top of the hill with the application of some common sense.

I got my fishing rod and crawled on hands and knees to the summit.

Descending was merely annoying, because it called into play the seldom-used muscles in the back of the thighs. At the bottom I gave them a short rest, then went on to the bank of the river where it was joined by the brook.

I sat down at the base of the giant Norway pine which was a marker for my own very private fishing spot. Lightning had long ago knocked off its top, and its trunk was scarred and fire-blackened. But it was still living and green-needled. I hoped that I had a small fraction of its character.

As I took off my shoes and stockings and rolled up my trousers, I had the queer sensation that time had done a magical back-flip. It was only yesterday that I had fished here, not a quarter of a century ago. I had really never been far away. I had never been sick. Any fears I had about future malignancy were groundless.

With clumsy fingers I attached a spoon to the leader and waded into the river on the gravel bar formed by the feeder stream. The water was cold and exhilarating. I didn't know whether wading was correct therapy, but it felt so good it had to be.

Where the bar sloped off into dark water, I halted. So far as I could tell, just below me was the deep hole where the northern pike used to lurk.

I made a practice cast upstream, away from the hole. The spoon shot through the air, halted as though it had struck a wall, and snapped back toward me in the granddaddy of all backlashes—a classic, intricate tangle of line. I picked away at it and finally got the line straightened out.

I made several more casts over unproductive waters, fabricated two more backlashes less obnoxious than the first, and then achieved a series of smooth throws, gaining distance each time. Now I was ready.

Bringing the rod up vertically to a high-noon position, I flipped the spoon slightly upstream and across the current. I let it carry downstream, reeling in just enough to keep it from snagging on the bottom.

When the angle of my line indicated the lure was below and beyond the hole, I began to retrieve it, with misgivings. Here I was using the old-fashioned method of casting in an era dominated by spinning tackle. Maybe my basic spoon was too dated to fool these new, knowledgeable generations of fish.

Maybe I was through as an angler, and—it followed—in every other way.

I could see the darting lure approach, flashing as it ascended toward the sunlit surface. And then there came another, bigger flash as a pike struck the old-fashioned spoon in its old-fashioned incomparable way.

I struck back, felt solid resistance and, laughing and shouting, let the fish run. I had come far for this moment.

The pike broke the surface threshing and shaking its head, then sounded. I let it sulk and dart around the deep hole. It leaped again, and abruptly quit. For sheer savagery and swiftness of attack, it's hard to fault a northern pike, but it isn't outstanding for staying powers.

I reeled in carefully until it was a few feet from me, at which point it made a final, frantic resistance, splashing and writhing like a wounded snake. Then it was over.

Pulling the tired fish close in, I reached down, slid my hand around its body close to the head and lifted it out of the water. It wasn't heavy; it wouldn't go over three pounds.

I removed the barbless hook from the pike's lower jaw. Then I restored the fish to its element, with a prayer of thanks. With sudden violence it once again became a projectile of grace and beauty, darting away toward deep water.

I waded back to shore and stretched out on the pine needles at the base of the big Norway. I had passed the final test. I knew what I needed to know.

All I had had to do was catch one fish, and I had done it. As fish went, it was small; but as a symbol of permanence and security, and as evidence that nothing had changed, including me, it was the biggest and best fish in the world.

Ahead of me lay the long road back, which very soon would involve an undignified crawl on hands and knees over a needle-slick hill. I had no misgiving about that, or about anything else in the future. I wasn't afraid of my next examination, of the biopsy, of cancer. I was scared of nothing now.

♕ January, 1958.

The art of photography

Unburdened by tradition, photography, of all the arts, is the unique medium of the modern day. Fortunately for the last generation, the practitioners of this new art utilized as their subject matter the raw material of journalistic event, and thus left us with a vivid document of history. Without it, we could never fully know the story of 1936-1961. In the first century of its history, photography produced standard portraiture and landscape likenesses. Gradually, the Europeans, who invented the "miraculous little box," began to experiment with it on a somewhat loftier level. Following technical advances in shutters and lenses, their cameramen heightened their results by interpreting what they saw in the lens instead of merely recording it. And so the cameraman became an artist.

From the aesthetic ferment of prewar Europe came such journalistic experiments as the **Berliner Illustrierte**—possibly the world's first true picture magazine—and such renowned names as Cartier-Bresson, Halsman, Blumenfeld, Brassai, Capa, Bischof and Karsh. Their influence spread across the Atlantic and by the early thirties strongly affected a growing new school of American photography.

Suddenly, in a great burst, photography was everywhere. The old-fashioned rotogravure section went out and the modern picture magazine rushed in. For the first time in our history, a government agency set up a separate department of photography—and so were born Roy Stryker's stunning picture files for the Farm Security Administration. The quick, versatile, unyieldingly honest camera became the quasi-official instrument to document the agony of the depression. Museums cleared their walls of the old masters of paint to display the new masters of film.

Hitler drove out of Europe some of its greatest camera artists; most emigrated to America, where they joined Steichen, Abbe, Weston, Bourke-White, Lange and the many more who made up a corps of enthusiasts—untrammeled by staleness or weary tradition, excited by the potential of photography and constantly reinfecting themselves with the virus of their own enthusiasm. From the realistic to the surrealistic, from the romantic to the naturalistic, the styles interwove into what is now unfolding as the tapestry of a thrilling art form. The world has seen nothing like it before, and, so long as its practitioners keep fanning their own flames of creativity, there seems little likelihood that it will soon be surpassed.

From its inception, CORONET had embraced the new art of the camera. The pictures on the following pages represent mere samplings of the many gifted cameramen whom the magazine has published in its quarter-century.

Motion Frozen   SYBIL SHULTON

Hills in a Haze
BURT GLINN

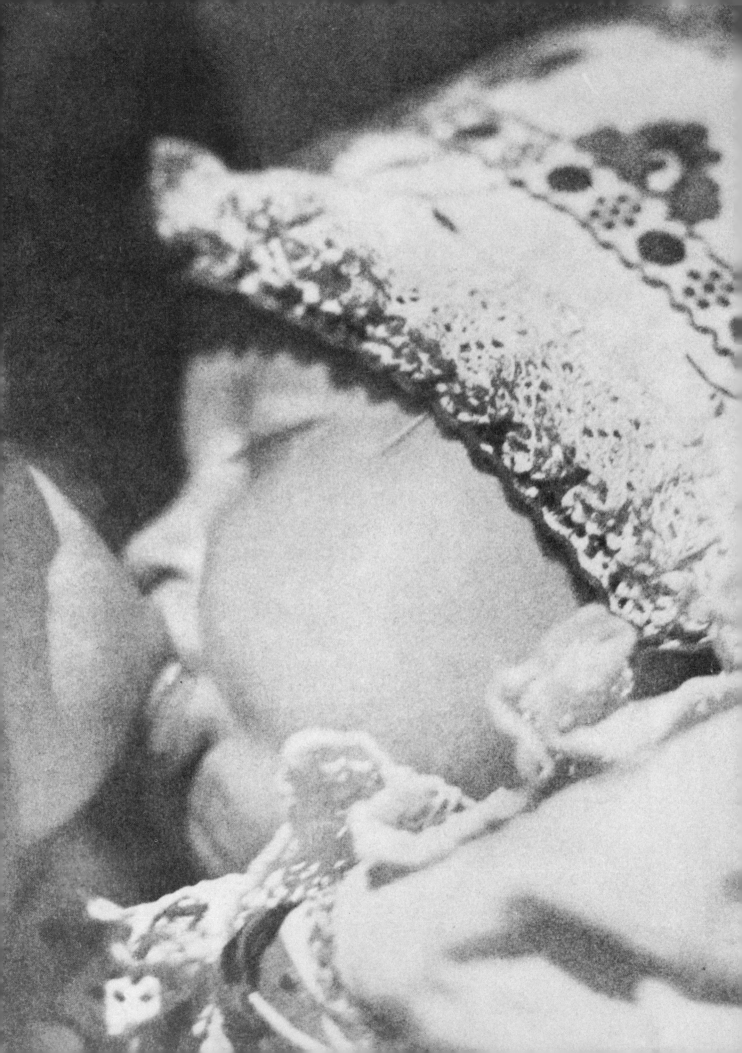

Courage   CHARLES TRIESCHMAN

The Story of Asia   ERGY LANDAU

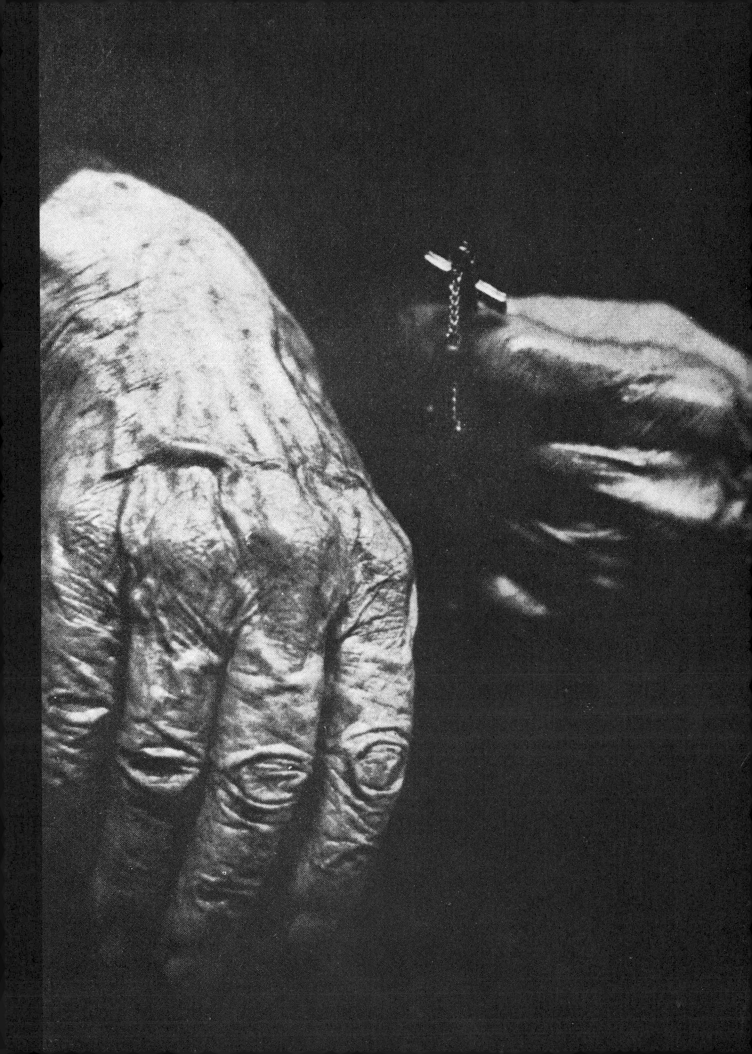

Pinwheel of the Stars   HERMAN EISSENBEISS

Soviet Monastery   EBERHARD SEELIGER

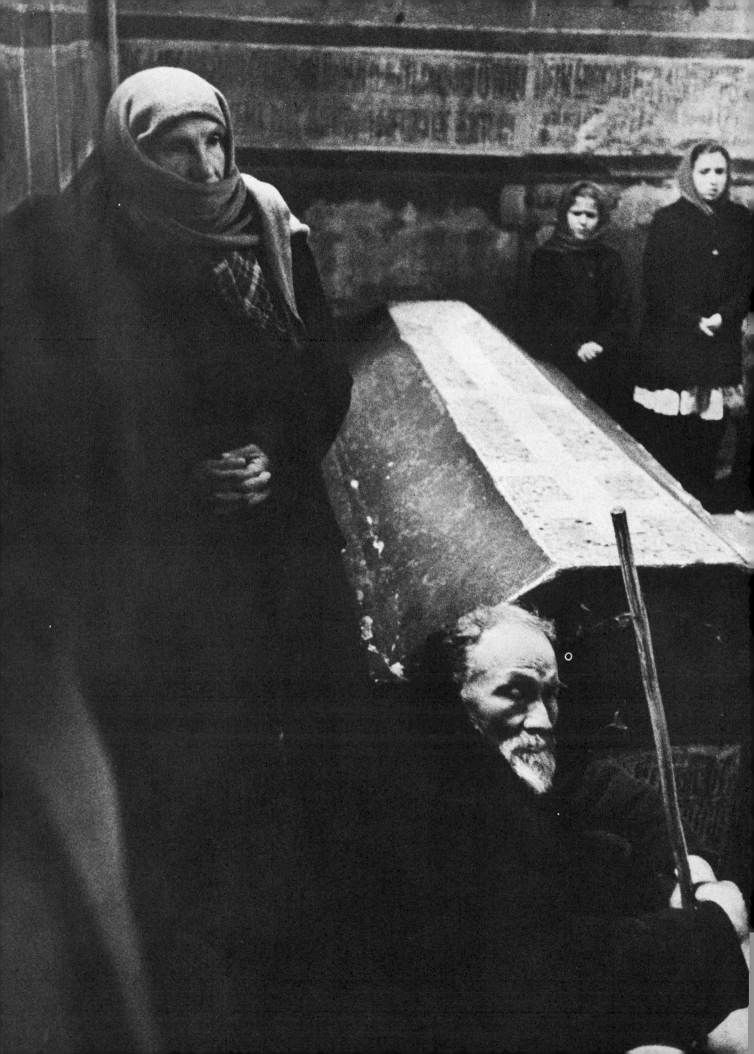

Bessie Love and a Pot-Bellied Stove

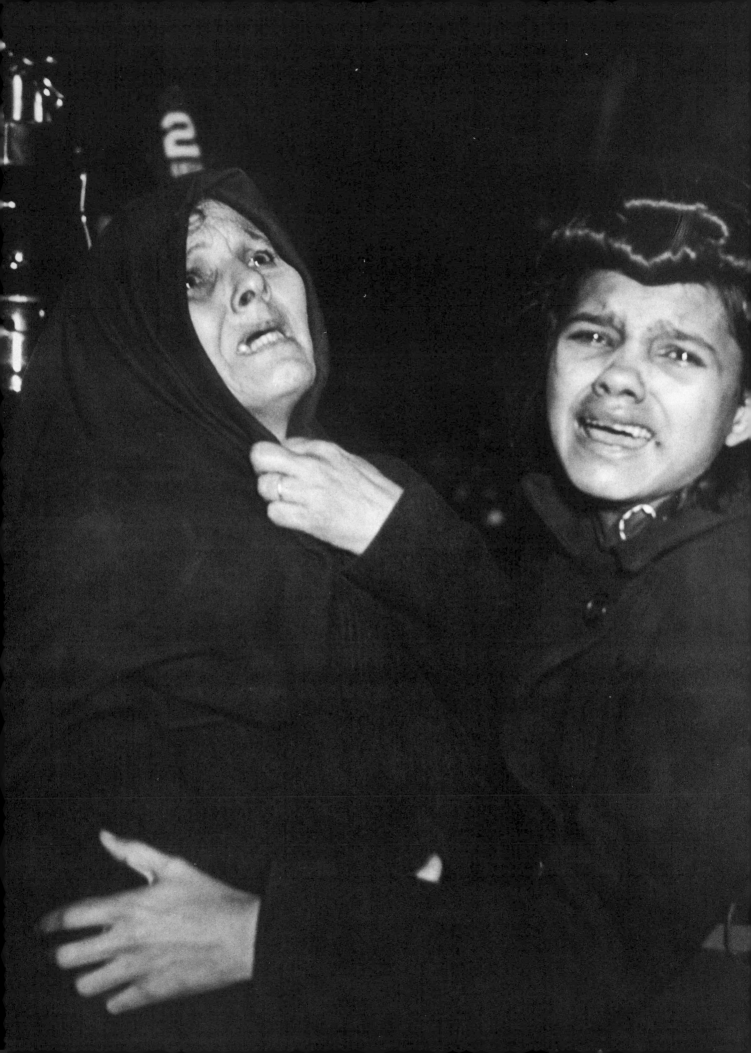

Loneliness in the City   HERBERT BAYER

Shore Patrol   KATHRYN ABBE

War
and
peace

During the twenty-five years, it seemed that we were always at war and that when peace came it was too short and served merely to set us up for new frustrations. The generation was born in bloodshed—Spain, Ethiopia, China. Then the Rhine-land, Austria, Czechoslovakia, until the entire earth caught fire in the horrors of World War II. Afterward came Korea, Indo-china, Hungary, Suez, Algeria, Cuba, the Congo and Laos. The guns never cooled.

We coined a special phrase to describe the strange peace: "the

Cold War." Riots, blockades, ultimatums and "summit conferences" that raised hopes only to dash them cruelly, made the postwar almost as nerve-racking as combat. The end of a war did not automatically bring an end to evil.

In so many ways this was a war generation: our marriages were war marriages and produced a bumper crop of war babies; the G.I. bill paid for the education of millions; war was the great theme of novels, plays and movies; we paid taxes and more taxes for defense; our population underwent unprecedented migrations, which in turn altered the political complexion of the land; everything from juvenile delinquency to the chaos of abstract art was blamed on the disrupting effects of war—and with evidence to support at least some of the charges.

But compensations followed. From the hell of nuclear fission as Hiroshima knew it, there was also opened the hope for outstanding advances in the atom's potential for medicine and industry—to lengthen life, relieve suffering and eliminate want.

The worst war gave birth to man's greatest hope for peace, the United Nations. Historians may yet find it possible to say that we learned a great lesson, one expressed by a man who flew on the Hiroshima bombing mission. "Nothing is gained by fighting a war. Nobody wins or loses."

If any one American symbolized our generation he was Franklin Delano Roosevelt, who led the nation out of a disastrous depression and through a terrible war; on the brink of victory F.D.R. himself became its casualty. In a memorable reminiscence, the dean of Washington press correspondents—whose "Thank you, Mr. President!" still ends White House news conferences—describes those sudden moments of agony which marked the end of a great man's life and of the era he captained.

Death
of
a
Leader

BY A. MERRIMAN SMITH

I SAW FRANKLIN ROOSEVELT START TO DIE.

It was a beautiful April afternoon in 1945 at Warm Springs, Georgia, and Bill Hassett and I were lazing on the front porch of his cottage, talking about Brunswick stew. Hassett was the secretary who made most of the trips with Roosevelt.

"I'll bet," said Hassett, "the President hasn't had any Brunswick stew in years. I think he'd enjoy some, too."

Next thing, Hassett and I were talking barbecue plans with Ruth Stevens, manager of the small Warm Springs Hotel.

The afternoon of April 12 was set for the party, to be given at the Pine Mountain home of Frank Allcorn, an Atlanta broker who had bought the hotel to satisfy his love of small-town life. We decided to limit the guests to the President's staff, the three wire-service men, and, of course, Ruth.

I spent most of the morning of April 12 on the mountain, helping Ruth and Allcorn get organized. At 3 P.M., I had to go down to Warm Springs Foundation and ran into Alice Winegar, Hassett's secretary. Alice looked a little strange as she darted across the street.

"You folks better be getting ready!" I yelled.

Alice didn't say anything. "What's the matter?" I asked.

"Nothing," she said. But I knew she was lying. Something must be brewing; yet it never occurred to me that a truly earth-shaking event was about to happen.

Later, I went gack to the Allcorn cottage, and at four o'clock the country fiddlers began to play. The first few guests were arriving. I walked to where a Signal Corps sergeant was sitting by his short-wave portable, put there for the Secret Service.

"How about letting me call the Little White House," I asked, "to find out if the boss is on his way?"

The sergeant handed me the microphone, and I spoke to Anderson, Secret Service agent on duty at the gate of the Little White House. "The President is supposed to be here in a few minutes."

"Yeah, I know," said Andy. "But there's nothing moving yet. Want me to give you a call?"

"No, I'll get on the Allcorns' phone and talk to Hackie." Hackie was Louise Hackmeister, the chief White House operator.

"Hackie," I said, "why aren't you people on the way?"

Suddenly her voice turned almost unreal. "I don't know, Smitty," she shouted. "But get the other two boys and go to the Hassett cottage as fast as you can!"

I ran out into the driveway, where Bob Nixon of International News and Harry Oliver of AP were standing together. Quietly I said, "Come with me." We headed toward a fast Signal Corps car. Then we saw Ed Clement of the local telephone company.

"Ed," I shouted, "get some circuits lined up to Washington!"

In a cloud of dust, we pulled up at Hassett's cottage and dashed inside. Hassett was standing near the fireplace, his face gray and mournful. On the couch were Grace Tully and her assistant, Dorothy Brady. Both were crying.

I picked up a phone resting on the living-room radiator. Hassett cleared his throat. "Gentlemen," he said, "it is my sad duty to inform you that the President . . ."

"Number, please?" said the the operator in my ear.

"Priority one—Washington," I said softly.

Hassett continued. "The President died at 3:35 this afternoon."

"Executive 3430," I finished to the operator. "My name is Smith."

I heard switchboards yanked apart, then the voice of the UP operator in Washington.

"Flash!" I roared into the phone. I could also hear Oliver and Nixon screaming because I had grabbed the living-room phone. Quickly, Hassett steered them to other instruments.

We dictated for a few minutes, then stopped to make notes, continuing this stop-and-go process for several hours. A third young man in khaki shirt and trousers helped us. He was Howard G. Bruenn, the Navy doctor who was with Roosevelt when he died.

Bruenn mopped his face and said with a hopeless shrug: "It was just like a bolt of lightning. One minute he was alive and laughing. The next minute —wham!"

"Did you see this thing coming?" we asked.

"It wasn't the sort of thing you could forecast.

He was awfully tired when he came down here. You saw him the other day—wasn't he in fine spirits?"

Yes, the President had been in fine spirits, but he looked unhealthy; his hands had trembled so badly that he could hardly get a cigarette to his mouth.

Two days before his death, the President was taking a quiet afternoon drive in his little open coupé. As I reined in my horse to let the car pass, Roosevelt bowed majestically to me and, in tones that must have been audible a block away, hailed me with: "Heigh-o, Silver!"

As far as I was concerned, those were his last words. Actually, he spoke his last words on April 12. It was before lunch, and the President was at work on official papers and posing at the same time for artist Elizabeth Shoumatoff. He had been in gay spirits. The war news was good that morning.

Suddenly he clapped his hand to the back of his head. "I have a terrific headache," he said softly. Then he collapsed.

Into the sunny room dashed Arthur Prettyman, the President's valet. He summoned a Filipino messboy, and they carried Roosevelt's sagging body to his small bedroom. Bruenn rushed in with George Fox, the Navy pharmacist who gave the President nightly rubdowns. Gently they removed Roosevelt's blue suit and put pajamas on his limp body.

Bruenn phoned his chief in Washington, who asked Dr. James Paullin, famous Atlanta internist, to hurry to Warm Springs. Paullin arrived after a wild auto ride, and his diagnosis agreed with Bruenn's —a massive cerebral hemorrhage. It was just a matter of time.

At 3:35 Roosevelt's tortured breathing stopped.

The night of April 12 was truly a nightmare—a horrible, discordant symphony of people shouting for phones, cars racing along dusty roads, the clatter of telegraph instruments and typewriters. I wrote until I thought not another word could come from my typewriter.

Mrs. Roosevelt arrived around midnight, so I

signed off my Washington wire and went into the village. There, sorrowing, miserable people sat along the curbstones, talking in low voices. Their faces were pictures of fear.

The cortege left the Little White House at 9:30 in the morning. A hot Southern sun bathed the green hills and valleys the President had loved so well. On the way to the station, troops from Fort Benning stood shoulder to shoulder, presenting arms. An honor guard walked ahead of the hearse.

At the Foundation, the square was thronged with hundreds of the President's friends. They looked at the procession with tearful eyes, then bowed their heads as the cortege passed.

First into the square was the Army band from Fort Benning. The roll of its muffled drums sounded dolefully through the still country air. The colors of each troop company carried black streamers to signify mourning for their commander in chief. Then came the hearse. The President's body was in a copper-lined, flag-draped coffin.

The polio patients at Georgia Hall were drawn up in a large semicircle around the driveway. Some were on crutches. Others in wheel chairs. Still others confined to their beds. There were no restrained emotions in this group. Their idol was dead. The world was at an end.

Mrs. Roosevelt had requested that the hearse pause momentarily at the entrance of Georgia Hall. As the vehicle stopped, a Negro Coast Guardsman, Chief Petty Officer Graham Jackson, stepped forward. Jackson was one of the President's favorite musicians and he had his accordion with him.

Tears were streaming down Jackson's cheeks as he began the soft strains of Dvorák's "Going Home." Children buried their faces in their elbows and wept loudly. Case-hardened nurses and doctors sniffled and looked at the ground.

There was old Tom Logan on the edge of the crowd. For fourteen years he had waited on the President at Warm Springs. As the white-haired Negro stared at the hearse bearing the body of his friend, his frail frame shook with sobs and he prayed aloud, "Lawd Gawd, take care of him now."

As the procession started to move again, Jackson edged closer to the slow-moving cars and began "Nearer, My God, to Thee."

At five minutes to ten, the hearse reached the train, where eight enlisted men, picked as a guard of honor for the trip to Washington, loaded the casket into the rear car. The train was beginning to move as I climbed aboard.

We passed a cotton field where Negro women were working on spring planting. I saw four of them kneeling near the edge of the field, their hands raised in prayerful supplication.

I thought of the President's prayer on D-Day when he spoke to God in behalf of our troops pouring ashore in Normandy.

"Some will never return," he prayed. "Embrace these, Father, and receive them, Thy heroic servants, into Thy kingdom. . . ."

⚒ April, 1950.

In 1936, as the shadows of war deepened, there was intense curiosity—and ignorance—about how it would be fought. Harold Kimmell, a military expert of that day, said it for many—that bombs really provided small threat to life during warfare. At the time, he was echoing the hopes of millions who longed for the tranquility of yesterday and committed themselves to head-in-the-sand thoughts that tomorrow's horrors could never happen.

The Bomb Bugaboo

BY HAROLD KIMMELL

OF THE MANY MORE OR LESS COMMON THINGS IN this world there are probably few that are more misunderstood and treated in an air of mystery than the phenomenon of explosion. In the mind of the layman, all war from now on will be nothing but a contest between great numbers of planes, and that nation which is so foolish as to build a battle fleet or to train more than a minimum number of infantry is defeated before the issue is begun.

Let us go into a few facts about the possibilities of this mode of waging war and perhaps some of these very popular theories will explode with greater violence than some of the bombs they describe.

Fortunately, enough is known of the chemistry and physics of explosion to analyze some of these wild statements.

Consider a principle that is of a very determining nature and one never considered by the bomb fanatics when they make their predictions about the effectiveness of their favorite. This principle is the one of confinement of explosion, and is known to all who have occasion to use explosives.

It is this one thing more than any other that limits the effect of the aerial bomb to superficial damage—except in very exceptional instances.

Oftentimes, when this subject is discussed, the question is brought up by someone asking why, if an artillery shell is capable of inflicting so much damage, cannot an aerial bomb of the same size accomplish as much? Two things give the artillery projectile the upper hand. An artillery shell is capable of doing considerable damage even though it does not explode, since it is traveling at a terrific rate of speed and strikes with tremendous force. This force is great enough to cause the shell to penetrate quite deeply, and if equipped with a delayed action fuse it will explode not upon striking the outside of the target but after it has penetrated deeply into it. Since this is true, the explosive is confined and is used efficiently.

Let us consider the aerial bomb and its limitations.

In the first place, the bomb is inherently a slow-speed projectile; it is not fired from a gun but is dependent upon gravity for any speed that it may attain. This speed would become very great in a few thousand feet of free falling if it were not for the resistance of the air. This retarding force is sufficient enough to limit the bomb to a speed that is not great enough to force it through any resistant material of any considerable thickness. Most aerial bombs will explode immediately upon contact. As a result the explosion is not confined and is for the most part wasted. In recent years a delayed action fuse has been developed for bombs and is intended to explode the bomb after it has penetrated into its target. The reasoning is sound, but since the bomb will not penetrate to any depth, the result is practically the same as though the contact fuse were used.

It is quite true that bombs have little difficulty in penetrating the roofs of dwellings and small structures, but they are very easily turned by fortifications and construction such as found in modern skyscrapers. Still another thing makes the unconfined explosion still more ineffective: the explosion for the most part is not in direct contact with the target, since the bomb is long and slender because of streamlining. Thus the fuse is in the nose and fires the charge upon contact, while all the rest of the bomb is above and out of contact with the surface, so that in effect that portion is exploding in air.

As an example of the effect of confinement, let us consider a rule used in blasting work. It is known to blasters that to blow a hole of a given size through a masonry wall it will require four and one half times as much TNT if placed on the outside than if the charge were placed in a hole within the wall.

A sixteen-inch naval gun shell weighs in excess of two thousand pounds and is capable of doing very serious damage. Basing deductions upon these facts, it becomes apparent that if a bomb is to compare with this shell it is going to have to weigh four and one half times as much as the 16-inch shell, or approximately nine thousand pounds. In the whole world there is not a bombing plane in production that will carry a bomb of this size.

The sensationalists also tell us that a fleet of bombing planes is capable of reducing the largest cities to small pieces of broken concrete and debris. This statement like many of the others that they make is not founded upon reasoning and is easily proved to be contrary to both theory and practical experience.

Any blasting engineer knows that to move or break up a certain amount of material of a certain type requires a very definite amount of explosive. When we consider the vast amount and type of material that goes to make up the modern city, we find the required amount of explosive to be of the order of trainloads rather than planeloads. In arriving at these figures, the fact that the planes that are to drop this load would probably be under heavy antiaircraft fire and be attacked by pursuit planes is not taken into consideration, but is figured on the basis of the best of bombing accuracy with the best of demolition equipment—a set of conditions that cannot be expected. And again what is to prevent the attacked city from taking cover under screening smoke? To strike a vital target the bomber must be able to see it. Smoke effectively prevents this while pursuit and attack planes go up to attack the invader.

The number of casualties to human life that may be expected from bombing cities is exaggerated enormously. The bomb would probably be put to a much more profitable use if it could be dropped alongside a ship and made to explode in the water against the side of the ship so as to give a torpedo effect, this being possible since the explosion would be backed up by the water.

The overenthusiastic writers referred to in this article are to be commended for their efforts to build up the national defense but are to be condemned for wanting to neglect all arms except the air service. War is a constantly changing art, and few if any are qualified to say what may be next expected to come to the fore and claim a substantial part of the world's population. But in spite of all the changes in the hundreds of years that have passed, one thing in war has remained unchanged. It is not enough to drive an enemy from the ground he occupies; it is necessary to then occupy the ground with our own forces to prevent the enemy's return. This is one job the airplane cannot perform but is the place of the man with the rifle. All other weapons are auxiliary to this one.

♛ December, 1936.

To victims of Nazi persecution, the war suggested little to laugh over. One of their outstanding spokesmen was the late Polish artist Arthur Szyk, himself a fugitive from a Gestapo dungeon. With savage sarcasm that bit to the bone, his drawings mocked and deflated the pompous bullies of fascism's "New Order." Szyk's work was so realistic that it still transmits a message of physical sensation; listen and you can almost hear the click of that Japanese warlord's shining teeth!

Ich bin der heilige Geist

DER UNTERMENSCH

A Madman's Dream BY ARTHUR SZYK

The black scare headlines from Europe
dismayed many Americans but did not deceive
or daunt Manuel Komroff, one of the foremost
literary figures of the Thirties. In 1938,
with uncanny accuracy, he forecast the sinister
course of events—and prophesied a golden
future when the bright sun of an "American
Renaissance" would warm the postwar world.

No
Bad
News
Today

BY MANUEL KOMROFF

BAD WEATHER CAN'T LAST FOREVER AND SOMEDAY I
hope to wake up in the morning, get the newspaper
from the door and read in big headlines: No BAD
NEWS TODAY. And that would be news indeed! And
I would like our young people to feel that a happier
time is not far off.

It is true that we are living today in times that
are filled with trouble. Many people are experiencing
a new kind of sorrow. Their ideals are shaken; their
hope in humanity is almost destroyed; their faith
in freedom and tolerance is lost.

Most of the bad news seems to come from Europe,
the cradle of our culture. A new kind of inquisition
has in the past few years come upon Europe—an
inquisition more terrible than the world has ever
known. If you would compare the inquistion of
Spain in the Middle Ages with the inquisition of
today you would realize that the old inquisitors were
really mild and decent people compared to those
of today. And the torture of the rack was nothing
compared to the horrors now taking place in Europe.

But still I am hopeful that a new and happier
day is not so far distant. The evil tide that is
swamping humanity is coming to its high mark and
soon, very soon, must recede. Napoleon, the arch
dictator of all dictators, only held the supreme power
for about fifteen years. Caesar also held power for
about fifteen years.

As paradoxical as it may seem, I firmly believe
that more dictatorships will mean less dictatorships.
The arrogant ideals of a dictator nation cannot bear
to have neighbors who also hold similar arrogant
ideals. When all want the same thing, then they
must become enemies. One can understand two
"supreme" races living side by side, but add half a
dozen more countries around them who feel the same
way and they must soon extinguish one another.
They can't all be the cream of the world. And that
is why I believe that a few more dictatorships will
mean the death of all dictatorships. But still that
will not bring peace to Europe. And it is important
for our youth to understand why the things now
happening in Europe are part of their old beliefs
and culture.

America has been settled almost entirely by im-
migrants from Europe. It was natural that the
culture and arts from Europe should have been im-
planted over here. But America is growing up, and
more and more do we realize that the old arts
and culture of Europe do not suit us. Geographically
and temperamentally, we have become a different
race. We live without intrigue—and this is something quite foreign to the European mind. Culture
without politics or intrigue has never existed in
Europe. Universities in Europe reflect the party in
power and professors are changed with the fall of
every cabinet. The paths of learning, like the paths
of a lion's den, point inward toward a centralized
state. Man is born in Europe to be trapped and to
die for his country. It is hardly possible for the
European mind to realize that a land can exist
where intrigue and political engineering are not
part of the daily cultural life of the people. It
is just as difficult for us to understand why we
cannot take the beautiful culture of old Europe and
leave the intrigue over there. The reason is that

64

they do not exist without each other.

More and more do we realize that in many fields the European design for life does not fit our land. We must begin again. And it is a good thing that we should cast about and see if the thing we are seeking has not already sprouted in our own soil. And what looks like a weed today may be a fine bloom tomorrow.

During the troublesome years following the Great War, some very important events have happened to us that lead me to believe that we have divorced our art and culture almost completely from that of Europe. We have discovered that we have an individuality and quality of mind that makes for a new culture. An abundance of talent has presented itself.

Literature, painting, music, architecture, drama and all the other arts—old and new—are very essential to the life and well-being of a people, a people become united through their arts, and they become significant when their art springs from their own soil. And so this new inquisition that has come upon Europe has really dug the trench between us deep and wide. I am sorry for all the pain and grief but I am not sorry that a gulf has grown between us.

An American Renaissance is definitely on its way, and that is one of the very encouraging things that I feel is in store for our younger people. And it is natural that this should happen at this time. The great period of Chinese art was born soon after the barbarians were driven out of China. The great Renaissance of Italy and Europe came immediately after the inquisition. The Impressionists and Post-Impressionists of France came directly upon the heels of the Franco-Prussian War.

Bad weather can't last forever.

♕ November, 1938.

The last war was bloody and impersonal; a soldier rarely saw the man who was trying to kill him. But that fact lessened human suffering not a bit. Behind each battle communiqué were intimate stories of heroism and pain. This one by famed combat correspondent Richard Tregaskis, whose book, **Guadalcanal Diary** became a World War II classic, describes the intensity of a wound—his very own.

Diary of a Wound

BY RICHARD TREGASKIS

THE FIRST SHELL OF THE BARRAGE HIT ME—AND THEN when consciousness came back, and I knew I had been badly wounded, I came to realize something I had long suspected: that there was absolutely no sensation of pain in such a situation. It was like a movie without sound.

Often I had seen badly wounded men—in Italy and the Pacific—and it had struck me that their eyes seemed to be filmed over by some barrier to pain. That barrier, I know now, was shock, the friend of the wounded soldier.

I knew, too, that shock had dimmed my perceptions, just as I had seen other men cut off from pain by shock. But though all my senses were dulled, I knew that I must catch up with Lieutenant Colonel William P. Yarborough of Staunton, Virginia, if I wanted to get off the mountain that night.

Colonel Yarborough and Captain Edmund Tomasik of New Bedford, Massachusetts, had gone a little ahead of me on our way back from the top of the mountain. I had stopped off for a few minutes to round up a day's notes. Then I got hit.

I knew that getting me off the hard rocky slope of Mt. Corno, west of the Italian town of Venafro, down the virtually impassable slope to the nearest jeep trail, a mile away, would take a crew of eight.

It did not seem likely that I would be able to find eight people to help me. The sense of self-preservation came strongly through my shock. Blood ran warmly down my face, but I half sat up and tried to shout to two soldiers who were running at a crouch a few feet away.

My own voice rattled faintly like a broken gramophone and I realized that the words didn't make sense. Surprised, I tried again, but I had lost my power of speech.

A shell was coming. I automatically grabbed the ground and listened. But this time too I heard the familiar sound muffled as if it were rattled nearly off the sound track, as if my whole head were joggling. The usually frightening sound of an approaching shell and the explosion were ghosts of themselves, almost comic.

A frightened soldier had skinned his way into the rocks next to me and I tried to talk, fumbling over the words, trying to say, "Can you help me?" coming out finally with the words, "Can help?"

Another shell burst farther down the slope and then the soldier's fear-wrought face was looking back as he ran away saying: "I can't help you, I'm too scared."

Then I realized that my chances of getting off that night depended on my getting up and walking. Blood still ran down my face and I knew I was badly hit. I saw my helmet lying on the ground, a hole like an open mouth in the front of it and another in the side. My glasses had been blown off but miraculously not broken. I put on my helmet and glasses unsteadily with my left arm because my right arm had been knocked out of action. It felt like a board against my side. I stood up and began to stagger down the rocky trail. I dropped my helmet and stopped to pick it up, thinking it would be a good souvenir if I survived—probably that was the only extraneous thought I had—except that I felt my pockets to make sure that I had my notes.

Then a shell was coming and I heard the same ragged, distant whistling and the rattling, loose explosion. I was on the ground for a little time and then I found a medical soldier wrapping my head in a bandage and saw that he had stuck my right arm with a morphine syringe. But I was not aware of the thrust of the needle. I picked up my right arm in my left hand and it felt like a foreign body. When I dropped it, it fell inert.

Then the medic was gone and I became again consciously alone and helpless. I got to my feet again, and stumbling, dropping my helmet time after time, picking it up with my left hand, talking my ape-jargon and with blood running down my glasses, I must have been a grotesque sight. . . . I felt something like relief at being wounded, even though I might die tonight. After so many close ones, my luck had at last caught up with me.

After having watched an all-day hand-grenade battle between the Germans and the Rangers on the Ridge of Mt. Corno, I had started down from the peak along the rocky trail.

On the long sweaty climb up the mountain to the box seat for the hand-to-hand battle, I had been struck by the continuous trail of blood sprinkled brightly on the calcite rocks. It was the first literal trail of blood I had ever seen over such a long distance. Nearly every day there had been casualties on this trail, particularly at one point where the Germans were able to bring a heavy concentration of artillery to bear. Yesterday from the foot of the mountain I had watched the dirty gray puffs of shellfire sprouting from the mountainside and had seen the wrecks of injured men. I hadn't thought that I would be contributing some of my own blood to this crimson trail.

However, here I was, badly wounded through the head and, as I thought, also in the arm.

Thinking back to that time I remember, however, that I was singularly unconcerned about my plight. I seemed vastly good-natured. Nothing seemed to disturb me—only the automatic force of

self-preservation seemed to be telling me what to do.

When the shells slacked off I climbed to my feet again, dropping and retrieving my souvenir helmet several times. Then I staggered down the rocky trail.

Like a robot unsteady on his feet but under directional control, I stumbled over the rocks, fell automatically each time I heard the approach of a shell, got back to my feet and went ahead.

Time did not seem to be moving fast or slowly; time seemed to be in neutral gear, but I knew that the distance I walked was long.

Around a bend of the trail I saw Colonel Yarborough, bending over a bleeding enlisted man who sat on the ground. With Colonel Yarborough was Captain Tomasik, and I felt a surge of pleasure at seeing them again, like a dog wagging his tail at the sight of some familiar person. Then I knew that somehow I would be able to get down the mountain that night, because I had found Yarborough. Fortunately for me, Yarborough and Tomasik had stayed behind to care for one of their men whose arm had been blown off a few minutes before.

From then on, down the long trail, Yarborough helped to support me. It must have been half an hour later that we reached a pleasant house and waited for transportation.

Still I tried to talk, uttering inane, unconnected syllables, lifting my paralyzed right arm in my left hand and trying to indicate where I thought it had been hit. They stripped the sleeve from my arm and it was untouched. Still the blood ran down my face and coated my glasses.

Across the room I saw a line of soldiers standing with fascinated, awed looks on their faces as they stared at me, the badly wounded man. Those fascinated spectators imagined more pain than I actually felt. Such is the friendly power of shock, and the stubborn will for preservation.

⚜ June, 1944.

War often propels writers along a thin line separating comedy from tragedy. During World War II, Bill Mauldin, Ernie Pyle and Marion Hargrove trod it with consummate skill. The bumptious bard of the Korean confict was the Navy's Bill Lederer, now famous as co-author of the sobering best-seller **The Ugly American.** But more in the irreverent Lederer tradition is this brash but affectionate dissection of the U.S. marines.

Our
Hilarious
Heroes:
Them
U.S. Marines!

BY COMMANDER WILLIAM J. LEDERER, USN

EVERYONE ASKS, "HOW THE HECK DO THE MARINES get that way?"

I tried to find the answer in military textbooks. No luck there. So I went into the field and started asking around. When the 1st Provisional Marine Brigade was getting ready to embark for Korea, I put the question bluntly to a group of them in front of a recruiting station. "Hey, how come you guys've got a good reputation?"

The veterans in the crowd didn't answer. But a beardless kid without any ribbons spoke up. "Mister," he said crisply, "we're respected because we're professionals."

I've heard this talk of "being pros" on posts all over the world. And the longer a Marine stays in service, the more firmly he seems to believe that either you're a professional fighter or a dead one. There's no place for amateurs.

It was suggested that it might be a good idea to expand the Marines to 750,000 men and have them act as occupation troops in Germany. Georgia Congressman Vinson put the proposition to General Vandegrift, then commandant of the Marine Corps.

"Sir," replied the General, "that's impossible."

"Oh, Congress would enact the legislation."

"But, sir," said General Vandegrift, "there aren't 750,000 men in the United States who are good enough to be Marines!"

When I was in Korea, I asked a Marine major, "Why are the Marines so good?"

"We get along okay," he replied, "because we've got discipline."

"What do you mean, discipline?"

"Well," he said, "there's the story of the Marine lieutenant who operates a rest camp. A company of battle-weary Marines came down from up north for a couple of days of relaxing.

"That night, about 2 A.M., it was cold, and the lieutenant sat in his jeep smoking and just keeping his eyes on things. Suddenly he was startled by a woman's scream. A girl with no clothes on ran from one of the houses with a Marine in pursuit. He wasn't in full uniform.

"The girl raced past the jeep. The Marine was gaining on her, but when he reached the lieutenant's jeep, he stopped and saluted.

"That," said the major, "is discipline."

The one thing all Marines accept is that their only function is to fight for the United States and the Marine Corps. Even the lady Marines catch the spirit. After the normal indoctrination, a group of Marines (female) were sent out to watch combat troops in maneuvers. After this, one of the Leathernecks (female) was handed a flame thrower. She strapped it on and let loose an arc of flame. Then she said, "Isn't there any place on this gadget to fix a bayonet?"

Marine officers generally are regarded as guys who have had more experience and know more soldiering than enlisted men. As of this day, 87.5 per cent of the officers on active duty in the Corps have served as enlisted men.

The Marine brass doesn't go in for quickie inspections of the front lines—they're up there all the time, with the combat troops. When Congressmen Hugh Scott and Henry Latham went with the Marines at the Naktong Bulge front, they found the commanding officer, Brigadier General Edward A. Craig, sleeping on the ground and eating exactly the same food as his men.

"Have you a headquarters with a bunk and mess table and orderlies?" asked the congressmen.

General Craig said, "When the rest of the Marine troops get bunks and tables, then we'll think about giving them to the officers too."

Because of their continued success in battle and out, the Leathernecks have developed a self-confidence which sometimes is offensive to other units of the service.

A social-relations professor, trying an experiment in morale for the Navy, asked permission to interview some Marines. His first contact was a rifleman who had just come off watch as a sentry.

"I'd like to ask you a question," said the professor, "about Marine officers."

"Be happy to help you sir."

"Suppose a Marine officer gave you an order, and then left the immediate area. Later, the officer realized he had made a mistake. He had given you a wrong order. What would most Marine officers do in such a case? Would they say nothing and let you carry out a wrong order—or would they come back and admit to an enlisted man that they had made a mistake?"

"Sir," replied the private, "what you asked me is what we call a hypothetical question."

"How so?" said the professor, whipping out his notebook.

"Well, sir, no Marine officer ever makes a mistake!"

Which is like the time an Army three-star general was making a courtesy inspection of a Marine artillery battery in Korea. Inspecting down the ranks, he found a USMC private who was a shell passer.

"Private," the general said, "suppose you were in a cold climate and the hydraulic-recoil mechanism on your howitzer froze. How would you fire the piece?"

"Why, General, sir, a Marine would never let his equipment freeze. That's impossible."

"But suppose you were way north and it *did* freeze. How would you then fire your weapon?"

"General," said the private, shaking his head, "you just don't understand Marines. That mechanism wouldn't dare freeze! Unless all of us was dead first."

A tenet of the Leathernecks is that they are prepared for any emergencies and must always practice for them.

During the peacetime years, there was a Marine general who had put on too much weight. So he took up riding. He would drive his car from his quarters to the stables which were outside the post. There he changed to riding clothes, got on the horse, and cantered back to his quarters. After a drink he rode back to the stables, showered, and then came home by auto.

One afternoon as he rode into the post, a Marine private, with his carbine set at the ready position, stepped out from behind a hedge.

"Advance and be recognized!" he ordered.

The general smiled. "I'm General ——."

The sentry cocked his rifle. "Dismount, advance and be recognized!" he repeated.

The general stopped smiling and dismounted.

"Show your identification card!" said the sentry.

The general didn't have it. It was back at the stables.

"Then you can't enter here!"

The general didn't argue; he mounted his horse and returned to the stable. Picking up his card, he rode back to the same entrance. Once more the sentry stepped from behind the bush.

"Dismount, advance and be recognized!"

Again the general dismounted, advanced, respectfully displayed his identification card.

"Proceed in, sir."

The general entered the post. Then he reined in the horse.

"Sentry."

"Yes, sir."

"This is peacetime. Who gave you orders to challenge everyone coming through this gate?"

"No one, sir. I was just practicing. My sergeant says that's the only way to become a professional."

That word, professional, comes up all the time. The Leathernecks operate like a ball club—doing everything neatly and taking advantage of all breaks.

A Corps news release tells of a company of Marines which had lost its light machine gun to the Korean Reds in a night raid.

"Let's get it back," a squad leader told his men. They moved out with the sergeant, away from the defense perimeter, soon sighted twenty-five Reds lugging the weapon along.

"I'll throw a grenade," volunteered one rifleman.

"No, you might damage the gun!" replied the sergeant. "Pick 'em off with your rifles."

That's the way the Leathernecks operate. You can't explain them. But from the Marine concoction of self-ridicule, horseplay, pride and fierce training comes the old Marine magic. It has a unique glow to it, a quality which is lyrical and intangible.

Marines somehow usually manage to win. When the Panama Canal was opened, the ships of the U.S. Fleet were lined up to be the first vessels to steam through the world's newest wonder.

As the fleet entered the channel, it was learned that two Marines had started earlier that day and already had paddled the length of the canal in a dugout.

The old Marine witchery has been boiling for almost two hundred years of United States history. The Marines accept it as normal procedure. It's like the sergeant who won a Medal of Honor in the Pacific for singlehandedly holding back a Japanese attack all night.

"Hell's fire!" he said, "if I had been on the ball and hadn't lost my pistol in the lagoon, I'd have brought back the whole damn company of them as prisoners. The colonel must be crazy recommending me for a Medal of Honor. The dumb knucklehead should have court-martialed me for losing my equipment!"

♛ January, 1952.

In his recent best-seller, **Exodus,** novelist Leon Uris touched on the final days of the Warsaw Ghetto, where, in 1943, Polish Jews waged a death struggle against overwhelming odds. Inspired by this heroic interlude, Uris returned to Warsaw to research and write this tribute to the ghetto's unsung heroes.

The Most Heroic Story of Our Century

BY LEON URIS

IN THE EARLY HOURS OF AN APRIL MORNING IN 1943, Nazi soldiers marched into the Warsaw Ghetto singing, confident they would clean out the Jews swiftly and mercilessly. Their leader, SS General Jürgen von Stroop, had vowed to his superiors that he would do the job in less than a week.

Suddenly, Von Stroop's jackbooted SS men came to a halt at Zamenhof and Mila streets. Squinting up at the rooftops, they spied a company of Jewish fighters looking down at them. Then a Jew, poised on the rooftop, lit and hurled the fire bomb that was the signal to open fire on the Nazis. The bottle crashed on the helmet of a soldier and turned him into a torch. This was the opening shot in one of man's immortal fights for freedom. It was the beginning of the most heroic battle waged against tyranny in the twentieth century.

I want the world to know the facts about this epic struggle—the facts as I learned them, despite Polish efforts to distort the truth. In the first part of my novel, *Exodus,* I touched upon the events in the Warsaw Ghetto during the German occupation; in the summer of 1959 I determined to delve more deeply into it. . . .

I went to Warsaw, and walked alone until I came to the desolate remains of the ghetto—an expanse of rubble and hard-caked dusty fields bearing no tree, no blade of grass. Upon this site once stood an incredible, vast human stockyard.

The ghetto had stood near the center of the city, 100 square blocks where over 500,000 people were herded behind a 12-foot brick wall, and systematically destroyed by disease, starvation and assembly-line murder in the gas chambers of the Treblinka.

Now, a few clapboard shacks stood on the site of a slave-labor factory which once manufactured brushes for the German Army. Here and there on the dusty field was an abominably constructed hovel, built from unclaimed rubble. I followed the line of the former wall on Stawki Street until I came to a large gray concrete building. Through its portals had passed more than 400,000 men, women and children bound for Treblinka. From here each day forty trains had hauled off six thousand people. Snarling dogs and SS men with whips crammed human cargo into the cattle cars. What grisly dramas had been played out on this spot!

I walked south again until I found the cemetery of what had once been the largest Jewish community in Europe. Here I found the one remaining stretch of the ghetto wall. Broken glass was cemented into the top, covered by triple strands of barbed wire. The cemetery was unkempt, covered with weeds, the tombstones in disarray from constant looting. Around me were the huge common graves of corpses picked up daily from the ghetto streets.

At the southern end of the ghetto, the Poles have built a large workers' housing development. The buildings had to be constructed ten to twelve feet about street level because the falling debris of the destroyed ghetto had raised the elevation of that entire portion of the city.

I searched for the monument which marked the uprising, and cut diagonally over a dusty field that was once Gesia Street. The monument was boarded up and sinking in the soft ground.

"Jew! Jew!"

A half-dozen Polish children threw rocks at me.

Back at the hotel, I locked my door and I fell into a troubled sleep.

On my last day in Warsaw, I returned to the ghetto to pay a final homage at 18 Mila Street, the site of an underground "bunker" the Jewish fighters had made their command post.

Mila 18 is now a junkyard. The proprietor is delighted with the extra source of income he gets by charging admission to sentimental Jews who make pilgrimages to a shrine marked only by a mound of brick and dirt, a stone tablet and a rusted German helmet. As I climbed the mound, I knew my journey had not been in vain. . . .

At the end of 1942 only fifty thousand Jews, slave laborers and a few on-duty officials survived in the ghetto. Among them, one thousand hard-core idealists —youngsters, mostly in their early twenties—had managed to arm themselves with a few dozen rifles, pistols and a single automatic weapon, smuggled in at great cost and risk. Some were even purchased from wounded German soldiers being transferred back to hospitals in Germany from the Russian front. Bottle bombs and water-pipe grenades were improvised.

In the first month of 1943 these desperate few struck. They seized control of the ghetto, disposed of their own hated police and the flunky Council and told the Germans, "Come in and get us."

At first, the Germans tried to coax them out with promises of decent work camps. The Nazis were reluctant to risk a rebellion which could explode throughout their empire. There were few takers.

Enraged at such defiance, the Germans called in General von Stroop. "Obliterate the ghetto," he was ordered. On the even of April 19—Passover, one of the holiest days in the Jewish year—Stroop's forces surrounded the ghetto. The Jewish fighters were outnumbered sixteen to one, the weight of arms against them almost one million to one.

Inside the ghetto the Jews celebrated their Passover in bunkers with the traditional Seder, the retelling of the story of the flight from Egypt's Pharaoh to freedom. On this night they faced another Pharaoh—with no hope of escape.

The last rabbi left in Warsaw conducted the Seder. Once a pacifist, he now said, "The truest obedience to God is opposition to tyranny."

The bunker beneath Mila 18 held some two hundred people, the Central Command of the Jewish fighters. In the bunker there was barely enough oxygen to keep a dozen candles burning. Six escape tunnels led out of Mila 18. Each of the six rooms was named for one of Poland's extermination camps: Auschwitz, Chelmno, Madjanek, Treblinka, Belzec and Zobibor.

The tormented Jews—men and women—poured a withering fire into German ranks with three years of pent-up bitterness spewing from their guns. These were the first Jews during World War II to fight as a people and rebel against the Nazis. Caught by surprise, the Germans fled, leaving their dead and wounded, and the first day marked a smashing victory for the rebels. On the second day the SS returned in greater force and with tanks. This time they walked into a land mine planted at the gates of the brushmaker's factory. On the third, fourth and fifth days the Jewish fighters ambushed German patrols and stopped their tanks. The Jews refused to be taken alive. Men and women flung themselves into their captors, pulling the pins of grenades.

At the end of the week in which victory had been promised, the Germans were compelled to change their tactics. They pulled out of the ghetto, and began an around-the-clock artillery bombardment. Each day, German patrols probed, but without success. By night they dared not even enter, for the Jewish fighters, dressed in uniforms stripped from German casualties, struck like phantoms.

At the end of the second week, Von Stroop gave the order to burn down the ghetto.

The Jewish forces which had used rooftops for passageways were now forced down into the bunkers. Communications were broken between fighting units. Each gram of food eaten, each drop of water drunk, each bullet fired, each casualty could not be replaced.

On the eve of Easter Sunday the sky around Warsaw was ablaze with the ghetto fire, but people beyond the wall closed their ears to the cries from within. The Warsaw fire department circled the ghetto to keep the flames inside the walls.

At the end of the third week's fighting, the ghetto area was leveled and sizzling. The Germans lifted the artillery and their patrols edged in. Starved, thirst-crazed Jewish fighters continued the battle in the rubble. Suicide attack followed suicide attack. But German power had to tell. Bunker after bunker was located and destroyed. The Nazis pursued relentlessly with dogs and detectors. Children were tortured before their mothers to force revelation of the location of a bunker.

With their food, water and ammunition depleted, they were cut off from their forces. The eighty surviving Jewish fighters took to the sewers, near boiling from the heat of the fires above. Hundreds of bodies floated about. The people plunged into pitch blackness holding hands in a chain, moving inch by inch through the slimy bilge. At times the canal pipe grew tiny, forcing them to crawl on their hands and knees for several hundred yards. In other places, the canal grew large and they walked on tiptoe through neck-high sewage. The line crept on for twelve hours beneath Warsaw until it came to the designated manhole. This was the agreed point for rendezvous with underground elements outside the ghetto who were to lead them to safe places.

Above them, they heard children playing on the streets. One man went insane from thirst and drank the water. He was dead in minutes. After thirty hours, help arrived and the ordeal was over.

There are only a few survivors alive today. All of them have tales of miraculous escapes. Some went on to fight as partisans. Others took part in

the Home Army's futile rebellion in 1944. Most slipped through a British blockade to Palestine and fought in Israel's war of liberation. General von Stroop and many of his confederates met their fate at the end of a rope as war criminals. Some are still at large.

For forty-two days and forty-two nights that valiant little force of Jews held its ground. That's pretty damn good when you consider that Norway, the Low Countries and Denmark each held for a total of only a few days. All of Poland lasted for only twenty-six days. Even after the Warsaw Ghetto was destroyed, men, women and children continued to fight on in the rubble for months until their strength gave way and they were rounded up.

Nothing compares with it. Not the Alamo nor Thermopylae. Never have two more unequal forces squared against each other and few times in history have unarmed civilians chosen to confront their hour of death with greater dignity. It was, indeed, a redemption for the humiliation suffered in the ghetto years. It has given us an eternal message. If we are ever faced with a similar situation, we pray we would have the courage to be among those last few who stood in defiance of tyranny.

♕ November, 1960.

With Old World cynicism—and wisdom—the distinguished French historian André Maurois wrote this sardonic essay on the absurdity and uselessness of revolution. He had no particular revolution in mind, only all of them. Perhaps the arguments he offered back in 1938 have since been vindicated by the course of history: "Everything changes, but nothing changes."

Futility of Revolutions

BY ANDRÉ MAUROIS

SOME DAYS AGO I MET A SPANISH WRITER WHOSE opinions had once appeared very advanced to me. I found him sad and discouraged. "I had no idea," said he, "what the violence and cruelty of mobs could be. Oppression and intolerance remain odious to me, but I have learned that a revolution is the most intolerant and oppressive thing in the world."

In the agreements between revolutionaries and intellectuals, there is often a misunderstanding which has been defined with a great deal of clear-sightedness by Denis de Rougemont. "It is very easy," he writes, "to hate and to condemn a certain order of things which vexes us. And it is very tempting to call this hate love for the people." But he goes on to show that the intellectual knows nothing of this class he thinks he loves.

Again we find the same idea in Gide: "As long as man is repressed, it is common to hope for much from him. There is the illusion that the people is composed of better men than the rest of deceitful humanity. I simply believe that it has been less spoiled, but that money could rot it like the rest. And see what is happening in the U.S.S.R.: this new bourgeoisie which is forming has all the defects of our own. It is no sooner come out of misery than it despises the miserable."

Laws do not follow customs quickly enough. "All revolutions," says Valéry, "come from the slowness of evolution." Finally a revolution breaks. It is what it must be, what all revolutions are: bloody, vigorous, absurd and in vain. The intellectuals are inevitable victims, and say when dying that the old regime was the best. Then, the crisis past, men reconstruct slowly, painfully, a society where the

72

same hierarchies and the same abuses are reborn under other names.

Mr. Herbert Morrison once began a lecture about like this: "We English Laborites are not a revolutionary party, because history teaches us that after a revolution one must begin by reconstructing what was destroyed. It is time lost. We prefer to accept the line of march such as it is today; we will try to go beyond it." This seems reasonable. But, alas, the first lesson of history is that the lessons of history have few hearers.

♔ June, 1938.

No modern revolution better typifies what André Maurois meant than that of Cuba's Fidel Castro. In 1958, while Castro's guerrillas were still fighting in the hills, CORONET sent Andrew St. George to their Sierra Maestra hideout. The then idealistic revolutionary wrote in pencil on a few yellow pages these words— his hopes for Cuba. The epilogue is all sadness. Fifteen months later his old friend St. George wrote how Castro had perverted his goals, turning his revolution into a totalitarian charade.

"Why
We
Fight"

BY FIDEL CASTRO

IN OBTAINING AND PUBLISHING THIS EXCLUSIVE article—the only first-person story written by me since we landed in Cuba on December 2, 1956— CORONET has given us the opportunity to state our aims and to correct the many errors and distortions circulating about our revolutionary struggle.

The single word most expressive of our aim and spirit is simply—freedom. First of all and most of all, we are fighting to do away with dictatorship in Cuba and to establish the foundations of genuine representative government.

To replace the unconstitutional Batista regime, we will set up a provisional government to be nomi-

nated by a special convention made up of the delegates of our various civic organizations. Once appointed, the provisional government's chief task will be to prepare and conduct truly honest general elections within twelve months.

The question has presented itself whether I aspire to the presidential office of this provisional government or the elected government which will succeed it. The truth is that, quite apart from my personal reluctance to enter the presidential competition so soon, our Constitution, as it now stands, would prohibit it. Under its age requirement clause, I am, at thirty-one, far too young to be eligible for the presidency, and will remain so for another ten years.

We do have, however, a number of program points which might serve as a basis for action by the provisional government. They are the following:

1. Immediate freedom for all political prisoners . . .
2. Full and untrammeled freedom of public information . . .
3. Re-establish for all citizens the personal and political rights set forth in our much-ignored Constitution . . .
4. Wipe out corruption in Cuban public life . . .
5. Sponsor an intensive campaign against illiteracy . . .
6. Land reform, but we will support no bill, however, which does not provide for the just compensation of expropriated owners . . .
7. Speedy industrialization of our national economy and the raising of employment levels.

Apart from political misconceptions about my own ambitions and those of our movement—we have been often accused of plotting to replace military dictatorship with revolutionary dictatorship—nothing has been so frequently misunderstood as our economic program. . . . Let me say for the record that we have no plans for the expropriation or nationalization of foreign investments here. . . . I feel that nationalization is, at best, a cumbersome instrument. Foreign

investments will always be welcome and secure here.

Industrialization is at the heart of our economic progress. Something must be done about the staggering mass of over one million unemployed who cannot find jobs during eight months out of twelve. They can hope to work only during the four months of the cane harvest. A million unemployed in a nation of six million bespeaks a terrible economic sickness which must be cured without delay, lest it fester and become a breeding ground for Communism. . . . And with rising living standards and growing confidence in government will come rapid progress toward political stability under a representative, truly democratic government. That, ultimately, is what we are fighting for.

♛ February, 1958

A Revolution Gone Wrong

BY ANDREW ST. GEORGE

THESE DAYS, EVERYONE GREETS ME THE SAME WAY: "What do you think of Castro *now?*" It's not a unreasonable question. During Cuba's two-year armed insurrection, I spent more time in the field with Fidel Castro than any other reporter—over six months. My visits delighted Castro. I had a two-year-old son (whose middle name is Fidel) and I had hardly ever seen him.

"Ah, Andrews," boomed Fidel, on one occasion, mispronouncing my name in a rush of affection. "I will be your son's godfather. We'll baptize him in the Church of the Angels when we win. Then you will come and bring your family to Havana."

This is not to say that Castro and I are no longer fond of each other. The chief of the police has orders to turn me loose whenever I'm arrested for taking pictures—six times during February and March.

Last March, I dashed up with my cameras to a midnight fight between Communists and Catholic students among the elm trees of the Plaza Central, only to be collared by a police corporal with a huge turkey-leg pistol. "March with me," the corporal said, "to the commissariat." At the corner of the park, a flock of teen-age boys, barely out of the lower grades of high school, surrounded us. Military intelligence agents, they carried submachine guns

and carbines with homemade pistol grips.

"This *hombre* is a foreigner," they told my corporal. "We have jurisdiction over foreigners."

By this time the mob was ten deep around us, and there were cries of "Let's finish off the son of a dog right here!"

The corporal steered me through the growling crowd with the barrel of his gun. When we got to the Third Precinct, I felt grateful to be in his hands.

One of the most terrifying experiences of my life happened in front of the Presidential Palace, under the North Terrace, where I once stood with Fidel on the night of his triumphant entry into Havana. Trying to photograph a rioting mob rocking a loudspeaker truck, I was half-carried, half-dragged around the plaza. Men and women swung at me wildly. A police sergeant and a fast-moving Army officer dumped me head first into the back of an Army jeep. "Another minute or two," the driver said, "and we would be carrying your corpse back here."

During the revolution, when dictator Fulgencio Batista was still on top, my reports—and the reports of others—were reprinted time and again and became the rebels' most important publicity. I had freedom to go where I wanted and to write what

I pleased. But when the revolution triumphed, its leaders had no further use for foreign newsmen.

My life grew more difficult. My phone functioned fitfully, requiring peculiar repairs and wiring. Overnight I became an "imperialist agent," instead of an honored hero of the revolution. Today, newsmen from the *other* side—Russians, Czechs, Bulgarians, Red Chinese—are inaugurating a new cycle as the "Heroic Correspondents of Our Anti-Imperialist Struggle."

My warm wartime friendship with Fidel would seem to be dead and forgotten, but that is not so. Fidel has found it difficult to forget the only magazine article he ever wrote, which appeared in CORONET.

What Fidel wrote could almost be considered a preamble to the revolution. It was reprinted in six Latin American countries, in eleven different publications. In Cuba, teams of young men from the Greater Havana Action and Sabotage Section of the Castro underground spent grinding hours turning out thousands of mimeographed copies which were circulated clandestinely.

Recently, the article has been re-appearing in the Cuban press, as a reminder of Castro campaign promises that have gone unfulfilled and ignored. One daily ran it front-page center, bordered in black.

The CORONET article has become a haunting image of the early high principles of a revolution that is going wrong. Yet he has never repudiated it.

In November 1957, I stood near a Cuban rebel forward post on La Mesa Hill, chatting with the commanding officer, Ernesto Guevara, an Argentine physician known as "El Che," who is now one of Cuba's most powerful men. We were talking of a friend, Captain Ciro Redondo, who had died in action a few days earlier.

"A real loss," said El Che. "When he came up here, Ciro wasn't a revolutionary, just a *Fidelista*. But here, we were making him a revolutionary."

That *Fidelistas* required El Che's indoctrination to be considered revolutionaries was significant news. Most informed observers now agree that Fidel's decision, halfway through the mountain war, to give El Che and his younger brother Raul Castro independent area commands was a fundamental mistake. As a result, when the revolution triumphed, Che and Raul controlled private armies much larger than Fidel's own force. Moreover, unlike Fidel's own happy-go-lucky outfit, these were politically indoctrinated troops.

There has been much guessing as to whether Raul Castro and Che Guevara are *bona fide* Communists. I happen to know that neither is a party member. But the thinking of both is described by Che's remark:

"The Communist philosophy is nearest to me."

Ernesto Guevara, a darkly handsome young man, has nursed a hatred for Western democracy from his teens. "I was for Hitler during the World War," Che once told me. "He fought the British, didn't he?"

By far the most bitterly remembered shock of Che's student days concerns a huge, drunken Ameri-

can sailor who tried to steal his girl at a Buenos Aires beer-garden dance. "When I tried to get up," Guevara recalls, still affected by the experience after ten years, "he put his hand on my head and pushed me down. I could not get up, no matter how I struggled, nor could I reach him. The waiters finally had to get him away."

Raul Castro has undergone no such traumatic experience. While still in his teens he volunteered to fight alongside U.S. troops in Korea. (He was turned down, probably because of his youth.) But during the last five years, Raul has become convinced that "The principal enemy of Cuba is the United States," and adds, "If I have to choose between capitalism and Communism, I won't choose capitalism."

On April 15, 1959, Fidel Castro left for a three-week tour of the U.S. and Latin America. While Commander Sergio Sanjegui, chief of operations of Army Intelligence, was busy with the security details of Fidel's trip, a lieutenant from Raul Castro's headquarters walked into his office and handed him a note of three typed lines: "Turn in your credentials, your gun and your uniform. You have been removed as Chief of Operations, G-2, and discharged from the Revolutionary Army." It was signed by Raul Castro.

Seizing the tactical advantage of Fidel's trip, Raul purged over thirty senior officers from the Army and the police. Rapidly he consolidated his hold over Cuba's armed forces. The most principled anti-Communist flag officer, Commander Huber Matos, was sent to prison with thirty-five of his staff officers; shortly afterward, the last wholeheartedly *Fidelista* officer in a top command post, the popular Army Chief of Staff Camilo Cienfuegos, vanished.

Perhaps Castro's greatest mistake has been his decision to reach for the leadership of the Communist-backed Left Opposition throughout Latin America. This has brought Cuba into ominous alliances with subversive groups in every Latin country, from Mexico to Ecuador.

Tragically, Castro probably does have the timbre of a great new Latin leader—the irresistible personality, the instinct for timely social reform, the sure touch with the masses. But as the result of his mistakes, Fidel Castro does not even rule Cuba today. Cuba is run by a triumvirate—Fidel, Raul and El Che. A combination of any two can box in the third, even if that third happens to be Fidel.

Raul and El Che have convinced Fidel that U.S. power is on the wane and that his only chance for Pan-American leadership is through a close political alliance with the Communist parties of the hemisphere.

Havana is now a hive of Communist and Communist-front activity. Moreover, to keep himself in the limelight, to keep the title of leader, to keep his own Cuban people united and militarized, Castro has launched his furious political and economic war against the U.S.

"We're riding a train without brakes," groaned a prominent Havana journalist to me recently.

It is hinted these days that Castro acts as if he

were Napoleon, that perhaps he is crazy. But the only psychiatrist ever allowed near him, a tall, elegant Latin American-born lady doctor, who was trained in the U.S. and is now practicing psychiatry in New York City, claims he's nothing of the sort.

"Fidel has unquestionably superior intelligence," she says, "good judgment, superb memory. He is a deeply anxiety-ridden man, very fearful of rejection, a syndrome that seems to go back to his earliest childhood, when his father Angel (a wealthy sugar planter) reportedly neither accepted nor acknowledged him, and his mother Lina (who had been employed in his father's house), I suppose, generally rejected him. This still disturbs his relations with other people on a personal level. It makes stability a difficult thing to achieve, when anything permanent, anything established or ordered must remind him of childhood's emotional disappointments."

As a Freudian afterthought she adds musingly: "It is my suspicion that his mother refused to breast-feed him."

The truth is, however, that Fidel even upset the established order of patient-psychiatrist relationship; instead of falling in love with *her*, as is customary, it was *she* who fell in love with her bearded patient.

"It was a brief romance," says the psychiatrist coolly. "It's all over now."

Yet many of Fidel's actions are probably influenced by an anxiety over a danger that is close at hand.

For all their fraternal front, the shadow of violence has never left the Cuban revolution's three new rulers. In 1957, when the small *Fidelista* landing force was scattered by Batista troops on its arrival from Mexico, Fidel, Raul and El Che were separated. Each took to the bush accompanied by one or two companions. And the Batista Government began spreading the rumor that Fidel had been killed or had surrendered.

"When the radio said Fidel had surrendered," Raul once recounted matter-of-factly, "I made up my mind to kill him if he had betrayed the revolution."

Later, when I repeated Raul's remark to Fidel, he said thoughtfully, "Yes, Raul would do anything for the revolution."

There are clear signs that Fidel is concerned with the prospect of sudden, violent death. When I flew with him in his private plane, he was startled by the sight of flames belching from the engine exhausts during warm up. The steward tried to reassure him that this was a common sight, but Fidel was worried. He ordered the engines stopped and questioned the sweating pilot for ten minutes before he allowed the plane to take off.

But unless he *is* killed—and there are those who say that his lungs and tongue would have to be clubbed to death separately—Fidel Castro will remain, as one observer put it, "A fact, a Cuban reality . . . the one man to whom Cubans have given

their mandate to conduct a social revolution."

There is little chance of Castro's government being removed, or even seriously shaken, by political opposition. The economy is groaning under the many shifts and changes. But it is by no means paralyzed. It may even go into higher gear under the impact of open and concealed Soviet technical aid.

At times, the depth of Fidel's popular support is shown in unexpected, touching ways. In the Havana Hilton, where the staff knows me, my clothes used to return from the hotel's dry-cleaning shop with slips of paper tucked into the pockets: "Be a good journalist Always speak true of Cuba Thank you God bless you."

"Castro is a better crowd manipulator than either Hitler or Nasser," says a correspondent who has seen all three. But Castro displays, even in difficult moments, a lack of personal cruelty; he has little of the repressive, repulsive harshness of the cartoon tyrant he is often made out to be.

When, not long ago, someone pleaded with Castro for a fellow revolutionary whom he had sent to prison for seven-and-a-half years, Castro began to count on his fingers worriedly: "How much time has he already spent in jail? Three months? Well, if he was given seven and a half years, he must spend at least six or seven months in jail before we can think of letting him go."

But, "Make no mistake, this is a dictatorship," says a U.S.-schooled Havana lawyer, who was once a fervent Castro partisan. "We have terror in Cuba. It's *not* violent terror, *not* gunfire in the streets. It's in the decrees and statutes that could send a man to prison and to a secret firing wall for opposing the government in any way at all. This terror is not being applied—yet. But it's here, written into law, waiting for the opposition to use real violence. Then, the roundups and executions . . . it'll be like anti-landlord week in Red China."

Many observers claim that revolutionary Cuba is a "dictatorship with a difference." Jean-Paul Sartre, the French writer and philosopher, who passed through Cuba recently, remarked, "The system seems to function this way: the people are confused; Fidel appears and tells the people what they want; the people decide Fidel is right. But what happens when Fidel is no longer around?"

My feelings are deeply divided about my friend Fidel. I still have great personal admiration for him. But I am alarmed and appalled by what has been happening to Cuba.

However, if Fidel recognizes his mistakes before it's too late, he and his country may still have a great future.

What I wonder is what Fidel—and Raul, and El Che, with whom I marched shoulder by shoulder through many moonless nights—will say to me when I return to Cuba.

⚜ July, 1960

She was just a little old lady in a sleepy Austrian town. But in a few words she summed up much of the reason for the Second World War. Martin Abramson, then a **Stars and Stripes** war correspondent, poked around the ancient town and discovered more than he had ever hoped for.

The Town That Changed Its Mind

BY MARTIN ABRAMSON

NEVER BEFORE IN ITS LONG, SOMNOLENT HISTORY HAD the little Austrian town of Braunau throbbed with such tension. The time was May 1, 1945, and across the placid Inn River, the 13th U.S. Armored Division prepared methodically to blow Braunau off the map.

Beyond the dubious distinction of having been the birthplace of Adolf Hitler, nothing much had ever happened to Braunau. Now, ironically, the war set in motion by its native son threatened to obliterate the city.

Only the day before, the fast-moving American columns had reached the river and sent a demand to the citizens to surrender. Die-hard Nazis had

blown up the bridge connecting Braunau with Simbach, where the Americans waited impatiently.

At eight o'clock that morning, the mayor of Simbach rowed across the river with an ultimatum for his friend, the mayor of Braunau. "Surrender unconditionally by noon," it read, "or your town will be destroyed." The mayor added his own advice.

"Give up, my friends, as we have done," he said heavily. "What is the use of resisting? We have already lost the war."

The morning hours ticked by. Never had the sunlit Austrian landscape looked lovelier.

At a quarter to twelve, three American artillery batteries zeroed on the town and waited for the signal to open fire. The minutes ticked swiftly by.

At three minutes to twelve three men climbed hastily into a boat on the Braunau side and began to row madly toward the Americans. From the boat they screamed frantically: "Wait, wait—don't fire—Braunau surrenders!"

That afternoon, American tanks lumbered through the sleepy streets of the town. Of the promised do-or-die resistance, there was no trace. What had happened in Braunau that desperate morning?

The German commander, a fanatical Nazi, had planned a last-ditch stand. In vain the worried burghers pleaded with him to save the town from destruction. When they staged a demonstration in the square, he marched in at the head of his troops and denounced the townsfolk.

"You will be disgraced before the world if you give up without a fight!" he shouted. "Braunau is everlastingly famous because it was the birthplace of our beloved Fuehrer. For the honor of his name, we must defend it to the last brick!"

"Maybe he is right," the citizens muttered to one another. "It *would* be a disgrace to surrender."

Suddenly, from the edge of the crowd, came a thin, quavering voice. "Adolf Hitler brought us no fame by being born here. He brought us nothing but misery. He is no good . . . he was no good from the beginning. You know that I speak the truth. Let us surrender!"

The voice was that of a little old woman known to every burgher. As her words died away, a noisy clamor arose. "Who are we to disagree?" . . . "Why should we worry about the Fuehrer's honor?" . . .

Swiftly the mood of the crowd changed. Somebody jabbed a gun in the back of the commander and led him away. His troops broke ranks and drifted into side streets. The mayor and two aides rushed to the river—and Braunau was saved. By a quirk of circumstance, Hitler's birthplace capitulated the very day the news of his own death flashed round the world.

The little old woman who had brought about the surrender shuffled back to her home, content to know that she had ended a story she herself had begun fifty-six years before. For it was then that Frau Rosa Hörl, in her capacity as town midwife, had delivered Adolf Hitler to the world.

❦ March, 1952.

On August 6, 1945, the crew of the
U.S. Bomber **Enola Gay** dropped the first
atomic bomb on Hiroshima, ushering in the
nuclear age. In that awesome moment of
truth, all previous weapons of war became as
nothing; the world could never be the same
again. Fifteen years later, CORONET tracked
down the thirteen crewmen who made history,
and recorded this memorable mosaic.

Fifteen
Years
Later:
The
Men
Who
Bombed
Hiroshima

The men of the *Enola Gay* were hand-picked experts, chosen
for intelligence, emotional stability and discipline. After
fifteen years the scene over Hiroshima is still sharp and clear
to them, and though they disagree on details, they are
unanimous on the point of whether they'd do the same
things again. The story begins on Tinian, at 2:30 a.m.,
August 6, 1945.

PILOT PAUL TIBBETTS: I was the only one that was
briefed from the outset. As different people had
functions to perform requiring knowledge of the
A-bomb, they were briefed to the extent that it was
necessary. There were perhaps four in the crew
that didn't know about it until we were in the air
on our way to the target. I crawled back in the back
of the airplane and briefed them all completely
several hours before target time. They were rather
quiet at first, and then as the impact of this thing
hit them, why, they became much more enthusiastic.

CO-PILOT ROBERT A. LEWIS: No, we knew we were
opening up a new age. I recall being briefed that
we were playing with uranium back in September
of 1944. The rest of the crew was told prior to the
mission. I know Tibbetts said many times that he
was the only one on board the ship that knew, but
this is a lot of baloney. Everybody knew.

BOMBARDIER THOMAS W. FERREBEE: Not many of the
crew had been on many combat missions. So I expect
they were a little nervous.

GUNNER ROBERT R. SHUMARD: Sure, I was scared.

TAIL GUNNER GEORGE CARON: On the long ride to
Japan I spent most of my time in the tail, chain
smoking, and sweating from the waist up and freezing from the waist down. I don't recall too much. I
know that I had my rosary beads that my mother

THE CREW TODAY

1. Pilot, Brig. Gen. Paul Tibbetts, Jr., 45, is a 23-year Air Force veteran. A Lt. Col. in 1945, he won first star this year, now commands the 6th Air Division, McDill AFB, Florida. He selected A-bomb crew.

2. Radar Counter Measures Operator, 1st Lt. Jacob Beser, 39, studied and taught at Johns Hopkins University in Baltimore, where he earns "five figures" in electronic defense work. Beser and his wife have four young sons.

3. Bombardier, Lt. Col. Thomas W. Ferrebee, 41, stayed in Air Force, serving in France before taking command of squadron maintaining electronic bomber equipment at McDill AFB. He's had four sons since the war.

4. Engineer, M/Sgt. Wyatt Duzenberry, 47, is heavier, has 18 years in uniform and fills same job today at Barksdale AFB, Louisiana. The Duzenberrys own a home in nearby Bossier City; they have two granddaughters.

5. Navigator, Maj. Theodore Van Kirk, 39, returned to Bucknell University, then joined duPont Co. in Wilmington, Delaware, as a chemist. Now a sales supervisor, he lives there with his two sons and a daughter.

6. Tail Gunner, S/Sgt. George Caron, 40, tried advertising in New York, then returned to prewar drafting job—work he now continues in Denver at $7,200 a year. He's put on weight, raised two sons and a daughter.

7. Radar Operator, S/Sgt. Joe Stiborik, 45, graying now, has lived in five states since 1945, is maintenance supervisor at the Alcoa plant in Taylor, Texas, where he lives comfortably with his wife and their two daughters.

8. Weaponeer, Lieut. Morris Jeppson, 38, pursued nuclear physics work in California, now is president of Applied Radiation Corp. —scientific-instrument makers—in Walnut Creek. Soft-spoken and balding, he's father of two.

9. Gunner, M/Sgt. Robert R. Shumard, 39, has kept moustache and sense of humor. A plumbing supply sales manager in Detroit and an Air Force reservist, Shumard is married, raises cats and owns his small home.

10. Pilot, Major Robert A. Lewis, 42, married and returned to prewar job with New York City candy manufacturer, where he's now plant manager. Four sons and a daughter fill family's Old Tappan, N. J. home.

11. Radio Operator, PFC, Richard Nelson, 35, studied business at University of Southern California. A salesman, he's active in local affairs in Wellesley Hills, Mass., has two daughters, likes colonial furniture.

12. Navy Ordnance Officer, Rear Admiral William S. Parsons, helped develop A-bomb fuse and armed bomb in flight. A director of Eniwetok tests and a Pentagon weapon expert, he died at 52 of heart attack in 1953.

gave me when I went overseas and I guess I wore them out a little bit!

LEWIS: We had Hiroshima as our prime target, but we had two alternate targets, Kokura and Nagasaki.

NAVIGATOR THEODORE VAN KIRK: The underlying factor in which city we would bomb was the weather.

LEWIS: Truman was in Potsdam and wanted us to drop the bomb on the second or third, but because of weather conditions we couldn't take off.

CARON: We saw the "gimmick," as we called it, in the bomb bay and it was a little bit different from anything we had ever seen. The security was so strict that I didn't look too hard at it.

WEAPONER MORRIS JEPPSON: The bomb was long and thin, about ten feet long and a yard in diameter. It was gray or dull green and a built-in five- or six-inch Navy gun fired one charge against the other. There may have been something scribbled on it, I don't remember, but definitely nothing obscene, as some reports had it.

VAN KIRK: We were all thinking, in terms of effect, how many times larger than a blockbuster is this thing. Is it going to be five times as large, ten times?

CARON: The colonel asked me if I had figured out what we were going to do that morning and I said, "Oh, hell, Colonel, we'll probably get in trouble with the security around here. I don't want to think." A little more chitchat came on and he decided to go forward, and as he started to crawl up into the tunnel I saw his foot sticking out so I reached up and yanked on his foot and he slid back into the waist section. He said, "What's the matter?" I looked at him and said, "Colonel, are we splitting atoms this morning?" He really looked at me funny then. It was just a lucky guess.

FERREBEE: We had a very good flight up to the target area. My part of the mission was very simple. I was able to see the target some distance out.

LEWIS: We made a single approach. It was about a three- or four-minute run. The bombardier sighted the target, which was the major military installation in the center of town. . . .

FERREBEE: Actually, it was the headquarters for the whole defense of the Japanese empire which had moved into Hiroshima.

RADIO OPERATOR RICHARD NELSON: There was a countdown to co-ordinate the dropping of instruments from the other aircraft with us. We sent out a steady signal, and at the end of ten seconds . . .

TIBBETTS: . . . the bomb release broke the contact and turned the transmitter off.

RADARMAN JACOB BESER: When they turned at the initial point the bomb-bay doors came open. Old Tom Ferrebee was up front giving us his countdown . . . and Bombs Away!

In Hiroshima that morning, volunteer workers were preparing firebreaks through the blocks of wooden houses. Thousands of families had been evacuated as a precaution against incendiary raids and the population of the ancient city was down to about 245,000. Earlier in the morning there had been a report of three planes in the vicinity, but the all clear had sounded and when the three B-29s appeared overhead, crowds stopped to gaze at three parachutes floating down from them. No one was prepared for what happened next, not even the men 32,000 feet above in the *Enola Gay*.

FERREBEE: Quick as I saw the bomb leave the aircraft I turned and said, "It's clear," and then the pilot immediately started the turn.

JEPPSON: I began counting seconds in my mind. We knew the fall time would be forty-seven seconds, but when I got to forty-seven nothing happened . . .

NELSON: We took a steep bank to the left, roughly 160 degrees, and dropped altitude to pick up speed. Everyone had put on Polaroid goggles.

CARON: It was a right-hand diving turn at just about the limit of the airplane's capabilities, quite a thrill. The turn really threw the tail around.

JEPPSON: Then I remembered it would take forty-seven more seconds for the shock waves to bounce back up to us, and just then it came. That wait was the most worrisome moment of the whole mission.

TIBBETTS: We got three jolts from shock waves that came up. They were perfectly visible, like an ever-expanding circle and they came from the point of the explosion upward. We continued right on around after the shock waves hit us so we'd come back at the target again and get a look at it.

SHUMARD: After that son-of-a-gun went off, I hope to tell you, we were really moving to get out of the way. I would say we were about a five- or seven-mile slant range after the bomb went off and we still felt the concussion.

VAN KIRK: Nobody saw the actual instant of the explosion because the plane was heading away from the target and we had been instructed not to look at the explosion because if we did the blinding flash would injure our eyes. After thirty seconds or so we turned the plane so we could take a look and see what happened.

CARON: I had the ringside seat in the tail. I was the first to see it coming. The shock waves hit the plane, bouncing it twice, and the colonel called back and asked me if I had seen anything yet, and I hadn't seen the actual mushroom coming up because the tail turret obscured the view of the impact point. But just as I said that, I saw this mushroom . . . it seemed to be coming at us, and I believe my words were, "Holy Moses, here it comes!"

SHUMARD: The flash even penetrated the glasses we had. The instant that flash occurred I turned my Polaroid glasses to where I could see clearly and it just seemed that everything was erupting right back up at us. I was scared that was "it."

LEWIS: There was actually no noise at all. There might have been on the ground, but we heard nothing.

VAN KIRK: The thing that amazed me was the cloud.

FERREBEE: By the time we had turned it was already even with us.

LEWIS: I think it took about three or four minutes to get up, and a very short time afterward it was well above our altitude.

CARON: I just kept shooting pictures. The mushroom itself was a spectacular sight, a bubbling mass of purplish-gray smoke and you could see it had a red core to it, and everything was burning inside.

FERREBEE: It was exactly the same as you've seen it in pictures, only that from being there you could actually see parts of things moving up in the cloud, parts of buildings or just rubbish of all kinds. It covered, I'd say, about a two- or three-mile-square area. You couldn't see any part of the city, just boiling dirt.

LEWIS: Where there had been a city and trolley cars and boats in the little channels that ran down into the city, all was obliterated with fire and smoke. I recall vividly the smoke and the fire that was climbing the mountainside. This was not easy to comprehend . . . to see a city disappear right in front of your eyes.

CARON: I was describing this on the intercom. I saw fires spring up, like flames on a bed of coals. And I was asked to count them. Count the fires? Hell, I stopped counting at about fifteen. That turbulent, bubbling mass looked like lava, covering the whole city, and it seemed to flow outward up into the foothills where the little valleys would come onto the plains.

BESER: Boy, that city was burning for all she was worth. There was all kinds of excitement, babbling back and forth. Paul announced over the intercom for the benefit of the crew what kind of weapon this was: "Fellows, you have just dropped the first atomic bomb in history." I was recording all that stuff. I had a disk recorder on board, for the benefit of the press pool. Somebody latched onto those disks. In the last fifteen years quite a few people have been trying to locate them. They'd be nice keepsakes.

I have never been able to verify this with anyone else, but Bob Lewis was quoted as having said, "My God!" over the interphone when it went off. I don't think Bob stopped there, and I don't think I'm quoting him properly, but I have a vague recollection that what he said was, "My God, look at that sonofabitch go."

LEWIS: I said, "My God, what have we done?" Meaning what has mankind done in designing and developing a bomb like this to destroy mankind. That is what I meant by that. People get the wrong meaning, that we immediately felt sorry. This was not the intent. The intent was that it was so enormous—human beings developing something to destroy a whole city at a time—it was utterly incomprehensible.

SHUMARD: There was nothing but death in that cloud. One fellow told me, "All the Japanese souls are rising to heaven."

VAN KIRK: The first thing was a sense of relief, and and the second thing was a sense of awe.

LEWIS: Our biggest thought, naturally, was our own safety. To get out of there and to get back safely.

TIBBETTS: There was a definite reaction of relief. With the relief was the point of view that here was the successful climax to about eleven months of demanding work.

FERREBEE: Captain Parsons and I had to get a report together to send to the President through Guam.

NELSON: We were tired, very tired, because we'd been up roughly thirty-six hours. But I can honestly say that there was much elation. I know I was elated, figuring that this would end the war.

Three days later a second A-bomb blasted Nagasaki, and on August 14 the Japanese surrendered. Relief and jubilation mingled with awe at the destructive force of the weapon. But gradually, as the Hiroshima casualties (78,150 dead, 37,425 injured and 13,983 missing) and the horrifying effects of radiation became known, the world began to face the moral questions raised by death on such a scale. Rumors spread that misfortune, remorse and even madness haunted the men who dropped the bomb like a curse. These stories were not true. Though one member of a reconnaissance mission which flew prior to the Nagasaki raid is in a mental hospital, the crew members of *Enola Gay* can speak for themselves:

LEWIS: We had hoped that if we delivered exactly on target it would involve military personnel mainly. Now, the bomb proved to be a good deal stronger than we had anticipated. It was unfortunate that so many innocent people were devoured by the weapon. But it was war, and it was an untried bomb, and it was just a case of war is hell, that's all. The same as Pearl Harbor, right?

ENGINEER WYATT DUZENBERRY: It was something we had no control over. Who am I to say the commander in chief isn't right? It was just another job we did.

VAN KIRK: Naturally I don't feel good over the tremendous amount of human suffering that's been caused, but under the same circumstances I would probably do the same thing again, and I would expect any crew in the Air Force to do the same thing.

NELSON: My wife received letters telling her how immoral a person I must be even to participate on a mission like this. I have had very, very intelligent people discuss the morals of this with me. I can understand people who feel it was unnecessary. I think maybe if they were there at the time they would have felt the necessity of it also.

RADAR OPERATOR JOE STIBORIK: We didn't know how many people we had killed or maimed but after we found out what we had done it did make me feel kind of bad. But if they had had it, they would have dropped it on us.

TIBBETTS: I have absolutely no feeling of guilt, quite contrary to some of the material that has been written about my being in an insane asylum because of remorse over this thing. I was directed to do it. If I were directed to do such a thing today, I've learned in all these years of military service to follow orders, so I'd follow them without question.

VAN KIRK: Recently quite a few girls from Hiroshima were brought to this country for plastic surgery. They appeared on a television show. Naturally, when you see these things, it gives you—I don't know what kind of a feeling it is—you just wonder whether this was all necessary. You don't feel good about it. I don't lose any sleep over it, except on these special occasions when I see something that reminds me of it.

SHUMARD: You don't brag about wiping out sixty to seventy thousand at one time. As my wife says, children too. And she's right. I don't think that at any time anybody's ever tried to accept a lot of glory for what they've done. It was a job that saved countless lives. Possibly if we hadn't done what we did there would have been an invasion of Japan. The boys who managed to get into occupied Japan after the war said that it would have been next to suicide if they had attempted to land.

LEWIS: The thought occurred many years ago that it might have been a good idea to drop it in Tokyo harbor to let them know we had something like this. But then again, second guessing is not a healthy thing. One very strong feeling I had was that I was sorry this bomb wasn't ready earlier, in February, when Iwo Jima took place. There was nothing but military personnel and it would have just about encompassed the entire island. That would have been a perfect target.

JEPPSON: It is possible that an advertised demonstration explosion to impress Japan could have been planned without the need for destroying a city. The risk, of course, was that the bomb might fail to detonate.

BESER: I spent many an hour digging through transcripts of the German Archives. I am Jewish, and I was interested in seeing for myself if some of the things that I had heard about really took place. My main regret is that the bomb was not available for the final subjugation of Germany. I think the German people earned the right to that honor more than the Japanese.

SHUMARD: I don't think you actually ever forget it. It's something that sticks with you.

NELSON: I have seen pictures of the victims. It is certainly not a pleasant thing to look at.

CARON: I have seen some movies showing the victims, some of the kids that were burned. That is the only time I might have had a partial feeling of guilt. I wish I hadn't seen them.

NELSON: I think that in retrospect we all have to do a little soul-searching to justify our acts on this mission, even though we were just flying an ordinary mission as far as we were concerned at the time. I feel that it has made me more aware that I have a responsibility, made me think that I have social obligations in my town, in my church, that I have to fulfill. These don't have to be any great moral things, but just participating in town gov-

ernment or in church or trying to raise my children the way I think necessary.

BESER: I probably am more conscious of the consequences of this thing. It has motivated me to a great extent in pursuing my life's work, which is defense, because I think that only through a positive, strong posture can we ultimately divert any disaster.

NELSON: The subject is becoming harder and harder to talk about now, as we lose sight of why it was dropped. At schools and churches they come right out and ask you whether something is right or wrong. Particularly in the high schools.

LEWIS: The question was raised that people who are exposed to radioactivity might become sterile. When Bob Caron came back he had a child right away. Then I got married and had a child fairly soon. We kind of joked about the fact that we either had not been exposed to too much or this was just a big hoax. I have five children.

SHUMARD: The last time I saw the *Enola Gay* was about 1948 or '49. I'm in the Air Force Reserve and we had occasion to fly down to Chicago, where they had an Air Force Museum. I saw this old 29 sitting there and as I walked by I patted her on the nose and kept on going. After, I got thinking, and remembered that number 82 we had on the nose. And I'll be doggone if it wasn't the same one . . . They're making a place for it in Washington at the Smithsonian Institution and it's down there now.

TIBBETTS: My mother is still living and in good health. Her maiden name was Enola Gay Haggard from Glidden, Iowa. When I was in college studying to be a doctor I always wanted to fly. In 1936 there was a family showdown on the subject. Most said, "You'll kill yourself." But my mother quite calmly said, "You go ahead and fly. You will be all right." In getting ready for the big one I rarely thought of what might happen, but when I did, those words

of Mom's put an end to it. So, how would you have named the plane?

It took the world one million years to progress through the Stone Age, Bronze Age, Iron Age and Machine Age. The Atomic Age arrived overnight and today mankind is still struggling to adjust and to comprehend its implications. The men who saw the new age born, high above Hiroshima, hope no one ever again will use this great power as they had to.

BESER: I have debated the issue many times, with clergymen of all faiths, with members of Congress, on public platforms. I have defended the entire operation and myself in the press and on radio.

TIBBETTS: If wars are going to be fought, you're going to win it with all the resources at your disposal. And if you're fortunate to possess powerful weapons, there's only one thing to do, and that's to use them.

BESER: I was the only man to go on both the Hiroshima and Nagasaki missions. I know, and history shows, that this wasn't an end to all wars: World War II wasn't over a year before they were popping at each other. I hate war, my wife hates war, my kids hate war, and this isn't just a truism: I mean it. But let's face up to it. Mankind has not yet developed a human animal that can live together without conflict. I certainly hope we've seen the end of global conflict, for I think the next time, when and if it comes, is going to set us back to the point where we'll be swinging by our tails from trees again. Literally, I can see no other way out.

FERREBEE: The weapons in the world today have much more power, but I doubt that one will ever be dropped, one single bomb, that changes things as much as that one did.

VAN KIRK: I think I have the same feeling that 99.9 per cent of the American people have: that this weapon will never have to be used for these purposes again.

♛ August, 1960.

WONDERFUL FOR RUSSIANS

Rich Aunt Anna has just returned
  from Moscow.
She learned about Communism from
  the hotel window.
She is terribly enthusiastic!
She would not care for it in this
  country.
For the Russians it was wonderful!

—O. S. M.

Survival of the spirit

Who can look back on the struggle of these years without feeling wonderment at the resources of the human spirit? The lesson is an important one: it is not what fate hands us but how we take it that counts. Wars, poverty, sorrows and failures cannot have great terrors; love, luck and laughs no counterpoise of bitterness for the man who has learned the values of the spirit. In the complex of daily living, all of us must hold fast to them or else we could never withstand the tireless assault of what the Greeks called Nemesis, the Victorians fussily termed "the fell clutch of circumstance," and we stoically slough off as "the breaks."

All of us can, if we open our eyes, glimpse eternity in nature and in the heart of a man which beats for the heart of another man. The great visionaries dreamed and doubted and dreamed more till they achieved, sometimes giving their lives for, the vision. In the process they left the legacy of reminder that men do have the capacity to make life sublime. For all men—the elegant or the humble—the goal is the same, the lesson changeless, whether its seeker is Dr. Harlow Shapley postulating new concepts as he gazes into fathomless space, or Edwin Way Teale marveling at an insect; Salvador Dali giving color and life to dreams of sleep, or a humble and brave youth offering new life from his own flesh to his dying twin. Sometimes it flashes in a terrifying and breathless moment—in a Hungarian cellar as a Soviet soldier raises his gun to fire, then wordlessly lets it fall and turns away and, in the act, grants life; other times with dawning revelation as a man soul-searches his conscience and perhaps risks his life to rescue a book from behind the Iron Curtain and thus bring the light of great thoughts to a world which otherwise would have been denied them.

In an age filled with turmoil and violence of such magnitude that lives by the millions were callously incinerated away, the earth's survivors might, understandably, have abandoned a belief in the spirit and thus fallen into a state of mass anonymity.

Fortunately for the human race, it did not happen that way. The spirit survived, perhaps with even more health than we can now realize. What we know of the brave ones who fanned the flame is their message, "Have faith; nothing can take loving from the living. No one can deny joy to those who give. Have faith and do not be afraid."

As the world prepared to plunge into a blood bath of cruelty and destruction, the value of a human life, the integrity of an individual, often seemed to be forgotten. It took the wisdom of historian-philosopher H. G. Wells to reassert the power of the human spirit, the intransigence of the human will.

"What Life Has Taught Me"

BY H. G. WELLS

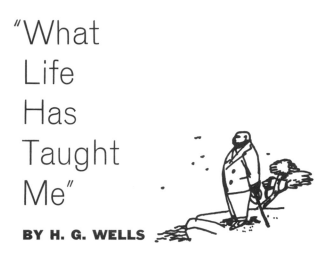

I HAVE FOUND LIFE AS A TEACHER RATHER APT TO begin with broad but unsound propositions, and then to qualify them and whittle them down, so much so, that at last they were the mere shadows and sometimes even inversions of the original assurance. At first, for example, life persuaded me that the whole world was made for me and absolutely secure, and that if everything was not exactly as I wished it, I had just to squall and things would be put right.

I gurgled and bubbled when the something that was not myself, the world about me, was complaisant, and I yelled at it, generally with excellent effect, whenever it failed me. And I grew up to the crawling, tottering stage of humanity without any serious disillusionment about my primary importance in the scheme of things.

Presently shadows came into my unqualified lordship. I think that they came first through dreams. I lived in a protective but expanding world, but somewhere in it there lurked something inimical, something to be feared.

In various ways, kicking and biting for instance, I battled against the powers of unbelief, and at adolescence I was still clinging to the conviction that I was central to my universe. But by then, my first innate self-confidence was sorely beset by an increasing swarm of incompatible facts, and the conflict had opened out and shifted its terrain.

The more I listened to the explanations of theology, the less I liked them. I could not bring myself to believe in some small-minded, personal deity, a sort of nursery-maid Providence, who could fetch and carry for me behind the screen of the stars, and when I turned from the infinitely great to the infinitely little, I found as little trace of any such friendly agent among the atoms. Sufficient to me, and more than enough for my powers, was my own little life. That was my job. It took me the best half of a lifetime to attain that much humility.

Our little lives go on, I had to learn, within a framework, silent, enormous and entirely inexplicable. We are bounded by the circling stars and by the dance of the atom systems, and though we do not possess, we belong. "You and your sort and your fusses are not everything; by our measure they are scarcely anything." The stars say that plainly to us and they say no more. They put us in our place and show no further concern about us. Because the universe has lost its subservience to us that does not detract from—rather it increases—our significance to ourselves. There is greatness and it reflects upon us.

The less I was able to shift the responsibility for my conduct to anything outside myself, to any outer law, commandments or leadership, the more I realized the intensity of my responsibility to my conscience, to an inescapable personal mystery within. I can explain conscience no more than I can explain the stars, but with every year of life I recognize its sole and imperative authority as to what I can do, may do and must not do. There are things I have to do to the best of my ability and things I will be damned if I do. To fail the former or to yield to the latter is a living death.

The humility that comes from a frank recognition of one's limitations and blunderings but which still keeps upright is the direct antithesis of pietistic self-abasement and surrender. One can be an ant in the dust and yet as proud as the devil in the face of king, party, priest, church, medicine man, know-all teacher, slaveowner or any other adversary to the liberty of being. I may be a midget but I will be damned if I will distort myself for any consideration whatever.

I have given this much space to the fundamental interpretation of existence to which life has brought me, because all the other lessons I have learnt can be made clear only in relation to that. One lesson I have learnt very slowly is to discriminate among my moods. I am still learning that. In my ardent youth I did not begin to suspect how inconsistent I could be. I said a thing and stuck to it, suppressing any subsequent questionings, and so I did many harsh, unjust or inconsiderate things and then justified them angrily. The fear of "weakness" is very strong in youth, and it takes us some time to learn the finer reality that at bottom our characters are all in a piece together and that we destroy something in ourselves when we suppress an inconsistency. That is not strength but egotistical pedantry.

Acknowledging our inconsistencies does not mean repudiating our responsibilities. When one does anything wrong one has to stand up to the consequences. The proper consequences of an error are, like it or not, frank admission and reparation. I have still the natural what-I-have-said-I-have-said disposition, but I find that life has taught me to hold things back for reconsideration whenever I can, correct more carefully and restrain my indignation when I am misunderstood. It is as natural as hiccups to believe that people who contradict or misunderstand you are animated by malice, and I have found the suppression of that disposition a difficult bit of self-training.

One series of lessons throughout my life has been the suppression of fear in a number of forms. One of them is the fear of pain. When I was young I used to have a shrinking horror of pain. I read about torments and I mused over instruments of torture. I used to think, "No. I could not endure that. I could not face it. I should squeal. I should give in. I should cringe and beg. And then what would be left of me?" "It" perhaps was the Inquisition—or Red Indians. My mother, dear woman, was humbugged by a half-crown dentist and several of my first set of teeth were prematurely extracted. That set a standard. What if that wrench was multiplied by a hundred, say, and prolonged!

But life has taught me that the possibilities of pain have been much exaggerated. You would not feel a tooth extraction multiplied by a hundred; you would not feel it multiplied by ten. Beyond certain limits the appreciation of pain ceases, just as the appreciation of light ceases beyond the red and violet of the spectrum. You can outface pain. Pain wavers more than you do, and beyond a quite low limit it blots itself out. Pain has no steadiness. Its onset is a disagreeable surprise and that is about the worst of it. If you can realize this simple proposition, "It will pass. It will surely pass," you will either find yourself presently on the other side of pain or else you will no longer be aware that it ever approached you. But for nearly every distressful phase of living, "It will pass" is a sure protection.

And another phobia that haunts the young and diminishes steadily as we learn more of life is the fear of death. That, paradoxically enough, is because the young cannot realize they will ever die. They think of death as living but in a muffled state.

The other day, reading some rather nonsensical stuff about immortality, I came upon an attempt to exaggerate the horror of death by calling it "eternal extinction." But there is no such thing as extinction that *goes on*, any more than there are countless pages after the end of a book. And in my youth I was tormented by such frightfully suggestive phrases as "the death agony." In ordinary death there is evidently a steady, merciful ebb of sensation, and even in a dreadful-seeming death such as being burnt alive, death must come as a complete cessation of pain.

Your death may be inconvenient or distressing for others, so that you should do your best to die considerately, but you will never know of it; it will never trouble nor inconvenience you. Death is a sleep and a forgetting; you will never know that you are dead.

The building up of this assurance that neither pain nor death can abase me if I refuse to be abased has been the fundamental shape of my life education. It is the backbone of my creed of Mystical Stoicism. Life has taught me very many other things in gross and detail, but this is as much as I can tell in the compass of one short article.

♕ May, 1939

The violence that for a time divided classless America into a land of suspicious "haves" and embittered "have-nots" produced a small band of modern martyrs, tough as nails and unforgiving. It also produced a guilt burden for the new generation with a social conscience, and the gap was not easy to bridge, as Sherwood Anderson's very personal, dramatic confrontation with Tom Mooney reveals.

Backstage with a Martyr

BY SHERWOOD ANDERSON

IT WAS SEVERAL YEARS AGO AND I WAS IN THE CITY of San Francisco. This was when my friend Lincoln Steffens was still alive, and he asked me to go see Mr. Fremont Older. As everyone on the Coast knows, the late Mr. Older had made a long fight for the release of Tom Mooney. Older had been, for many years, the best-known and, I'm sure, the best-loved newspaperman on the coast.

He was very insistent that I go out to San Quentin prison to see Tom Mooney.

But why?

What could I do for him?

However, I went, and Ted Lilienthal went with me. He drove me out. Ted, with Leon Gelber, runs a delightful book store in San Francisco.

We went to the office of the warden. I told him who I was, that I had been sent to him by Older, that I had come to see Tom Mooney.

The warden was a large, heavy-looking man. When I had told him my mission, he sat for a long time looking at me. Then he made a little motion with his hand.

"Another one to see Tom Mooney, eh?" he said.

He leaned forward, pointed a finger at me. Ted, a shy man, had gone into a corner by himself. What the warden said made me feel a little foolish.

"This Tom Mooney," he said, "I know nothing about it. I don't know whether he is guilty or not. I didn't try him. I'm the warden of this prison. People keep coming and coming to see Tom Mooney.

"Hell, man," he said, "I got a lot of other boys in here. Some of them would like to have people coming, now and then, to see them."

It was something to think about. It was no doubt true. What could I do for Tom Mooney?

Then I thought of something. At the time, during the same labor war on the Coast, when they had convicted Tom, there had been two others also convicted.

There was the man called "Smitty" and there was one of the McNamara brothers. They were in for life. Not much chance of their getting out.

They had blown up a newspaper office down in Los Angeles. There had been people killed.

It hadn't been planned that way. There was this bitter labor struggle. They had planned to blow up the building when it was unoccupied, but things had gone wrong.

"Sure we're guilty. We did it."

When I mentioned the names of the two men, the warden's face lighted up. He smiled.

"Sure you can see them. They're a couple of swell eggs."

They were brought in, two healthy-looking, quiet men, and we began to talk, pulling shy Ted into the conversation, the warden leaning forward to listen.

They were both curiously alive, intellectually alive. They had done something, terrible enough, earlier in their lives and were paying for it. They knew my books, the books of other men of my time. They discussed them with me, asked questions, were filled with intellectual curiosity.

They mentioned some of our outstanding writers. What sort of guys were they? What about Hemingway, Faulkner, Dos Passos, Dreiser? How did these fellows live? What did they look like? Did I know them?

Ted and I both were taken into what seemed to me a kind of warm friendliness, the warden leaning forward to listen, apparently warming himself in it.

They were there and they were gone.

"Well, so long, men."

A kind of heartiness. The warden weakened.

"Oh, I guess I'll have them bring in Tom. Why not?"

He seemed to give the order for Tom's coming a little wearily, like a bartender humoring a drunken man.

And then Tom came. He was dressed in white, with a black flowing tie. He marched in. I cannot help what I felt. To me he was a bit the bad actor, let's say playing the part of Napoleon.

So I was Sherwood Anderson, eh? He strode across the room to me, a finger pointed at my face.

"So you are Sherwood Anderson?" he said again. His finger seemed about to run into my eye and I drew away, but he followed.

"You quit what you are doing," he said. "You be the American Zola. I'm the American Dreyfus."

That was about all. We didn't stay long. I tried to introduce him to Ted Lilienthal, but he dismissed poor Ted with disdain.

As I have suggested, that is about all I can remember.

He had come into the room and he went out, striding out as he strode in. He left us curiously flat.

It wasn't that we doubted his innocence. Why should we? There was apparently plenty of evidence that he was innocent.

But had his innocence, his martyrdom done that to him? We had no way of knowing.

There were the other two who were guilty. Two guilty men who knew they were stuck.

So warm and friendly.

And then Tom—the innocent one.

"I'm the American Dreyfus. You be the American Zola."

Well, you who read this, figure it out, if you can.

ꟿ July, 1940.

IMPUDENT TOMMY

Throw impudent Tommy out of
    Sunday School!
The teacher was telling about the
    rewards of hard work.
Tommy mentioned some people who
    were not rewarded.
He mentioned some people who were
    rewarded for no work at all.
Throw impudent Tommy out of
    Sunday School!
        —O.S.M.

The author, who carved the wondrous sculptures on the giant cliffs of Mt. Rushmore and thereby "got as close to heaven as man can reach," pays homage to all those humans who refuse to allow matter, even natural, to dwarf their dreams.

I Molded a Mountain

BY GUTZON BORGLUM

THE "MAD" DETERMINATION TO DEAL WITH A MOUNtain of granite as if it were a block of stone in your own studio—the great outside wonderful world as your workshop—the sun, moon and even the stars as your light—the subject of your creation the mass action of civilization—this was first conceived in the South when I obtained a commission to do the Confederate Memorial at Stone Mountain.

I was consumed with both physical and spiritual fear at the thought of the long years of purely material work ahead of me before I reached the surface of the figures into which I must carve the characters of Generals Lee, Jackson and their host. Every sculptor with whom I discussed my problem advised against the undertaking. But this only provoked a challenge in me and gave me a will that dared not fail—a will that did not fail.

So you see it was Stone Mountain which opened the door for me to a new and larger form of memorial. And it awakened in Doane Robinson of South Dakota, historian of the Northwest, a patriotic desire that the record of the development of the great Western democracy should have a mountain monument, too.

In response to his request in 1925, my son Lincoln and I first went to the Black Hills, where, equipped with guides, horses and camping outfits we started out to find a piece of rock suitable for carving. A shoulder of granite facing southeast was a necessary condition, because on it would be carved my figures. And since the sun, north of the equator, is a Southern gentleman, moving to the south in his westward course, I wanted as much of him all day on all my figures as was possible. If sculptors who build monuments north of the equator would think of this, our monuments, whether sculptured figures or ornamented buildings, would be more successful.

After two weeks' search, camping in the open, scaling seemingly inaccessible granite cliffs, we started to climb the grandest of them all, Mount Rushmore. This was no easy task, for the last one hundred and fifty feet was almost perpendicular rock. Only with great difficulty did we manage to find a toe-hold. But by pyramiding three men on the shoulders of each other, the top man with a lariat found a rock where a rope could be looped over a projecting sliver of rock, and we finally reached the higher floor. Breathless and with torn hands and broken nails, we collapsed on top, glad to lie resting in the sun.

And then suddenly a new thought seized me —a thought so great it frightened me, forced me to my feet—a thought that was to dominate all my carving: *the scale of the mountain peak!* We were 6,200 feet above sea level, 500 feet above all surrounding cliffs. We looked out over a horizon literally leveled by the workings of time on this upper world. I had not realized that there was another scale here different from the lower world— a scale that existed unknown and unused by man. Here the Earth aspires, forgets the valleys, assumes the form and dimensions of related sister planets; mighty storms hew and shape these lonely peaks as they reach away from the little farms and valleys.

And it came to me in an almost terrifying manner that I had never sensed what I was planning— its dimensions—and how unrelated to the gods were the little people below. I had never dreamed in terms of this outer, larger world, and yet here I was planning to carve the gods of the valley, of my race, of my little world, into the dimensions of these planetary forms. The thought struck me as a rebuke. I realized that I was not of them, that I belonged to that smaller people—the little race of two-legs in the valley. I felt a new fear.

The vastness that lay here demanded complete remodeling of the grouping I had been dreaming. I must see, think, feel and draw in Thor's dimensions. The mountain was beginning its work.

The rest of the story can be repeated here more briefly. No less important than selecting the location was finding a subject justifying the task. As I have often said, the carving of mountains should not be undertaken by anybody, anywhere, except for the purpose of recording great and important events in the history of the people who form the surrounding civilization. And so we chose a memorial symbolizing the creation and the extension of the republic—the forming of the government by Washington and Jefferson—the saving of the political union by Lincoln—and finally, the completion of the unfinished work of Columbus by Theodore Roosevelt who, by cutting the Panama Canal, united the west and east oceans.

Having determined our subject, our location and the important question of lighting, I proceeded to make models on a scale of an inch to the foot of finished carving. Then began the difficult problem of locating the figures on the mountain. Back in New York, when I was making the colossal head of Lincoln, there was a colored woman who cleaned the studio. She had swept around that block of marble for weeks when one day her gaze traveled up to what I had been doing. "Why, Mistah Borglum!" she exclaimed in astonishment. "How'd you know Mist' Lincoln was in that stone?" That has been our problem: we knew that Washington and the others were in that rock, but how to find them?

The surface rock of Rushmore is rough, indented with fissures and occasional infiltrations of feldspar and other minerals. I found that the cracks generally run diagonally, about seventy feet apart, and I could place the heads between them. However, the cracks and irregularities of the stone have made it impossible to finish any one head until all were carefully determined, for we never knew what changes we might find to be necessary.

The Black Hills are far from the labor market of skilled stone carvers. Indeed, there are few of these anywhere. But on the other hand, western South Dakota is rich in mines, and from miners we drew our crew of workmen. Many of them have been with me for years and have mastered the difficult problem of how to remove stone by blasting, yet without injuring or jarring the rock.

The men work in harnesses, suspended over the side of the rock at the end of a steel cable operated from a winch at the top. A sudden gust of wind or a kink in the cable may give a driller an unpleasant moment or two, even though he is strapped in and could not fall out even if he became unconscious. I had a very severe jolt not long ago, and my whole nervous system sustained a severe shock.

The work goes on in almost any weather except during severe cold and thunderstorms. A couple of years ago, although the sky was clear above our mountain, lightning from a storm several miles away exploded the dynamite a driller was preparing for a blast and threw his cable out into space. He had the presence of mind to kick the rock with his feet, having his knees bent, as he swung back, and thus avoided a nasty accident. Two other workmen narrowly escaped injury from the same thunder bolt, and now we don't work with dynamite if there is a storm anywhere around.

I spoke of the infiltrations of other deposits. At the end of Lincoln's nose we ran into silver and lead, but not enough to interfere with the design. Washington's collar had to be carved with special care, owing to the large size of the feldspar crystals, larger in the Black Hills than anywhere else. About four years ago, on Roosevelt's cheek, a red substance was encountered which Dr. Connolly, of the South Dakota State School of Mines, thought might be a rare mineral called allanite. Fortunately it occurred in the hollow between nose and cheek and could all be removed as part of the design. The Black Hills are known to have a greater variety of minerals than almost any other locality in the United States.

Many years ago, we used to climb to our work at the top of the mountain—eight hundred steps up very steep ladders. We had no money for a proper hoist—engineers had said that an adequate system of scaffolding and elevators would cost more money than we had for the whole memorial. I estimated that it took the men from fifteen minutes to half an hour to get their breath after the climb before going to work. That meant a loss of from fifteen to thirty hours a day in a group of sixty workmen, to say nothing of the exhaustion. We had always had a bucket running on a stout cable to ferry the drills back and forth, a distance of fifteen hundred feet to the blacksmith shop, and finally, after eight years of climbing, I had the carpenter make an open box, capable of holding four men, to replace the bucket. At first I rode up and down alone, for the Commission forbade the workmen to imperil their lives and even tried tactfully to keep me from riding in it. Now the box has been strongly reinforced, together with the cable carrying it, and all but the most timid ride in it. The cable will carry a load of twenty thousand pounds.

It might be said in passing that the human element in carving is as difficult to deal with as the granite. I am proud to say that we have never lost a man in our fourteen years of hazardous work, and I took pleasure in pointing out a comparison of this record with that of the government at Boulder Dam, to a government official who had reported to Washington that I did not take sufficient care of my men.

But it is public response to the memorial that has thrilled me most. Last year, approximately 300,000 tourists visited Mount Rushmore. They came from all walks of life and showed varying degrees of emotion. One little old lady, plainly a New Englander, grasped my hand at the door of the studio one day. She was sobbing, and my wife put her arms around her to steady her.

"Mr. Borglum, may I shake your hand?" she said. "I never knew America was so great!"

♛ August, 1941.

Despite the carnage of war, the materialism, the ever-faster pursuit of money, in this time, as in every time, a flight for a single life could capture the imagination and marshal tremendous energies and resources. The baby was only twelve inches long and "hadn't a chance," but within him flickered the precious flame of life—and it had to be saved.

The Precious Life of a Preemie

BY KATHERYN WITHERSPOON

BABY ROBERT BROWN WAS ONLY MINUTES OLD WHEN he was wheeled through the door marked PREMATURE NURSERY in New York's Flower-Fifth Avenue Hospital.

"Poor little fellow," Dr. Robertson, the hospital's resident physician in pediatrics, said, and shook his head. "He's too small to last more than a few hours."

"Don't be so sure, doctor." There was challenge in Nurse Carey's tone as she lifted the tiny infant from the portable incubator. "Isn't he cute? He must be about the smallest we've ever had."

She put him quickly in one of the nursery's Isolette incubators reserved for newborns under four pounds, placing him on the folded diaper his body was too frail to wear.

"He's just a six-months baby and so full of mucus he hasn't a chance," Dr. Robertson said. "The mother bore another preemie two years ago that lived only nine hours."

They looked down through the transparent plastic hood at the baby lying in the warm incubator like a little sparrow, all ribs and legs and arms. His head was finely shaped, with pointed chin and delicate nostrils, but his weazened skin gave him the wise look of a little old man.

"Here are his identification bracelets."

The doctor handed the blue and white bead bracelets to Nurse Carey. Ordinarily they were put on a newborn's wrists in the delivery room, but any unnecessary handling would endanger the life of a preemie this size. Nurse Carey tucked them into a recess adjoining the head of the mattress.

A cleaning maid in green uniform, bustling in to empty the wastebaskets, paused to peer over their shoulders.

"What a little one!" she exclaimed. "Why, he's a living doll." She crooked a playful finger at the baby. "How big was that littlest girl we had?"

"One pound fifteen ounces," Nurse Carey answered.

"One fifteen—and you should see her now." The maid puffed out her own fat cheeks imitatively. "Can we—will this one—?"

"Small girls seem to me to do better than small boys." Nurse Carey shrugged. "Somehow, the boys we've had didn't seem able to make it. We've never had a boy this tiny live, and only one girl. Our smallest boy was two five. I'd say this baby has about one chance in a hundred."

"Poor thing—"

He lay there quietly, his rib cage rising and falling as he breathed, exhausted from the shock of birth. His ribs beneath his thin skin resembled small ridges of fine sand along the seashore. His umbilical cord, tied off, hung to one side like a sea shell. His deep blue eyes were serene.

But suddenly he began breathing with difficulty, and his color changed rapidly to blue-black.

"He's got to be suctioned," Nurse Carey called. "Let me have the aspirator."

A student nurse brought her a delicate blown-glass oval, with a glass trap inside. A long glass cylinder extended from the top, with a rubber tube suspended from the bottom.

Nurse Carey reached through the incubator portholes and placed the rubber tubing in the baby's mouth. Then she put the upper glass cylinder in her own mouth and inhaled gently. The suction of her breath drew the mucus that was choking the tiny throat to safety in the glass trap.

Satisfied that Baby Brown was free of mucus temporarily, Nurse Carey took the aspirator to the sink and washed her hands. . . .

Baby Brown was one hour old when Nurse Carey raised the shade covering the window that looked out on the corridor. She smiled at the father waiting there, and silently pointed to Baby Brown's incubator.

The father looked eagerly at his little son fighting for life. Pride and love shone on his face—then he seemed to remember. He turned away quickly to hide the tears. . . .

Baby Brown was four hours old when Nurse Carey noticed the drop of blood on his umbilical cord.

"I've got to tie his cord tighter or he may bleed to death," she told the student nurse.

She took a sterile string, or cord tie, from the cabinet. Working through the Isolette portholes, she tied it around the baby's cord. Her practiced hands knotted the string with ease, but the umbilical cord, which was like thick gelatine that would dry up and fall off naturally in time, was so fragile that it quickly broke.

More drops of blood appeared as the student watched, horrified.

Nurse Carey hid her own tremors. With a second tie, she started all over again. Fortunately, there was enough of the baby's umbilical cord left to hold the new string. This time it did not break.

Baby Brown was twenty-two hours old when Nurse Carey came on duty the next morning. She was early.

"I could hardly wait to see if he was still here," she said to the student on duty. "I telephoned last night to find out just before I went to bed. Every hour he lives, his chances get better."

"When do we feed him?" asked the student nurse.

"Not until he's about ninety-six hours old," Nurse Carey told her. "That's when the real trouble can start because you never know how they'll take it. The stomach fills up and creates pressure on the lungs. It can interfere with breathing, or cause mucus they can't get out. Even if they bring up the mucus, it may fall back down the trachea into the lungs and cause pneumonia to develop."

"Lucky they're born with enough food and water stored up in the bodies so they can last awhile without anything," said the student nurse.

"If they're going to die, I'd rather it was before we started feeding them," Nurse Carey said. "It's hard after that."

"You shouldn't take it so to heart."

"If you don't love babies, there's no sense in working with them," Nurse Carey said.

Dr. Starr, a brisk, pretty woman pediatrician, the private doctor on the case, entered the nursery.

She appraised Baby Brown for a long moment. "I don't know, Miss Carey. I don't think we should put bells on—yet. But he does look more active. If he lives a week, then I'll start being thrilled."

Baby Brown squirmed vigorously, his feet in the air, and managed to turn over on his side.

"See that?" Nurse Carey smiled. "He doesn't want to leave us."

"You can weigh him tomorrow if he's still going," said Dr. Starr. . . .

Baby Brown was forty-six hours old, and still going strong, when the weighing began. It was a delicate process. First, Nurse Carey placed the scales on top of the incubator. Then she took a rod with a hook on the top and one on the bottom. Attaching the top hook to the scales, she lowered the rod throught the weighing hole in the top of the Isolette and attached the lower hook to the hammock that held the baby. Thus the baby would be weighed without leaving the warm safety of his incubator.

Intently she watched the dial move to one pound fourteen ounces.

"He would normally have lost about two ounces since birth," she figured. "That makes him around two pounds when born."

Then she placed a tape measure on the mattress beside him as he lay straight on his back. He measured twelve inches long. . . .

Baby Brown was ninety-five hours old when preparations started for his first feeding. Dr. Robertson inserted in the baby's left nostril the smooth plastic tube used to feed preemies under three pounds.

The baby became very much alive and struggled beneath Nurse Carey's restraining hands while the doctor worked.

"There, there," he soothed. "This doesn't hurt at all."

Actually the tube is so comfortable that it can be left in place for a week at a time. Then it is removed and a clean tube placed in the other nostril. This adds to the preemie's chance of living, because it cuts down on handling. The tubes of hard rubber formerly used had to be inserted and removed with each feeding.

Feeding would begin after Baby Brown had become accustomed to the tube and could breathe easily with it.

"Do you think he'll be able to take feeding?" the student nurse asked.

"We'll soon find out. . . ."

Baby Brown was exactly ninety-six hours old when breakfast time came. Nurse Carey placed sixty drops of lactose and water in a syringe fitted with an adapter over the open ends of the tube. The liquid flowed automatically through the tube, descending at the rate the baby took it.

The caps of the nurses almost met as they leaned forward to watch.

After four minutes, all the liquid had passed from the syringe into the stomach. Baby Brown had had his first breakfast.

But he soon began to fuss and breathe harder. Then he turned blue-black. He had regurgitated. The feeding had passed into his lungs.

Nurse Carey suctioned him and told the student to telephone Dr. Robertson that he'd aspirated his feeding.

Dr. Robertson came immediately. "He has an aspiration pneumonia," he said.

He prescribed penicillin injections twice daily,

steam to be increase in his incubator, all feeding stopped for twenty-four hours.

As Nurse Carey injected the life-saving penicillin into the little body, Baby Brown cried.

The telephone rang and the student nurse quickly moved to answer it.

"It's Miss Green," she said. "She wants to know if you'll take her shift at eleven tonight and let her take your place in the morning. Her aunt's critically ill."

"Tell her yes," Nurse Carey said, almost with relief. . . .

Baby Brown was a hundred and eleven hours old. It was midnight and all was quiet as Nurse Carey moved about the nursery, watching the preemies sleeping peacefully.

These were her own babies now. They would go out into the world, strong and well and living, never remembering, never knowing that it was to her care they owed their lives.

She bent over Baby Brown's incubator. His rib cage had stopped moving. She looked again, sharply, to be sure. He was no longer breathing.

She snatched up the telephone. "Give me Dr. Robertson. Hurry, please!"

"Hello," the resident pediatrician answered sleepily from his room.

"Baby Brown has stopped breathing."

"I'll be right up."

Quickly, Nurse Carey suctioned the baby and began artificial respiration.

Dr. Robertson appeared in a few minutes. He rushed to the Isolette where Baby Brown lay as in death, eyes staring open, and thrust the extra-long stethoscope through a porthole.

"He's still living."

Nurse Carey moved aside and the doctor continued the artificial respiration.

"Drop some mineral oil in his eyes," he told the nurse. "The air will dry them out, wide open like that, without any fluid from blinking. If he lives, we must save his sight."

As he moved the tiny legs in rhythm up to the chest and down, up and down again, Nurse Carey took a medicine dropper and carefully covered the eyes with the mineral oil.

"Give him three minims of caffein sodium benzoate to stimulate respiration, and increase his oxygen with a funnel," Dr. Robertson said.

Up and down, up and down went the little legs, but still Baby Brown lay as in death.

Dr. Robertson listened again for the heartbeat. All was silence.

"It's stopped beating," he announced. "There's nothing to lose now. I'm going to inject adrenalin directly into his heart."

Nurse Carey brought the hypodermic and skillfully he plunged the needle into the deathlike body. Then he started working again, up and down, up and down, with the tiny legs.

Still there was no sound. Brain damage would occur if the vital organ did not start pumping in a matter of seconds now.

He listened again. "I think I heard it!" he exclaimed and went back to the artificial respiration with renewed hope.

Doctor and nurse worked on, silent, efficient. Then Baby Brown made a little gasp, the first intake of air of his own in at least thirty-five minutes.

"He's breathing," Nurse Carey muttered, trying not to cry.

A few minutes more of artificial respiration and the little rib cage was moving again under its own power.

"I could have pronounced him dead," said Dr. Robertson. "But I felt something was still there. Technically, he *was* dead for about three minutes. If he survives this crisis, I thing he'll make it. . . ."

Baby Brown was three months old when Nurse Carey placed him in his mother's arms for the first time. He weighed five and a half pounds, he was eighteen inches long—and he was dressed to go home.

Baby Brown fumbled the back of his tiny hand against his open, seeking mouth. He made murmurations of happy sounds. His feet wiggled. He made cak-cak-cak noises with his mouth, and gave the pleading scream of a baby well-pampered.

"Use a slow nipple on him," Nurse Carey told his mother in parting. "He eats well, but he needs a lot of sucking."

To Baby Brown she said simply: "Good-by, Robert. Don't forget me *too* soon."

♛ May, 1956.

With the postwar world came a crop of new children—most of them, according to their parents, and some, according to their teachers —properly deserving of the sobriquet "bright child." All were concerned about how he should be handled. Abraham Lass, an educator who taught thousands belonging to others and who raised two of his own, offers a prescription compounded of his experiences.

The Way to Raise a Bright Child

BY ABRAHAM H. LASS

DAVE WAS ONLY FOUR, BUT EVERYBODY WAS CONvinced that when he grew up he'd be something important. "You'll hear from Dave," they said.

He started out in elementary school like a house afire. His teachers loved him because he was so bright, so eager, so interested in everything around him, and so far ahead of the others. He knew all the answers to all the questions—and he had questions the teachers couldn't answer.

But, in fourth grade, something happened to Dave. He began to lose interest in school. When he wasn't dawdling or daydreaming, he was getting into minor troubles with his fellow pupils. His grades plummeted from the high nineties to just average.

In high school and college it was the same story. Dave seemed to have developed a "slow leak." His grades were mediocre, his accomplishments indifferent.

Dave is working now as a clerk in a large business organization, purposeless and dispirited. When he was four, he was full of infinite promise. He could have become almost anything—but this.

It's too bad about Dave, too bad nobody seemed to know or to care about what was happening to him. It's too late to do anything about Dave now. But it's not too late to do something about today's Daves.

Dave was a bright child. Today's bright children are our greatest natural resource. They are tomorrow's leaders, creators, inventors, scientists, engineers. The kind of world we'll have tomorrow will depend upon what we do to give all our bright children a chance to develop their wonderful powers and talents.

At best, we don't have too many bright children. We can't afford to waste even one. In our elementary schools today, there are only approximately 500,000 bright children like Dave, and about 150,000 in our high schools.

About 2 per cent of our children getting ready for school are bright or very bright. Your child may be one of them.

Here is a composite picture of the bright child drawn from various sources including the famous Stanford University studies of gifted children, the authoritative work of the late Professor Leta S. Hollingsworth, the observations compiled in New York University's Counseling Center for Gifted Children. No one bright child will have all these characteristics. But if your child has a number of them, the chances are that he is bright.

He's an early starter. He begins to walk early—sometimes at nine or ten months. He talks early, well and much; and in fairly complete, mature sentences. He becomes interested in reading very early, often learning to read with little or no training. Bright children frequently teach themselves to read when they are five or even younger.

He has an insatiable curiosity. He asks more questions, more intelligently, more insistently and more persistently than other children do. And he isn't put off with pat answers. He is especially curious about birth and death, and very early feels a need to have the universe explained to him.

He has many interests and pursues them with great persistence for long periods of time. He becomes the prince of collectors and hobbyists. Stamps, butterflies, birds, animals, photography, engines, rocks, seem to have a special fascination for him. He tends to spend a great deal of his time alone with his collections and hobbies, or in the company of a few select children who share his interests and enthusiasms.

As early as nine or ten, bright children tend to develop an unusual interest in numbers, atlases and encyclopedias; and in games that require thought, like chess and checkers.

His intellectual abilities are unusual and develop early. He seems to remember everything he hears, sees or learns: Latin names of species of birds, fish, prehistoric animals; fluctuations of the stock market; batting averages; characteristics of the chemical elements; makes of cars; types of airplanes.

He shows mature insight into problems and has an uncanny knack for sizing up people and appraising their motives. He has a great capacity for abstract thought and for generalizing about such matters as birth and death.

He is generally younger than fellow students in his grade. And his knowledge is generally far greater than the average child in the grade is expected to achieve. The late Professor Lewis M. Terman, one of the world's greatest authorities on the bright child, estimated that more than half the bright children "have already mastered the curriculum to a point two full grades beyond the one in which they are enrolled." Hence he tends to seek the companionship of older children and adults.

His vocabulary is large and very often unusual. He is sensitive to words and ideas, and quite naturally links them together. When he talks, he sounds "grown-up," or "like an encyclopedia."

He doesn't care much for "rough" group games like football and soccer. He prefers sports like tennis and swimming. Generally speaking, the bright child does not excel in activities requiring great physical or manual skill. But, contrary to popular opinion, he is on the average healthier, stronger and larger than other children.

If you think you have a bright child, have him tested by some reliable, recognized testing service or psychological clinic to make sure. Practically every college or university has such a clinic or can refer you to one. The larger and better schools and school systems have personnel and facilities to do their own testing.

If the tests verify the fact that you have a bright child on your hands, rejoice. You're going to have a wonderful time raising that kid. For there's nothing quite so exciting as watching a bright child develop. But you and he will have problems to contend with.

Fortunately for you and for him, however, there

is enough expert advice at hand for you to do an intelligent and effective job of raising your bright child, giving him every chance to realize his great and varied possibilities and grow into a successful, happy human being.

Here is what the experts say will be his major problems:

He's likely to have school problems. Partly because he is bored with the ordinary school routines, partly because his interests aren't adequately challenged by the school program, and partly because he feels misunderstood, overlooked and resented. His revolt against school may express itself in restlessness, daydreaming, getting into mischief, cutting classes, defiance of school authorities.

The right school and the right teacher can head off many of these problems. By providing a program of challenging, creative, varied activities, the bright child will find useful and enjoyable outlets for his energies. Give him a teacher who understands what he wants and needs, and school will be a joyful, stimulating experience.

He's different, so he's going to have social problems. He'll need friends his own age. And it won't be easy for him to find these friends, for he's a marked man. His companions will sense it—and they will let him know in the unmistakable accents of youth that he's different. They'll call him "genius." They'll poke fun at his tastes, at his vocabulary, at his ideas, because they resent and fear those who are "different" from them.

Your cue is to see to it that your child learns to do all the things other children can do and enjoy. Normalize him. Provide the experiences that will give him more in common with other children his age. Teach him to skate, to play ball, to swim, to dance, to box, to wrestle. Encourage him to take part in group games. Let him know that you are proud of his achievements in these directions.

Remember that every child wants to "belong," to be accepted by his group. If he's a good sport, he'll belong—in spite of his differences. As a matter of fact, he'll be respected for his differences—provided he can do what the others can do.

His intense interests tend to drive him in upon himself. In extreme cases, the bright child comes to prefer his narrow world of books, hobbies and a few friends to the larger world around him. This smaller world is more comfortable, more congenial, more manageable, more predictable. Here the child is master of all he surveys.

So make special, planned efforts to get your child out of sedentary, withdrawn routines. See that he gets some kind of outdoor exercise every day, preferably with boys his own age. Take him to zoos, museums, points of historical interest—anywhere so long as he is expanding his experiences in the larger world in which he must learn to live.

If you're beginning to feel a bit apprehensive about raising that bright child of yours, don't be. Bright children are tough and sturdy. Like children in general, they can "stand the gaff" very well.

You can help him by observing these golden rules:

1. Accept your child matter-of-factly. Don't let him think that he's extraordinary, something "out of this world." Encourage him, give him every opportunity to develop. Stimulate his interests. Do everything you can to let him try his wings. Watch him grow. But don't, by showing him off or by excessive and indiscriminate praise, let him develop into a little prig.

Teach your child that others have abilities and talents that he should respect, that—in short—he is not the center of the universe.

2. Don't project your own frustrations and failures on your child. Respect him for what he is—even if he isn't what you want him to be. His happiness will lie in developing his innate talents and abilities. Your cue lies in what he wants, not what you are hoping he will want.

3. Let him be a child and have a long, slow taste of the joys of childhood. Don't push him into adult activities until he's ready for them. Don't pressure him. Teach him to relax and enjoy simple, earthy things—and simple, earthy people, too.

4. Answer all his questions. Keep his curiosity alive.

5. Give him regular duties and responsibilities. Don't let him develop a superior attitude toward homely and necessary chores.

6. Let him follow all the hobbies he wants. Lifelong interests and careers often develop out of these early hobbies. Try (if you are able to) to keep him to one hobby at a time.

7. Give him lots of books. And don't worry too much about the inferior books he reads—or even the comics. Few, if any, bright children get permanently caught by the comic books or the not-so-comic books. It doesn't take long to outgrow them.

8. Prepare him to be resented by those less able than himself. Get him to recognize calmly and without rancor why he will be called "long hair" and "egghead." Teach him to "to take it"—philosophically and with good humor.

9. Give him all your love and understanding. He needs every bit of it. In this respect he is just like the rest of God's chillun.

꙰ June, 1957.

Waif
to
Woman

BY JAMES T. FARRELL

With the
brilliant insight
that made
"Studs Lonigan"
a modern classic,
novelist
James T. Farrell
tells the story of
Marilyn Monroe—
the orphan
who fashioned
a glittering dream
from the dark
shadows
of her childhood—
a period
re-created by the
imaginative lens of
photographer
Carroll Seghers II.

MARILYN MONROE HAS BECOME THE SEX DOLL OF millions of masculine fantasies. This is mighty healthy for the box office and makes the men happy —at least in their dreams. The story of her rise should make Horatio Alger regretful in his grave. He was born too soon, and merely wrote about virtuous shoeshine boys instead of orphaned girls. But hers is no Horatio Alger story. Had she been a character in a novel by Charles Dickens, she would have evoked pity and tears instead of provoking riots in Japan and near hysteria at airports. Helen of Troy's beauty launched a thousand ships. Marilyn Monroe's makes men whistle and scream. A woman with a childhood such as hers, however, could have become a name in a case history instead of on the marquees of movie houses the world over.

MEMORIES OF EARLY CHILDHOOD. CHILDREN SHOULD watch out, or the goblins of James Whitcomb Riley will get them. But this is no goblin; it is a demented woman neighbor trying to suffocate the sin and evil out of a two-year-old girl named Norma Jeane Baker (Marilyn Monroe's real name). She would have succeeded had not other neighbors dragged her away in time. The illegitimate child of an emotionally disturbed mother and a father she never knew, Norma Jeane might as well have lived her youth in the frigid Arctic as in California's sunshine. She lived in more foster homes than she can remember, scrubbing strangers' dirty floors—and existing in an atmosphere where the warmth of human relations rarely penetrated. Movie queens are the new royalty of America, the fairy princesses of the twentieth century. But what does their success mean to them? What are their real personalities? The Parisian **chanteuse** Mistinguett used to remark that she was made of good material. Her legs were once insured for three million dollars. Like her, Marilyn Monroe is made of good material: her legs, body and doll-like face are the most cele-brated physical attributes in the world. They won her instantaneous film success. How does one live up to such fame—how does one find a way to carry such burdens day after day? From waif (in the following simulated pictures) to woman, from rags to mink in the Hollywood Garden of Eden, can all this be, in reality, a search for identity? Or an escape from it?

MANY OF NORMA JEANE'S CHILDHOOD DAYS WERE spent as a drudge in a foster home. At one stage she was sent to live with a group of English actors—or,

rather, would-be actors—scratching for a toehold in Hollywood. Her foster parents staged wild parties (above), made little Norma Jeane clean up after their tawdry roistering, and gave her empty whisky bottles to play with. These were the years of the Great Depression. And Los Angeles County made a businesslike arrangement with people in need. It paid them $20 a month for taking care of its wards. Norma Jeane soon became a virtual commodity. But she found the surprise of love for a brief interlude. In later years, she had no memory of any brothers, sisters, aunts or uncles. But she could never forget one particular merry and affectionate "mother" in one of her foster homes, who gave her, for once, love and laughter. Finally, the world became too much for Norma Jeane's mother. She was committed to an institution and her little girl dragged to an orphanage. Here she scrubbed toilets—at five cents a month. Then she was promoted: assigned to wash

100 plates, cups, knives and forks three times a day, seven days a week, at a dime a month. With the money, she bought ribbons for her hair. For the most part, though, shuttled from home to home, her emotions became sewn up in a sense of guilt. She had panics. She stuttered. In one home she used to hide in a shed, and dream her fantasies (right). Yet even here, in the darkness, the seeds of her career were stirring, struggling upward to the light, growing into the shape of tomorrow.

IS IT DREAM, OR REALITY? THE NEIGHBOR, A "FRIEND of the family," who attempted to rape Norma Jeane when she was six? Our memories of childhood can frequently play tricks on us. To an utterly neglected waif, hungry for affection, even a horrible act of violence can be a mark of attention. Yet who can know how deeply such a hurt seared her spirit, as it certainly tormented her body? The years passed. A dab

of lipstick, a few awkward smears of mascara—and subtly her face changed. Her spirits soared. But she did not yet know what magic she possessed. Not until the boys ogled, squirmed and shouted when she walked into class in a borrowed sweater did she begin to sense power. Norma Jeane was on her way. It takes society and adults, themselves often malformed, many years to destroy a happy, laughing child. And yet this is not easily done. Nature gives the child the instinct and will to survive. Nature gave this to Norma Jeane Baker—together with a beauty that would attract and, beyond attraction, fascinate. Somehow, despite the searing experiences and bitter disillusions of her youth, she had survived. But for what? The formula is: Boy Meets Girl. But what if the meeting is not on celluloid? In many prosaic weddings like this one, the couple sinks into gray anonymity. The boy is an aircraft worker. Norma

Jeane's foster parents pressed her into the marriage. The neglected girl would become the wife of a man who needed her as much as she needed him. This was practical. But Norma Jeane needed love even more than bread. Her husband went off to sea as a merchant seaman during World War II; at home, she sprayed paint in an aircraft factory. The divorce came later.

SHY AND INARTICULATE, JOE DIMAGGIO WAS ONE OF the greatest baseball stars of his time when he met Norma Jeane, who by then had become Marilyn Monroe. Their marriage was the happy ending of a Technicolor film, but they had nothing to say to each other, nothing to give. Marriages like theirs have an unreal quality. But the needs, the emotions, are real. A baseball player and a movie queen can symbolize the daydreams of anonymous millions.

But, tragically, the same dream image tantalizes—and fades....We construct lie detectors and fantastic machines which calculate and predict. But science has yet to build a meter to measure anguish. A woman knows anguish when she loses her second husband—as Marilyn Monroe lost Joe DiMaggio—but it gave her an insight into herself that could be won at no lesser pain. "I want to be an actress, a real actress." This was no woodshed fantasy. She began to fight for herself, to grow. Could a waif play a woman out of a Dostoevski novel? Now Marilyn Monroe could reply: "Hasn't my whole life been a prelude to Dostoevski?" She ignored those who laughed at her. But there were those who did not laugh—among them, playwright Arthur Miller, the poet of the frustrated, and, therefore, the poet of her own aspirations. The two were married, and for a while, Marilyn seemed to find happiness. But life runs on, and its threads are many and complex. Marilyn, the waif, is a woman. But too often now her face is seamed with doubt and stained with tears, for the key to her identity still remains an elusive grail.

Phenomenal advances in all fields of science were made in this eventful quarter century. Medicine held out the promise of a longer, healthier life, and opened the door to a future with undreamed of miracles. No medical area is more intriguing than that which permits transplanting of organs, opening the possibility of a "bank" of vital parts from which the sick and injured could draw replacements. The pioneering experiment in this wonderful work had a drama all its own, as a young man gave all of his heart and a piece of his body to save his twin.

A
Brother's
Gift
of
Life

BY AL HIRSHBERG

AT PRECISELY 8 A.M., TWO DAYS BEFORE CHRISTMAS, in the amphitheatre of Boston's Peter Bent Brigham Hospital, surgeons bent over the wasted form of twenty-three-year-old Richard Herrick.

On a table in an adjacent operating room lay his twin brother, Ronald.

Richard Herrick, of Northboro, Massachusetts, was a victim of nephritis, a disease which causes inflammation of the kidneys. His had ceased functioning. Uremic poisoning coursed through his body. He was dying.

His twin, Ronald, on the other hand, was in perfect health—and he had two functioning kidneys.

Normal life can be maintained with one kidney. (One person in a thousand is born with a single kidney.) If one of Ronald's could be successfully transferred to Richard, Richard might live.

True, in all medical history no such transplant had ever been completely successful—but here there was a chance.

The kidneys are pink, bean-shaped organs about five inches long and three inches wide. They are located on either side of the spinal column, behind the abdominal cavity below the center of the back.

Each kidney and its vessels is imbedded in fatty tissue and surrounded by fibrous tissue which helps to hold it in place. It is connected to the renal vein, the renal artery (a branch of the aorta, the main trunk from the heart) and the ureter (a tube that leads from the kidney to the bladder).

The kidneys are key organs in the body's waste disposal system. Urine is formed in them and sent, via the ureter, to the bladder, where it rests until ready to be eliminated.

Medical and surgical teams co-ordinated by Dr. John P. Merrill, head of the hospital's world-famous Kidney Research Laboratory, had studied Richard Herrick's condition thoroughly while providing him temporary respite by use of an artificial kidney.

However, his own kidney continued to deteriorate. It was finally concluded that if Richard and Ronald were identical twins, Richard would have a better chance of survival than any previous kidney transplant recipient.

But there a new problem presented itself: it is impossible to establish beyond doubt the identity of twins. Identity can only be disproved. All the doctors could hope to do was establish the probability of identity.

Through birth records, it was established that the brothers came from a single placenta, a characteristic of identical twins. Skin grafts and chemical tests all pointed to the probability of identity.

Although the doctors felt reasonably sure of a better-than-even chance of success, they were very mindful that not one but two lives were at stake. The element of risk is always present with major surgery. And even if Ronald's part of the operation moved smoothly, he might be sacrificing a kidney for nothing.

Ronald knew this. But he also knew that his brother had no chance whatever otherwise.

On the morning of December 23, 1954, Richard was wheeled into the amphitheatre, Room 2 of Peter Bent Brigham Hospital's operation section. Ronald was taken into Room 1, separated from the amphitheatre only by a small scrub room where surgeons prepared themselves for operating.

The amphitheatre had a small balcony, with seats holding about fifty spectators. Less than twenty-five professional persons had been invited to watch the kidney transplant.

Dr. Joseph E. Murray, specialist in plastic surgery at the hospital, was in charge of the surgical team in the amphitheatre. Dr. J. Hartwell Harrison, head of the hospital's urological service, headed the team in Room 1.

Both teams worked slowly, carefully, methodically. The spectators could hear every word, but few were spoken except for an occasional low-pitched, clipped order, a brief comment or question about progress in the other room.

In the spectators' balcony, tension mounted. Medical history might be in the making.

In spite of his weakened condition—he weighed less than one hundred pounds, his blood pressure

was high, his heart faltering—Richard, under a local anesthetic, was standing his ordeal remarkably well. In Room 1, Ronald lay on the table, his kidney exposed and ready to be taken out.

At 10:15 A.M., two hours and fifteen minutes after the double operation started, a surgeon in the amphitheatre asked, "Are they ready?"

"Yes," one of the others nodded.

"So are we," said the surgeon. "Will you tell them in the other room, please?"

A surgeon in Room 1 began the removal of Ronald's kidney. He clipped off blood vessels, cut the connections which led to the renal vein, the renal artery and the ureter. He lifted the kidney from Ronald's body and wrapped it in sterile gauze. Then he placed it on a sterile sheet on a surgical tray.

Another doctor wheeled the tray through the scrub room and into the amphitheatre.

The kidney, pink when first removed from Ronald's body, began to lose color as the blood drained from it. Even as the surgeon in the amphitheatre picked it up to study it, the kidney took on a bluish tinge, like the lips of a child who has been in cold water too long.

The operating surgeon had to decide exactly at what angle to place it in Richard's body, exactly how it should be attached, exactly which vessels to tie off and which to connect.

The kidney was to be placed within Richard's abdominal cavity—just below and behind the appendix—instead of where his diseased kidneys were. It was a natural enough location. There was room, and connections to artery, vein and ureter could all be made from there. The diseased kidneys would be removed later.

For fifteen breathless minutes the surgeon studied the kidney. Then he nodded his head. He had decided.

"All right," he said quietly.

For the next forty-five minutes, the team in the amphitheatre worked on the grim jigsaw puzzle, following the plan that had been formulated in the previous fifteen minutes.

Behind them was the research in kidney transplants that had been going on for years, the failures and frustrations in the laboratory, the endless transplants planned and theorized on paper, the transplants made on animals, the previous thirteen transplant attempts on humans made at the hospital and those attempted elsewhere—all the work and study and experimenting that had been going on for years.

If Ronald's kidney would properly function in Richard's body and give solid indication that it would continue to do so indefinitely, great impetus would be given to research in kidney diseases. Success would prove beyond doubt what had only been theory before—that a kidney transplant would work when it involved identical twins.

During the forty-five minutes it took to connect Ronald's kidney to Richard's body, the only sounds in the amphitheatre were the gentle hum of the electric clock on the wall, the brief, calm instruc-

tions of the operating surgeon, the occasional click-
ing of instruments.

Then the surgeon straightened wearily. He was
done. "Now you're going to see this pink up," he
said.

As he spoke, the kidney, now receiving blood from
Richard's heart through the newly connected renal
artery, began to lose its blue tinge. Seconds later, it
was a healthy pink. The tension relaxed.

From the depths of the operating table, in a
startlingly clear voice, Richard said, "I knew it
was going to help."

At just past eleven o'clock, the surgeon bent over
to sew the ureter of the transplanted kidney to the
opened urinary bladder. This would guarantee
normal function. It was the final major connecting
link. (A plastic tube passed from the kidney down
the ureter and out of the bladder in order to collect
the urine separately from the transplanted kidney.)

Forty-five more minutes went by. Then, without
straightening up, he commented, "It looks all right."

Observers waited tensely for the clinching evidence of success. The kidney had been placed on Richard's body, it was connected in all the necessary
places, it looked a natural pink, but would it function?

As they watched, urine formed in the new kidney,
moved through the ureter and was collected through
the plastic tube which emptied into a small bottle
. . . a truly exciting moment for all. The five-and-a-
half-hour operation was over. Richard had a kidney
that worked.

As the weeks passed, Richard grew stronger every
day. All evidence of uremic poisoning and heart
failure disappeared. His blood pressure dropped
dramatically.

He left the hospital on January 29 and returned
in April for the removal of one of the two diseased
kidneys still in his body. Two weeks later, he was
back home in Northboro, well on the way to recovery.

The final step in the series of operations that
saved Richard Herrick from certain death was
taken last June, when the other diseased kidney was
removed. Only after that had been accomplished did
the doctors concede that the twin transplant was a
complete success.

Today, Ronald and Richard, now identical to the
point where each has only one kidney, are normal,
healthy young men. Inseparable, devoted, they find
it unnecessary to put their feelings into words.

Perhaps doctors at Peter Bent Brigham expressed
it for them when they released a statement last
December 25, which read: "The Herrick twins have
been an inspiration to us all in their unflinching
willingness to share their lives in such a vital way.
No better example of the spirit of Christians can
be found."

♛ December, 1955.

The era produced its heroes, some of them
bemedaled for killing, others honored for great
philanthropies. But often true heroism was
quietly performed without spectacular
recognition. No greater sacrifice could have
been made by one man for all men than
Mario Ponzio's piecemeal gift of his life.
The saga of his protracted agony, suffered to
make the world a better one, takes on
the aura of a modern crucifixion.

The Noble Agony of Mario Ponzio

BY GEOFFREY BOCCA

LAST SEPTEMBER IN TURIN, ITALY, A TALL, WHITE-
haired, rock-jawed doctor closed one of the most
courageous chapters in medical history. He was
Professor Mario Ponzio, daring pioneer in the attempt to cure cancer by radiology. He had paid for
it finally—after nineteen operations for radium
burns—with his life.

The end was a long time in coming. As Professor
Ponzio grew daily more helpless he sat in his laboratory at the Institute of Radiology in Turin University, working with little more than his eyes.
X-ray photographs were placed before him; he
looked at them, gave instructions, and they were
taken away. Every now and then he said, "Cigarette," and an assistant placed a lighted cigarette
between his lips.

One day just before the end, a pretty girl entered
the institute and asked for treatment to remove a
blemish from her cheek. A friend had recommended
that she come, but she was doubtful.

"Are you sure," she asked, "that radiology will
take it off?"

Professor Ponzio gave a great roar of laughter
and rose to his feet. "It ought to, my dear young

like all great boons to medicine, they carried a sting in the tail. X rays not only penetrate flesh, they also burn and destroy it. Nor do they give warning. They are invisible, have no temperature, odor or "rhythm" to remind doctors who may be exposed to them overlong of their danger.

When Italy entered World War I against Germany and Austria, Ponzio joined the Alpini, Italy's crack mountain regiment, as a doctor and a radiologist. At the disastrous Battle of Caporetto his incredible ordeal began. Wounded soldiers arrived in cartloads at the field hospitals. Ponzio, rushing from one case to another, was one moment a doctor and the next a radiologist. Leaving the operating room, he hurried to the X-ray room. Since time was of the essence, he ignored the clumsy protective gloves lined with lead and exposed his bare hands carelessly to the deadly rays.

After a few months, the first bad blisters began to show. But by then he had other things on his mind. He had fallen in love with one of the wealthiest and most beautiful girls in Turin, Imelde Tregnaghi, educated in England, fluent in half a dozen languages. The handsome soldier and lovely socialite were married in 1917. It seemed a brilliant match for both.

By the end of the war, the condition of Ponzio's hands had deteriorated sufficiently for him to qualify for the medal which Italy awarded to mutilated soldiers. He wore the badge of the *mutilati* proudly in his buttonhole.

A civilian again, his researches continued. He pioneered in what he called the study of radiological "disymmetry," the change in the direction of the ray once it enters the human body, an action which he described as similar to the refraction of light when it enters water. What this meant, according to Ponzio, was that a foreign body detected by X rays in the human body is not actually where it appears to be in the X-ray photograph. Ponzio was one of the first to establish formulae for the exact location. He also broke new ground in the biological action of secondary radiation, and in the means of measuring ultraviolet radiation.

Everything he learned he told, in more than 250 books, articles and reports. Few men in his class of research have been so prolific in their teachings and writings.

New worlds of healing opened when he began to attempt the cure of cancer by radium. His reputation spread beyond the borders of Italy. Meanwhile, risks had to be faced—or ignored.

His associates protested against the recklessness with which he continued to expose himself to X rays, but he could not help himself. The leaden gloves and the various other protective devices hampered and infuriated him.

"It's all nonsense," he said. "It's a risk of the profession. Every radiologist suffers from burned hands in one degree or another."

This was true enough. But the radiologist knew, and so did his wife, that his enthusiasm had been

lady," he said. "It took all this off." The girl saw for the first time that the doctor had no left arm at all and that his right hand had been amputated at the wrist.

Fame and adulation worried Ponzio much more than death, or the long years he spent in contemplation of it. Though his fellow scientists watched in helpless horror as he was slowly consumed by the spreading ulceration of radium burns, he never complained. Yet he was no saint. He was quick-tempered, with strong likes and dislikes, and his sense of humor tended toward the macabre.

Mario Ponzio was a brilliant, and a strange, man. Born in 1885, he become a doctor in 1910. Handsome, well-built, he had the typical young Italian's passion for sports and was an expert mountain climber. Yet he hated to treat sick children. Their suffering was too personal.

In 1915, Dr. Ponzio began studying X rays, which had been discovered only twenty years earlier. Of much shorter length than visible light rays, X rays were able to penetrate living tissue and enable scientists for the first time to see rather than merely estimate what goes on inside the human body. But carried perhaps beyond the point where cure remained possible.

In 1925, he underwent his first operation—for the amputation of part of a finger of the left hand.

"So—" he shrugged. "Four fingers are enough."

Before Ponzio a great future had opened. He was invited to lecture about cancer and radium in the United States and the Soviet Union. He had founded the Institute of Radiology in Turin. He became a co-founder of the Italian Society of Medical Radiology. The French gave him the ribbon of the Legion of Honor.

But the amputation of part of his finger did not stop the rot. Year by year the ulcerations bit deeper and deeper.

"There can be only one end to this dangerous experimentation," a colleague warned him. "And you know what it is as clearly as I."

Ponzio replied, "One must balance what a certain span of life is worth with what one can accomplish in that span. I have no alternative."

He was under no illusion. If he stopped working, his life might be saved. He continued his researches, but he took up two curiously significant hobbies: astronomy and the study of the Far East. (Without setting foot in Asia he began to acquire one of the finest collections of Buddhas in Italy.) Friends found it oddly touching that the professor, as his sickness imposed on him more and more physical limitations, should turn his thoughts toward the stars and the land beyond his reach.

World War II burst on Italy just as the Institute of Radiology in Turin was about to start an ambitious project of expansion. In 1943, a high-explosive bomb, dropped by Allied Air Forces seeking the giant Fiat works, landed squarely on the institute and reduced it to rubble. Ponzio wandered about the ruins disconsolately. "We must start again," he muttered. "We must start again." So preoccupied was he with the disaster that, returning home, he scarcely noticed that his apartment, too, had been bombed and reduced to a single habitable room.

At the end of the war, the hammer-and-sickle went up on all houses around the institute, which was centered in the heart of "Red" Turin. But Communism affected Ponzio as little as fascism had. His hands hurt him constantly, but he hid his discomfort with humor. The shyness which he had shown with sick children now manifested itself at any time when his courage was praised.

In 1947, the fourth finger of his right hand was amputated; seven years later, three fingers of the left hand and half the right hand. Ponzio called the operation "my manicure." The following July came the most terrible operation of all: the amputation of the professor's left arm, shoulder and collarbone.

"The operations I have had did not harm me," he told his anxious pupils. "I have the comfort of having contributed with my work to the development of radiology. I am old and I am going to retire. You must continue. . . ."

He had scarcely recovered from this operation when what remained of his right hand had to go too.

From that moment, Ponzio was dependent for everything on his wife and staff. In the past he had been a figure of professorial untidiness. Now that his wife dressed him he became immaculate. He arrived at the institute every morning clean-shaven, his linen spotless, his tie never off-center or imperfectly knotted. His presence had become a living example of courage and dedication to other scientists, but their admiration only increased his shyness.

In September, 1955, the President of the Italian Republic, Giovanni Gronchi, awarded Ponzio the Gold Medal for Civil Valor, Italy's highest honor, and one usually reserved for the dead. The medal was to be presented by the Mayor of Turin at a ceremony in the city's beautiful Palazzo Madama. Thousands of Turinese crowded the square for the occasion and the professor's car was blocked.

"Look at all those people," he said, interested. "Who are they waiting to see?"

"Why, Mario," Signora Ponzio cried in exasperation, "they've come to see *you!*"

In his younger days, Ponzio had been impatient of food and drink. Now he began to enjoy the role of host. Scientists came to dine and scholars to argue. His home was open to both pupils and patients.

Once a peasant from Trieste knocked on the door and begged the professor to look at his daughter, who had cancer of the mouth. Ignoring his other guests, Ponzio took them both in, examined the girl and packed them off in his car to the institute, where treatment was begun which put the girl on the way to recovery.

In the winter of 1955, a partial paralysis of his remaining arm set in. Sleep became impossible. But worse than the pain was the sense of urgency which had kept him going for so many years. He was planning to open a new institute which had been granted the name Mario Ponzio Institute. There was so much to do, and clearly so little time to do it in.

Ponzio flung himself into a killing schedule of work. He never missed a day at his laboratory and at home in the evenings he continued his researches, dictating notes and papers to his wife.

In February he traveled to Belgium to receive an honorary degree from the University of Louvain. In March he was in Paris to receive the Gold Medal of the Antoine Béclère Foundation. In April he participated in every meeting of the International Congress of Radiology in Geneva. In the first days of May he went to Rome as chairman of the Council of the Italian Society of Radiology.

All this activity had its inevitable result. The finest physicians in Turin were called and agreed that science had nothing more to give to the man who had given his life to science. Ponzio had been expecting this moment for a long time, and it came almost as a relief. "I have suffered too much," he said, admitting it for the first time.

At 6:15 on the evening of September 8, 1956, at the age of seventy-one, the long ordeal of Mario Ponzio came to an end.

ₘₐy, 1957.

A casualty of our age was the family doctor, with his battered black bag. Everybody became a specialist, and the specialties grew ever more compartmentalized. As with all change, the benefits were not unmixed, as a physician laments in this sentimental look backward.

The Doctor's Little Black Bag

BY PAUL H. FLUCK, M.D.

NO OTHER PIECE OF LUGGAGE SO INTRIGUES THE MINDS of Americans as the doctor's tool chest. For, if you should deny that the stork brought you, you would be forced to admit that the doctor's black bag probably did . . . or so the story goes.

Few have been privileged to look inside one of these ancient satchels. Even today, when exposés of the most intimate nature are published everywhere, the doctor's bag and its mysterious contents remain as impenetrable as ever.

In the twelve years that I have lugged these infernally heavy packsacks up and down the stairs of New Jersey homes, I have packed, repacked and unpacked the blasted things until I know well (if others don't) every gadget in them. When a fuse quits on short notice, I stumble to my medical kit to find a light, rather than risk breaking my neck searching any other cubbyhole in the house.

My first medical bag was a beauty, and I packed it lovingly. I folded and refolded my stethoscope until it lay in comfortable coils among the lesser articles. My sphygmomanometer (blood-pressure outfit to you), my otoscope, my rubber hammer, (doctors *do* use a rubber hammer), my transilluminator (flashlight, you would call it) and assorted containers for accessory tongue depressors, swabs and medicines, all lay at rigid attention under the snaky stethoscope.

My first call found me proudly swinging that beautiful case as I walked toward the uncertain steps of a weather-beaten house. My first patient (I never saw her) disappeared through the back door as I entered through the front. The family thought she was crazy, although I'm not too sure. All this transpired years ago, but I can still remember feeling rather glad that the immaculate contents of my bag had not been disturbed.

Specifically, my medical kit, equipped for action, carries a gross weight of some 20 pounds. In it, there are exactly 182 different gadgets, accessories and medicines, not counting pills. In winter, it really bulges when I try to shove an extra dozen sticky bottles into its groaning cavities. The cost of replacing this medical haversack would be well over $225 at today's prices. (And yet doctors leave these things in unlocked cars.)

Today, alas, the doctor's bag is taking its final bow, swiftly moving toward the exit, pursued by drug-hungry patients and government regulations. Few doctors care to fill out the quadruplicate forms and pay the inflated bills that accompany the stuffing for their luggage.

These days, a prescription pad solves the supply problem for doctors all over the country. Patients buy their own iodine, bandages and headache tablets. A midget stethoscope, a condensed version of the elaborate blood-pressure contraption, a thermometer, and perhaps one or two other instruments may all be carried in a coat pocket, or in the Zipper case that gives the "New Look" to your doctor.

It is perplexing to answer the questions of diagnosis with the meager contents of my brand-new case. And it is tougher still to find a druggist who will welcome my prescriptions in the witching hours. So it is that, when drugstores are dark and the shadows hide the "Old Look," doctors will still be seen lugging their ancient bags up creaking stairs.

There have been persistent rumors of a better-organized twenty-four-hour pharmacy service. Should this modern blessing materialize, America's most intriguing and mystical luggage will vanish from storybooks and doctors' hands alike. Nevertheless, the bulging black bag—the black bag that brought Mom and Pop—has earned eternal retirement under the attic eaves, plus the decoration of cobwebs that it will someday proudly wear.

♛ December, 1949.

MR. BRANDELL'S BREAKDOWN

Mr. Brandell keeps himself fit.
So he tells his doctor.
He plays polo—golf—tennis.
He skis and skates a little.
He diverts his mind with dancing.
It's not the work at the office!
It's "keeping fit" that seems to get him.

—OTTO S. MAYER

For many, the period was a time of almost unbearable suffering and dislocation.
Our shores once again became a haven for the oppressed and the opponents of tyranny.
Beginning again is a heartbreaking task, and to sustain herself, the daughter of the immortal Russian novelist found strength in this simple creed learned from her father— a philosophy that remains timeless.

My Father's Legacy of Wisdom

COUNTESS ALEXANDRA TOLSTOY, as told to Floyd Miller

WHENEVER I FIND MY LIFE BECOMING TOO COMplicated, I think back to the advice given me by my father, Russian author Count Leo Tolstoy: "Simplicity . . . simplicity . . . simplicity!" he used to say over and over to me, and to himself. Sometimes he would vary the lecture by saying, "Work . . . nature . . . love of man." He believed that man must not only be in tune with nature, work with her seasons by planting and harvesting, but also that he must live in simple dignity and freedom. Freedom above all, he said, for without that the rest is meaningless. As my father's secretary, I observed how nature was his strength and inspiration. His routine was inviolate. Each morning he arose at eight o'clock and immediately walked out into the woods to sit on a tree stump or his favorite bench and contemplate the coming day. At nine he ate a breakfast of coffee and bread, then entered his study, where he wrote until one in the afternoon.

After that, he rode across the countryside on horseback or labored with the peasants. The more difficult the writing had been in the morning, the harder he would till the soil in the afternoon. He was a powerful man and could keep pace with the hardiest peasant, sweating and laughing, his long beard whipped by the Russian winds as he plowed or sowed or reaped. And in the end he would return to his desk to write, refreshed and renewed by this intimacy with the earth and the simple men he loved and respected.

It was not until years later, after I had come to America, that I fully understood Father's advice. But even as a child I tried to emulate him, not only because I loved him but because I saw he had the courage and the greatness to live as he said I should.

Born to the Russian nobility, he had inherited Yasnaya Polyana, the huge family country estate, with hundreds of serfs, vast herds of livestock and a great house cared for by fourteen servants. He owned a town house in Moscow, but disliked high society and the cities and retired to Yasnaya Polyana. There he freed his serfs, created schools for their children and lived on the estate, which was operated as a working farm. And there he had thirteen children. I am his youngest daughter.

Despite the beauty and opulence of Yasnaya Polyana, my childhood was an unhappy one, for I was afflicted with deep feelings of inferiority. I worshiped my father and was eager to attract his attention and praise, yet whenever I did so I was not certain I merited it. Father never punished us or even gave us orders; he merely advised and suggested. But his soft-spoken words carried more weight than the sternest discipline, for we knew he was wise and just.

One spring morning when I was about eleven, he wandered into my bedroom before breakfast. I was looking out the window while a servant made my bed. Later that day he took me aside. "Sasha," he said, "it is not seemly for a healthy young girl to sit in idleness and let an older woman make her bed." To this day, I make my own bed.

Another afternoon I was playing tennis with a visiting Japanese writer. Father, who had been cutting wood, put down his saw to come and stand beside the tennis court. Without looking at him, I knew he had something to say to me. I paused between serves to turn to him. He told me there was a pregnant peasant woman who was awkwardly raking hay in a field.

"I do not like to watch my daughter play tennis while that woman must work," Father said. We grabbed up rakes and joined the woman. Only after the entire field had been raked and the hay delivered to her cabin did we return to the tennis court. And thus I learned that leisure must be earned to be fully enjoyed.

These lessons did nothing to strengthen my ego, however. The fact that Father loved all men seemed to reduce my own stature. This was particularly true at Christmas time. We always had a decorated tree in the great hall of the main house, and on Christmas Eve the children gathered around it to sing carols and receive their gifts. Not only the Tolstoy children, but all the peasant youngsters as well. Father always seated them in the front row and gave them preferential treatment.

That Father loved me I never doubted, but I wanted ever more of his love and attention, and never dared demand it. Yet often it came to me,

E. Karlin

unasked for, when I needed it most. One such time was when Mother disciplined me for falling into a mud puddle while wearing one of my good dresses.

Clothes were of no importance to my father; he usually wore a simple blouse with a wide leather belt, rough pants and high boots. His clothing was utilitarian, worn to keep him warm and not for personal adornment. But my mother, the Countess, was determined that her children should be perfectly groomed. When she caught me sneaking into the house with a mud-spattered dress, she spanked me.

I ran outdoors, wild with that helpless despair of childhood in the face of adult injustice. I decided to kill myself and started toward the river. On the way I got my feet wet and, thinking how that would further displease my mother, I turned back to change my boots. Halfway home I came upon my father. I stood in miserable silence while he looked at me with his kindly, knowing eyes. He did not ask what had happened; he allowed me privacy for my hurt. Yet he knew how to remove the pain. He touched my cheek with his fingers and said, "Sasha, everything will be all right."

My heart soared. I would have welcomed a spanking every day for the reward of his comforting words.

I was twelve when I realized that his great love for mankind had a compartment just for me. A game revealed it. One night after dinner, he announced that we would have a poetry contest. Mother gave us four rhyming words and Father instructed us to write a poem employing those words. "I'll be the judge," he said, "and will award a prize to the winner. When you finish your poem, fold it and place it in the bowl without your name on it. The judge does not wish to be accused of favoritism."

Soon all the poems had been placed in the bowl. One by one, Father solemnly studied them. At last he decided upon the winner. As he began to read aloud, I realized it was mine. I was the winner! I was seized with panic. "I have no right to win," I told myself. "I cannot possibly be the best."

My father completed the poem, then said, "That is very good. Who wrote it?"

There was silence. His eyes traveled slowly around the table until they came to my scarlet face. I was discovered! I burst into tears and fled.

But from that moment I gained confidence and over the next few years Father and I became increasingly close. When I was sixteen, my older sister Masha left home to be married and asked me if I would like to take her place as Father's secretary. I could not reveal to her or to anyone, how deeply moved I was. Leo Tolstoy was already the leading literary figure of Europe; his novels, *War and Peace* and *Anna Karenina*, were being hailed as masterpieces. But there could be only one personal secretary . . . and it was to be me!

Father was a perfectionist who revised, revised, revised. His handwriting was so eccentric that often even he could not read it, and during those first few days many a page was smeared with my tears as I struggled to make intelligible copies. But I mastered it. Eventually I learned shorthand, and when the Remington Company sent us one of its first machines, I learned to type.

Aside from being his secretary, I organized schools on the estate for the peasant children and taught in them. One day when I was preparing some lessons, Father touched me on the shoulder and said, "Sasha, you find this fun?"

"Fun, Father?"

"I mean, is it play? If this is only play, it is not worth doing. No man can feel achievement unless he does difficult work."

I assured him it was both work and difficult.

Father died in 1910, making me the executrix of his will. His last instructions were that I was to sell first rights to all his unpublished works, then use the money to buy Yasnaya Polyana from my brothers and sisters and give all the land to the peasants. He could not know that within a decade they would lose it to the Communists.

Had my father lived another ten years, history might have been changed. Beyond doubt, he would have played a leading role in the Russian Revolution, giving direction and vitality to the democratic forces and perhaps preventing the Bolsheviks from taking power. Had he lived and *not* defeated the Bolsheviks, they would have killed him, for he loved the peasants and would never have stood idly by while they lost their land.

I continued to live on at Yasnaya Polyana after the Revolution. The government turned the big house into a museum, and beside being the curator I was engaged in the extensive work of editing and annotating my father's writings. But year by year, the Bolsheviks began a campaign to make Tolstoy their own, distorting the facts of his life and the meaning of his work.

As Tolstoy's daughter, I enjoyed some privileges and immunities, yet I knew that my ultimate fate would be either betrayal of my father's principles or prison. So in 1929 I fled to Japan and then to America.

At middle age I found myself uprooted, torn from all that was familiar and precious. Then I remembered my father's advice: "Work . . . nature . . . simplicity." These were verities not just for life in Russia, but for America too.

I bought a farm in Connecticut and began to raise chickens. I found the smell of the wind, the swing of the stars in heaven, the sound of a boastful cock at dawn were the same here as at Yasnaya Polyana. I was home.

One day an old friend, Tatiana Schaufuss, came to me and said that many thousands of my countrymen had fled Russia and were in desperate need of rehabilitation. As she spoke, I realized that I had fulfilled only part of my father's maxim: I had nature and simplicity, but not difficult work.

I joined Tatiana Schaufuss, and in 1939, with the help of many dedicated and generous people, we established the Tolstoy Foundation for the rescue and rehabilitation of refugee Russians. Since then we have helped nineteen thousand persons to find a meaningful life. Many have been routed through the Tolstoy Farm outside Valley Cottage, in New York, where they work until they can find regular jobs.

They labor in the fields and eat the simple but abundant yield. They sleep through the night, knowing that if they are disturbed it will not be by the thud of military boots and a rifle butt against their bedroom doors, but only by the call of the hoot owl that lives in the caverns of the barn, or the throaty courting of frogs among the lily pads in the pond. They come to the farm wounded in spirit, but I can see the tension and fears drain out of them and the beauty of the human spirit well up again. They have been cured, as I was, by my father's advice: "Work . . . nature . . . and love of man."

♛ November, 1960.

In the bitter years of the cold war, both sides fought with invective and with weapons to a skidding standstill. But, for the free world, the crack in the armor of the enemy—even more than Hungary—was the victory of a book over the Communist monolith—**Doctor Zhivago.** A victory, also, as this story reveals, of a man who risked his life and found himself a new one as he labored to put Boris Pasternak's monumental work onto printed page beyond the Iron Curtain.

The Book That Shook the Kremlin

BY MELTON S. DAVIS

IT SEEMS FITTING THAT RUSSIAN AUTHOR BORIS Pasternak, whose writing has been called a great act of faith, should have had his towering novel, *Doctor Zhivago*, spirited out of the Soviet Union and published by a Communist who had to reach within himself to match that faith.

Doctor Zhivago is a terrifying panorama of Russia's revolutionary agonies and, more important, an impassioned denial of the godless materialism that is the crux of Marxism. Its publication so infuriated the Soviets that when Pasternak was awarded a 1958 Nobel Prize, they at first refused to let him accept it branding him "a pig," "a snake" and "a black sheep in a good flock." Since released in an American edition, it became our number-one best seller; its U.S. publisher, Pantheon Books, estimates that one million copies may be sold.

Today it is obvious that this ideology-shaking book would never have seen the light of day had it not been for Giangiacomo Feltrinelli. The story of how this came about is full of intrigue, political threats and earnest soul-searching. At thirty-two, Feltrinelli is the youngest publisher in Italy, and probably the bravest. Though a Communist, he chose to place artistic freedom above party discipline, and through him *Doctor Zhivago* was won for the West. To do so, Feltrinelli—a slim, intense man who wears horn-rimmed glasses—had to stand up to the Italian Communist party, largest and strongest west of the Iron Curtain.

In 1956, when he brought about his *Doctor Zhivago* coup, Feltrinelli was only twenty-nine and had been in the publishing business for just one year. His father, a banker, died when Feltrinelli was about twenty-one, leaving a fortune in landholdings, building materials and other enterprises. Since then the firms have been run by administrators while Feltrinelli now devotes his time to publishing.

Feltrinelli was a natural for Communist recruiters. Mussolini was riding high, and young Giangiacomo was impressed by Communist resistance to the hated Fascists. At night he would go outside and scribble on the walls: *"Abasso Mussolini!* Down with Mussolini!"

In November 1945, while still in school, he volunteered for the Italian Army, which by then was fighting alongside the Allies. Thanks to the English he had learned as a child, he was assigned to liaison with the American Fifth Army and saw combat around Bologna. He left the Army as he entered—a private.

Feltrinelli had by that time become a Communist. "I was against that class in Italy which had backed fascism, which was against the working man, against land reform, against change," he explains. (Similar views, incidentally, are expressed by Pasha, a character in *Doctor Zhivago* who turns to Marxism as a reaction against overcrowding, deprivation and the "indifference of the rich.")

For a while Feltrinelli wrote for left-wing publications, and in 1954, started financing a line of inexpensive paperback books on economics, history and sociology. This brought him into close contact with the Communist co-operative bookshop, Rinascita, which distributed the volumes. Finally, in 1955, he went into publishing on his own.

At the beginning of 1956, Communist party chieftains decided to send a representative to Moscow to forge stronger ties with Soviet literary circles. The man chosen was Sergio D'Angelo, who had been running the Rinascita Bookshop in Rome. D'Angelo speaks fluent Russian and is an expert on Soviet affairs. Feltrinelli, who knew him from the bookshop, asked D'Angelo to keep an eye out for any Russian works that might bear republication in Italy. As Feltrinelli's man in Moscow, D'Angelo became one of the main protagonists of the *Zhivago* affair. Even now he is reluctant to discuss it—obviously afraid of endangering Russian friends. But part of the story can only be told by him.

"Not long after my arrival in Moscow in 1956," D'Angelo says, "I heard a broadcast announcing that a new book by Boris Pasternak would shortly be published." Here was news. Pasternak, Russia's greatest living poet, was again preparing a major work after twenty-five years of silence. No foreign correspondent thought the matter worth reporting, since few people in the West had ever heard of him.

To D'Angelo, however, the announcement was significant. In February 1956, Khrushchev had already made his eventful speech denouncing Stalin. There was hope for a thawing of repressive Soviet policies. Pasternak again in print would be an important manifestation of this change. D'Angelo quickly wrote to Feltrinelli.

"I wanted to make sure," he says, "that he would have the chance of being the first Western editor to publish the book."

Feltrinelli immediately told D'Angelo to contact Pasternak and secure the manuscript and world rights to the book. But finding Pasternak, D'Angelo discovered, was a difficult task. People who knew him were reluctant to admit it, and when they did, they hesitated to reveal his address. Finally, D'Angelo managed to meet the Russian author in a small office which Pasternak maintained in Moscow. A few days later, Pasternak invited D'Angelo to his home at Peredelkino, about twenty miles from Moscow.

Pasternak had always liked Italy and Italians—his second wife is half-Italian. On the porch of his small wooden house, surrounded by a forest of birch and pine, Pasternak signed a contract granting Feltrinelli world rights to his book. Then he went into the house and brought back a copy of the novel, saying, "I gave another copy to Goslitizdat (the Soviet state publishing house). I haven't the

slightest idea when it will be published."

If D'Angelo had sent the novel by mail—as he normally would have—the typed script would probably never have arrived in Milan. Instead, Feltrinelli had made arrangements for a rendezvous in Berlin. D'Angelo put the manuscript in the bottom of his suitcase—not, he says, to smuggle it out, but only because he didn't want to crush his shirt collars. The two men met on West Berlin's fashionable Kurfürstendamm and D'Angelo handed Feltrinelli a string-tied parcel about the size of a newspaper folded into four parts.

On his return to Moscow, D'Angelo discovered that the Russian authorities knew that the manuscript of *Doctor Zhivago* had left the country. Important people, he was told, were upset about it.

Back in Italy, Feltrinelli, too, found that the atmosphere had changed. Letters began to arrive from Russia. One asked to have the manuscript returned to Pasternak "for revisions." Others suggested it would not be wise to publish the book. Then, in the fall of 1956, Feltrinelli was summoned to the office of Palmiro Togliatti, the extremely literate Italian Communist party boss. "I want you to hand over that novel by Pasternak," Togliatti said brusquely. "I don't think you should publish it."

"But, why?" asked Feltrinelli, taken by surprise. "In my opinion, it is a very good book."

Togliatti, apparently acting on instructions from Moscow, insisted that even Pasternak had changed his mind about having the book published. When Feltrinelli refused to return the manuscript, Togliatti angrily threatened him with expulsion from the party and withdrawal of all support from his editorial enterprise. He urged Feltrinelli to send the manuscript back to Russia. The younger man remained firm. "I must think it over," he said.

"At least," said Togliatti, "promise not to publish it without telling me first." Feltrinelli consented.

For several months, no more was heard of the matter. Then in January 1957, Feltrinelli received a letter from Goslitizdat in Moscow, asking him not to publish the book in the West until their own publication date—tentatively set for September 1957. Party officials in Rome called Feltrinelli several times to make sure he would honor the request.

Feltrinelli, replying through D'Angelo in Moscow, wrote that he had no intention of exploiting the book for anti-Soviet purposes. He also assured the Russians that he would wait until September 1, 1957.

It was not until much later that Feltrinelli discovered that the Russians had already refused to publish the book. They returned the manuscript to Pasternak on October 24, 1956. It had been accompanied by a bitter letter in which five Soviet literary lights branded the book "a squalid, malicious work full of hatred for socialism."

But the Communists still had to convince the recalcitrant Feltrinelli. As D'Angelo tells it: "September 1 was near and the party was using every possible means to prevent the book's publication. But Feltrinelli kept saying that he would wait only

until the date agreed upon. At this point a surprise card was played. In the middle of August 1957, Feltrinelli received a telegram signed by Pasternak, saying, 'Please return my manuscript as I consider it not a mature work.' "

Now Feltrinelli had to make a big decision. Should he take the cable at its face value and send back the novel? In his safe, along with the manuscript, were several letters from Pasternak which seemed to contradict this last message. For some time, particularly after the Hungarian rebellion, Feltrinelli's faith in the party had been shaken; he had been subjected to what he calls "the greatest pressures." Undoubtedly, Pasternak also had felt the turn of the screw—and even more forcefully. Today it is believed that Pasternak was told either to telegraph Feltrinelli within twenty-four hours or face arrest.

"To Feltrinelli, and to me," says D'Angelo, "it seemed that Pasternak had not done it of his own free will. We felt sure he would not deny his own work."

Feltrinelli had other reasons for believing that the Pasternak telegram had not been sent voluntarily. Sometime earlier he had received the Russian author's autobiography which, in its last pages, contained this sentence: "I have just finished my major work, the only one of which I am not ashamed, and for which I will answer without fear, *Doctor Zhivago.* . . ."

Still Feltrinelli hesitated. If he published the book, he would be severing connections with his friends and colleagues. Besides, what would happen to Pasternak if he published the book? Did he have the right to gamble with another man's freedom, and possibly his life?

Feltrinelli's final decision came from the book itself. At first, he had not thought it particularly anti-Communist. But then he began to find answers to questions he had long felt like asking. Feltrinelli had already published several books on what he calls "the disconcerting reality of our times—man against machines." In *Doctor Zhivago* he found the soul's need overshadowing economic need.

"Here was a newer, sharper meaning for human values," says Feltrinelli, "something that is needed now when each of us is pitted against superorganized society. In my view, man is fighting for his soul. This book, I believe, helps one to fight." If this were so, Feltrinelli reasoned, Pasternak surely would want his voice heard. After all, he had written that it was not the function of the writer "to serve principalities and powers, communism or capitalism." This could only mean that the writer's responsibility was to himself as a man. If, thought Feltrinelli, he, too, was to be an individual, he would have to publish the book.

Not until a year later was he to know how correct his judgment had been—when photographs showed the joy with which Pasternak had greeted news that he had won the Nobel Prize.

Meanwhile, Feltrinelli sent a carefully worded reply to Pasternak's telegram. Agreements had been made with two foreign publishers—Gallimard in

France and William Collins Sons & Co. in England. It was now too late to rescind these, he wired, expressing his regrets.

But the Russians made one more attempt to prevent publication. A delegation of Russian writers came to Italy, ostensibly on a holiday. It was led by poet Alexei Surkov, secretary general of the Union of Soviet Writers. In Milan, Surkov had a turbulent meeting with Feltrinelli in which he berated the publisher for not returning Pasternak's manuscript. When Feltrinelli stood firm, Surkov stormed out empty-handed.

Furious, the Russian called a press conference, inviting only newspapers of the extreme Left. "I have just seen an Italian publisher," he sneered, "who is about to publish a novel which has never appeared in Russia; . . . the author has tried in vain to get his manuscript back from this publisher. We Soviets are amazed that the wishes of an author can be so shamefully violated."

Then, as if by chance, he recalled another occasion, many years ago, when a book by Pilniak—which had been turned down in Russia—came out abroad. This allusion was greeted by an embarrassed silence. Even the Communist journalists remembered that in the period of the great purges, Pilniak had ended up in front of a firing squad!

In November 1957, *Doctor Zhivago* appeared in Italian bookstores. Reviews were unanimously laudatory. Even party-line critics reviewed it in glowing terms, although when word finally reached them that the book was banned in Moscow, they flip-flopped shamelessly to pour abuse on Pasternak. Within a year, however, over 120,000 copies were sold, although few Italian best sellers reached the 30,000 mark. The success of the book made Feltrinelli Italy's third largest publisher.

There have been several attempts to isolate Feltrinelli from Italian intellectual life. But he takes comfort in a phrase of Pasternak's that "only the isolated seek truth and break with those who do not love it enough." On November 6, 1958, almost three hundred Italian writers, painters, journalists and stage and screen personalities called on the West to boycott Soviet cultural activities until Pasternak was allowed to work freely. It was only after this that the Communist party started to attack Feltrinelli frontally.

There had been other, subtler attempts to discredit him. One, according to the publisher, was the mysterious publication in Holland of a clandestine Russian edition of *Doctor Zhivago*. On the frontispiece—without his permission—was Feltrinelli's name. Copies were handed out at the Brussels World's Fair last summer. A strange side light is that the Dutch publisher claims to have handed copies to a messenger sent by Feltrinelli. Feltrinelli denies sending any messenger and further insists he never gave the Dutch publisher the Russian text. Recently, in ads taken in *The New York Times* and six leading European newspapers, the Dutch firm admitted publishing the book without permission and reaffirmed Feltrinelli's rights to it.

Feltrinelli has not been happy about attempts to use *Doctor Zhivago* as political propaganda. He thinks this can only worsen Pasternak's position. Besides, he feels that the book's meaning transcends the cold war. As Pasternak himself says, "My novel was not intended to be a political statement. I wanted to show life as it is, in all its wealth and intensity. I am not a propagandist."

The circumstances under which *Doctor Zhivago* came to the West have evoked almost as much controversy as the book itself. One of the thorniest problems is the definition of the phrase "world rights." Some Americans insist they have the right to use the book for films or TV since no copyright agreements exist between the U.S. and Russia, and because Feltrinelli only owns book publication rights. Feltrinelli says that he owns *all* rights and the fact that no agreement exists between the other two countries means nothing, since he is Italian. In any event, royalties are being scrupulously paid into accounts set up for Pasternak. They will even-tually come to about $1,000,000.

How deeply Giangiacomo Feltrinelli himself was affected by *Doctor Zhivago* was shown in November 1958, when he publicly announced that he had left the Communist party a year earlier "for various reasons, the last of which was definitely the Pasternak affair."

Others are following his example. Oddly, their defections are being carried out quietly. There seems to be something in the book which impels Communist readers to re-examine their position. That this forceful statement of faith in the human spirit came out of Communist Russia was a miracle. That it has helped readers to find themselves is another. That it raised doubts among the Communist faithful that may never be stilled is perhaps the greatest miracle of all.

Doctor Zhivago may have finally provided Western intellectuals who are still tied to the Communist party with a new belief by which they can become free.

♕ May, 1959.

Godliness comes in strange shapes and forms. To Lajos Zilahy, free Hungary's leading novelist, it appeared in the compassionate, Biblical countenance of the Communist tommy-gunner who spared his life. "In the blistering hells of war, he carried in his heart forgiveness for everybody. . . ."

The Christ-Faced Soviet Soldier

BY LAJOS ZILAHY

IN THE FALL OF 1944, GERMANY HAD ALL BUT LOST the war. The victorious Red Army was rolling toward the west in Rumania, in Poland and in the eastern part of Hungary.

By late December, when the forces of Marshals Tolbukhin and Malinovsky had completely encircled Budapest, they sent emissaries to the Nazi general defending the city calling upon him to surrender in order to avoid needless bloodshed and destruction. The German general, in reply, had the Russian emissaries shot.

At this news, the populace went into the cellars as into the grave. And the siege of Budapest began.

We were forty-two in our overcrowded cellar,

123

sleeping on chairs, on tables or on the concrete floor,
fully dressed in winter coats. Our food supply was
dangerously diminishing, but our "butcher shop" in
the back yard was open day and night. It was the
corpse of a horse, killed by a bomb, frozen stone-
hard in the cold winter. We were without water, and
used melted snow for drinking and cooking.

During these days of Dantean inferno, the house
above us received three small bombs and seventeen
artillery shells. But more than bombs, we dreaded
the "defenders" of the city, who fought not the attacking Red Army, but the populace. Acting as
"military police," they dragged the Jews from their
beds during the nights, led them barefooted in
pajamas to the Danube shore, shot them and threw
their bodies into the ice-packed river. They were
hunting for Western-minded "liberals," too, and for
everybody whom they suspected as being anti-Nazi.

We in the cellar were anti-Nazis without exception, armed with false documents. There were Jews
among us, Social Democrat workers, butlers, house-
maids and rich aristocrats, men, women and children: the most mixed society, but now in complete
equality and brotherhood.

All of us had reasons to fear the Gestapo and the
"military police." The Nazi newspapers had revealed
my dark past: that before the war I had spent
several years in England and the United States,
where my novels were published and my plays produced. This was enough to prove me a dangerous
"pro-Anglo-Saxon" individual, a liberal, a Jew-
hireling.

During the long, dark days we paced the narrow
confines of the cellar like caged animals, obsessed
by a single thought: when would they end—the
bombardment, the Nazi terror, the starvation? But
who would liberate us? Only the Soviet soldiers. And
we had every reason to dread that moment.

After the emissaries were shot, the Soviets sent
Ukrainian divisions against Budapest, giving them
forty-eight hours of free looting, as a revenge. The
German and Hungarian Nazi troops had burned
thousands of small Ukrainian villages, committed
horrible bestialities.

The news found its way to our cellar that the
Ukrainian troops had already occupied the suburbs,
and in some places they had simply opened Tommy-
gun fire when they entered the dark cellars. On
January 18, they reached the neighboring streets.

Around noon, a voice shouted desperately, "Here
they are!"

We rushed to the little broken windows of the
cellar. A single Soviet soldier was climbing over the
back-yard fence. He stood in the snow and looked
around, huge in the thin fog, a nightmare vision.
He was the victorious Red Army; he was Ukrainia,
coming to take her revenge. He wore a high, ice-
gray fur cap, and across his chest hung the dreaded
Tommy gun.

We watched him breathlessly. He stepped closer
to the half-eaten corpse of the horse, and examined
it for a few seconds.

When he slowly started toward the door of the

cellar, we quickly lined up and stood almost at attention in deep silence, immobile, except for the moving lips of the women who were praying mutely.

The door swung open and the Soviet soldier entered our dimly lit cellar with a small flashlight in his left hand. In his right he carried a big black revolver.

The yellow circle of the flashlight went from face to face. With our unkempt, stubbly faces we resembled stage figures in Gorki's *The Lower Depths*, exaggerating the garb of misery. As a contrast, Countess P.'s huge diamond earrings glittered in the flashlight, but it passed over them. It seemed that the Soviet soldier, a typical, primitive Russian peasant with a drooping sun-bleached mustache, was not interested in jewels. His weather-lined face was extremely sad, tired, ageless.

The light stopped on the greenish-white hollow face of a ten-year-old girl. Her mouth was half-open, frozen in a mute scream of panic. For a few seconds the yellow circle of light remained on her starved face, a strange golden halo.

The Soviet soldier pocketed his flashlight and revolver almost in the way a doctor does when he finishes his examination, but his face did not reveal what he would do. The high, ice-gray fur cap bent through the doorway as he left without a word.

We stood in silence. It was obvious that he would return with more soldiers. And what would happen then?

He came back in a few minutes, alone, without his Tommy gun. He had brought a heavy black loaf of military bread, almost a yard long, and he put it on the table with a shy, awkward movement. I watched his plow-ridden hand with its broken nails. Then he walked out sheepishly, without looking at anybody. We were liberated.

That night I was asked to write the lead article for the first free newspaper, *Szabadsag*. I began it by describing the scene with the Soviet soldier and the bread. I wrote:

"It was a Biblical moment. There was a man, a primitive Ukrainian peasant, whose village had been burned, his people killed by Hungarian troops. He was authorized by Soviet marshals for free looting; he could even have killed us without any consequences. His humble, sad face made the impression upon me that he was one of the many millions of Russian peasants who still go every Sunday to their Orthodox Greek Churches under the bright-colored, onion-shaped cupolas, who in remote villages in their little mud farmhouses still kneel before the mite-lighted icons. I don't know the name of that Soviet soldier, and I am afraid I will never meet him again. But I, and all of us in the cellar, will remember him forever. In the blistering hells of war, he carried in his heart forgiveness for everybody, and when he brought us bread instead of revenge, as he put the bread on the table with that shy, awkward movement, his sad, humble face reminded me of the face of Christ."

My article had a tremendous effect on many readers. I received a lot of letters, unanimously saying: "Just wait, you dirty Communist, we will hang you together with your Christ-faced Soviet soldier."

I was not surprised. Not everybody was as lucky as we were. Though killing was rather rare, robbing and especially raping were general. The populace of Budapest learned in the first days what Russian liberation was.

After the failure of the coalition government, the Communist party came into power in 1947 and I left Hungary for the United States.

Seven years later, the "Christ-faced" Soviet soldier rose up in New York to haunt me. My wife and I passed our examination for citizenship, but we were not called to be sworn in. A whole year went by.

My lawyer was pessimistic. "I know what the trouble is," he said. "Your last novel, *The Angry Angel*, dealt not only with the Communist, but with the Nazi terror, too."

He handed me a small Hungarian Nazi paper, published in Europe.

"He is the same Zilahy," said an article, "who wrote his famous editorial about the Christ-faced Soviet soldier. It is our duty to silence Zilahy."

Then my lawyer continued, "These Nazi groups don't like the idea that a novel in six major languages speaks about their past. Their policy is today: let's forget what happened—now we are the 100 per cent, most reliable anti-Communists.

"I'm afraid they are flooding the American authorities with letters, and not only from Europe."

An investigation was begun of me and my wife. At that same time, all of my works were on the black list in Budapest, and I was attacked in the Communist papers as a traitor to my old country, who had left the "People's Democracy" for the United States. The investigation went on for almost two years.

On a November afternoon I was sitting again before an investigator in the Immigration and Naturalization Office for another long interrogation. From the previous questionings, I already knew what were the accusations against me. I had been the president of the Hungarian Sovietic Cultural Society. (True.) My photo had appeared in *Pravda* sitting on the sofa with Russian Marshal Voroshilov, then head of the Allied Control Commission in Hungary. (True.) I was the editor-in-chief of a Communist daily. (False.)

The investigator was a clean-shaven, bespectacled, soft-spoken, but very cold, unsmiling man.

"Did you ever write an article about a 'Christ-faced' Soviet soldier?"

"Yes, sir. I did."

"Were you under pressure when you wrote this article? Would you or your family have been in danger if you had refused to write this article?"

"No, sir. Nobody told me what to write."

"Why did you write that his face reminded you of the face of Christ?"

I closed my eyes for a moment before I answered. All my memories came back very vividly. The sad, peasant profile as he put the bread on the table.

The deep silence, then the sob of a woman. The whole tragedy of mankind flashed through my mind as in a slow, tired voice I described the scene in the cellar.

There were a few seconds of deep silence, then the investigator asked coldly, "Now, knowing more about the Soviet terror, do you revoke this article?"

I felt that my citizenship hung in the balance. What shall I answer? I wrote the truth. I wrote what I saw: a ray of Christian love in that dark cellar.

I am sure I was pale with emotion. I felt that a great injustice was being done . . . to whom? Not only me, and not only by this American investigation, but by our present world situation to the whole of mankind. To the "Christ-faced" Soviet soldier, and me, too. I was persecuted by the Nazis as a pro-American. I had to leave Communist Hungary because I became again a suspicious pro-American. And now, after ten years here in the United States, I had to answer questions like a criminal. I felt deeply hurt.

"I will never revoke my article," I said. "And if I do not receive my citizenship because of that article, I will never be sorry that I did not become an American citizen!"

I sat down. I felt that I had lost my battle. I must give up the United States. But where to go? Where start a new life under the disillusion and humiliation that we were not worthy of being American citizens?

It was five o'clock when I finally left the Immigration Office and headed toward the elevator. I heard steps behind me, but I did not turn back. When I wanted to push the down button, a hand forestalled me. I turned—it was the investigator. He extended his hand, looked into my eyes and said, "Mr. Zilahy, I'm on your side. God bless you—good-bye."

Outside on Columbus Avenue it was raining. A woman seized my arm. She was in tears.

"Oh, Mr. Zilahy . . . I'm so sorry for you. . . . I understand so well your article about the Christ-faced soldier. . . . I strongly believe myself that there are good-hearted people in the Soviet Union, too. . . ."

She was the little stenographer who had taken my testimony during my questioning. She accompanied me to the bus stop, holding my arm, supporting me as if I were a wounded man.

In the bus, I said to myself absent-mindedly, "This is America."

In ten days we were summoned again to the Immigration Office. The investigation was closed. We were 100 per cent cleared.

Two weeks later we were sworn in as American citizens.

♛ March, 1958.

In every town there is the inspired tinkerer who will try anything once. This one, like his counterpart in 1937 or 1962, believed as he kept tinkering, "We ain't reached the limit yet."

He Never Flew

BY R. E. KORNMANN

THERE WERE SCREWS AND WIRES ON THE KITCHEN table. Pop Bill shoved them and frowned at me.

I recognized the scowl—lifting of the right brow, slight flaring of his nostrils and a peculiar pout of the lips—as a signal that something surprising was about to happen. He gave the big mass of twisted wires another push and lifted a mysterious bundle from the floor onto the table.

Slowly his grease-stained fingers undid the wrappings while I hopped from one foot to the other in anticipation.

The fingers paused. Pop looked at me sternly. This expression meant disapproval. I put both feet on the floor and for a while was quiet, though I slowly rolled a screw round and round on the table with a grubby forefinger.

The unwrapping continued and at last there emerged a shiny cylinder about which was wrapped copper wire, smoothly shellacked; along the top of the coil the shellac had been scraped away to form a bright furrow, above which ran a brass rod. And atop the rod was an impressive knob.

Also, there was a lumpish-looking stone that Pop Bill called a galena and unpacked reverently, and a thin wire that, with his most fierce scowl, he called "the cat's whisker."

He tightened screws and frowned and glared and pouted and, after a long minute of tickling the galena with the cat's whisker, while he held a flat disk to his ear, finally stood erect. He put the disk against my ear.

There was music!

"That," said Pop slowly, "comes all the way from Pittsburgh."

Pop was always the first in the neighborhood to own any new mechanical contraption. We had the first player piano in the village, the first shower bath, the first carpet sweeper. Ours, too, was the first and only stereopticon machine in Leaville.

I remember the stereopticon machine particularly because of the extraordinary clumps of gray something that he somehow mixed with something else to give light to the projector; a terrible odor and a hiccoughing noise came out of the can that held the mixture at every performance of the machine. Pop Bill gravely assured all of us, Nana Het and Aunt Kate and Second Cousin Alley and me, that the noise meant the whole shooting match would explode at any instant.

Much as I enjoyed the excitement of the darkened room, the white bed sheet hung against the wall on which appeared magically enlarged "S'Matter Pop" comic strips out of the New York *Globe* and scenes from the Holy Land, I expected to be catapulted suddenly skyward. This gave a deliciously terrifying zest to the entertainment; I trembled partly with dread and partly with the chill of the strawberry "snowball" that coldly burned in my hand. Even yet, strawberries inevitably remind me of acetylene fumes.

We survived the stereopticon without injury, and lived to have our bones jolted in a Stanley Steamer, a steam-propelled automobile. Fortunately we were all indoors getting ready for an extensive excursion to Elmhurst—a distance of twenty miles each way —the morning the boiler exploded and wrecked the car.

This startling display of the power of steam roused all Leaville. But it couldn't daunt Pop. Within six months we rolled along the turnpike to Elmhurst in an imported Renault—pushed by gasoline this time—and only paused to change tires twice in the three hours' drive there and back.

Things seemed to happen all at once after that.

An open-air movie show—high board walls, cement floor, rain-ruined seats—opened across the street, and at dusk all Leaville with the exception of the pillars of the M. E. Church came to occupy the seats, to discourage mosquitoes with lighted punks and to groan at the misfortune of Clara Kimball Young, cheer the heroism of Maurice Costello and roar at the pie throwing of a little man in a derby whose name was Charlie Chaplin.

But Pop Bill hammered and thumped upon our roof all of one Saturday afternoon. At twilight, frowning mysteriously, he led us up the narrow stairs from the attic. A high platform had been erected near the edge of the slanted roof and upon it were chairs. Gingerly Nana Het and Second Cousin Alley and I followed him along the narrow planking before the chairs; somehow each achieved a terrifyingly elevated seat upon the platform. Henceforth, every clear night, the whole family (with the exception of Aunt Kate, who trembled at the very thought of venturing upon the roof) enjoyed the show gratis while our feet dangled three stories above the King's County Turnpike.

Movies in those days were full of portentous notes written in flourishing long hand; and alas, we were too far away from the screen, on our lofty platform, to decipher these. Pop, however, solved this by somehow combining the lenses of his now unused stereopticon to make a spy glass. Through this he peered—like an anxious mariner in a crow's nest—perched upon his chair, and read the significant words aloud. Far away the movie piano— (played by Al Lockhart's girl, Mealie) tinkled the "Skater's Waltz," while he intoned the forged message that brought prison and terrible disgrace to the nervous young man in the high celluloid collar.

Best of all, Pop liked the travelogues. But he laughed only occasionally during the pie-throwing scenes and then grudgingly; his favorite among the comedians was Al St. John, a blond young man who did incredible things on a bicycle.

Those were thrilling nights, but the days were no less exciting. Rumpel's Butcher Shop installed an electric meat chopper; Jurgen's Grocery rivaled it with an electric coffee grinder and Huger's Confectionery, not to be outdone, put in an electric ice-cream freezer that by its subterranean thumping made the glasses on the soda bar rattle. But Pop's was the first household in the village to be wired for light.

This marked the beginning of a new era. Came an electric sewing machine, then an electric waffle cooker. Next we got an electric laundry iron and an electric comfort pad for Aunt Kate's rheumatism which, incidentally, that apprehensive lady never dared to use. Even the stereopticon machine was dragged out of the cellar and restored to favor with an electric bulb replacing the odorous acetylene arrangements.

On Christmas an electric train went dizzily round and round the base of our tree, stretching a marvelous finger of light before it. The tree itself was a glory of uncountable electric bulbs.

And all that winter and until the summer when Nana Het died, you could see the light that flashed on and off in our window behind the ground glass sign of Pop Bill's name with the awesome word ELECTRICIAN underneath it.

He turned out the sign after Nana Het was buried. He went to his job at the shop in New York but no longer sought after odd electrical work in the neighborhood of Leaville.

Just recently I saw Pop Bill for the first time in six years. After I went away to school, he said, and Aunt Kate and Alley went back to New Bedford to Grandpa's, he just let everything go and started traveling. He has been around the world three times; worked as a maintenance man in a pressroom in Shanghai, helped to set up elevators in Vladivostok and helped to construct an electric ferry that was hopeful of running between Malmo, which is in Sweden, and Copenhagen, Denmark.

In Dundalk, on the Irish Sea, he repaired bicycles and motor bikes; at Montpellier on the Gulf of Lions he worked side by side with a man who was inventing a marvelously rapid wine-press.

Now his chin was grizzled with gray and when he frowned lines that I did not remember formed beside his eyes; but his excitement at meeting me after so long had made him talkative—he who had been taciturn and grim.

He wanted to see the airport, he said. In the bus going there he talked aimlessly of the carefully guarded fire that night and day, behind a tin fence, burns off the surplus coffee beans in Rio.

Then, irrelevantly, he spoke of a man named Josie with whom he had installed oil-pumping machinery at Baku, south of the mountains on the Caspian Sea.

"It was a queer kind of business," he said, frowning at the memory, "because the water, you know, is actually more than eighty feet below sea-level."

We had got to the airport. As we got off the bus a silver wing glided overhead. Before us were planes, warming up; even as we walked toward them, one took off with a roar like an angry dragon.

"They wouldn't let me fly," said Pop Bill savagely. "Claimed I was too old to pass. Out in Frisco that was."

"I've never been up," I confessed shamefully.

His eyes were on the plane that now grew smaller and smaller toward the south. "Greatest thing in the world," he growled; "you're missing something.

"Why that new one they got, the big one, y'know, averages 'bout two hundred fifty a n'our."

Suddenly and somehow sadly I recalled the Stanley Steamer, the Renault, the first top-heavy Hudson, the brass-banded Ford and all the other high-bodied, thin-tired cars that had chugged me through adolescence and childhood.

"Pop Bill," I asked, "do you remember—?"

But I stopped because he was not listening. Eyes full of profound admiration, he gazed absorbedly to the south. The windy sky was empty where the plane had so lately throbbed.

"Gone, gone already," he whispered, "gone clean outa sight.

"But, hell," he exclaimed, "that's nothin'. Say, listen, there's a little Dutchman in Augsburg—Southa Germany, y'know—that's actually got together a plane that goes by rocket power. He claims it's gonna do six hundred when he gets it workin'."

"But, Bill, why should anyone want to travel that fast—even if he could?"

The old frown of disapproval came back. I was a little boy, again, being reprimanded for impatience. He did not answer the question, but turned slowly back to the field where yet another bright monster stood, sun glistening on its rounded flank.

"Believe it or not," said Pop to no one in particular, "we ain't reached the limit yet."

As he walked away, hands in his pockets, pipe stuck stubbornly between his teeth, the plane toward which he sauntered no longer looked so impossibly big. Pop, a little man with grease beneath his fingernails, seemed somehow to have dwarfed it.

♛ August, 1937.

JUSTICE

There is a justice outside courts we know,
I saw it in my barn and stood below.
A mother swallow and a father swallow
Came almost faster than my eyes could follow
Through the high window, never both together,
And so not able to tell each other whether
This young-one fed the last, or that or that,
And neither stopped to judge which crop looked fat,
But each shot in and fed the proper one,
The emptiest, and back out in the sun.
The wide bills opened at the selfsame angle,
The five necks rose from out the hairy tangle
In the nest the same height at the sound
Of wings that told the blind food was around;
It would have taken Solomon to say
Which bill was widest and hungriest that day,
And yet there never was a single miss.
One bird was there, bent down and gave the kiss
Of parenthood, was gone, and in its stead
The other came, a new wide mouth was fed.
Any man who saw it would confess
This was a lovely chain of righteousness.
—ROBERT P. TRISTRAM COFFIN

Nature's symbolism tells man truths about all life. Survival of the fittest is the rule of the deadly Darwinian struggle waged endlessly among all living creatures. But, as the denouement of the struggle between the scavenger and its mortal enemy reveals, victory goes not always to the strong.

The Battle of the Great White Shark

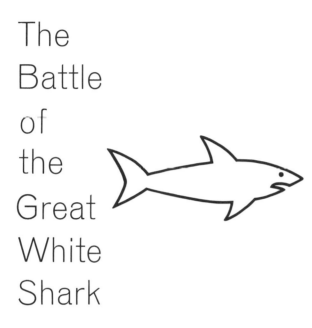

BY S. ROBERT RUSSELL

FORTY MILES OFF SHORE, IN THE GULF OF MEXICO, our commercial fishing boat, *Celsa*, wallowed soddenly, her dirty canvas hanging limp in the dead calm, her ancient Diesel dead. The four-man crew labored over the stubborn engine and cursed their luck. I could offer only halfhearted sympathy, for as a paying passenger making the trip to study marine life, I felt sure this interlude in calm waters would prove exciting. From my vantage point on top of the cabin, I surveyed the sea.

The blazing August sun made the water transparent for one hundred feet straight down before it fogged into smoky translucence.

Deep down in the haze I spotted a cigar-shaped shadow. It was so small it hardly caught my eye. But as it rose toward the surface a terrifying change took place. That which had seemed only inches long grew to feet, then yards and finally, when the sail-like dorsal broke water, it had become a blood-chilling monster as long as our boat, a full thirty feet from snout to wide-forked tail. It was the great white shark, *Carcharodon carcharias*.

Gray-white, horrible, he was a direct descendant of gigantic ancestors. Deadly, broad, serrated daggers gleamed ivory-white in the sardonic-grinning,

half-opened mouth, as symmetrical as the teeth on a cross-cut saw. Along one side an even row of small round scars, like healed machine-gun bullet wounds, gave testimony that a giant sawfish had once driven home a telling blow.

He circled the boat. Down on the deck the men jumped up with a yell when the high, pointed fin passed by, cruising around us.

For a time he swam aimlessly, then, swerving, he streaked toward a large patch of seawood.

Lying half-awash, comfortably bedded atop the seaweed, was one of nature's weirdest freaks, *Mola mola*, the oceanic sunfish.

She looked, from small, pouting mouth to high dorsal, much like any full-bodied fish. But from the dorsal where her body should have tapered off into a tail was—nothing. She was almost exactly half a fish, a tailless head and body, something nature had absentmindedly left incomplete. She was small, as such freaks go, measuring three feet up and down.

Carcharodon skirted the seaweed, scented the thing sheltered on it, reversed in a whirlpool of foam and struck.

In an instant the seaweed patch erupted into a boiling, foaming maelstrom. Brown clumps flew spinning into the air. *Carcharodon*'s terrifying jaws opened and clamped shut, lightning fast. His battery of jagged-edged knives sheared into *Mola mola's* leathery skin and locked. Another great swirl and *Mola mola* disappeared as completely as though she had never existed.

Carcharodon plowed out of the seaweed. Streamers trailed from tight clenched jaws, beardlike.

It was soon after that the engine gave its first thump. As the explosions shattered the quiet and vibrated through the depths the towering dorsal fin sank slowly beneath the surface.

Our cargo was beginning to smell. There was no use taking it in. For a time I helped the fishermen shovel the fish overboard. The exhaust skipped, quit, started and skipped, and the *Celsa* crept toward harbor as I searched the water for another glimpse of the tremendous white shark.

He did not surface again nor could I locate him below us, but I visualized him matching our poor speed effortlessly, slashing and gorging on our catch with ravenous gluttony.

Unloading tons of big fish by hand is slow work. The engine constantly balked and stopped. As a result it was late afternoon when the last fish was jettisoned and the Galveston north jetty lay close in, dead ahead. There the engine died finally. The captain sent a man forward to throw the kedge over. We then could signal for a tow in.

I mounted to the deckhouse roof, convinced that the huge shark had followed our trail of fish, and wishing to have a last glimpse of his spine-chilling bulk.

Inshore on the flats lay an old wreck. To seaward of it a school of porpoises surfaced, blew and fed around a slow-moving shrimp trawler. Not far from us swam a mother porpoise and her pup.

It was feeding time for the pup. He nudged and butted his mother insistently. Finally yielding she stopped, rolled over slightly until her starboard flipper came out of water.

Female porpoises have two exposed teats which they extrude, pump full of milk from an internal reservoir and discharge into the offspring's mouth. I watched, delighted at the luck my trip had brought, for few men have seen a porpoise pup being nursed.

Then, a commotion twenty yards away attracted my attention. A bull porpoise surfaced noisily with a large flounder held loosely between his jaws. Throwing back his head quickly he sent the fish spinning into the air. He retrieved it almost as it struck the water and repeated the performance again and again. Finally abandoning the shredded fish, he dived and almost instantly zoomed into the air in the series of spectacular leaps that is the main act in a male porpoise's courtship.

Suddenly a tremendous, shadowy form materialized in the depths nearby. It was the great white shark. Possibly the abandoned flounder had settled close enough to be detected by his marvelously acute combination senses of taste and smell.

In any event he swam directly toward the mother porpoise and her nursing pup. He seemed in no hurry and completely unaware of their presence.

But the porpoise, her every nerve alert while nursing, sensed his approach. She whirled, panic-stricken, to an even keel. As she did, her flipper smacked the pup smartly across the head. Frightened, bewildered by the undeserved chastisement, he darted away from her protecting side—straight toward the shark!

Carcharodon saw the tiny porpoise, swerved and surged ahead to meet it. Death was quick and merciful for the little pup.

The frantic mother, tearing after him, twisted and dived instinctively. That lightning reflex saved her. Her conical teeth were grinders, useless to tear and slash, quite incapable of ripping through the shark's tough, denticle-armored hide. But nature had given her another weapon. The actions since her forebears had first left land for a marine existence had fused her neck vertebrae into almost solid bone. Her hog-like snout made a perfect battering ram.

She smashed into the shark with the force of three-hundred pounds moving at almost forty miles an hour. His great bulk quivered under the impact. He whirled, jaws clashing. She twisted away from his boiling rush with far superior speed and agility.

As she dodged, the bull porpoise charged to her aid. Nearly twice the weight and infinitely more powerful than the female, he blasted into the shark well aft, almost at the anal fins. The smash was so terrific that the huge tail was lifted a full yard out of the water.

Then the mother drove in again from the opposite side. She hit the shark above center, slid up the smooth side, shot ten feet into the air and struck the water on her back. For a split second she floundered, confused. In that brief interval the shark spun, jaws snapping. Knife-edged teeth slashed multiple grooves along her side and chopped the end of her port side flipper.

Around them the water boiled and swirled. Foam spread in a widening circle. Mud from the bottom, only fifteen feet below, slowly changed the clear water to a dirty yellow.

A half mile north the other porpoises had abandoned their feeding and were playing, blowing and diving around the shrimp boat. Abruptly, as if in response to an inaudible signal, they surfaced and charged in echelon, straight for the boiling, foam-flecked whirlpool.

So great was the urge for speed that they swam almost on the surface, submerging only slightly in long undulating dives. Two flashed cleanly into the air in shallow, speed-accelerating leaps.

Outweighed and outweaponed, the female porpoise and her new-found champion fought on desperately. The tide of battle was slowly turning against them. Six inches had been sheered from the great bull's starboard tail-fluke and a row of jagged furrows, from dorsal fin aft, ran red.

He charged in fury, struck high, ricocheted in turn from the plunging, rounded back and burst into the air in a long, shallow flight. His landing split the surface fifty feet distant. The shark plunged toward the weakening female.

He might have caught her, but before the chase had run twenty yards, the charging school of porpoises struck with the impact of galloping Cossacks. The sound of sodden, smashing blows was like a boxer's dripping gloves smacking against flesh but amplified to thousands of pounds.

For ten explosive, water-churning minutes the porpoises tore in, struck and retreated like a pack of dogs holding a bear at bay. Like a bear the shark would make short slashing stands; then, as his adversaries drew back, attempt to run for safety. And each time the school, circling to seaward, drove him toward the beach.

A blindly charging young bull failed to elude the champing jaws. That was the beginning of the end. As the shark slowed to crush his victim the mother porpoise charged for the monster's most vulnerable spot—his gill slits. She was squarely on target.

At forty miles an hour her hard snout drove through the leather-tough protecting strips on his starboard side as though they were paper. Her head bored in eyes-deep. Her powerful jaws clamped. Thrashing free she brought with her a whole mouthful of crimson gill tissue, as all important to the shark as lungs to a man.

Blood pumping from the gaping opening dyed the water.

As if on signal the entire school concentrated its attack on both gills. One tough snout after another drove in, lightning fast. Teeth clamped, ripped and withdrew. Within a minute the port gill was also gushing red.

There was a cataclysmic upheaval. Chunks of mud slung spinning into the air. Silt-yellowed water darkened to reddish brown. A ghastly, sneering head climbed straight out of the water until the huge flippers came into view. It hung there for three long seconds, ruptured gills spouting redly. Frightful jaws gaped wide, then crashed shut with the report of two planks being slapped together. A convulsive shudder shook the crumpling hulk. It toppled backward, quivering weakly, and settled toward the bottom.

One by one the porpoises withdrew, all but the still raging female and the big bull. Time after time she surfaced, then dived, and by the water's turmoil I could visualize her slamming into the flaccid bulk on the bottom. The male, as if in patient understanding, made no effort to dissuade her but circled slowly as if waiting until her fury was spent.

Finally she turned from her vengeance and swam to him. For a long minute they lay quietly. Then swimming side by side they followed the others.

The sun had set, and the quiet bay was purple with the reflection of fading twilight, when a power boat whose skipper had caught our signals finally towed us into port.

"Didja get a good catch?" he asked the member of our crew who tossed him the tow rope. Our man replied in disgust that the trip had been a complete bust. I had the sense to keep quiet, realizing my commercial-minded boatmates could hardly share the most rewarding day I had ever spent on the Gulf.

♛ May, 1945.

Each generation has its angry white knight of social criticism, whose lance pricks the bubble of ignorance and complacency. Ours is Philip Wylie, whose blast at "Momism" made the nation wince. More recently, Wylie turned his anger and caustic pen on the sickroom Peeping Toms who seem to dance wildly around the private fire of someone else's agony, as if to reassure themselves that it isn't happening to them.

We Are Making a Circus of Death

BY PHILIP WYLIE

WHEN PRESIDENT EISENHOWER SUFFERED HIS HEART attack, Dr. Paul Dudley White, a world-famous specialist, was summoned to Washington. He soon gave out a hopeful statement about his patient. But he added information for which no one had asked: the President's bowel movements, Dr. White said, were normal. Evidently someone questioned the need for such news, for the eminent physician later explained with bare-faced blandness, that the American people were very much interested in bowel movements.

Perhaps some are. But I am one American who is not in the last interested in the bowel movements of others, Presidents included. I thought Dr. White's unsolicited discussion of the matter was absolutely uncalled for. I felt it must have been exceedingly embarrassing to President Eisenhower. The President is but one of many public figures who have recently been obliged to expose their agonies to the prying press and the glaring gaze of television. John Foster Dulles, our former Secretary of State, died of cancer—after the world had peered intimately at each sorry step of his decline.

While Mr. Dulles was in office and in good health, I disagreed violently and publicly with his policies. But I never belittled his superb courage and my heart went out to him in his final months. He was a well-bred, highly educated man—and human. No one will ever know how much inner suffering was added to his terminal distress by having to endure it in the same lurid limelight that followed his steps when he was well—and the busiest man on earth.

Let the reader ask himself how *he* would feel in such a situation.

Suppose *you* were stricken by an incurable disease. How would you react if your every symptom, pain, treatment and brief remission were submitted to public scrutiny? How would you like it if, while you were trying to recuperate in the Florida home of a friend, the press stormed your refuge like troops attacking a beachhead? Imagine that, as a last-ditch measure, radioactive gold was injected in your veins—and then try to imagine how you'd feel if the newspapers reported you'd become temporarily so radioactive that your visitors had to keep ten feet away from you to be safe from the rays you emitted?

Assume also that you, like the late Mr. Dulles, had established a world-wide reputation for energy, dauntlessness and durability, only to become a na-

131

tional exhibit to the pitiful fact that cancer can and does bring the strongest among us to our knees, no matter what courage is in us. Wouldn't you think it morbid and cruel of the public to stare at your inchmeal disintegration?

Of course you would!

And yet, while Mr. Dulles lay dying, the surfeit of his personal calamity was not enough for the press, radio and TV. A celebrated entertainer discovered, after surgery, that a pain in his chest was due to lung cancer—and, again, all the world was allowed to watch and listen while Arthur Godfrey, in openly admitted terror, was wheeled to the operating room. During the ensuing hard days, Mr. Godfrey tried to co-operate with the inquisitive press. He even wrote down for a presumedly ghoulish public his deepest emotions. He tried to describe the clinical details of his surgery.

It is time to ask ourselves a question about the ruthless public attention given these famous men, and others, nowadays. Do the people of America really want to sit at the bedside of every stricken great man and every sick celebrity, listening to and looking at each successive detail of their tragedies —however grim, gruesome or intimate—without any regard for the feelings of the victims?

Has the American press, radio or television any duty—let alone the right—to invade the operating and hospital rooms of important people?

Is the American public that heartless or that neurotically curious? Must leading Americans give up the last shred of privacy, the last iota of dignity and even a chance to die in peace, simply because they happen to be famous?

Robert C. Ruark, the syndicated columnist, writing about the coverage on the late Secretary Dulles and Arthur Godfrey, says: "Ten years ago you wouldn't read that a man had cancer. . . . The evil thing has finally come out into the open, to where you can write about it."

Up to a point, I agree with Mr. Ruark. Until quite recently, a superstitious, ignorant, large fraction of the American public believed that cancer was so awful that it should not be mentioned even when it became the cause of death. Cancer victims were reported to have died of "a lingering illness," as Mr. Ruark also notes. A major part of an enlightened, modern campaign has aimed at bringing cancer into the open and at recognizing it early so that anyone afflicted by it will have the best possible chance of recovery.

Why was such a campaign necessary? Why was the mere word "cancer" nationally taboo? The answer goes back to dark and horrible notions held by earlier generations. Many thought the affliction was evidence of a secret, sexual misdeed and showed that the stricken person had led an evil or vile life. So when cancer occurred, family fear and pride united to hush up the presumed proof of its victim's wicked past.

Today, we know substantially more about the disease. We know it has nothing to do with sin, sexual or other. We also know it is not—as some

dreaded—contagious. We know that the best hope we have of dealing with it, and of curing it, is to bring into the open the basic facts about the disease and to encourage everybody who even thinks he may have cancer to see his doctor.

Even so, there is a measureless difference between the public admission of cancer and the public examination of every step of the cancer-afflicted individual's suffering. It helps humanity to learn that the late Mr. Dulles suffered from cancer, and that Godfrey and—more recently—General Nathan F. Twining, Chairman of our Joint Chiefs of Staff, have been operated on for lung cancer. By such announcements, other worried and perhaps still-superstitious people are led to take their symptoms to capable doctors. But who is helped, in any fashion, by an ensuing account of tribulations that used to be held a man's private business? *Nobody*.

When the President suffered his heart attack, it was vitally important for the world to know two facts: the nature of his illness and the prognosis— that is, how the President might be expected to respond to treatment. Those two facts—and those alone—were of critical importance because many affairs of humanity hinged upon them. Both facts were given to the world the instant they were surely ascertained. There was no need, afterward, for the world to listen to elaborate medical talks about the minor symptoms of the President—or to hear about the normalcy of his bowels.

Dr. White's confiding of such a personal datum appalled the press of Britain. That such a needless and intimate fact should be published in American newspapers made the British think we had lost our sense of decency, discarded all feeling for privacy and revealed ourselves as unspeakably vulgar.

And countless Americans of sensibility agreed. They have begun to react violently to the clinical avidity of our press, radio and TV. Thus Arthur Krock, writing recently in *The New York Times* about the public spectacle made of the illness of the late Mr. Dulles said: ". . . the time is overdue to return . . . to the proprieties of the sickroom."

It seems abnormal, from the standpoint of mental health, to want to read masses of surgical, medical, psychological and other torturesome detail about ill persons, however notable. And it is carrying the sacred right of press freedom to the edge of mental disease, to gather and broadcast such information.

Nobody has a right to invade the privacy of a sufferer, whatever his ailment or however important his name. Our free press should never presume it has the license to mount a deathwatch and to dispatch as news the step-by-step approach of dissolution. Only vultures may stand naturally, leering at the twitch-by-twitch decline that turns a thing alive into their distressful prey: carrion. Such behavior is beneath a human being.

How could so many of us have fallen into so depraved a state?

The causes are varied. One is an overzealous desire of certain sick persons, or of those who speak for them, to keep the press completely informed. But

the agents of the press and of all other media of communication ought to have the sense to omit complete information that is unnecessary, embarrassing or overdetailed. Pity and compassion on the part of newspaper reporters once kept them from their present ghoulish acts. They knew, for instance—but did not say—that Babe Ruth was dying of cancer and Lou Gehrig of amyotrophic lateral sclerosis. Those two brave men, the reporters also realized, could still read the papers and would be humiliated to have their doomed circumstances set before the public. The reporters of that era were right.

When some of his friends visited Babe Ruth toward the end, it was announced on the radio that they wept at the sight of their hero, shrunk from '225 pounds to 100 pounds." According to Mrs. Ruth, when the Babe heard about that broadcast he cursed the man who made it and said bitterly, "Hell, when I'm dead my bones will weigh more than 100 pounds."

It is hard enough to bear a slow death; but to bear it under feverish public stare must be as ignominious to a decent man as to be stripped, tarred, feathered and ridden through the streets on a rail.

For a sick man or one dying—however great—surely has one right greater than all other alleged rights: the right to be a *private* citizen for as long as he wishes.

Certainly, if the destiny of other people impinges upon his state, a stricken leader—but nobody else—has a further duty. He owes it to those who depend upon him to let them know the bare facts of his situation. It was rumored, for instance, that Franklin Delano Roosevelt suffered from an incipient heart disorder. If so—and if he knew it—I think it should have been told to the people—for the nation might then have been better prepared to face the consequences of his subsequent death by stroke. And surely, the long illness of Woodrow Wilson should not have been shrouded in silence while a mystified world wondered, waited and, in the perplexing period, lost hold of its ideals.

But even in such rare, crucial instances, nobody needed the kind of news people are getting today about stricken celebrities. These frequent bulletins, fulsome as hospital records, are useful only to the doctors in attendance. The public has no right to them. And certainly their publication has a bad effect on any sufferer unless he is such an exhibitionist he insanely believes it good publicity to have the masses examine X rays of his liver and photographs of his gallstones.

It is, to sum up, a brave and honorable public service of the stricken to announce the simple fact of whatever disease it is that threatens and perhaps ultimately ends their lives. From such unadorned announcement, all people gain a noble example and the medical statisticians gain useful data. Among national leaders, such simple announcement is mandatory. But to add more detail is to bring a death to dignity itself by robbing death of dignity.

There is, already, too much violence and misery, murder, mayhem and sensationalism in our press, on our radio and on our TV screens. Such loud merchandising of calamity tends to make us callous.

That is why, perhaps, we have not yet done what we should do, whenever the candid cameras and klieg lights are carted into the sickroom of some notable: rebel with our individual voices. These, united, would yank the vultures out of the sickroom and give the patient what he most needs: peace, privacy, rest and quiet.

Only a fool would want that sort of attention, and only an idiot could bear it. Disease is not a proper occasion for charivari. Most of the important men among us are neither fools nor idiots. And even if a shameless public should desire to peer upon renowned agony, none but veritable pimps of communication would cater to such an appetite.

So let's restore to sickness its privacy and to death its necessary dignity. For if we do not, we shall have taken a major portion of dignity and of value not just from death but from life, also.

꿔 September, 1959.

PLEA FOR PERSONAL ATTENTION

Stand on the corner of any city street,

And watch the parade of the freaks pass in review.

It is not the born deformed, the maimed, the ailing,

Nor the ill in mind, of whom I speak.

It is the unwieldly with fat, the man,

Huge-stomached, who has not seen his toes in years;

The shapeless woman waddling like a duck;

Round, bending shoulders and the leading chin,

Long arms hung ape-like, and the genuflecting knees;

The concave chest and jutting hips. . . .

It is the puffy nose, the bloodshot eyes;

It is the face meant to be pleasant to the sight,

The body formed for ease and grace in motion,

Neglected to become impaired and ugly.

It is the many who, inert and meek,

Let life misshape and mar them, of whom I speak.

—IRMA WASSAL

What is it like to die? We know that feeling only once, and then it is usually too late for objective analysis. But in 1957, famed British author Joyce Cary—doomed by a progressive paralysis and given limited days of life—pondered what it was that had made his life worth while. In these, his last written words, his courage and calm acceptance of the irrevocable in an era of anxiety and fear are rare and inspiring.

A Great Author Faces Up to Death

AN INTERVIEW WITH JOYCE CARY
by Graham Fisher

I HAD ALWAYS HOPED TO DIE SUDDENLY, AS WITH A bullet through the head. But in a way, this illness of mine might be regarded as lucky; I might have had a galloping cancer. This thing gives me some more years for work, is almost painless and doesn't affect the brain.

Solace? I don't need any solace. I've got my faith and I've got my work. I don't see why anyone should moan when he's had his life. Life is given to us. It is a free gift. We do nothing to merit it.

I've had a good life, a happy marriage, a happy home, devoted friends. I've been a very lucky person and I have nothing to complain of now.

This thing started immediately after the Viscount crash at London airport last year. The Viscount I was on took the wrong runway and hit a lot of building material just as it was leaving the ground.

No one was really hurt. I didn't feel hurt at all at the time and went on by the next plane.

I first noticed something wrong while I was out in Greece and Cyprus. I had two small falls, though I didn't pay much attention to them at the time. I was told by my doctors that I had temporary brain damage which would pass off, the sort of thing a jet pilot gets if he pulls out of a dive too quickly.

But when the disability increased, specialists revised this opinion and said that what I had was disseminated neuritis and I must have had it a long time before it began to show its effect. This is a form of paralysis which, at least at present, has no cure. It is progressive, but varies in the speed of its progression.

I had started on a novel in 1954, *The Captive and the Free*, before this thing began. I am going on with that now.

Will what has happened affect what goes into it? The main lines of this novel have been laid down for years and all the chief scenes are already written, so that if recent events affect it, it can only be in detail. The novel is about religion and deals partly with faith-healing, for faith-healing raises some of the fundamental problems of religion; for instance, the question of miracles and of what we mean by omnipotence.

Personally, I do not believe in what are called physical miracles. That is to say, any interference in the natural order of things, so far as it is revealed by scientific research. I know, of course, that science rests on an assumption of consistency in material nature. For instance, the proposition that all men are mortal cannot be proved true until all men have died, but this criticism of the scientific position seems to me rather frivolous.

A fundamental objection to physical miracles is that they make God responsible for all evil not due to evil will, that is to say, for all bad luck. When a child dies in agony of meningitis its misery is due simply to bad luck and not to anybody's wickedness. God could not abolish the power of doing evil because if he did he also would have to abolish the power of doing good. The world would be a machine; there would be no evil . . . and no goodness, no happiness and no grief, for machines feel neither.

But if physical miracles are possible, there is no reason why any child should die in agony. To believe in their possibility makes God responsible for evil.

What has happened to me has not changed my perspective on anything. I have had the same religious views from at least the age of thirty, and the same values on life.

Do I believe in God? I believe absolutely in God as the ground of love, beauty and goodness. These are personal things which can only exist in personality; that is why we think of God as a person.

These feelings exist universally in human nature, and human nature is part of a universal nature. As soon as one realizes this very simple fact . . . that there is personality in nature . . . it becomes the most important thing in nature. It is certainly the most important thing for humanity, because men live to satisfy their feelings. They use their brains only to create a world satisfactory to their feelings.

And, again, personality cannot exist in a machine. It exists only in the free world, the free soul, with power of moral choice, power to create its own answer for each moral situation, always unique.

The word "soul" is highly ambiguous. For me, a man's soul is the character of his personality, good or bad. It is partly inherited, as the fundamental emotions and intuitions of human nature, and partly formed by his education and his own moral choice.

Of course, this free creative mind can also plan evil and does so every day. Also, since it is perpetually at work inventing new ideas, new processes, new politics, the world is always full of insecurity. We live among perpetual changes. Nothing ever stays fixed. This is the price we pay.

We owe what makes life worth living—family affection, achieved ambition—to the same factor of free creative personality as makes for all the injustice, insecurity and change that infects all existence. They belong together in the free world. It is no good complaining of bad luck for luck is also the field of our freedom.

Do I believe in an afterlife? There is no real evidence either way. That is to say, I don't believe or disbelieve. I certainly don't count on it and I can't visualize it. If there is such a thing, it must obviously be quite strange to our ideas. If there is no afterlife, then death is final. I don't believe in reincarnation.

At present, I'm finding out what a lot of things you can do without when you have to. I used to live a very active life, enjoying all kinds of sport: sailing, punting. I used to walk three or four miles a day in the country or the parks. I used to go to the theatre. But I don't miss those things. I haven't time to miss them.

My one real regret is not having finished some of the novels I've started. I should like very much to finish some of these, but I shan't look at them until I have finished my present novel.

I don't know exactly how much longer I have to live, but I do know that I've got much more to do in the time than I shall ever be able to do.

I went to art school once for two years. I intended to be an artist. I'm sorry I haven't had time to carry on with it, but this writing job takes up all your time. I wish I'd had time for art as well—I miss it—but I'd need to have another life for that.

Is there anything I regret not having achieved in life? Not really. I'd have liked my novels to have been rather better. Every book I start I think is going to be wonderful—a masterpiece—and then when it's finished I'm always disappointed. If I'd another life, I'd rewrite the lot.

Language is never adequate to express feeling. Words are just marks on paper, after all. Music is much more powerful in the direct expression of emotion—much more exciting—but not so precise. The novel has to give the fact as well as the feeling, the scene of actual life, as well as a judgment upon that scene.

Would I be willing to barter the books I've written

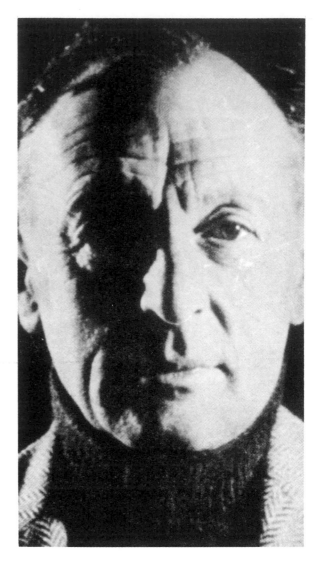

for a few more years of life? No, I wouldn't. It isn't that I think my books are so good, but they're me. They're something I have done with my life.

Has my illness revealed any difference in the world? Nothing very definite except the tremendous amount of goodness in people. I've had letters of sympathy and kindness, sometimes without even an address given. I receive extraordinarily kind letters from complete strangers nearly every day. Friends come in to see me, write to me, send me flowers. So do my children. In fact, I have been rather embarrassed by all the sympathy and to-do.

When the newspapers quoted me as saying that I was ready to die, one of my friends—a woman—remarked, "Well, we are all ready to die." And that's quite true. What's more, it's a very important truth.

It is very important that people should realize that any week may be their last . . . that next week they may be smashed up in a motor accident or knocked out with polio.

Do I mind dying? Of course. I mind very much. But I look upon the time I have left as a gift. And I am very busy.

♛ January, 1957.

Freedom was the dominant issue of the times. Abroad it united peoples and nations in a common cause. But here in America, another fight for freedom became an abrasive, divisive force. The school-integration controversy split the land and the people. And, as in every such struggle, there were innocent victims—such as the children of an embattled Virginia county, the only one in the U.S. without public schools.

Blackout in Prince Edward County

BY LUCY DANIELS

HE IS TALL FOR HIS FIFTEEN YEARS, LEAN AND handsome. His dark eyes still look down with the shyness of boyhood, but the singing voice in his throat is powerful. If he had continued doing well in school, there might even have been a chance for the musical training of which he dreamed. But today those hopes are nearly forgotten. Where can anyone go without an education? For this boy is a Negro living in Prince Edward County, Virginia. And there are no schools for Negroes in Prince Edward, none at all.

In the summer of 1959, rather than yield to a Federal court order for integration in the larger of its two white high schools, Prince Edward's board of supervisors cut off funds for all twenty-one of the county's public schools. The result: seventeen hundred Negro children and fifteen hundred white children with no facilities for education; *the only county in America without public schools.*

Prince Edward's white citizens hastily set up private schools for white children in churches and vacant business buildings. But no schools have been provided for the Negroes. Some seventy of the older ones have been sent away—to relatives in nearby counties or to Kittrell Junior College's high-school division in North Carolina. A few Negro mothers have tried teaching their children at home, but in most cases they lack both the textbooks and the education. So there are hundreds like the fifteen-year-old singer who have already lost a year of school.

"Sometime I work a day," the boy says. "Sometime I go hunting. But mostly I just hang around home." By "home" he means this dimly lit little room with its rusting wood stove and small television set. From the kitchen next to it floats the customary fragrance of hot ham fat and boiling greens. His older sister feeds a bottle to her baby. His mother patches a pair of overalls.

"Yes, I worry about his schooling," she says. "Nowadays you can't get a job without it." But she cannot afford to send him away, and she will not apply for one of Virginia's state tuition grants for private schools. "No, I'd worry . . . I don't understand."

Up and down the muddy back roads of Prince Edward there are many more homes like this, and people who don't understand. Not all Negroes either. For, in Prince Edward, where the population is about half and half, Negroes and whites often live on adjacent farms. The poverty is shared by white and black. Also the prosperity.

Despite the closing of the schools, life in Prince Edward moves on nearly as languidly as ever. So many Negroes flock to town on weekends that "no nice white lady goes shopping on Saturday," but there has never been violence. (Not a lynching in the history of the county.) Voices on both sides vow there will be none. And judging from the attention both whites and Negroes have paid the law throughout their struggle, it would seem they are right.

However, there *has* been a change in Prince Edward. A middle-aged Negro baker, who has lived in Prince Edward all his life, each day meets white men he has known for years. Do they still speak? "Sure. There's nothing else to do. . . . But their smile is guilty now," he says. "I see that the same white man I once would've fought for don't care about us. . . . Still, white man smiles at me, I smile back. I won't be the one to show it."

Probably the reason for the lack of both violence and communication is the power wielded by extremists of both groups. Both speak clearly and determinedly, but neither hears the other. And the moderates—the Negroes who prefer segregated schools to no schools; the whites who would settle for public education with token integration—do not speak at all. So segregation is maintained by the same white businessmen who control everything from religion to politics in the county.

J. B. Wall, publisher and editor of the Farmville *Herald*, speaks for them. He has lived in Farmville all his sixty-one years. Wall declares with an impatient sweep of his cigar, "We aren't going to break any laws but there's no such thing as token integration; it all leads to amalgamation. And we won't have it."

The Reverend L. Francis Griffin, Baptist minister and co-ordinator for the National Association for the Advancement of Colored People in Prince Edward, is the spokesman for the other side. A heavy-set, light-colored Negro just over forty, he served in the Army during World War II and returned to Farmville to succeed his father as pastor of the First Baptist Church.

"We never got what was due us," he says. "But in the late '40's things reached a climax. Crowded conditions in the colored high school were intolerable. So we went to the white school board and asked for a new school.

"They agreed about the conditions but said there was 'no money.'

"They dragged their feet like that for years. And all they did in the end was put up eight tar-paper shacks that were cold and leaky."

In 1951 the Negro children staged a two-week strike, refusing to attend those tar-paper schools. And a letter was written to N.A.A.C.P. officials asking for help. The N.A.A.C.P. went to work in Prince Edward and the Negroes finally did get a new high school. That school, completed in 1953, cost $900,000. Now, however, it is as empty as the unused yellow school buses beside it. And its towering brick façade bears the same "No Trespassing" placard as the tiny weather-beaten schoolrooms with matching outhouses which dot the countryside.

John W. Booker, another Negro minister, actually favors segregation. Booker preaches in four rural churches, but never mentions his convictions in his sermons. Big, with graying hair, Booker has lived on the same farm (which he owns) all his sixty-five years. He has a ready laugh, but when he talks about Prince Edward, his lined face grows sad—"It's pitiful. You got to be particular what you say."

And certainly many Negroes seem to be "particular." One weather-beaten frame house in Farmville on a winter night shows not a ray of light; not a paper rustles to suggest that it is occupied. Yet knocking on the door brings a voice from within.

"Who is it?"

The visitor gives his name.

The sound of a bolt turning. Then the bright face of an adolescent girl appears in the crack. "Yes, please come in. Reverend Griffin came by, and Mama's expecting you."

Inside, the room is bright (there are black curtains at the windows) with the flickering of oil lamps and kerosene stove. Besides the animated face of the teen-age girl, there are five smaller, pinched faces with wide, watching, bead-black eyes. And "Mama" is a small, hard-faced woman with the same darting eyes. She has agreed to talk, but she cannot.

Do you worry about your children's education?

"I couldn't say."

Do you think the public schools will reopen?

"I couldn't say."

Would you rather have segregated schools than no schools at all?

"I couldn't say."

In fact, there is only one thing she will say— "Being uneducated is like being heathen." She echoes without knowing the words of Lester Andrews,

white businessman and chairman of the now functionless public school board: "Two things have been overlooked—the children and education."

Undoubtedly, Andrews' fellow segregationists would disagree with him. For the county's fifteen hundred white children *are* going to school. The Prince Edward School Foundation, which now operates eight private schools (two high, six elementary), was organized six years ago, immediately after the Supreme Court's integration ruling. All but three of its sixty-sixty teachers are holdovers from the public system, paid the same salaries as before. So far these schools have been financed on contributions—materials, time, books and money. No tuition has been charged. Administrator Roy R. Pearson claimed he had enough funds on hand to meet the schools' annual budget of $305,000.

No itemized account of this money is available to the public. Reportedly, a major portion comes from the $1.80 per $100 school-tax refund which all Prince Edward citizens were urged to contribute. Most white families—with or without children—have paid this; some much more. But Pearson says some children attend the private schools without contributing.

Teachers say that disciplinary problems are at a minimum in the new schools and that some classes are a month ahead of schedule. Parents, too, seem generally satisfied; but some are concerned about the long mornings of classes—8:30 A.M. to 1:30 P.M. —without a lunch break. And the classrooms are makeshift and inconvenient. Scattered about in neighboring—but not adjacent—churches, warehouses and civic club buildings, all are adequately lighted and meet Virginia's fire regulations. But they are overcrowded and hampered by inefficient equipment.

In some the study tables are simply doors with legs of metal piping; in others they are Sunday school kindergarten tables with blocks of wood under their legs to adapt them for weekday use by older children. Elementary school children keep books in pillowcases attached to the backs of their chairs.

One eighth grader tells of how "large mice" molested her home room. "It was awful." She shivers. "But the boys brought poison and rat traps, so they're mostly gone now." The books are the same as those in use throughout Virginia. The bespectacled, substantial-looking teacher is the same one they would have had in the public school.

Each child sits erect at his wobbly desk—a unique collapsible contraption hinged to the back of a folding bridge chair. There is very little whispering or passing of notes. For these children have been made to understand this year is one of public emergency; that the success—or failure—of the private schools depends upon them.

And so far they have met that responsibility. At first because it was something like an adventure. Now, patiently, obediently, perhaps a little wearily. Under the private system they are deprived of many of the pleasanter aspects of school. No physical education. No lunch periods with their friends. No extracurricular activities.

Still, Administrator Pearson, retired oil specialist turned educator who has a daughter in the sixth grade, says: "I want my daughter to go to segregated schools, because I know white and colored can't sit beside each other without becoming infatuated."

To such statements Griffin replies, "That's the white man's guilty conscience speaking. We don't want to socialize. We just want our rights as human beings."

Even loyal supporters of the private schools say a more permanent setup is necessary. The churches won't lend their buildings forever; $305,000 is a big bill for fewer than half the families in Prince Edward to meet annually. So local leaders are talking of reopening the white schools next fall in permanent buildings. Where the money will come from, they do not say. But they hint that tuition will eventually be charged.

There have been insistent attempts by white citizens to help Negroes organize private schools. But Prince Edward's Negroes turn thumbs down on all such ventures. "To accept," Griffin explains, "would be compromising on our right to integrated public education. The white men want us to set the precedent on the state's tuition grants—which they haven't yet dared to use—so that they can take advantage of them."

"Anyway," Griffin adds, "they could never actually organize schools for Negroes. All but two or three of our teachers have left the county. Besides, most of our ministers are for integration and would never donate their church buildings as the white ministers have done."

There are many pressures. A couple of years ago one of the county's leading contractors, a Negro, found it advisable to run an ad in the Farmville *Herald* saying he was not a member of the N.A.A.C.P. A college professor, who quickly questioned the wisdom of closing the public schools, has changed his way of talking since he tried to get a loan for a house. A white Presbyterian minister, who spoke out for integration, was asked to leave.

But these pressures are rarely obvious. There are only two things the Prince Edward elite hate openly —the N.A.A.C.P. and Governor J. Lindsay Almond. Three years ago they wined and dined Governor Almond; he was going to save Virginia from integration. But now that the Governor has abandoned massive resistance for a more compromising position, he is called "Benedict" Almond in Prince Edward.

Yet, Prince Edward's white citizens are still Virginia cavaliers. They never forget what is proper— even in revenge. One housewife protests that the integrationist minister was "by no means forced out. And when he left, we gave him $500 and a sterling-silver tea service."

What the future holds for Prince Edward no one there will venture. As the white citizens try to make their private school permanent, the Rev. Griffin predicts it will take a long legal battle to reopen the public schools. Certainly not this fall.

"There's just one thing sure," Minister John Booker says with bitter laughter. "Half the white folks and half the colored folks are going to hell over integration."

ꟿ August, 1960.

In the austere object lesson of his work in Lambaréné, Albert Schweitzer embarrassed Western man into awareness concerning the purpose of the Christian path and made him feel shame for his reluctance to tread it. Schweitzer—perhaps accidentally, perhaps with the wisdom of the prophet—selected the fastness of Africa as the center of his lesson, the same continent which was to explode against injustices whites visited upon it and reform itself into self-governing states undreamed of even twenty-five years ago. With the irony of history, it was significant that the little boy who figures so movingly in the following story was a young Negro of the Western world, whose guileless dream reached around the earth to the old man in the dark continent.

To Dr. Schweitzer— With Love

BY MORTON PUNER

DR. ALBERT SCHWEITZER STUDIED THE TELEGRAM THE native boy had handed him. It had taken almost twenty-four hours to get from Naples, Italy, to his ramshackle forty-five-building hospital compound at Lambaréné on the west coast of Africa. Unexpectedly, it asked Dr. Schweitzer when he would be able to accept nine thousand pounds of medical supplies "from the Italian people." It was signed, "Lt. Gen. Richard C. Lindsay, United States Air Force."

Dr. Schweitzer wondered, "How did this happen?" The world-famed philosopher, humanitarian and Nobel Peace Prize winner would soon find out. And so, too, would the rest of the world: how a thirteen-year-old boy from Waycross, Georgia, named Robert Hill, had a noble idea and acted upon it; how he enlisted the help of NATO and the Italian and French air forces and how his idea inspired the generosity of thousands of people.

Bobby Hill had come to Italy in April 1958, with his family to join his father, Henry Hill, staff sergeant at the Naples headquarters of Allied Air Forces Southern Europe (AIRSOUTH). AIRSOUTH is a NATO air arm made up of people and equipment from France, Greece, Turkey and the United Kingdom as well as from Italy and the United States.

Bobby Hill played outfield in the Naples Babe Ruth League, got A's and B's in the local Forrest Sherman School for American personnel. He learned of Albert Schweitzer in a book, *The World of Albert Schweitzer*, by Erica Anderson and Eugene Exman, which tells how the great man gave up the comforts of Europe to practice medicine and his philosophy of "reverence for life" in the primitive African jungle.

Bobby was particularly struck by the story of Schweitzer's quest for peace. He thought about it a lot, the way a thirteen-year-old will, and then, one day, asked his father for money to buy medical supplies for Dr. Schweitzer. Sergeant Hill gave him five dollars, promised him more, but asked, "How do you expect to get the medicine to Africa?"

Then Bobby had his idea. One evening he wrote to the commander of AIRSOUTH.

Dear General Lindsay:

I have read in the newspapers about people wanting peace. My father has told me about NATO, and that it is also for peace.

I read about Dr. Albert Schweitzer's help to people in Equatorial Africa. . . . This is why I am writing to you. I think that by helping others we can have peace.

I want to help Dr. Schweitzer. I asked my father to buy some medicine and he said he will buy all he can afford if there is a way to get it to Dr. Schweitzer. I thought that if any of your airplanes go where Dr. Schweitzer is, they would deliver it for me. Maybe some other people will want to give some medicine too. . . . I have not told my father I am writing you but I am sure he wouldn't object.

Thank you, General, if you can help.

ROBERT A. HILL
13 years old

The general replied two days later, assuring Bobby that he would get the medicine to Africa. He also said that he was getting in touch with the program director of RAI, the Italian radio network, which has a program, *Ventiquattresima Ora* (Twenty-fourth Hour), broadcasting worthy appeals for assistance. The general added: ". . . do not become discouraged . . . there are always many people who want to help one another."

Bobby's letter was read—in English, French, German and Italian—on the RAI the following Sunday night at eight. Then Bobby was invited to appear on television to tell, through an interpreter, of his project.

The radio appeal was made on June 14, 1959. Within three weeks, medical supplies valued at more than $400,000 poured into Naples. The big Italian pharmaceutical firm of Lepetit made a huge contribution; the rest came from individual donors. Italian doctors screened the gifts to make sure they were suitable for French Equatorial Africa.

Fifty small cash gifts came from children, in amounts ranging from 500 lire (about 80 cents) to 10,000 lire (about $16). Almost all came with letters, such as the one from an eleven-year-old boy: "I do not know what medicines to buy but I am glad to offer my savings of 1,500 lire. I hope that other children will do likewise for humanity."

General Napoli, chief of the Italian Air Force, offered a transport plane to take the medicine to Africa. The French Air Force also offered a plane. It was at this point that General Lindsay sent his telegram to Dr. Schweitzer.

Dr. Schweitzer soon learned that Bobby was a Negro. One of the people the doctor had served for so many years was now helping him. He wrote his gratitude to General Lindsay.

Dr. Schweitzer also asked: Did the medicines need refrigeration? How much space did they take up? He was afraid that he couldn't handle a huge amount. Perhaps, he suggested, the supplies should be deposited with the Libreville Medical Service "to benefit all the doctors in (the province of) Gabon." He also asked permission to send some to a hospital in Peru bearing his name.

The Italian doctors who had screened the supplies had done their work well, however. There was little need for refrigeration of the material selected. And it was suggested to Dr. Schweitzer that since the supplies had been given to him, it was proper for him to receive them—and then dispose of them as he saw fit. Dr. Schweitzer notified General Lindsay that he was prepared to receive the supplies—and Bobby Hill.

The sixteen-hour trip to Lambaréné was Bobby's first flight. A second French plane, jammed with newspaper correspondents, joined the airlift. Soft-spoken, shy Bobby was the only child among more than thirty NATO officials and journalists.

There were incidents. Lieutenant Colonel Frank McWalters, who looked after Bobby, tells of two.

"*The Nigerian Times* had carried Bobby's picture, and when we got to Kano everyone seemed to know him. Once, an African stopped Bobby on the street and said, 'Don't trust them, Bobby. I am a nigger, and you're a nigger to them—no matter what they say.'

"Later, I tried to figure out what effect the man's words had on Bobby," Colonel McWalters said. "I don't think they hurt him. He's aware of prejudice against Negroes. But that doesn't mean he distrusts all white people. He seems to judge them the same way he judges Negroes—as individuals, worthy of his trust and affection unless they show otherwise."

Another incident took place at the Libreville hotel. At 2 A.M. a tribal chieftain strode into Bobby's room and awakened him. "Boy!" he shouted. "You're black and I'm black. We're brothers. Give me the truth. Who told you to write that letter to the general?"

A bewildered, sleep-filled Bobby Hill answered, "Nobody told me."

The chieftain then switched languages, hurled a quick stream of French at the boy. "I'm sorry," Bobby said, shaking his head. "I can't understand a word you're saying. I'm an American and I can only speak English."

The man retreated from the room. When Colonel McWalters caught up with him, the chieftain explained that he was opposed to French control of Equatorial Africa. He had been sure that Bobby was a French agent, that the whole episode had been concocted "to divert the attention of Africans from their real problems." But Bobby's obvious honesty and bewilderment convinced him otherwise.

Bobby Hill and the medical supplies reached Lambaréné on July 17. Still vigorous at eighty-four, Dr. Schweitzer, wearing an incredibly rumpled white suit, met Bobby and his party at the airstrip carved out of the 100-foot-high jungle.

The white-haired old man came forward, kissed the boy and said, in French, "How beautiful a child he is." He took Bobby by the hand and led him to the hospital to show him the patients the medicine would help. A Dutch nurse acted as interpreter.

Neither the difference in age nor in background seemed to be a barrier between the old man and the boy. Dr. Schweitzer was plainly delighted to see Bobby Hill; Bobby was thrilled to be in his presence. At a luncheon, the doctor thanked those who had contributed "in my name and in the name of the many who will need this medicine." He added, "I never thought that help would come to me through a little boy."

Bobby Hill spent two days at Lambaréné. Before he left, Dr. Schweitzer gave him a rosewood box for his mother. Inside was a note to Mrs. Hill: "Any mother who can bear a child like yours deserves my highest esteem—Albert Schweitzer."

The Bobby Hill story is not over.

Letters from many countries continue to reach him. Typical is one from a woman in Vomero, Italy.

Dear Little Boy:

When I was a child I met a boy of your race in Calabria. Everyone looked at him without speaking and made him unhappy. One day I went to him and started to talk. Together we understood the sea, the sky, the beauty of things. And he was no longer unhappy. . . . You represent the soul of all the children in the world. Bring my love with you to America. . . .

꟔ April, 1960.

One reaction to the menace of Communism in the postwar world was McCarthyism—the witch-hunting, oath-taking brand of patriotism that sowed suspicion and alarmed the nation at the very time its full energies were most needed. A few courageous voices, reaffirming the freedoms of our forebears, rallied men of good will to halt McCarthyism and work instead to fight Communism by making America stronger. The then junior Senator from Massachusetts was one, when he used CORONET's forum to attack college loyalty oaths, an early call to President Kennedy's New Frontier.

Let's Get Rid of College Loyalty Oaths!

BY JOHN F. KENNEDY

IN 1776, BENJAMIN FRANKLIN—FULLY AWARE OF the risk—decided to entrust secret plans of the American Revolution to a French agent. He believed the man's word of honor that even British torture would never wring these facts from him. What more could he ask? "He would have given me his oath for it," Franklin reported to the Continental Congress, "if I laid stress upon oaths. But I have never regarded them otherwise than as the last recourse of liars."

Franklin knew that many an American agent had hypocritically taken the new British oath of allegiance. On the other hand, he knew that little could be expected from those colonists with Tory sympathies who had been compelled by their crusading neighbors to take oaths supporting the Revolution.

Unfortunately, the American nation born in that year of divided loyalties has rarely heeded Ben Franklin's sage advice. In times of crisis to the

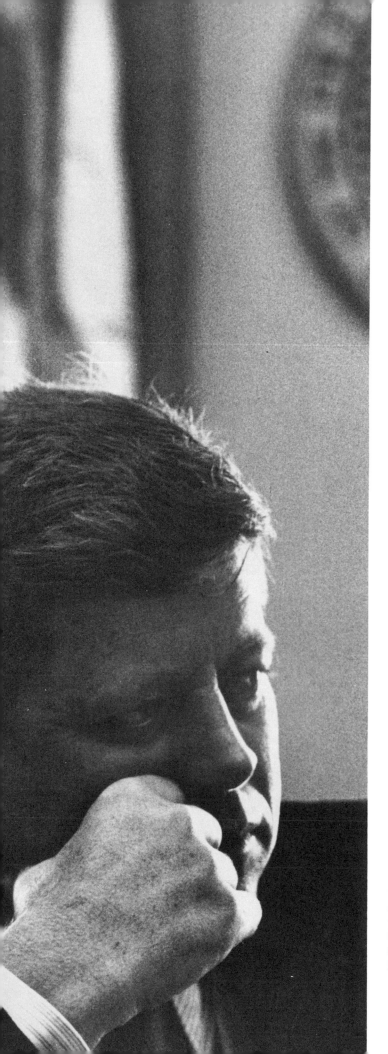

state—times of war, insurrection or suspected subversion—both federal and state governments have repeatedly sought some swift, convenient and reassuring means of publicly identifying and compelling citizen loyalty. Elaborate loyalty oaths and affidavits—going far beyond the simple pledge of allegiance or the oath to uphold and defend the Constitution—have inevitably been the answer.

But there is no evidence that they have ever contributed substantially to the security of the nation.

Yet overzealous patriots keep trying to legislate loyalty. The latest example of this is the case of the National Defense Education Act of 1958, which contains a welcome program for student loans.

Many bright students, whose talents this nation needs to develop in competing with the Soviets, require financial assistance to continue their studies. But today, if those needy students attend Harvard, Yale, Mills, Grinnell, Sarah Lawrence, Oberlin, Swarthmore and a dozen or so other schools—including some of our best science laboratories—they *cannot* obtain a federal loan.

These colleges and universities are refusing to participate in the loan program. They need the money—they know their students need the money —but they refuse to administer one of the bill's strangest provisions: a section which requires every student, teacher, scientist or other scholar applying for a loan to not only sign the customary oath of allegiance, but also to sign a vague, sweeping affidavit declaring that he does not *believe in* or support any organization which *believes in* or teaches the overthrow of the government by illegal methods.

How can our universities police this affidavit they find so distasteful and humiliating? How can they investigate what organizations their students might "believe in," and what those organizations believe? If a student does not belong to a subversive organization, might not his beliefs still be contrary to the affidavit? Which methods of overthrowing the government are illegal and which are not?

No one can quarrel with the principle that all Americans should be loyal citizens and should be willing to swear allegiance to our country. But this is quite different from a doctrine which singles out students—and only those students who need to borrow money to continue their education—as a group which must sign a rather vague affidavit as to their *beliefs* as well as their *acts.*

The president of Wisconsin State College calls it "unnecessary and distasteful." Father Michael J. Walsh, the president of Boston College, says it "represents a lack of confidence in the youth of the country." Mills College in California would not accept these funds because this section "invades the privacy and questions the integrity of individual belief." President Nathan M. Pusey of Harvard called it "vague in intent, useless in effect, inappropriate in context and insulting to the very group Congress seeks to encourage." Oberlin College declined all loans under the program because, its president stated, "it cannot compromise its historical devotion to freedom of expression and belief."

In introducing a bill to repeal this provision last year, I called it "a futile gesture to the memory of an earlier age." Between the end of World War II and the end of the Korean War, a rising tide of fear and suspicion engulfed many Americans. The detection of Communist agents and the erection of new standards of loyalty and security were no longer left to responsible authorities. Neighbors, fellow workers, faculty members, Federal employees, friends—anyone might turn out to be "Red" (or be said to be by someone). Easy answers and convenient scapegoats were sought—and provided—in a troubled time when the answers (How did the Russians get the bomb? Why did we lose China?) were not easy.

But one easy answer was the oath. Those who took it were loyal; those who refused were not. What could be simpler? And so countless hundreds of new oaths sprang up, administered by federal, state and local bodies: oaths for schoolteachers, oaths for notary publics, oaths for professors, students and scientists and, in one state, a loyalty oath for professional wrestlers.

Finally, the furor died down—the atmosphere changed. Senator Joseph R. McCarthy of Wisconsin departed from the scene and the American people turned their attention from oaths of loyalty to the more positive tasks necessary for strengthening our national security. But in the summer of 1958, one relic of this earlier era crept into the National Defense Education Act.

The historical background of this kind of special oath is not confined to the recent era of hate and suspicion.

The first soldier in Washington's army to hang for treason—in a plot to capture the Continental Congress—had sworn to two special oaths of loyalty.

During the Civil War when Congress extended special oath-taking to itself, the only result was the resignation of a loyal but indignant Senator from Delaware, James A. Bayard. Another reluctant oath-taker, a civil servant in the Census Bureau whom a Congressional Committee had cited for disloyal feelings, enlisted in the Union Army and lost his sight at Gettysburg; while another Federal employee, when apprehended for disloyal conduct and asked about his oath, replied: "I could take 500,000 such oaths, as they amount to nothing."

In the post World War I era, New York's famous Lusk Laws included oaths among other special tests of teacher loyalty. But after only two years they were repealed, dismissed teachers were reinstated and Governor Al Smith called the laws "repugnant to the fundamentals of American democracy."

Nearly two million W.P.A. workers were required to swear their loyalty in the unsettled days prior to World War II, before they could pick up their tools and rakes. After the war, when the Taft-Hartley Act required special non-Communist affidavits from union leaders, Harry Bridges took the oath—but John L. Lewis, a fighting anti-Communist, would

not. Among the federally employed scientists working on secret weapons projects who took a special oath was David Greenglass, convicted atomic spy.

This is hardly historical justification for the imposition of a special oath on student-loan applicants today. And the history of special oaths in other lands should also have taught us a lesson. The student affidavit of disbelief is directly descended from the hated test oaths imposed centuries ago by successive contenders for the British crown. Under Charles II, for example, no one could teach at a university or school without taking an Anglican oath—and also an oath that the earlier oath imposed by Oliver Cromwell was unlawful! Article VI of our own Constitution reflected the fear of test oaths which had driven many to these shores.

In the 1930's our universities benefited from Italian professors fleeing Mussolini's requirement that all faculty members take a special oath stating that their teaching would be aimed at instilling devotion "to the Fascist regime."

The tragic fact is—as the history of loyalty oaths demonstrates—that the affidavit will not keep Communists or other subversives out of the student-loan program. Card-carrying members of the Communist party will have no hesitancy about perjuring themselves in the affidavit. I am proud as a U.S. Senator to reaffirm my own pledge to uphold the Constitution and Flag. But I regard a special affidavit as to a person's beliefs—imposed on average citizens who have no special position of trust—as a wholly meaningless, impractical weapon against real subversives. This is particularly so when they are singled out because they cannot afford the tuition their classmates can afford.

It is all very well to ask: "Why not sign, if you're not guilty?" Most students will sign. Most universities will participate. Those who reject loans may be dismissed by some as overconscientious or as eccentrics, nonconformists and chronic dissenters. But I thought the purpose of this Act was to attract into scientific and other vital pursuits the best talents of the country, the most inquiring minds, the most thoughtful students. How can we if we exclude the overconscientious, the eccentrics, the nonconformists and the chronic dissenters? What is the purpose of a provision that in operation could result in some Communists getting loans and some non-Communists dropping out of school—in some talented, needy students being included but some equally talented, equally needy—and equally loyal —students being left out?

There is a very real danger that this unnecessary, futile gesture toward the memory of an earlier age will defeat the purposes of the National Defense Education Act. Unlike the Soviets, we cannot take steps to keep our brightest minds *in* scientific careers—but we might take steps that keep them *out*.

If this affidavit remains on the statute books, we will have cause for concern about the chances for success of the entire National Defense Education program, with some of our leading science-trained institutions and best-known colleges refusing to participate. They know that once they accept this precedent of federal dictation as to the beliefs of their scholarship or loan applicants, a tradition of American education will have been shattered.

I would be concerned about those students who did sign the affidavit. We want their minds to be free and flexible, searching out new ideas and trying out new principles. But a young student who has sworn—under penalty of a federal indictment for perjury—as to what he privately *believes* (and what he thinks some organization he believes in believes) is likely to be rather cautious about changing his beliefs or joining new organizations. Other students may feel that federal inquiry into their beliefs is so unrealistic as to be meaningless—and, in their minds, oaths of allegiance as well as sworn affidavits will be dangerously cheapened.

Perhaps a few perjurers will be caught under this requirement. But we already have enough anti-Communist, antisedition and antiespionage statutes to catch these few students, if any, without damaging—in the minds of millions of other students—their respect for free inquiry and free government.

If William Penn or Benjamin Franklin or Henry Thoreau attended college in America today, I doubt that they would sign this affidavit, despite their great loyalty to this country. And our effort to develop the best minds of the country needs all the Penns and Franklins and Thoreaus we can attract. Never before have we tried to legislate orthodoxy in our colleges, sought to put students in jeopardy for their private beliefs or assumed a scholar is disloyal until he swears to the contrary.

Surely this is not the way to "catch up" with the new Russian excellence in education, science and research—by imitating their objective of teaching students *what* to think instead of *how* to think. What kind of security is it that assumes all is well because thousands of affidavits are signed: do we really believe that loyalty can be reduced to an automatic formula, coerced and compelled instead of inspired?

I think it high time that we recalled the words of Mr. Justice Hugo L. Black: "Loyalty to the United States can never be secured by the endless proliferation of loyalty oaths. Loyalty must arise spontaneously from the hearts of people who love their country and respect their government."

♛ April, 1960.

After Freud, our era was never the same. The reassuring world of "facts" was shaken, and a deeper reality was pursued in the world of dreams. Nothing expressed the mystery, the incongruity of Freud's new continent of the mind quite like Salvador Dali's surrealism, here employed as an esthetic microscope to examine the new language of psychoanalysis.

Dream World

BY SALVADOR DALI

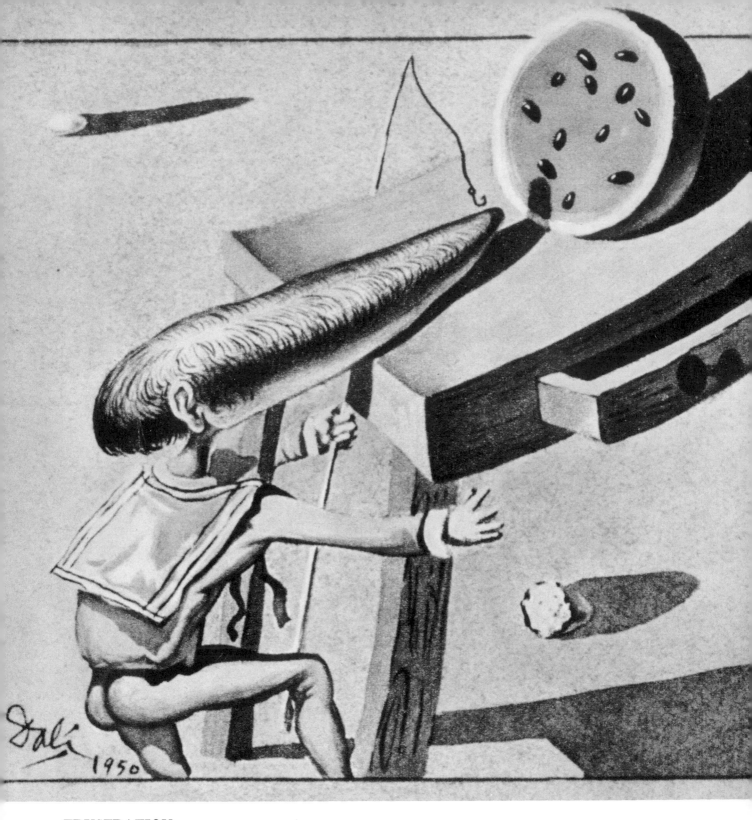

FRUSTRATION

NEARLY EVERYONE HAS DREAMT OF some ineffable delight, forever tantalizing, forever just beyond his reach. To the poet, it is a ravishing phrase; to the miser, an effortless million; to the glutton, a masterpiece of culinary art. More modest in his desire than any of these, the boy in this picture is no less ardent. He wants a water-melon. He wants it so badly that he not only reaches out and fishes for it, but even allows his head to be changed into a sort of tool, designed specifically for the attainment and consumption of water-melons. Frustrated desire has deformed him physically, as it has so many others spiritually.

LOVE

SUPPORTED BY THE CRUTCHES OF human impotence, the wheel of life spins inexorably. Its stops are few—until it reaches the last stop of all. When we are born, it pauses long enough to take us on, and then it stops again, this second time enchanted into momentary stillness by the miracle of love. While we stand enraptured beside our beloved, seeing the moon and the vast night sky, as it were, for the first time, the decrepit wheel dangles its crutches idly and seems to burst into fantastic bloom. This is the magic hour, and when the spinning begins again we scarcely are aware of a faint, ominous creaking noise.

DISINTEGRATION

DEEP IN EACH MORTAL LURKS THE fear of his own mortality. One day, numbered either in the calendar on his desk or in some calendar not yet printed, is ringed in invisible ink. It is the day of his disintegration. He knows, and in imagination approaches it with cautious steps, as though it were a wild beast hidden in a thicket.

Dreams often help to reassure him in his conflict with inevitable death. The common one, reproduced here, seems to say, "Behold, it is not so bad, after all. Even though you should be hurled off a cliff into eternity, the experience will be no more painful than the simple falling apart of a statue..."

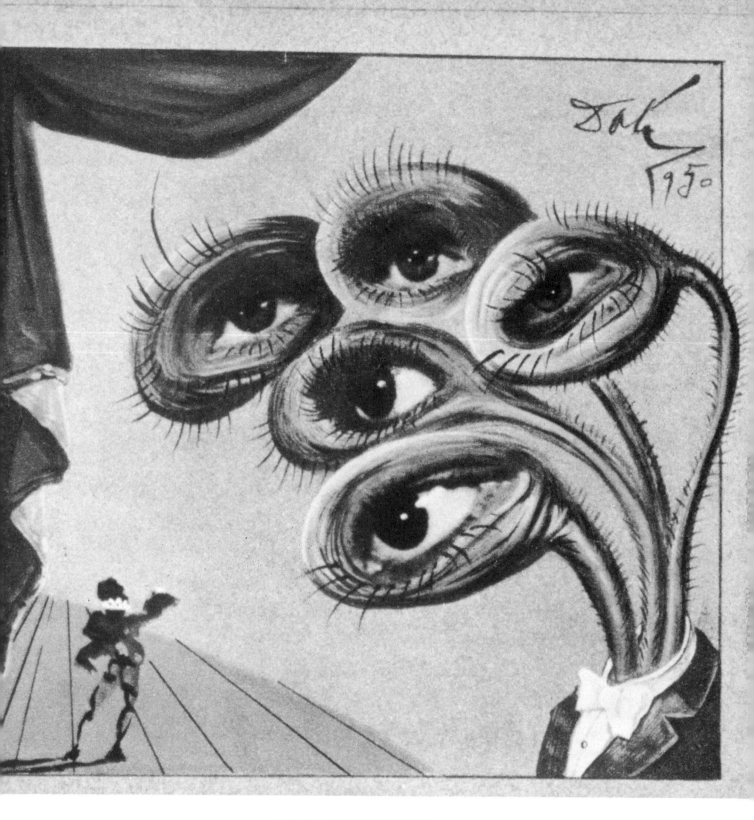

WISH FULFILLMENT

WHO CAN BOAST THAT ALL HIS DE-
sires have been realized among the
experiences of waking life? Sometimes, unknown even to ourselves,
we long for the impossible—to be
loved, protected, and applauded.
Denied expression in the everyday
world, these fugitive wishes produce their own extravaganzas in
our dreams. There, miraculously,
we hold the center of the stage.
As in the above painting, all eyes
are on us, and, although these eyes
are anonymous, even grotesque,
they flatter, for plainly they belong
to important people. We can tell
that by the distinguished evening
clothes from which they sprout.

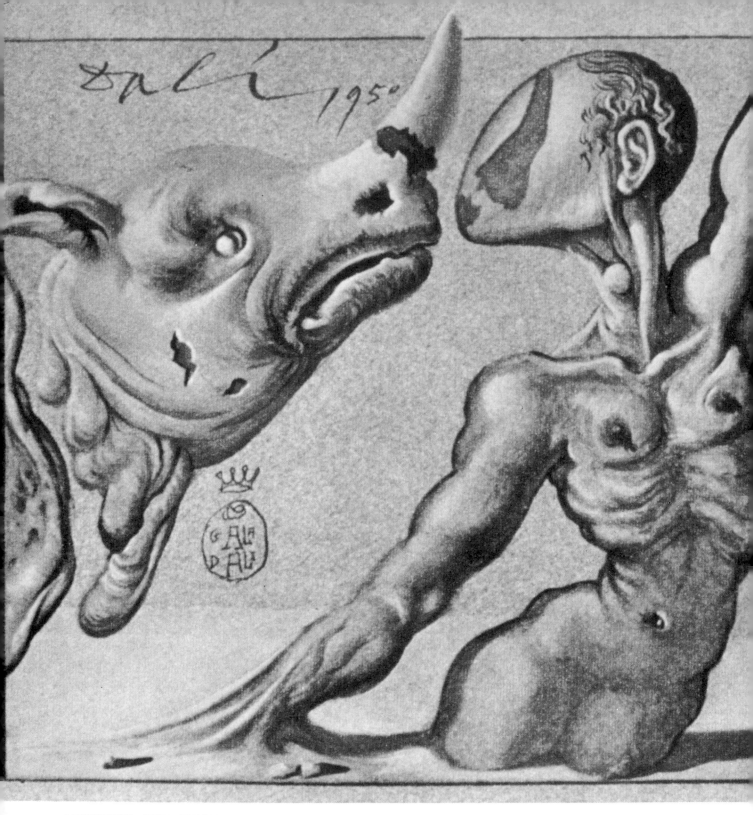

ANXIETY AND FEAR

BUT, IF DREAMS CAN FLATTER THEY also can terrify. Fears, as deep-seated, as irrational as many of our wishes, also haunt us; sleep releases them from the prison of the unconscious, and they, too, have their moments in the forefront of our minds. Feeling ourselves weak, threatened and pursued, we try to flee and succeed only in sinking deeper into quicksand. We become faceless, writhing symbols of terror. Then, suddenly, a monster materializes beside us! Horned and ugly, it is a composite of all the threats to mankind from the beginning of time. We cry out in horror—and awake from nightmare!

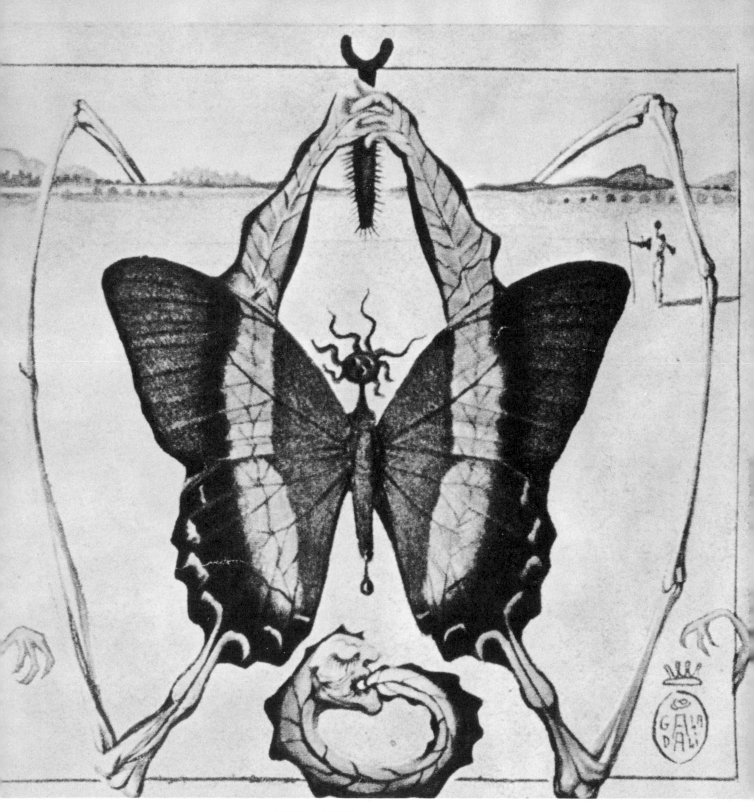

CREATION

AMONG THE RAREST AND MOST GRA-
tifying of dreams are those which
shadow forth our powers of creation. Sometimes they are actively
creative (Coleridge, for instance,
dreamt the famous poem, *Kubla-
Khan*, and was awakened by a
tradesman pounding on his door
—which is why the poem was
never finished). Sometimes, as in
the painting above, they are passive. Then, embracing vast dis-
tances—which, we feel, we can
traverse at a single step—they are
filled with mysterious yet pleasing
symbols, with symmetrical objects
and singing, harmonious lines.
From dreams like these we rise up
smiling and refreshed.

This hearty, optimistic approach to the "dream world" of scientific aspiration shows how science can make a liar out of itself— and all others who say "it can't be done." Atomic energy, rocketry, interplanetary travel—these are some of the futuristic subjects of the "dreamers" of 1937.

Never, Never Land

BY GEORGE W. GRAY

EDWARD E. SLOSSON USED TO SAY THAT WHEN A NEW idea is proposed to the world it starts with a handicap of about one billion eight hundred million adverse votes.

Nor are the croakers of "impossibles" only the self-seekers, who fear that their private interests may be imperiled by change, and the uninformed, whose natural inertia is fortified by ignorance. Always the clamor is reinforced by the expert opinion of some authority on the subject who learnedly declares it can't be done. On occasions he will cite arithmetic, algebra, geometry and even metaphysics to prove that the result aimed for is inherently unattainable.

It is surprising to find how many eminent men of science, distinguished discoverers and inventors, men of far vision, have put themselves on record in some stultifying expression of pessimism.

Even Edison was not free of this myopia. In 1906, when wireless telegraphy was operating in a feeble way, he was asked, "What is the outlook for wireless telephony?" The great innovator answered, "It does not exist." A few months later some wireless operators on ships off New York were astonished to hear voices and music in their earphones in place of the usual rasp of dots and dashes. Lee DeForest had attained his first radio telephone, and was testing it by a broadcast of a phonograph record— perhaps even a record of Mr. Edison's manufacture.

Equally eminent authorities voted against the airplane.

Lord Kelvin, whose adventurous science made the transatlantic cable a reality after several practical men had botched the job, was sure that a flying machine was a physical impossibility. He proved it to his own satisfaction by the laws of physics.

Kelvin's pronouncement was seconded in America by the eminent mathematician, Simon Newcomb,

chief astronomer at the Naval Observatory. Just as ostriches and other birds above a certain weight do not fly, so machines above a certain avoirdupois would be incapable of lifting themselves in sustained flight. Newcomb suggested that if successful airplanes were attained they must of necessity be small lightweight mechanisms like watches. "If the watchmaker can make a machine which will fly through the room with a button, then by combining ten thousand such machines he may be able to carry a man," ventured Professor Newcomb, on the same principle that "a sufficient number of hummingbirds, if we could combine their forces, would carry an aerial excursion party through the air."

Since these authorities failed so widely in their estimates of what could be managed within the law of nature, we need not take too seriously the shrugs with which some present-day authorities react to the mention of other human dreams.

There is very much alive today, for example, the dream of interplanetary flight. It is not new, to be sure, but is one of man's oldest anticipations, as the Greek legends of Daedalus and Icarus show. The problems involved are beyond those of aeronautics, just as the problems of telephony were beyond those of telegraphy—but the lessons of successful aerial flight are giving pointers and hints and warnings and guides to a future technique of space navigation which the specialists have named "astronautics."

A space ship cannot be just an enlarged airplane, or a multiplication of planes—on the analogue of Professor Newcomb's harnessed flock of hummingbirds. Since it must leave the atmosphere and navigate the vacuum of interplanetary space, it cannot depend on propeller, rudder and other air-minded devices, but must substitute some entirely different principle of propulsion and steering. When I mentioned the rocket to a professor of aeronautics seven years ago, he laughed outright. "Are you asking me to discuss the rocket as a practical power device?"

Why not? The steam engine, the dynamo and the gasoline motor were feeble toys once. Each had to advance from infantile beginnings through step after step of experiment and improvement before the present efficient types were attained. Rocket research is occupying the time of a few pioneering physicists today, and the engineering is advanced beyond that of 1930. In another seven years we may look for courses in rocket engineering in some of the more progressive schools. I believe the Yale Rocket Club is the first college group to attain the rank of an affiliate of the American Rocket Society, but others are on the horizon. With regard to the highly futuristic subject of atomic energy, I must add the caution of certain eminent authorities. There are those today who say that this dream is completely wild, who point out that more energy is required to smash atoms than is released from the relatively few that get smashed, and that therefore hope of atomic energy as an economic source of power is futile, never to be attained.

Can a scientist afford to use the word "never" in

a serious sense? I doubt it. Remembering what happened to the forecasts of Newcomb, Kelvin and Edison in the cases cited, and to other pessimistic prognostications of learned experts of earlier generations, seeing how adaptable is nature, and marking what the ingenious techniques of man have accomplished within her iron law, I object to the recognition of any "never, never land" of science.

As George R. Harrison has said, "Just because a man is an authority on the universe is no reason why he should speak with authority on eternity."

The important rule to remember is that science predominantly is positive, progressive, affirmative —and that a negative attitude has been so often discredited in the history of its various techniques that negativism is no longer to be taken seriously. The conquest of matter, the conquest of space, the conquest of aging, even the conquest of death—who would dare write "never" to a one of these dreams? The least difficult may require the efforts of generations of experimenters yet unborn, but nature must yield if man perseveres.

♛ September, 1937.

As we busily prepared to conquer the unknown of outer space, a few sober men began to consider what sweeping changes tomorrow's revelations would wreak on life on earth. For example, Dr. Harlow Shapley, our greatest astronomer-philosopher, believes there is life on other worlds—and that man may have to abandon the cherished conviction that God smiles on him alone. Thus, yet another great era in man's history of himself may begin.

The Riddle of God, Man and Outer Space

BY DR. HARLOW SHAPLEY

FOR CENTURIES, ALMOST SINCE THE DAY HE CLAMBERED out of the primeval ooze, man has looked to the sky and wondered: "In this universe of stars, space and time, am I alone?" After a half century of studying the heavens, I am struck by the inescapable conclusion that there *is* life in outer space; there must be. The laws of science leave me with no other belief.

I would estimate that there are more than one hundred quintillion radiant stars in the sky—100 followed by 18 zeros! Suppose that only one star in 1,000,000 has a family of planets. And suppose that only one in 1,000,000 of these stellar families has a planet like Earth. There would still be 100,000,000 planets suitable for life—or one planet for every trillion stars. And this is a conservative estimate.

Man's first reaction to disturbing truths about his relative insignificance within the universe usually is: "Don't bother me. Life is difficult enough." Fortu-

153

nately, however, this initial response is soon supplanted by curiosity, surprise, respect and wonderment. People begin to ask: "What will this do to my importance in the world?" "What will this do to my religious beliefs?"

The possibility of life in outer space does open a Pandora's box for humanity. For if, indeed, we are not alone in the cosmos, we must reexamine our philosophical and religious concepts—and abandon some of them, if need be. Many of our venerable religious beliefs are based on the limited view of the universe that prevailed before the telescope opened the sky and the microscope opened the underworld of atoms and cells. The prophets of antiquity had no reason to believe man was not God's supreme creation. But their vision was myopic, as we now see. Doubtless our vision is also deficient. But we do recognize that we are acting in a play far grander than foretold in bygone times. Reverence then had to be supported with imaginings and superstitions. But the facts of today far transcend the fictions of yesterday. To be reverent, we no longer need the crutches of superstition. Now, many of our old dogmas seem too earth-bound, too egotistically man-centered. With our earth, moon, planets and bright stars exposed as motes in one star-filled galaxy among millions, is it not foolish to cling blindly to the notion of a one-planet God? To me, the idea that some omnipotent deity smiles on Earth alone has doubtful validity.

As matters stand, there is only one basic question that still baffles us: "*Why* is there a universe?" Many exclaim, "God only knows!"—apparently this is "restricted" information. But scientists, somewhat incorrigible, ask *why* only God should know—why must we accept the suggestion that secrets must forever remain secrets?

I am unwilling to attribute the origin of life to unquestioned divinity. Nature has given us mental equipment. It seems unnatural not to use it—even if it means dispelling cherished ideas. Mystery invites observation and analysis—and the mystery of life strikes me as a challenge worth meeting.

If there is some grandeur in man's position in space, I fail to find it. Life—the biochemical adventure that has occurred on our undistinguished planet during the last three billion years—could have transpired on other planets circling other stars. No, our glory must lie elsewhere. This means we should openly question the vain and tedious line that man somehow is something special, something superior. He may be. I hope he is. But certainly it is not his prestige in space, his energy or his abilities that make him unique.

Actually, man has made far less of an impression on the face of the earth than the tiny animals of 100,000,000 years ago. They, at least, contributed their shells to the making of the chalk cliffs of Dover, and produced considerable limestone all over the planet. Seen from the moon or Mars, the earth must look very much the way it did in primeval times. The advance and retreat of glaciers and ice sheets have been the chief visible changes—and man

had nothing to do with them.

One could conceivably imagine biological monsters on another planet—monstrous in physique or in ingenuity—that could level off the mountains, melt the ice caps, dispose of the rivers and seas, perhaps alter the orbit of Earth. But man is not of that brain and brawn. We are equipped with powers far short of those that often enrich our imaginations. In fact, we are rather feeble-minded compared with what we might be—compared, indeed, with what may exist elsewhere.

All right, so we are comparatively inconsequential; what is so humiliating about that? The gazelle runs faster than we do, the hippopotamus is larger and the dog can hear better—does this degrade us? No, we easily adjust to these evidences of inferiority and still maintain a feeling of importance. After all, it is a magnificent universe we live in. To play a role in it—however humble—should be enough.

The origin and persistence of life on this or any other planet is one of the wonders of the world. Until recently, its beginnings seemed to be science's greatest unsolved problem. Now it is no longer a deep mystery. We have bridged, at least in part, the gap between life and the lifeless by using the already known mechanics of nature; supernatural "intervention" is not required.

A few years ago, several American scientists, following the lead of Russia's A. I. Oparin and the Englishman, J. B. S. Haldane, began to speculate about the conditions on Earth when life first appeared. It became clear that Earth's primeval atmosphere was quite different from what we now have. There was marsh gas, ammonia gas, water vapor and a tremendous amount of hydrogen. Oxygen was scarce or nonexistent. The absence of free oxygen was a valuable clue in the solution of the mystery of life. In those early days, there were several energy sources available for the building of complicated big molecules out of simple ones: lightning, gamma rays, volcanic heat and ultraviolet sunlight.

Suppose we confine the four gaseous constituents of the primeval atmosphere in a container and bombard the mixture with a continuing electric discharge. We would then be using lightning and primitive gases as they were used thousands of millions of years ago. In a University of Chicago laboratory, Dr. Harold Urey and his graduate student, Dr. Stanley Miller, carried out this experiment. A deep pinkish glow appeared in the container after a week's bombardment. An analysis was made by Dr. Miller, who found that many compounds had been produced. Among them were amino acids—the building blocks of proteins—which in turn are the materials of living bodies.

Much hard work is yet to be done, but we are now confident that life will emerge whenever and wherever the physics, chemistry and climate are right. But what about life in others worlds? Does it exist? And if so, what is it like?

Varieties of life other than ours are possible. We

can rule out the sun and other radiant stars as sites for life. They are too hot. In sunspots and some of the cooler stars, we find evidence of simple molecular compounds, but no evidence of those delicate structures that compose protoplasm, the life substance in our world.

Planetary surfaces appear to be the likeliest places for life. But the following conditions must exist:

1. Water must be available in a liquid form—not cold ice or hot steam. Therefore the distance of a livable planet from its star—its source of light and heat—cannot be too great or too small.

2. Some atmosphere is necessary. Therefore the planet's mass must be large enough to retain important gases. Hence we must eliminate all comets, meteors, asteroids, small satellites and wandering atoms and nebulae.

3. The atmosphere must be oxygen-rich, if air-breathers are contemplated, and it must not contain poisons in sufficient abundance to kill off the air-breathers. Hence, no more strontium 90 than we now nervously endure, nor too much carbon monoxide.

4. The planet's orbit must be approximately circular. Otherwise the temperature range throughout the planet's year would be unendurable.

5. The planet's rotation must be such that the nights are not too long and cold, and the days not too long and hot.

6. The nourishing star must be reasonably constant in energy output. An exploding star would kill all organisms on its planets.

7. Life must somehow get started. This is the most important condition. We can trust evolution to diversify life into its myriad forms.

For various reasons, all the planets in our little solar system disqualify themselves as havens for life. Although the popular belief is that seasonal changes on Mars prove the presence of vegetation, no one now believes that highly developed life exists on that inhospitable red planet. Algae, fungi, mosses —that is about as far as any student of Mars cares to go—and that is too far, in my opinion.

It looks as if the only place in *our* solar system suitable for life as we have defined it is right here on Planet No. 3. But our solar system is just a speck in the cosmos, which stretches toward infinity; who can say that someday we will not find life in another distant galaxy?

But planets are not the only possibilities for life in outer space. There must be millions of astral bodies bigger than the largest planet and smaller than the smallest star. I call them "Lilliputian stars," and some of them could be of the right size and temperature to retain liquid water on their surfaces. They also could be massive enough to hold a life sustaining atmosphere.

If life inevitably starts when the physical conditions are right, then some of these Lilliputian stars may have life on their watery or rocky surfaces. If so, that life must be vastly different from that which we know. There would be no natural violet-to-red light and, therefore, presumably no sense of vision. The surface gravity would be great and any living organisms would have to adjust to enormous pressures.

Many religious men try to dismiss this view of the universe as mere speculation, insecurely founded. They cannot seem to recognize that the God of humanity is the God of gravitation and the God of atoms. But at least they should entertain the possibility that there may be other higher beings somewhere in the cosmos who can attain the same intellectual and spiritual rating we now arrogate to ourselves.

With our confreres on distant planets; with our fellow animals and plants of land, sea and air; with the photons and atoms that comprise the stars; with the rocks and waters of all planetary crusts; with all these we are associated in an existence and an evolution that inspires respect and deep reverence.

We cannot escape humility. And as groping scientists and philosophers, we must be thankful for the mysteries that still lie beyond our grasp.

♛ February, 1961.

Every new invention spawns its claque
of enthusiasts and its "realistic" critics, such
as this talented composer who predicted for
1955 a dismal world in which creative music is
destroyed by the black box of television.
Happily, the generation outdid itself; never
before in our history has the concert stage,
the opera, the symphony, the world of
creative music enjoyed such an enthusiastic,
live following—even while television keeps
coming on stronger. And for the failure of his
gloomy prophesy, who would have been
more pleased than the late author?

Music in 1955

BY GEORGE ANTHEIL

IN THE FUTURE MUSIC WILL CERTAINLY BE MADE BY
machines. Music is an art involving not only the
human soul but the most abstract of celestial mathematics as well, and it adapts itself almost too easily
to man's engines.

Those who spoof against the machine and the
machine-made music of the future, spoof I fear
against the Wall of Inevitability. The great orchestra director Stokowski, who is undoubtedly one
of the very greatest orchestral leaders of these
times, seems, year after year, to lose just about as
much interest in his human Philadelphia Orchestra
as he gains in his Westinghouse mechanical one.
This great modern musician has been ever quick to
realize which way the future lies, and it is of double
interest to note that he has now given himself almost completely over to new musical scientific research. For him there is apparently no doubt that
music's present pathways have reached the complete
end of their ropes, and that music must now blaze
new trails, if it hopes to remain virile.

We can safely say that the present-day youth
of this country have exactly the same attitude
toward symphonic music that they have toward the
radio as an electrical and mechanical instrument—
they are neither interested in what makes it go nor
in the wires and tubes in the back of the box. They
are interested rather in the quality of entertainment that comes out of their loudspeakers. They
don't give a damn about what makes it go. The new
generation is growing up with as little interest in
the *visual playing* of the symphony orchestra as it
has, apparently, for the insides of its sports road-
sters. Frankly most of our young people care not if
they *never* see a symphony orchestra in operation.

Mr. Average Listener, however, is a little older,
and in his day he has vaguely, at least, heard about
the "cultural influence" of symphonic music.

How will he get music? Like the small gardener
who has not a large enough garden to raise all his
own vegetables he will have to get his greens canned.
But—and this "but" is of greatest importance
—the canning will no longer be the unmusical
canning of the past, but a new and musical canning
of a highly superior order. And the new methods of
the canning will not be alike to the old at all but
will present new and exciting angles and a highly
startling fidelity to the original, so startling, in
fact, that one will not be able to tell the copy from
the human performance. And unlike the past, canned
music will not be the subject of invective. It will,
rather, be quite the rage.

Just how will this come about? In this way—
orchestral, solo and vocal music will no longer first
be played and registered, but will be cut *directly*
into the disk or sound-ribbon. We shall use the
sound wave direct. More exactly, the specific sound
wave of an oboe playing, for instance middle F
sharp and quite *ppp*, is always the same. There can
be, of course, various types of oboes, but there can
only be one middle F sharp. And *ppp* will remain
forever *ppp*. The exact outline of this oboe sound
wave will be but an infinitesimal part of a vast new
musical ABC's, and if a sound-wave typewriter is
ever invented—and its invention is inevitable—we
shall soon be able to *type* every kind of instrumental
and vocal sound instantly into a reproducing record
without the medium of a voice or orchestra! Minus
the cost of rehearsing a hundred trained men in a
half-dozen rehearsals and without putting up with
the temperament of a fluffy opera singer, music
will be "typed" directly into a moving ribbon of
sound much the same as moving-picture music is
now recorded upon a film; the process, however,
will be a somewhat finer one using a higher vibra-
tion rate of sound reproduction. (If this light-ray
recording process is eventually adapted most probably the new ultra-violet instead of white light will
be used; this will insure practically perfect reproduction!)

In a word we shall no longer need to *play* any
specific instrument to secure any specific sound
wave. Although it might seem heretic to say so,
mere human playing or singing will be soon, if
desired, entirely dispensed with.

Many will certainly complain that this method
of orchestral reproduction will become too mechanical. Let me add therefore that every shade of
musical meaning will now be easily producible; we
need only to perfectly assemble the sound waves.
The engineer (our new musical typist!) "cutting"

these sound waves will have before him a score so perfectly marked that not even the slightest nuance will be neglected; he will blend these fixed tones in exactly the same proportion as, for instance, a Stokowski or a Toscanini marking this score before him, has indicated. Stokowski, let us say, has made every indication exactly; there is not a phrase, nor a pause, nor a rubato neglected; every last *ppp* or *ff* is in its place. The slightest graduation in tempo is firmly marked from second to second in exact metronomic indications. This score would then be followed to the dot.

It is perhaps a rather horrible thought to think that music can and will be so mechanized. One must reflect, however, that even those little imperfections so lovable in the living beauty of music still performed by human hands can be "cut" oh, so easily into the superlative reproductive "canned" music of the future. Remember, too, that the art faker of today can duplicate every last crack of the canvases of the old masters; they can make a new painting so exactly like an old one that even connoisseurs are often hard put to it to distinguish one painting from the other. If public taste so desires, orchestral records of the future (although they have never been recorded from an actual orchestra) will certainly be full of those lovable little imperfections and crudities so dear to the heart of the music lover who pretends to recognize, blindfolded, the superlative performance of one great artist from another. They will simply be cut in.

That the sweeping inventions now being developed will certainly eliminate, in part, the human orchestra is no longer a matter for speculation. Everyone who has the slightest idea of that which is going on day and night in the great electrical-musical laboratories of the world knows that the orchestra of the past is a thing already doomed. It is not a matter, any longer, of what may be, but of what will be.

Mr. Average Listener wants masterworks, and plenty of them. And for him we shall develop the new Dial-Television-Phonogram.

This will not be a radio-operated affair. It will be, rather, a cable job; it may well be, eventually, connected with your telephone company and you will probably, in the end, merely turn a switch at your telephone and dial upon this same telephone dial a symphony instead of a telephone conversation. This will then be played upon your televisionic loud-speaker.

And at your side you will have an enormous red "telephone book," only it will not be a telephone book. It will contain, instead, the dialing number of every opera, symphony, song and sonata upon earth, played, sung, and directed by every authority in the world worth hearing, and you will be able to hear these works, and see them too for that matter, at any time that you most feel like it. You will no longer need to sit in uncomfortable opera or concert-hall seats or rush through dinner to get there in time; you will never again listen to music that does not fit your mood.

In 1955 it is extremely probable that the radio will have been absorbed by television, and moving pictures will surely be quick to follow and combined with this wonderful invention upon whose threshold the world has already placed one tentative foot. In 1937 we are still in the dark ages, but by 1955 the phonograph will have disappeared as thoroughly as the player piano of yesteryear, and dialing system and new coaxial cables will be everywhere, absorbing everything and reproducing everything. There will be no new musical comedy but that will have its *première* in every home.

I, for one, believe that the purge and the revolution of the oncoming mechanical age to be a healthy one, and one which will again give the original immortal fire of great music at least a fighting chance. Music will be music—and not gossip.

At any rate, most of us alive today will soon see what happens. It is harmless enough to calculate, make graphs, suppositions and forecasts from the data already at hand, and to note that the handwriting already on the wall is in a good clear honest hand, reminding one of the writing of automobile mechanics.

♕ December, 1936.

THE BROOKLYN ARTIST

The Brooklyn artist moved to Greenwich Village

He thought it would be good for his art.

He drinks gin and lives with Mimi.

It could have been arranged in Brooklyn.

—Otto S. Mayer

To a lady with a houseful of kids and the most original funnybone of the Sixties, those housewives who struggle with their interiors with such frenzy must seem the Helen Hokinsons of the New Frontier. Author of **Please Don't Eat the Daisies** and the stage hit **Mary Mary,** New Rochelle's star triple-threat mother is offered almost none of the luxury moments to afford for herself such desperate doings.

Decoration by Desperation

BY JEAN KERR

AS A RESULT OF A RECENT IMPARTIAL SURVEY TAKEN among my friends, I have discovered a number of significant facts about home decorating that I am perfectly willing to share. The whole subject comes up because this is the time of year when a lot of people discover the appalling fact that in the bright sun of spring the apartment looks even more depressing than it did in the gloom of last November.

The problem confronting the average housewife today is not whether she's going to decorate. Of course she's going to decorate. The problem is *when*.

In general it is safe to list three situations in which it is advisable to redo the living room: (1) when you have the money; (2) when you don't have the money but are planning to go on a quiz program; (3) when you don't have the money and there's not a chance you're going to get it but if you have to look at the speckled blue wallpaper one more day you will go smack out of your mind.

Having decided that you are going to go ahead with the project, you come up against the really ticklish question of *how*—in what color and in what style. And it is a curious fact that even those women who ordinarily intimidate their friends by the absolute conviction they bring to all subjects suddenly develop vast areas of insecurity the moment they have to say whether the ceiling should be painted lighter or darker than the walls.

I know one woman of unusually strong character who selected a college for her son in a single afternoon and who has always been able to plan a dinner for sixteen in five minutes. In a beauty parlor, when the manicurist asks her what color she wants her nails, she can glance at a rack of nineteen bottles of nail polish and announce "Carioca Pink" without a second's hesitation.

She is, as I say, exceptional. I was all the more surprised, then, to meet her in a department store recently on what was her seventh visit to that establishment to select an upholstery fabric for one wing chair in her living room. Gone was that brave air of decision and dispatch. Before me, adrift in a sea of samples, sat a broken figure pathetically waving swatches of damask and asking advice from total strangers.

To avoid this sort of thing it is helpful to get the advice of a decorator. The decorator invariably arrives with a notebook and an air of pained preoccupation. He tiptoes cautiously around That Tragic Error, your living room, and finally flashes a sympathetic smile that seems to say, "Thank God, you called me. Another month and it might have been too late."

Then he speaks: "My dear, you have a small, dark room with very poor fenestration. I see pale, silver ash." And you say, "I thought turquoise—with maybe a touch of pink."

At the mention of the word "turquoise" a look of such pain washes over his face as to suggest that he is suffering a sudden gall-bladder attack.

He dismisses your suggestion with the contempt it deserves and marches over to your small, charming fireplace. He taps it with his pencil. "Victorian, of course."

"Oh, yes," you burble helpfully, "it is perfect Victorian. The fireplace is really the reason we bought this house in the first place."

"Well"—his manner is now brisk and to the point—"we won't have any trouble with that. We can rip it out and put in sheetrock." You fire the decorator.

At this juncture you may be tempted to ask your husband for advice. Don't. Husbands have two different approaches to home decoration. First, there is the constructive but useless attitude: "Blue is such a pretty color, why don't you make everything blue?" Then, there is the destructive but useless attitude: "Oh, do what you want, but for heaven's sake, don't have a lot of bloodshot petunias hanging all over like your sister Helen."

There is no point in explaining that those petunias are carnations and that they repose on a hand-screened English linen that costs $18.75 a yard.

You might look for help in the tonier magazines, although the pretty people in those four-color layouts don't seem to live like the rest of us. They apparently spend all their time out on terraces or patios, chastely broiling filets over new and expensive-looking braziers.

This outdoor life is undoubtedly sensible. How else would they get the vigor necessary for springing out of that curious low furniture they keep in the living room?

Once in a while you do see a picture of an attractive traditional room. Just last month I came across a room done entirely in seafoam green and chalk white. The only color accents were one red apple and a bright red magazine on the coffee table. It was lovely. Of course, you would have to be continually replacing that apple, and down through the years somebody would be bound to inquire why you still had that 1935 copy of *Charm.*

Then there are those "How To" pieces. I read a splendid one some time ago entitled "There Are Treasures in Your Attic." It told how a number of enterprising women had transformed forgotten monstrosities—dilapidated furniture, old nail kegs—into "Conversation Pieces."

One canny lady rescued a battered dresser and hacked it into three sections. The bottom section she covered with plywood and parchment paper to make a "very quaint" coffee table. The middle piece, after it had been sanded and pickled and equipped with cunning little brass handles, became a night table. And the top section, a drawer with a mirror over it, was sanded and stained and hung in the entrance hall.

In this way she had *three* conversation pieces. As I see it, when this giddy carpenter has guests to the house, they'll spend the whole long night talking about the furniture.

Did you know that properly treated old nail kegs make a charming pair of end tables for a rumpus room? If you shouldn't happen to have any old nail kegs in your attic, you can buy them—with the nails—for $19.50 apiece, and then, of course, you'll have all those nails.

But we are digressing. Even if you are going to redo your living room, you'll probably have to put up with most of the furniture you already have, including that sturdy sofa you bought in 1923. Therefore, it will be mostly a matter of slipcovers, drapes and paint.

When you go to pick your fabrics, it is best to go to a large department store where nobody will ever wait on you. This way you are left alone for hours to mull over rolls of fabric. In a regular fabric house you get such excellent attention that it is impossible to make a selection. By the time the salesman has arranged twenty-eight samples on the rack, you begin to get a feeling of mounting panic that you are *never* going to like anything and that this lovely man is going to know you for the failure you are.

In this situation, I find it very helpful to divert the salesman. I usually say, "Yes, it's lovely—but I have to consider whether it will go with my pink grand piano."

The salesman is now definitely diverted. In fact, he is shaken to his foundations. In a moment he will be suggesting, in a strained voice, "Lady, the racks are over there—why don't you just look?"

In due time you will have selected material for your slipcovers, picked out a darker color for the drapes and a lighter color for walls, and dropped the whole confusing assortment at an upholsterer's. One day seven months later everything arrives, and it's beautiful—or maybe it isn't. You can always do it over again in twenty years or so.

March, 1956.

For men who project ideas, the urge to predict the future in terms of the knowable is overwhelming. And the chances are that someday, perhaps in 2009, people will read these predictions and smile with condescension at the timorous hopes of the writer—no differently than we do today at his predecessors of 1911.

How We'll Live Fifty Years From Now

BY RALPH BASS

ON A WARM SPRING AFTERNOON IN THE YEAR 2009, Dr. and Mrs. John Wade, of Alexandria, Virginia, leave home about 5:30 in order to drive to a dinner party. The party is in West Newton, Massachusetts. They will be there in under an hour.

Dr. and Mrs. Wade and their hosts in West Newton, Mr. and Mrs. Henry Cabot, live in the largest super-city in the Western Hemisphere. This extends from Bangor, Maine, to Richmond, Virginia, and contains scores of millions of people. Old cities have ceased to exist as they once were. With the huge spurt in population they have grown together.

All of this has been made possible by improved transportation. As population growth accelerated, people moved farther and farther from the old cities until the metropolitan areas met and merged into a tremendous megalopolis. Had it not been for this improved transportation and accompanying spread-out, cities as they had once existed would have been suffocated by traffic.

By 1959, for instance, commuting to New York City from the suburbs had become a daily agony for millions, while on the West Coast engineers estimated that if all the 1,500,000 passenger cars in the Los Angeles area came out at the same time they would completely fill the 12,500 miles of street!

But now, in 2009, the 150th anniversary of the oil industry, transportation in the super-city—and all over the world, in fact—is swift and easy beyond the dreams of the bygone twentieth century.

A citizen may drive his oil-powered vehicle from one end of the eastern megalopolis to the other in about the time it took a resident of New York to go the fourteen miles by subway from Coney Island to Times Square fifty years before.

The Wades will ride to the Cabot house at 600 miles per hour in a conveyance that speeds along on a cushion of air just above a monorail. The machine is jet-propelled, powered by an oil derivative or, perhaps, by a fuel cell. The fuel cell, which was in development back in 1959, converts petroleum or hydrogen and oxygen into electricity *without* combustion by passing the material through electrodes with twice the efficiency of the best gasoline engine. Both public and private transport use monorails. (Some big commercial airlines utilize atomic energy, but for smaller vehicles the atom is still impractical. Meanwhile, improved kerosene and gasoline serve very well.)

Moreover, in all transportation devices, hundreds of parts are made from petroleum derivatives. In the Wade's car, for example, upholstery, glass, even the body are derived from oil. The motor is made of a self-lubricating plastic. Others motors are of light metal with permanent lubrication locked in. In any event, the old practice of changing oil every thousand miles is a thing of the long-forgotten past.

While oil is still an important source of heat and power, the emphasis in the oil industry has changed. The Wades and Cabots live in a world of petrochemicals. In the Cabot home, for example, the dining room is beautifully paneled in what appears to be solid chestnut—a wood long extinct in New England. It is a plastic which cunningly simulates the original, and may be washed easily with an oil-derived detergent and water. The plastic upholstery of the chairs, sawed into the desired shapes, is softer than foam rubber. The wall-to-wall carpeting, easily cleaned by washing, is a fabric synthesized from oil. The plumbing, durable and never rusty, is of plastic.

The house itself is constructed of colored asphalt and plastic bricks or sheets, the parts delivered whole and put together in a few days. Like the insulation, these parts are made of materials derived from chemicals.

These petrochemicals upon which the Wades and the Cabots rely for so much of their existence are produced by an amazing process known as polymerization, developed a half century earlier. Polymers are synthetic chemical compounds that evolve from the mixing of gases and a catalyst, a chemical agent, that brings about changes in the molecules and atoms that make up the gases. There are many different kinds of polymers—some are hard, others elastic, some transparent, others solid. Their great variety is responsible for the myriad uses to which petrochemicals can be put.

By 1956, more than 3,000 synthetic chemicals had already been evolved, and new ones were being added at the rate of 400 a year. Three years later, more than 2,500 different commercial products were being developed from petroleum, chalking up a profitable total of $7 billion a year. Petrochemicals were used in shaving cream, TV sets, men's suits, sugar, soap, light bulbs, automobile tires, floor covering, vitamins, anesthetics and water rafts.

But the Cabots and their guests know all about these and many others. All their lives they have worn clothes synthesized from chemicals, light, durable, stainproof and washable. Their lawns are brilliant green; oil-based coloring, harmless to vegetation has been sprayed on. Their vegetables and flowers are lush and brightly hued, protected against blight and insect enemies by oil fungicides and pesticides.

Since the Cabots are a conservative family, their house is not too different in appearance from those of the preceding century, despite its novel building materials. Some of their friends, however, are more venturesome. One has an antigravity house that floats in the air, catching the vagrant breezes. Another has built his house on a turntable that pivots to face the sun. Several have enclosed their homes and gardens with glass domes, thus providing air conditioning throughout.

When Mrs. Cabot invited her dinner guests she had no menu problem. All she had to do was press a number of buttons and food moved automatically from a freezer to an oven where it was cooked by high-speed microwaves. Later the dishes would be washed by ultrasonics. The food itself is far more nutritious than the fare of a half century before. Oil-based proteins are added to meat and other dishes. Food is plentiful, since improved fertilizers made from petrochemicals enrich the soil in which the crops grow. Even farming is much more efficient—one man at a computer-console plows a dozen fields by remote control.

Obviously the Wades, the Cabots and their friends live in a vastly different world than that of their grandfathers. They take for granted wonders that

were barely imagined fifty years before. There are the gigantic solar mirrors, six miles in diameter, that reflect the sun's rays to various portions of the earth as required. Mail between cities is delivered by satellites, with local mailmen leaping from street to street with the aid of one-man rockets strapped to their backs. Almost everyone carries a radio telephone in his pocket, and home phones are all equipped with TV. This can be embarrassing on occasion, and there is less sitting around in the evening in informal costumes.

On ocean liners, life boats are equipped with rockets that spray oil on waves over an area of almost 100,000 square feet, facilitating rescue operations and lessening the danger of capsizing. Ashore, people carry folded-up airplanes on automobile trips, inflating them when they wish to take to the air. If they get tired of the color of their automobile they can change it in a jiffy with an electromagnetic ray gun.

Automation has set in with a vengeance. In restaurants, full-course dinners are prepared and served without a soul in sight—except the button-pushing patrons. Vending machines make change promptly and accurately for any bill denomination, now and then setting off an alarm at the sight of counterfeit currency.

In outer space, farmers develop crops on satellites, growing food in tubes filled with chemical solutions, while back on earth, doctors project electrocardiograms on walls during operations, permitting them to keep watch on heart action.

Of course, many of these changes were anticipated a half century before. In the libraries of the megalopolis can be read a 1957 statement of rocket pioneer, Dr. Wernher von Braun. As with so many prophecies, the actuality came fifty years earlier than forecast:

". . . the earth will be surrounded by a whole family of artificial satellites," von Braun said. "They will be of a great variety of sizes, brightnesses, purposes, nationalities, orbital altitudes and orbital inclinations. Some of the satellites . . . have taken over the mailman's job. They receive messages radioed up to them while over one city, country, or continent, and play it back while over others. . . . A few such communication satellites will handle the entire volume of private and official mail communications between all points on earth which are more than five hundred miles apart, and no message will require more than one hour from sender to recipient."

Inevitably, in the late 1950's, there were also some jocular predictions, none of which, fortunately, came true. One group of architects had said that "homes of the future will be dumbbell-shaped, with the parents at one end and the children at the other." In 2009, architects were making the same prophecy about 2059—and it became pretty clear that someone was indulging in wishful thinking.

But most of the forecasts in the late 1950's were on a serious, almost solemn level. The terrifying potentialities of world-destroying weapons apparently fostered sober thought.

"If man survives," Dr. John Weir, associate professor of psychology at the California Institute of Technology, had said, "he can look forward to learning more about himself in the next hundred years than he has in the preceding million. He could discover the causes and cures of sickness and pain, of hate and destruction. He could come to realize his true biological potentials. He could learn to circumvent many of his limitations. He could learn how to change himself. . . . Even today, we can dimly foresee and can speculate a bit about some of the possibilities."

Not all of Dr. Weir's prophecy had come true by 2009, but he still had fifty years to go. In any event, he had done a lot better than Jules Verne who thought eighty days around the world was fantastic speed, only to be outfoxed by the airplane engine. And there was the case of the Louisiana Purchase when one statesman predicted that the territory would probably not be fully occupied be-

fore the year 2600. The railroad locomotive took care of that prophecy.

The year 2009 witnessed three developments of outstanding benefit to mankind. The least important was the creation of robots with enough artificial intelligence to carry on routine but time-consuming chores. The next, a greater boon, was the grafting of electronic organs of hearing and sight to the nerve ends of the blind and deaf, restoring perfect vision and hearing.

But the greatest of all, perhaps, was the development of new astronomical devices to explore the universe and determine, once and for all, whether it was truly infinite or had definite boundaries. This represented man's final reaching out toward the stars.

Like those who lived before them, many people in 2009 were content with what they had, fearful perhaps of the future. But there were others who were animated by the spirit of the great English biologist, Thomas Henry Huxley: "Those who refuse to go beyond facts rarely get as far as facts."

♛ December, 1959.

The corrosiveness of modern life, the feeling of suffocation as our cities and suburbs crept cancerously into the countryside, the smog in the air and the pollution in the streams—all of these things fed a new yearning for the simple beauty of nature and made our greatest nature writer, Edwin Way Teale, an author of necessity. Here, his explanation of the simple world of nature made the complex world of man easier to tolerate.

Kingdom of the Night

BY EDWIN WAY TEALE

ONE EVENING WHILE I LAY ON THE GRASSY BANK OF a Maine lake, watching the ebbing colors in the western sky, I began to follow, in my mind's eye, the steady, westward sweep of the twilight.

A thousand square miles around me at that very instant were sinking into the dusk. From then on, until the whole continent was in darkness, each succeeding minute would bring sunset and then twilight—the old age of the day and the youth of the night—to vast areas of countryside. Beyond the ridges, beyond the sunset, beyond the boundaries of the night, untold millions of human beings would be affected in many ways by this swift transition from light to dark.

As the shadow of night spreads silently and swiftly westward across farms and cities, highways and lakes, how varied are the emotions it creates! How different is its meaning for the mother beside the bed of a sick child, the sailor taking his watch on the Great Lakes, the laborer lighting his pipe at the end of his working day, the policeman making his rounds, the child putting away his toys, the student switching on his study lamp—night so familiar in aspect to all, so varied in meaning to each!

Arriving suddenly in mountain valleys and coming with deliberation on the wide plains, the night would advance its western fringe from my far-Eastern lake shore across the breadth and length of the continent. I could visualize an immense shadow as it raced across the miles.

It was darkening the waters and the sand and the rocks—where the gulls were coming in—all along the Eastern seacoast. It was adding gloom to the Great Dismal Swamp and the Okeefenokee and the mangrove wilderness of the Shark River. In cities and towns and villages, it was bringing out the street lamps and the glare of neon signs. Lights were coming on everywhere, lights in innumerable forms.

The black-block silhouettes of farmhouses were being pierced by rectangles of yellow. Lanterns were beginning to bob about in mountain barnyards. Airway beacons were commencing their night-long circling. And the shafts of brilliance from locomotive headlights were spearing down long stretches of shining rails.

In a thousand scattered communities, street lights were picking out pedestrians, passing cars, wandering dogs, fluttering moths. In misty areas, they were glowing and diffused. In towns where winds swept along the streets, the lights were casting shadows that raced and checked and raced back again endlessly as lower branches of trees tossed and plunged in the gusts.

On the mountain roads of New England, the twin beams of auto headlights were rising and falling and winding about along miles of highway. They were picking out sudden glowing points of colored light as they struck the eyes of wild animals by the roadside.

Darkness was bringing with it the red glare of furnaces and the cool pinpoints of the stars. Night was coming to Boston and Portsmouth and New York and Baltimore and Savannah; it was coming with clear weather and cloudy, with rain and with the hot dust settling on parched roadside weeds.

The Hudson River and Chesapeake Bay and all the convoluted inlets of the Georgia low country were losing the sheen and the coloring of the sunset hour. Down the length of the Shenandoah Valley, farms and orchards were disappearing from sight. All the land east of the high Alleghenies was now embraced within the dark boundaries of the night, within the natural realm of the bat, the owl and the whippoorwill.

As unhasting as it was inexorable, twilight was spreading ever westward over the ball of the earth. It was blending its deepening gray with the smoke of Pittsburgh; it was adding to the gloom of deep Appalachian valleys. Over vast areas there, the growing darkness is unrelieved by a single lamp. But when the moving shadow reaches the wide Ohio plain, the clustered lights of towns and villages spread away in luminous spots on the darkening surface of the level land.

The Great Lakes slip into darkness. The shadow speeds down the winding course of the Ohio River. It crosses Georgia; it engulfs the hill towns of Tennessee. Cypress and Spanish moss and the black waterways of the Louisiana bayous and swamps join the Great Dismal and the Okeefenokee as part of the kingdom of the night.

From Minnesota to the deltas of the Gulf, the Mississippi—bisecting a nation—glows faintly long after its banks are lost in blackness. All the land from the outermost islands of the Maine coast to the plains of Kansas and the beginnings of Texas have now experienced, once more, the old phenomenon of nightfall.

Beyond the Mississippi, farmlands, flat and fertile, endless miles of growing corn, the rich wealth of the nation's breadbasket—all these sink into dusk while the shadow races on and reaches the approaches to the Rockies. Even before the last of the plains towns are engulfed, the communities on the eastern skirts of the mountains are plunged into darkness. They are in the shadow of the great range beyond them. The sky above is luminous long after the land below is enveloped in the shadows.

The burning glare of the salt flats in Utah subsides as the tide of the earliest dusk sweeps across them. The geysers and the mud springs of Yellowstone begin to fade and become indistinct in the gloom while, far to the south, the shadow spreads upward along the muddy Rio Grande and stretches across the Great American Desert.

All the wide and infinitely varied land that makes up Southern California—the truck farms of the Imperial Valley; the avenues lined with ferny pepper trees; the wharfs and fishing docks of the San Diego waterfront; the city of Los Angeles, ablaze and sprawling—all this area, in its turn, is swallowed by the accumulating shadows.

And, farther north, along the Sierras, on the rocky headlands of Monterey, in the great forests of the far Northwest, trees of many kinds—twisted cypresses, towering redwoods, great Douglas spruces—all merge into the darkness just as the million oaks of New England, the elms of Ohio, the sycamores of Indiana, the cottonwoods of Kansas and the high, wind-shaped cedars of the Rockies have faded into the landscape before them.

Long after the surf, that white surf on the bluest of brilliant waters, has sunk—with the whole of Monterey Bay—into deepening twilight, the upper reaches of the towering coast redwoods are still lighted by the sun. Even after the incandescent disk has flattened itself against the rim of the darkening ocean waters and has slowly sunk from sight, their tips are still lighted.

Then they, too, rise in dark silhouette against the sky, and only the peaks of the mountains behind are touched by the sun's rays. The shadows, rising along these magnificent ramparts, overwhelm the peaks in a sudden rush.

Day, for our continent, is at an end. From coast to coast, it lies within the boundaries of the night.

ⴟ November, 1949.

It was called by some "The Age of Anxiety,"
a time of pessimism and a dark future.
To the fearful, America's great liberal
spokesman hurled ringing defiance; to the
eager he offered a joyful challenge to
experience the zest of living in a period of
excitement and purpose.

If
I
Were
Twenty-one

BY ADLAI E. STEVENSON

Stevenson at twenty-one

I HAVE OFTEN WONDERED WHAT MAGIC LIES IN THE
age of twenty-one. The day before our twenty-first
birthday, we are considered immature, uninformed
and not responsible. Then suddenly, a strange al-
chemy remakes our legal and moral selves: overnight we become independent, self-sustaining and
competent citizens of the Republic.

One day we are, for all practical and lawful
purposes, children. The next, we select Presidents,
send men to jail and sometimes inherit the right
to squander money which, until now, has been
prudently denied us.

Whatever it is—the twenty-first birthday is about
as decisive and pivotal a twenty-four-hour spate of
time as any man is apt to have in his life.

Actually, we all know that twenty-one is no more
than an arbitrary, imaginary equator marking off
youth from manhood and womanhood. Society said
long ago: There has to be *some* point at which to
refurbish voting lists and cut umbilical cords—and
twenty-one seemed to be a happy figure. And I suspect that it was selected by solemn, elderly gentlemen profoundly mistrustful of radical, impetuous
youth to whom anything younger than twenty-one
would be risky indeed.

In my case, however, I cannot recall that I was
impressed by the significance of this magical age.
To be sure there was hilarity and the twenty-one-
candle cake. There was my diploma—in sight at
last. And there was the privilege of voting. There
was also the sudden opening of a Pandora's Box
of decisions: would I teach, be a reporter, a rancher,
study law . . . ? And while the prospect of earning a
living and supporting a family must have been sober-

ing, I can't remember feeling any acute anxiety
about the future or doubting my adequacy to meet
whatever challenges the years would bring.

It wasn't long though before I skidded to a tentative stop, chastened by the realization that all
of the regalia of maturity I had acquired was
largely symbolic. How very unfortunate, I now
chide myself, that twenty-one had to be wasted on
me when I was so young.

Yet—what do I know now that I didn't know at
twenty-one?

Whatever it is, as I once tried to put it, it is for
the most part incommunicable: "The laws, the
aphorisms, the generalizations, the universal truths,
the parables and the old saws—all the observations
about life which can be communicated readily in
handy, verbal packages—are as well known to a
man at twenty-one as at fifty-five. He had been
told them all, he has read them all and he has
probably repeated them all—but he has not *lived*
them all.

"What he knows at middle age that he did not
know when he came of age boils down to something
like this:

"The knowledge he has acquired with age is not
a knowledge of formulas, or forms of words, but
of people, places, actions—a knowledge not gained
by words, but by touch, sight, sound, victories,
failures, sleeplessness, devotion, love—the human
experiences and emotions of this earth and of one's
self and other men. Perhaps, too, a little faith, a
little reverence for things you cannot see."

Yes, there are things I would do differently if I

were on that equator-like dividing line of twenty-one again. I think, I like to think, that rather than breathing a sigh of relief at blessed release from classrooms, I would begin educating myself, in earnest. I would rediscover the nearest library—and many of the books I had glanced through with one eye on the report card and the other on the next game. I would try learning, for learning's sake—not for my diploma's—or my parents'—or my ego's.

I would look hard for the inner meaning of the great classics instead of playing a guessing game with my examination questions. I would read, read, read. I would soar where curiosity took me, not just where the recommended reading list pointed. I would be guided by a hungry mind, not by the instinct of competition and survival. And I would question—question everything.

Looking back, I feel that, more than by any other single factor, imaginative, healthy youth is characterized by rebelliousness. It's a good thing, and normal to inquiring youth's uncorrupted vision of pure justice and goodness. It is good for man at every age to seek, to question, to rebel—to keep alive and up to date in body, mind and spirit. Change and progress are the fruit of our re-examination of the methods, attitudes and customs we have taken for granted; they are the fruit of rebellion and rejection of the old.

Our century cries out for boldness, imagination, experiment—for people, as I have said before, "who take open eyes and open minds into the society they inherit."

But in the impetuous rebellion of youth against all the evils that the children of God have contrived, I would go slow. Of course our twenty-one-year-old need not, must not, swallow whole all the tribal beliefs, modes, manners which have been poured on us by parents, teachers and friends. But neither would I automatically throw out whatever I had been told to accept on faith—whatever didn't yield a simple satisfactory explanation to superficial study. I would try to keep twenty-one the age of the suspended final judgment, the re-evaluation of our moral and political environment.

As a matter of fact, I don't think my generation at twenty-one rebelled against much of anything. We were just emerging from the First World War and we thought we were on the threshold of everlasting peace and prosperity. It was the age of "flappers," cynical materialism—and normalcy!

But if not of rebellion, it was a period, I think, of irreverence: there was too little of God and the eternal verities in the air when I was twenty-one and too much talk just of getting a job, making money, somehow, anyhow, and having a good time. It was smash and grab, and devil take the hindmost.

Today, at twenty-one, I would try a little harder and a little sooner to understand that it is not public demonstrations of reverence but the content of religious convictions that really matters; that there are absolutes of religion and morality by which we shall be judged; and that we need God all the time, not just when we are in trouble.

There are so many things I would do if I were twenty-one again, or at least *should* do! I would, for instance, participate actively in the political life of my community, my neighborhood, my block. How easy it is to look down disdainful twenty-one-year-old noses at politics and politicians! But that is to default in the basic, never-ending fight for democracy. Far better to get to work in the political party of our choice—to let rebellion and reform do battle in the arena, not the grandstand.

If we are prepared to fight and to die for our democratic ideals when they are threatened from without, why not fight and live for them when they are threatened from within? They always are. And the basic struggle takes place every day, and in your own town.

That is why, since twenty-one, I have learned never to underestimate the precinct captain. He is more effective, in his field, for good or for ill, than a July 4 political orator who throws back at a noise-deaf crowd the platitudes it wants to hear. There is no more eloquent expression of democracy than a sincere man persuading his next-door neighbor to vote for his alderman.

I now know that the most elemental expression of our belief in democracy is exercising our right to vote. A genuinely free and an honestly informed people will ultimately triumph over intolerance, injustice and evil from without or within. But a lazy people, an apathetic people, an uninformed people or a people too proud for politics, is not free. And it may quickly be a mob.

While paying deference in this atomic age of infinitely complex problems to the specialist and the technician, I would avoid an easy acceptance of another's thinking.

After all, the great issues of the day are not technical, they are moral. And in a thriving, full-bodied democracy, the moral issues are best decided by a consensus which can only evolve when people —and I mean all the people—reason together, reason aloud, reason their way to clarity of judgment and unity of purpose. How often we have observed the great body of public opinion slowly, clumsily perhaps, arrive at moral decisions which are wiser than those reached swiftly, smoothly by specialists—or computing machines.

And, speaking of specialization, at twenty-one I would not take any job just because the pay is good or the practical prospects bright. The world's work is vast. Each man who labors at his own job to his best ability, happy in his work, has a dignity that cannot be classified. There is no second-class citizen—or worker—in our great nation. The artisan stands equal to the judge; and the truck driver's contribution to a free, strong nation is as indispensable as the comptroller's.

Einstein once wrote that if he had it to do over again, he would have been a plumber. How much better off many of us—less gifted than Einstein— would really be if we resisted the snobbish temptation to take while-collar work and followed instead a natural bent to work with our hands and muscles! There is incomparable satisfaction in building, repairing, conserving, producing with our hands. It brings most of the beauty and utility in the world. And how much happier many people would be to go home at night with dirt under their fingernails instead of inkstains on their fingers, tired instead of nervous!

No matter what job I took at twenty-one, I would not go into it with the conviction that it would be my last. I would not be afraid to experiment in the search for satisfaction. And while I know how hard it is, I would dare to take on bigger assignments than I was sure I could handle, and I would try to work for bigger, better men than I.

To trade integrity for a quick promotion or to sacrifice self-respect and conviction for the boss' favor is a price I would not pay. Better to be fired for the right cause than to sell your talents for the wrong one. You won't have an opportunity to *try out* your ideas and ideals, unless you resist the temptation to *sell them out*. Conscience is a fragile thing. It dies easily but the pain lasts forever. You have to live with yourself, and hypocrisy is an uncomfortable companion.

If I were twenty-one I would try a variety of things on the side to see where my interests led me. I would seek a hobby quite different from my work.

For health and well-being I would also take up a sport. Even if our participation is crude, even embarrassing, there is more health and physical satisfaction in playing games badly than in watching professionals play them well. And I say (with self-conscious concern) that I fear there may be some correlation between the fat that accumulates around our middle and the fat that invades our heads.

So, in my recreation as well as my work, I would start at the beginning of adulthood to develop the whole me, with an aim at perfection but an understanding that the aim, not the achievement, is the important thing.

If I were twenty-one I would hope for a prompt realization that doing for others is not only a Christian obligation, but also life's greatest satisfaction. A neighborhood boys' club would especially interest me at twenty-one because too many of us get interested in juveniles, not to prevent delinquency but because of delinquency. Our interest comes too late.

Most young men nowadays find their lives interrupted by several years of military service. It seems to me that a young man who fully understands that each generation must pay a price for the freedom to make its choices would accept this duty with enthusiastic loyalty and eagerness to make the most of it. I would learn the soldiers' or sailors' or airmen's trade, and seize this chance to make new friends among men of widely varying interests and beliefs. I would study with fresh curiosity the new places I saw, nor overlook the opportunities for education and skills which the services offer. I would wear my country's uniform with pride and try to bow gladly to discipline in the knowledge that a team is often more important than an individual player. Our greatest batters have to know how to lay down a sacrifice bunt.

Growing up in this Age of Anxiety, the Age of the Hydrogen Bomb and international hysteria, I would expect of my country's leaders good sense, maturity and consistency in dealings with friends and enemies alike. I would accept in good faith the proposition that while all the ordinary peoples of the world want peace and a better life, the aims and methods of the Western and Communist leaders differ widely. And I would also try to remember that no other people have as much as we do: that misery, ignorance and desire still afflict much of the world, and that we dare not lower our guard while working for the peace and well-being of all mankind, regardless of race, color or geography.

Finally, and most of all, I would try to understand, to know, to feel, the hopes and fears of my contemporaries rich and poor, from town and country, that I might better share and influence my generation—a generation destined to live in an exciting, perilous golden age.

There is nothing so fine as to be twenty-one and an American. One is for a fleeting instant—and the other is forever. So live—decently, fearlessly, joyously—and don't forget that in the long run it is not the years in your life but the life in your years that counts!

♔ December, 1955.

Manners and morals

The turmoil of our times—war, depression, revolution human and scientific—has obscured the profound changes wrought on our manners and morals. Social currents run deep. They are identified by no historic dates, battlefields or key inventions. Yet they fix the pace of every age, whether the Victorian or the "Roaring Twenties." Ours is not an exception.

Perhaps not enough time has elapsed for a fair evaluation of the essence of this quarter-century. Certainly it is easier to measure its pace than to fix its character. We note with assurance that decisive changes were begun, that fundamental values were questioned. Yet, like Newton's law, every action seemed to evoke an equal and opposite reaction.

Nowhere was the pressure for change greater than in our sexual attitude and practice. Freud parted the curtains; Kinsey ripped them away. Young people, sociologist Ira L. Reiss noted, seemed to be adopting a pattern of sexual permissiveness but with deeper affection. Even as divorce ended one marriage in four we saw, concurrently, a return to large families. The impersonality of urbanization was balanced by a move to the suburbs, which encouraged family unity and a richer participation in community affairs.

The contrasts were remarkable. Juvenile delinquency aggravated our urban problems, yet in many cities student sit-ins—white as well as Negro—demonstrated their idealism fighting for racial equality. The thousands of young people who rushed to join the Peace Corps demonstrated their deep concern, in another way, with moral issues. The quiz show and "payola" scandals, the mink coats and deep-freezes of Washington "ten-percenters," pricefixing in big industry and graft in big unions made the front pages. But more people joined churches than ever before and they encouraged their leaders to speak out on issues of national interest hitherto avoided by the ministry. On the political scene, the fresh spirit of F.D.R. and Robert A. Taft outlasted the sour cynicism of Huey Long and Joe McCarthy.

The swirl of social change swept us about and frequently bewildered us. But it was on a note of faith in changeless values that John Steinbeck, whose novel **The Grapes of Wrath** stands as the indignant cry of the Thirties for social justice, addressed another great moralist of our day, Adlai Stevenson. Their moving correspondence in this chapter sums up both the dilemma and the hope of our time.

HEINRICH KLEY

In an age of omnipresent "communication" and "modern conveniences," the greatest luxuries sometimes seemed to be simplicity, privacy and quiet. Television, the phenomenon of the period, added to the intrusion.

But, ironically, even TV's most distinguished commentator pleaded for surcease.

Let's
Leave
Each
Other
Alone

BY EDWARD R. MURROW

DURING FEBRUARY, WE OBSERVE A NOTABLE HOLIDAY in honor of George Washington. However, for a nation that prides itself on efficiency, we have allowed our general holiday situation to fall into a deplorable mess.

Different holidays in different states; no consistency, no scheduling; and no holidays at all for people like myself in the news business. Hence, I should like to propose, half seriously and in a holiday mood, yet another holiday. This would be a national holiday (it could be either in winter or summer), which would be very appropriate in these times when we don't know where we're going. This holiday would be designed to remind us where we have been—of what the "Good Old Days" were really like.

The provisional title for this holiday would be "Let's Leave Each Other Alone." On this one day, no one would work, except firemen and skeleton hospital staffs. There would be no electric light, no hot and cold running water. All trains would stand on sidings; all aircraft would be grounded. No newspapers would be published; radio transmitters would be silent; television screens would be dark.

For twenty-four hours, all telephone exchanges would close down. No mail would be delivered, no telegrams transmitted. It would be impossible to buy gasoline, or cigarettes, or soap. Streetcars, buses, subways and taxis would be immobilized. The whole country would be immobilized.

If a Senator made a speech, only those within the sound of his voice could hear him. If the Russians made a threatening gesture, we wouldn't know about it till the next day. Important news, such as marriages, divorces and who was seen dining with whom at what night club, would just have to wait for twenty-four hours, by which time who was dining with whom wouldn't be news any more.

We do not pretend to know what would happen during this "Let's Leave Each Other Alone" holiday; but we would guess that the average citizen could catch up with national and international affairs without much trouble, once normal facilities were restored. And meantime, there would have been twenty-four hours of silence, immobility and, perhaps, contemplation.

A few families might have become acquainted again. Some letters might have been written, with attention to style and detail. Parents might have remembered stories to tell their children. Some conversation might have grown where there had been no conversation for years. There might have developed an increased appreciation of the modern wonders of electric light and transportation and drugstores.

A few people would have discovered that they can walk a few blocks or climb a few stairs. The postman and the taxi driver, the pilot and the engineer, would be held in new regard. In the eyes of the younger generation, the men and the industries that created these marvels that we take for granted would increase in stature.

This could be a day for the compiling of a personal mental and spiritual inventory, when the individual could take counsel with his conscience, his family and his neighbors. The secondary and superficial distractions would not be there. There would be enough hardship and inconvenience to send him back next day into this civilization of steam, scurry and scamper with an improved appreciation of the mechanical aids available to him for either use or abuse.

It would be a day with time for remembrance, for the counting of blessings and for the making of worth-while resolutions. For some people, the waiting time would be hard—waiting for the light and the water and the radio and the TV to come on again. But probably the strongest argument against our proposal for a "Let's Leave Each Other Alone" holiday is that too many people might come to like it and be reluctant, as is the case with all holidays, to see it end.

♛ February, 1954

The late William Caine's wry, fantastical wit earned him a devoted following among (as he would have said) "conoozers" of the comic in England. CORONET introduced his work to America with this set of cartoons lampooning man in his most vulnerable, ridiculous attitude—feeding.

Cartoons

BY WILLIAM CAINE

BUCKWHEAT CAKES

"This is an American business man finishing his breakfast. He has just eaten a grapefruit, two pounds of Vitamoats, planked blue fish, ham-and-eggs Maryland Style, a porterhouse steak, a golden-back terrapin, a canvas-back duck and a dozen hot dogs. He is now winding it all up with his plate of buckwheat cakes. The jug is full of maple syrup. The Negro who has just carried in the cakes probably will not be eaten. But take fair warning: Beware of the man who eats a good breakfast."

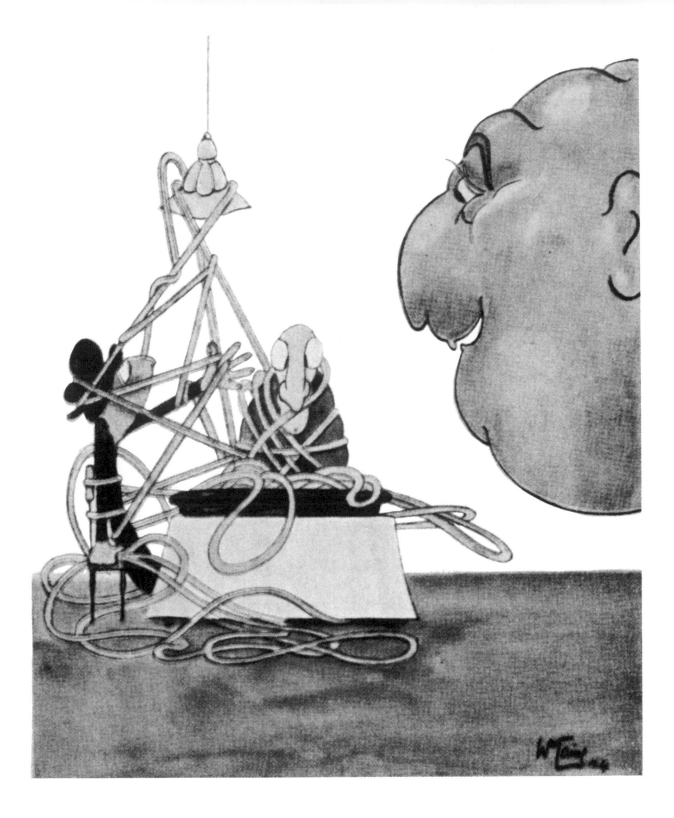

SPAGHETTI

"This is the way English people eat spaghetti. Italians do it more cleverly, but they have the advantage of knowing the language. Spaghetti is a fine appetizer; the exercise is so stimulating. Quite the best artistic representation of spaghetti-eating is an antique statue-group of an old man named Laocoön and two boys trying to get away with a yard or two of it. Spaghetti is made of water, flour and india-rubber in equal parts. The holes down the middle of it are made first to provide a foundation and then the paste is built up round them. Vermicelli is young spaghetti. It doesn't strangle. It chokes. Macaroni is old spaghetti. It gets inside you and stays there, laughing, till you die."

KETCHUP

"Ketchup keeps the British Empire going. For consider, unless we
eat, we die, don't we? Now if the Race is to be continued, we mustn't
die, must we? Therefore if the Race is to be continued, we must eat,
isn't it? Very good. All right. But if we couldn't taste our victuals, we
wouldn't care much about eating, would we? Ketchup enables Britons
to taste what they eat. Were it not, accordingly, for Ketchup the British Nation would become extinct from sheer lack of interest in its
meals and then the British Empire would go phut. Thus, these Britons
are nourished and the British Empire is maintained. Unfortunately,
the worst of it is that those who manufacture sauces are maintained
too. But Heaven will have it so and what are you going to do about it?"

ASPARAGUS

"Asparagus was not well thought out. Its intentions are excellent, but they carry it such a very little way. A food which is only one-half per cent edible cannot be said really to have come off. A strawberry goes absolutely all the way, unless you are threatened with appendicitis and mayn't eat seeds. An egg, again, does almost as well as it is possible to do and of a mutton cutlet very little is unassimilable, while a potato is absolutely all food. Asparagus is, however, very nearly all handle. This is not right. In fact, it is dead wrong. If Asparagus had been properly pondered it would have been made the other way round. Still, it was a bright notion and it lays us under many obligations."

THE VULTURES

"It is no use for you to look for birds in this picture. The title is metaphorical. Every explorer who has died in the desert will tell you that without the vultures he simply wouldn't have known how to dispose of his body. The meaning of my picture is that to a waiter a customer is not a human being, but a repast. It's your money he wants, not your love, not your reverence, not your admiration. This picture is a sad one, I know—pessimistic, if you like—but the decorations are to blame."

The changes sweeping the nation sometimes missed, for a while, the tranquil corners of rural America, the hometown America which the great author Sherwood Anderson chronicled in his **Winesburg Ohio,** and about which he nostalgically reminisced in this Virginia memoir.

Virginia Country Squires

BY SHERWOOD ANDERSON

THERE WERE THOUSANDS OF THEM. IN SOME STATES they were called "justices of the peace," in others "squires." Virginia squires held the little neighborhood courts in which were tried the chicken stealers, the small damage suits—as when a farmer's horse gets into another's corn—the assault cases, some of the liquor cases, petty thefts of all sorts. When I was a boy we had a squire as a neighbor. He had a tremendous voice.

The man was an early riser and in the summer was abroad at five. He stood on his front porch. Seeing a neighbor three or four blocks away, he began a conversation. His voice rang through the little town and honest citizens, awakening, cursed the squire.

Still the man was liked. He laughed with his whole body. His fat belly shook and he waved his arms. He had a trick he could do with the muscles of his stomach. He drew it in and then let it fly out. Grasping a small boy he embraced him enthusiastically. The stomach was drawn up, taking the boy with it, and then it was let fly. The breath was knocked out of the boy. He fell to the ground and the squire stood over him, roaring with laughter. All the bystanders laughed too. Such a man could be elected squire over and over. No one could beat him.

The squires are nearly all small farmers. In Virginia, where I now live, three squires ruled over each squirarchial district. The size of the district was fixed quite arbitrarily. In our county we had three such districts and therefore nine squires, while in the next county, but slightly larger, there were seven districts and twenty-one squires.

The squire received no salary but was paid one dollar for issuing a warrant and two dollars for trying a case. When the prisoner was found guilty he must pay the costs, the squire's fee, the fee to the officers who serve the warrants, and the witness fees.

The court of the squire was held in the winter in a farmhouse living room and in the summer on his front porch. In most of our Virginia farmhouses there is a bed in the living room. The squire's wife is working in the kitchen. You can hear the rattle of pans. When the case interested her, as for example when the fatherhood of a illegitimate child was to be determined, or when there was some other misdemeanor that came directly into the world of women, she came in her kitchen apron, and stood by the door listening.

There was always a crowd present. Men and women had come from all the neighboring farms. In the summer, children were playing on the lawn before the house and the women had fixed themselves up. They sat stiffly on chairs brought from the house, in their stiff clean calico dresses. They whispered to each other.

The squire's court was the theatre of the countryside. Here the tragedies and comedies of the neighborhood were played out to an appreciative audience. For the smaller cases there was rarely a lawyer present. The country people are suspicious of lawyers. They are a necessary evil, at times, but it is best, when possible, to go on without one.

And the squires were also happier when there were no lawyers present. A lawyer is always telling you how to do things. He has ideas about the procedure of a court. He brings law books with him. "In such and such a case, State of Vermont, volume so and so, page so and so."

"Eh! The devil! What have we to do with Vermont?"

In a squire's court the man or woman being tried is personally known to the squire. "Well, Jim—or Lizzy, what about it, eh? Do you agree to tell the truth, the whole truth and nothing but the truth?"

Often several people are talking at once. Lizzy has had a fight with Martha Smith. On Sunday evening Martha went to church and got to flirting with Lizzy's husband. Lizzy saw her talking to him in the road. Then, on the next day, Lizzy and Martha met in the same road. There were words and a fight started. Lizzy got a black eye and Martha had her face scratched. It was Martha who took Lizzy with a warrant.

"I wasn't doing a thing. I ain't that kind of a woman," Martha says.

She begins to testify, and in the midst of her testimony makes a statement that seems to Lizzy an untruth. "You lie," screams Lizzy from her place on the squire's front porch. Both Lizzy and Martha have to be held back by their friends or they would go at it again, right in the squire's court. The man about whom all this fuss is being made sits sheepishly under a tree. The other men are laughing at him. He is filled with resentment. His wife should have gone on home about her business. He and the woman Martha weren't up to anything. Now the men of the neighborhood are whispering together and laughing. His wife has got him into a fine mess.

The squire may not pass on a case involving a felony, where there is a prison term hanging over the accused. He may, however, ask questions, find out if there is enough evidence to justify the man's being sent to court or to the next meeting of the grand jury. During prohibition most of the liquor cases became felonies. The stiff penalties they put on for violations of the liquor laws, cut down the number of cases that formerly belonged in the Squire's court. It cut his income.

In the court of Squire McHugh, who is an old man of eighty-two, the case of Jim McGrew is being heard. Jim is a thin-lipped, smiling man of forty-five, who has a slight limp. His case has attracted wide attention, and neighbors have come to court from all the surrounding cornfields.

It is such an unusual case, that the sheriff, who took Jim and his two sons, Harold and Burt McGrew, has come over from the county seat, and the county prosecuting attorney has come.

It is obvious that these two men are bent on convicting Jim and his sons, who are accused of chicken stealing.

But Jim is slick, with a hard, good-natured slickness, difficult to get past.

There have been chickens missing from the neighborhood for months. It isn't a question of a few chickens. Mrs. Sullivan, a widow, lost fifty-two fine hens in one night, and John Williams, a prosperous farmer, lost thirty.

The henhouses were safely locked at night and there was no noise, not a sound. On the night when Mrs. Sullivan's hens disappeared she was lying awake. Se declares she did not sleep a wink all that night. She remembers having locked the door to the henhouse. They were just gone. Not a sound from the henhouse.

In these days, when almost anyone can own a cheap car, a carload of chickens may be lifted in one neighborhood at night and be a hundred miles away by daylight. A man, who looks like a farmer, drives up to a dealer in poultry in some distant place. He sells the chickens, gets the money and leaves. The hens are shipped off to a distant market. How are you going to identify chickens after they get into the dealer's shipping crates?

The man named Jim McGrew lives in a little house on the side of a hill and has six children. They are all in court, with Jim's wife, and look like a brood of young foxes. All of them have sharp eyes, like Jim's, and you can get nothing out of them. The whole neighborhood knows that Jim never works. He lives in one neighborhood until it gets too hot for him and then moves to another. Wherever he goes things just disappear.

He's slick. In spite of themselves the squire and the neighborhood farmers, who have gathered in, admire his smartness.

They might have got him one time—there was a henhouse, filled with fine friers, back of a rich man's house—but for Jim's brood of kids. When Jim operated he could scatter kids all over the neighborhood.

People said they had a system of signals. A dog barked or there was the mew of a cat. Then Jim got out into the road and came moping along, as innocent-looking as you please.

He likes to smile at the sheriff with that cold smile of his.

"What are you doing here, Jim?"

"Well, Sheriff, if you want to know the truth, I came out here to get some whiskey. A man was going to sell me some. I guess he saw you here and he lit out."

Whiskey indeed. Jim was after the friers.

The prosecuting attorney is after something now. He scents a liquor case. "Where does he live, that fellow who was going to sell you that liquor? What's his name?"

"I don't know." That smile is playing about Jim's lips.

The prosecuting attorney is asking him to describe the fictitious man who was to sell Jim the liquor.

"Well," Jim drawls, "he had two gold teeth, like you got, and had gray hair, like the squire there." He points out the more respectable men present. The fictitious whiskey seller had eyes like this one, wore a hat like that man over there, had on a suit of clothes like the man leaning against the tree.

In the squire's court everyone talks when there is something to say. The squire can't be too dignified. He is a man of the neighborhood. He stops the procedure of the court to borrow a chew of tobacco from the man accused. He and the sheriff and the others will get the man if they can. It is a game. Most law cases, even in the higher courts, are a good deal that way.

In the case of Jim McGrew, the prosecuting attorney had something up his sleeve. He and the sheriff had got Jim and two of his brood of kids on a country road at midnight, two or three nights before. It is true there were no chickens in the car that night but Jim had in the car several empty bags and there was a heavy wirecutter.

And now, almost any night, for two weeks, there had been chickens missing from henhouses in just that neighborhood. The henhouses had all been stapled and locked and the staples had been cut with just such a heavy wire-cutter.

They had taken Jim and his kids to jail and one of the kids had talked.

Then afterwards, when he was brought into the presence of his father, the boy had tightened up. "Yes, I did say we stole the chickens but it was a lie," the boy declares. He says he was betrayed into telling a lie. There had been a trick played. They had made the boy think his dad had confessed. It is all right, the Prosecuting Attorney says, smiling at Jim, who smiles back at him. "Maybe we can't get you this time Jim, but we have got the kid."

He explains to Jim that he can send the boy up for what he calls "perjury." The idea frightens Jim. Perjury is a big, dangerous-sounding word. Jim gets up from his seat on the grass, his back against a tree in the squire's yard, and calls his wife to one side. The prosecuting attorney is smiling at the sheriff and the old squire is smiling. They have got Jim. Jim's wife is a heavy woman with a shrewd face. She and Jim whisper together.

"They can get the kid for telling a lie, eh? Can they send him to jail?"

"Well, I guess they can send him to the reform farm."

"Huh," says Jim, "one of my kids going off there, eh?"

Jim comes back and, calling the prosecuting attorney to one side, holds another whispered conversation.

The crowd is tense now. "You ain't got no case against me and you know you ain't, but I don't want one of my kids stuck. You went and scared the kid and made him tell a lot of lies. What is the least you will give me if I come through?"

It is agreed that the prosecuting attorney will ask the squire to be as light as he can on Jim and Jim confesses. It is to save his kid. They have got Jim this time but all the men in the crowd feel a certain sympathy for him. The squire feels it too. He will let Jim off light. And so Jim makes his confession to the squire and to the men and women gathered in the squire's yard. He makes it as dramatic as he can. After all, even in a chicken-stealing affair there is such a thing as art, and Jim is an artist.

He tells how it was done, how he and the kids have been working, how he got Mrs. Sullivan's chickens and John Williams' lot. There was a night when he and his kids got the chickens right from under the sheriff's nose. They had their car parked within a quarter mile of the house.

Jim is making the sheriff cringe a little as he tells his tale. He takes a shot at the prosecuting attorney, too. "We would have got yours if you had kept any chickens," he says. Then he takes the jail sentence that has been agreed upon with his characteristic cold little smile and is marched off.

As for the people who have come to the trial, they all feel they have got a good show. They go away along the road talking it over.

"After all, he stuck to his kid," they say, as they go back to the fields and to their work in the corn.

In Virginia, recently, they have done away with the country squires. All the minor cases in the state are now handled by a special trial judge. He is an employee of the state and gets a salary. The fee system has been abolished. There is little doubt that abstract justice is now getting a better break but there has been a loss too. These Squire courts were our folk theatres, ourselves and our neighbors the actors.

Their disappearance has taken something very colorful out of our lives.

♛ March, 1938.

DANCE OF YOUTH

HEINRICH KLEY

DANCE OF AGE

178

No topic was taboo to the questioning, seeking
spirit of this generation. The foundations of
the worlds of politics and business had been
rocked; why take traditional moral laws for
granted? In his characteristically forthright
style, Havelock Ellis, prophet of sexual freedom,
raised anew an issue which must make
controversy for generations to follow.

The
Question
of
Abortion

BY HAVELOCK ELLIS

THOUSANDS OF UNNECESSARY DEATHS EVERY YEAR,
homes destroyed, lives physically ruined, mental
calamity without end, as well as a "moral pall," as it
has been termed, cast over the relations of doctors
and their patients—that is what we witness today
even in those countries which consider themselves
the most "civilized."

Imagine a visitor from Mars arriving and survey-
ing this scene. Would he not ask why law had not
stopped this easily preventable state of things? And
imagine his astonished horror when he found not
only that the law was not so invoked, but that this
unnecessary human misery was absolutely and entirely due to laws!

Today, on the one hand, to procure abortion is a
criminal offense which the law punishes in the
severest manner. In most of the United States
resort to abortion is punishable under any circumstances, except when the life of the pregnant woman
is threatened. In England, for a doctor to perform
an abortion, except when the mother's life is threatened, is a criminal offense which may be punished
by penal servitude for life: even to aid in such an
attempt is a misdemeanor punishable by penal
servitude for three years.

Yet, on the other hand, what in real life do we
find? We are concerned with a proceeding which is
below the social surface, so that we cannot secure
exact statistics. But there is no doubt as to the
extreme frequency with which this law is disre-
garded. For the United States, where abortion has
been said to be more common than in any other
country, Taussig estimates the total annual number

of abortions as about 700,000 with an annual total
of over 8,000 deaths, most of them due to illegal
interference. As regards Great Britain and other
European countries, even when no figures are
hazarded, criminal abortion is everywhere found to
be common.

But that is not the whole of the question. Theft
is common, but most of us admit that it is wrong,
if not a "sin." The punishment for abortion is
graver than for theft, yet few people, certainly few
women, regard it as wrong. Every doctor receives
visits from pregnant women who ask him to bring
their condition to an end, without seeming to realize
that they are inviting him to risk spending the rest
of his life in prison. Every village in the land holds
pregnant women who, without the slightest hesitation, obtain unwholesome drugs, which destroy their
health and perhaps that of the offspring they bear,
in the frequently vain attempt to induce abortion. In
England so dangerous a drug as lead is recklessly
taken for this purpose.

An experienced physician, not himself of the
younger generation, has stated that most doctors of
the younger generation today believe that abortion
is not always an evil act. There have indeed long
been, as some of us know, occasional physicians even
of repute, so tenderhearted and humanitarian, that
they have been willing even at their own peril to
break what they felt to be an evil and outworn law.

The English law is, however, as has lately been
from time to time pointed out, in a very unsatisfactory and even ambiguous condition. To procure abortion in Great Britain, is only legal when done to save
the life of the mother and after the seventh month
has passed. It is a mistake to suppose that it allows
any consideration for the mother short of danger to
life; the law is blind to all the anxiety, trouble,
disease, and subsequent constitutional risks, short of
danger to life, that pregnancy sometimes involves.
Moreover, as Dr. Killick Millard has pointed out,
the law in addition to its "preposterous severity,"
counts it "murder" if death follows, which is merely
a "legal quibble," since there is nothing the operator
is so anxious to avoid as the death of his patient.

At last we have reached a stage in our civilization
when it is possible to face the situation. In some
countries, indeed, a vigorous opposition to these
effete and mischievous laws was set up a considerable time back and supported by medical and legal
experts. In Russia practical progress became rapid
as a result of the clean slate presented to the government after the Revolution of 1917. In Leningrad
in one year (1933) eighty thousand abortions were
registered, and an English medical observer was
much impressed by the dexterity and speed with
which they were carried out. Unauthorized abortion
remained a crime, and the new legislation proved
an unqualified success. Maternal mortality and
morbidity diminished, as also cases of uterine hemorrhage, while puerperal sepsis (of which the most
virulent forms are due to abortive attempts) was
also said to have decreased.

In Great Britain, where the inability to regard

abortion as a crime is almost universal among the general population, the demand for a change in the law is constantly becoming more outspoken.

But though leading obstetricians are in favor of a change in the law there are still wide differences of opinion among the profession generally, since the professional forces of conservatism and inertia are always strong.

In the United States there is no doubt that opinion favorable to change is rapidly gaining strength both in the medical profession and among the general public. Professor Taussig of St. Louis, long an authority of this subject, holds that the present illegal abortion in its varying degrees constitutes one of the gravest maternal problems of all the countries of which we have definite knowledge. He severely criticizes the laws of some states, "often confused in their wording and illogical in the penalties inflicted." But he believes that mass opinion in the United States is at last prepared for considerable changes in the laws.

That such is the case, and even among the representatives of religion, I have evidence in a letter received very recently from an American minister, writing to me on behalf of himself and his wife. They have three children; they must have no more; they are anxious to eliminate even the slightest shadow of a possible unwanted pregnancy. They know all there is to know about contraceptives, and they know their uncertainty. They desire that complete freedom in their relationship which would permit it to be a spiritual adventure. "At least," he declares, "we ought to have the assurance of available immediate and safe abortion, although we know that abortion is a threat to a woman's psychic nature, which tends to enfold lovingly."

Such a statement from a minister of religion is a significant sign of our times. There are indeed limits within which abortion is likely, as a rule, to be restrained. But Taussig is of the opinion that legal recognition should be given to any abortion performed by any regular practitioner of medicine, after consultation with another such practitioner to confirm the desirability of such abortion, provided it is performed in a licensed hospital and for the purpose of preserving the mother's life or health, or in cases of the physical depletion (which is a fairly elastic term) or the moral irresponsibility of the mother.

It is along such lines as these, though there are variations of method, that legal reform is slowly proceeding in some countries, especially of Northern Europe.

That is where the question stands today. There is here a wrong to be righted, as even the opponent of abortion admits. It may be true that we live in an evil world. But, even at the worst, there are points at which we may today work hopefully, and leave that world a happier place than we found it.

May, 1938.

In the wake of the war came a revival of orthodox religion, and the evangelical appeal of popular preachers brought new vigor to the churches. The fervor carried with it, however, a reactive wave of intolerance, and as laws and traditions were ignored, one non-conforming group suffered.

The Right to Be an Atheist

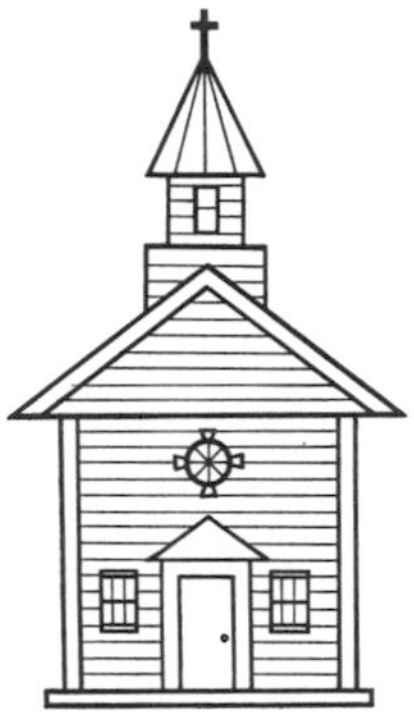

BY THE RIGHT REV. JAMES A. PIKE

THERE IS NO SUCH THING AS AN ATHEIST. BUT THERE are people who believe they are atheists, and they have as much right to their "religion" as other believers. They are of postive benefit to the church. What is more, there are many atheists within the churches. Do these statements confuse you? What they say certainly does not jibe with the customary understanding of atheism as the denial of God. Atheism a religion? A benefit to the church? Many atheists within the churches? The answer to each question is yes, I believe, and this belief indicates why I am concerned about the protection of the rights of atheists. Let me explain.

As a Christian and a bishop I am, of course, interested in the promotion of my faith and church. But I long ago learned that real faith cannot be forced, that real religious allegiance, to be of any worth, must not be compelled. I learned this from personal experience. I chose, as a young man, to leave the church in which I was born and raised. I became an agnostic, believing in no consciously accepted credo. Then, after further study and maturity (as I now see it), I joined the Episcopal Church, left the practice of the law and in due course was ordained an Episcopal priest.

I value the freedom I had to be "nothing" as highly as I do the freedom I had to become "something" again. To me, religious freedom is hollow unless it includes freedom to be not "religious."

This freedom is not always fully granted to atheists in our country today. Despite the fundamental guarantees of our Constitution, many state and local laws limit the right of atheists to hold office, teach school, even to testify in court. I earnestly believe that to defend the rights of this group in our nation is to strengthen liberty for all.

Actually there are fewer and fewer announced atheists anywhere. They have largely gone underground—not in a scheming sense, but with a "couldn't care less" apathy. More admirable, and useful to the cause of sound religion, is the articulate, self-conscious atheist. His concern with fundamental issues is important and what he has to say to the "religious" is important.

About ten years ago, when I was Chaplain of Columbia University, a Barnard sophomore told me with sadness (and, I suspect, a touch of pride) that she no longer believed in God. "Tell me," I retorted, "about the God you don't believe in." When she had finished I was able to say reassuringly, "Cheer up. I'm an atheist too—as far as *that* God goes. Now let me tell you about the God I believe in."

What had happened to this young lady has happened to many others who have lost faith. The God she didn't believe in was something like the one confronting me from a persistent correspondent who calls himself an atheist. He delights in quoting to me from the most bloodthirsty passages of the Old Testament. He wants to "make a thing" of disbelief in the God he heard about as a child.

So-called "atheists" have a good deal in common with a heavy proportion of "believers." The God in which many adult Christians and Jews believe is as inadequate as the one the "atheists" deny. The point is well summed up in the title of J. B. Phillips' book, *Your God Is Too Small*. For many it is the image of their overly stern father; for some he is their overly indulgent grandfather; some see him as a tribal god, a protector of Americanism or a regional way of life (white supremacy, for example); for still others he is a "Mr. Fixit"—not generally relevant, but useful in emergencies.

Atheists are good for churchmen because they are a challenge to allegiance to too small a god.

What is a god? A focus of aspiration and meaning. The pagan and mythical gods of antiquity met this definition. The worshippers of Baal were preoccupied with the multiplication of flocks and crops, and of people to tend them. Venus, the goddess of love; Ceres, goddess of the harvest; Mars, god of war; Mammon, personification of material riches —all served the functions of a God for people of various temperaments. This is not just ancient history: today we are not lacking in Baal-worshippers (we call it production); Venus-worshippers (sex and beauty); Mars-devotees (nationalism); Mammon-followers (money). For some—the least attractive of the lot—*self* is the God.

The recent presidential campaign served to remind us that the atheist is America's "forgotten man" when it comes to equality and tolerance. Richard M. Nixon, in repudiating anti-Roman Catholic bias, expressed this when he said that anyone *except an atheist* should be eligible for the presidency.

No one spoke up for the estimated 36.6 per cent of our people who are affiliated with *no* church. Since no atheist was running, the issue wasn't debated. It is, however, a clear contradiction of the Constitutional prohibition (Article VI, paragraph 3) against a religious test for public office. Very few today would flatly assert that the rights of atheists should be suppressed; but many Americans—including most of the "atheists" within the churches— would agree that an atheist should not be eligible for the presidency.

The problem is not merely one of popular prejudice. It is actually written into state law. In Maryland, Pennsylvania, Tennessee and Arkansas, in order to hold public office a man must believe in the being of God. In many places, testimony of a witness in court may be impeached if it can be shown that he is an atheist.

In Maryland a would-be notary public named Torcaso, who has alleged he could not in good conscience take the oath of belief in God, was, after a series of court contests, barred from the office by the State Court of Appeals. The question is now going up before the U.S. Supreme Court, where I hope Torcaso will be vindicated.

The status of atheists under our Constitution needs clarification not only in cases like Torcaso's, but also in regard to courtroom testimony, conscientious objection to war (which, to be recognized for draft exemption, must be religiously motivated) and qualification of teachers. In New York City not long ago, the Board of Superintendents of the public schools sought to require all teachers to manifest a belief in God before their classes. Fortunately the plan was defeated—through the combined efforts of the Episcopal diocese, the Protestant Council, the American Jewish Congress, as well as others.

It's not what a man says he is, but what he puts first in his day-to-day choices that counts.

As Jesus said, "Not everyone that saith unto me Lord, Lord, shall enter the kingdom of Heaven, but he that doeth the will of my Father which is in Heaven." It is quite possible for a man to be conspicuously "religious" and still assiduously seek to frustrate the will of a God who has "made of one blood all nations," and with whom there "is neither Jew nor Greek . . . neither bond nor free," and who is "no respector of persons," to quote some familiar Biblical texts.

This is a powerful reason why the man who calls himself an atheist should not be deprived of any rights in our society. If rights are limited to Christians and Jews, then by all means let's really enforce this test and in each case be sure that the supposed "religious" man really is what he professes to be.

This obviously carries the point to absurdity. It would require a team consisting of an expert theologian, psychoanalyst, biographer and perhaps a private detective to guess at the truth. For it is only to Almighty God "all hearts are open, all desires known, and from whom no secrets are hid." That is why we shouldn't say that a candidate for public office should be barred because he doesn't profess a standard-brand religion. Who knows finally what any candidate's god really is—or are? We can only look at his record on particular issues.

In my ecclesiastical life I have met many "Christians" who, when it came right down to it, couldn't care less about what their faith really involved.

I have met fewer "atheists," but many of them really cared about ultimate questions, and this is an important part of being religious. Often their real god or gods, worshipped unconsciously, were the same as those worshipped (out of church) by many Christians. One could wish for these atheists that they knew the real God of the Bible. But one could wish this for many Christians and Jews as well!

♛ April, 1961.

IN FLAGRANTE . . .

. . . DELICTO

The revolution in sex begun in the Twenties is still going on apace and is perhaps the most significant social movement of the times. Certainly it has caused the greatest furor. But, as a Bard College sociologist argues, the new ways may bring men and women into greater harmony.

Our Changing Premarital Morals

BY IRA L. REISS, Ph.D.

NEW FORCES IN AMERICA TODAY ARE WORKING TO alter our age-old standards of sexual conduct. Traditional codes of chastity and male privilege are being challenged. Research points toward increasing liberality in relations between men and women in the decades ahead. In principle we restrict sexual intercourse to marriage. Nevertheless, Dr. Alfred C. Kinsey found that vast numbers of men and women he interviewed had engaged in premarital sex. Traditionally, there exists a *formal* standard of abstinence for all, and an *informal* standard of freedom for men only—popularly called the "double standard." Now another, not openly and not generally accepted, view has appeared. This is the belief that premarital relations are all right for *both* men and women when a stable relationship with engagement, love or strong affection is present. This standard can be called "permissiveness with affection."

At the outset let me explain that a sociologist does not argue what is "right" or "wrong." These are questions for each person to decide according to his religious and moral conscience. The sociologist examines human behavior to learn what people actually *do*, and why.

In studying sex we have found that the Judeo-Christian traditions to which we are deeply attached are not accepted everywhere as the natural law for all men. In parts of India, for example, women were allowed to take several husbands, while among Moslems, men may have many wives. The early Christians looked on love between husband and wife as a potential distraction from the love of God. Women of the Hopi Indians are the first to make advances in courtship, quite the opposite from us. Each of these groups would regard the customs of the others —including our own—as peculiar.

Research in the field of premarital sexual behavior is only about thirty years old. One of its limitations is that it isn't fully representative of all parts of American life. Most of the samplings have been from white, higher-educated city people. There is a real danger in generalizing too glibly from these studies to the over-all American population. Yet, though inadequate, they can be useful in understanding future trends.

It is in this spirit of sociological research that I wish to report on the findings concerning an important trend in our lives. I make no moral judgments. Naturally, it is not possible to forecast the future with absolute certainty. Many factors, such as a resurgence of orthodox religion, could check the trend toward permissive premarital sexual behavior. But, I believe, along with a number of important religious leaders, such factors will have to become much stronger than they are now to have widespread effect.

Our heritage of sexual attitudes has come down to us from the ancient Hebrews, the Greeks, Romans and early Christians. They have been altered in the Age of Chivalry and the Industrial Revolution. Most recently they were revised in the Roaring Twenties. The decade of the Sixties will likely see further important changes.

Many of the basic ideas in the Western world can be traced to the Hebrews. Although harems of concubines are mentioned in the Old Testament, a single wife became the favored form of marriage. But marriages were not supposed to be the result of love. They were arranged by the parents, usually for social and economic reasons. Abstinence was even then the formal standard, but in practice the punishment for a woman's transgressions was worse than for the male's. Much of our own double standard in America dates back to this influence from the Hebrew culture.

The double standard was entrenched in Greece as well. There was a special class of well-educated mistresses, called "Hetaerae," for men's sexual pleasures, though adultery was forbidden to wives. The Romans idealized their mothers and virginal women. During the second century B.C., women began to gain in status and legal rights. But the double standard, though weakened, still prevailed. Cato said: "If you take your wife in adultery, you may kill her without a trial. But if you commit adultery . . . she has no right to raise a finger."

The early Christians of the first two centuries accorded marriage, family life, women and sex the lowest status of any known culture. They taught that man should prepare for the Second Coming of Christ, and ignore the temptations of sex.

As St. Paul wrote: "It is good for man not to touch woman. Yet for fear of fornication let each man have his own wife. . . . But this I say by way of concession, not by way of commandment. . . . He

who gives his virgin in marriage does well, and he who does not give her does better." The Christian influence gave our culture a sense of sin associated with all sexual behavior outside of marriage. This Christian influence continues to be powerful.

It was not until the Middle Ages that the concept of romantic love introduced tenderness and affection into the relationships between men and women. Yet in many places outside of the Western world, the notion of romantic love is today laughed at as impractical.

Many other peoples cannot conceive of picking a life-mate on the basis of an emotion. But the courtly love that began with the troubadours of France and came to us by way of the Norman invasion of England, is fundamental to American sexual standards.

Romantic love challenged the traditional parent-arranged marriages. By the end of the nineteenth century, especially in America, young people were marrying for love. The Industrial Revolution at the same time completed the process of breaking up the old, countrified ways of life. In the industrial cities, young people could live their own lives, freer from the control of parents or of small-town gossip. And women, taking jobs, became more independent.

Love marriages gave rise to the system of dating as we know it today. The intimacy of dating helped men and women find the person they could best love and live with. Chaperones went out with high-buttoned shoes, and in a freer atmosphere couples gave more rein to their emotions. At the same period women achieved more equality with men in every field. These modern movements weakened the hold of the double standard and of abstinence.

It was in the rebellious mood of the 1920's that "the new sexual freedom" took root. The rapid changes in our society had uprooted many of these men and women and left them somewhat disillusioned and indifferent. Others—simply against repression of any kind—were waging war against Victorian restrictions, armed with the new freedom of Freud's ideology.

Again, during and after World War II, many restraints were loosened. Young people were often far from their homes, mixing with others of different backgrounds at home and abroad. And a new frankness in discussing sex in schools and in mass journalism allowed them to take part in the debate concerning our traditional standards.

Countering these factors are the teachings of the church, the influence of parents and the formal pressures of community opinion. During the past century, due to these conflicting pressures, the choice has more clearly become abstinence or permissiveness for *both* men and women. Forty years ago, Americans began increasingly to choose the latter, though not openly.

In a group of one hundred students I studied a few years ago I found that ninety per cent said they would prefer another code to the double standard. However, many added that they would go along with it, since they did not "want to try to change the world." Such attitudes are often the first steps toward more open rejection, and, in fact, the greater freedom in sex practiced by women during engagement or serious love affairs is a clear modification of the double standard.

Abstinence, like the double standard, has also seen some of its main supports weakened in our fast-changing society. Science has controlled conception and disease. Psychiatry has shed new light on guilt feelings. Social condemnation has been tempered. In the last fifty years, as Dr. Kinsey and others have shown, the number of young people who pet, but stop short of intercourse, has increased greatly.

So, just as the double standard has been modified, abstinence too has been revised to accept petting when affection is present. It is obvious that petting can be close enough to intercourse to tempt one to cross the line; once the line is crossed in behavior, adjustment of beliefs often follows. Nobody likes to feel guilty, so people develop beliefs that will justify their actions.

One signifcant aspect of the trend toward more sexual freedom should be emphasized: the biggest increase in premarital sex involves partners drawn together by feelings of love, rather than just physical gratification. These relationships can lead to marriage, and they have less of the purely sensual in them than the casual contacts common to the double standard.

Data from a study by Professor L. M. Terman indicate that men have experienced a sharp increase in the amount of sexual intercourse with their future wives. Men who formerly would not go "all the way" with their fiancées because they were "good" girls are now indulging with them more and more. Men have stopped being "so double standard" and women have become less strictly abstinent.

Although our premarital behavior today is not radically different from the 1920's, those who engage in affairs do it more openly. This is another mark of the transition of permissiveness with affection from an informal, tolerated custom to an established standard. In the same way, while the total following of abstinence and the double standard has decreased, the people who support these codes today are allowing more freedoms in their relations.

The new attitudes toward sexual freedom have come to America later than to some other Western countries. Sweden has long accepted permissiveness with affection as one of its standards. It grew out of a kind of "bundling" custom that was more liberal than the bundling of eighteenth-century America. Bundling in America disappeared as our nation moved from farms to the cities. The courting scene shifted to the parlor, and finally to the automobile. More sexual liberties seem to be taken in the automobile than were ever taken beneath the blankets of the old-time bundling beds!

Nevertheless, there is evidence to indicate that even in the puritanical days of eighteenth-century America premarital intercourse among engaged couples was not too uncommon. In Groton Church, Groton, Massachusetts, there is a record that sixty-six out of two hundred couples confessed to their minister that they had committed fornication. Up until recently some people were quite proud of their ancestors for having two distinctive initials—C. F. —following their names, like a degree, in church records. Pride changed to embarrassment when it was discovered C. F. stood for "Confessed Fornication."

A Swedish student of mine has told me that he believes American girls are much freer with sexual favors than their Swedish counterparts—up to the final point. A Swedish girl, he said, regards "heavy petting" as far too intimate unless she is seriously affectionately involved and therefore intends to go all the way. In this sense, one might say that although American women are more virginal than the Swedish women, they are still more promiscuous sexually!

No one could have foreseen the great changes that occurred in the last few generations. The changes in the next few generations may be equally surprising.

The new postwar generation, particularly the upper and middle-class educated group, is far enough removed from the past, and deeply enough involved in the newer permissive thinking to take it for granted. I believe that with each succeeding generation, the new outlook will be more securely rooted.

What are the alternatives? Our society, with its lack of chaperonage, its anonymity, its defense of the individual's right to his beliefs, its freedom for young people and growing equality for women, doesn't seem a fertile ground for the maintenance of an abstinence code. Nevertheless, social behavior is often unpredictable. And it is certainly true that the state of research and the incomplete evidence so far collected is far from foolproof. The movement toward permissiveness could boomerang and produce a strong reaction that would check its development. I can only say that there is at present little evidence to justify that expectation.

College graduates probably will spearhead the new trend. College men more often choose their sexual partners on the basis of affection than that of physical gratification. Also, college women seem to have the longest periods of courtship, due to their later ages at marriage. This means they have more time to become involved in a premarital love affair. It also means that college people have more time to spend evolving their sexual beliefs.

The rate of change will surely vary for different parts of the country—being the slowest in the more rural regions, such as the South. The highly urbanized areas of the Northeast and West Coast will likely lead in the changes.

These changes are a trend—not an inevitable movement—representing a shift of direction in the long line of our social history. This line has never been a straight one. In the past, just as today, our evolution in attitudes toward sex has followed a winding course. The forces propelling the present trend may be counteracted by other forces—for example, a revival of orthodox religion—leading in a different direction.

At each of these turning points the sections of society which are most closely bound to the ideas that are challenged feel distressed by the rejection of their standards. Sometimes they blame the new generations, and call them wild or immoral. These are not the terms used by the sociologist; his task is to describe the changing character of behavior in our society.

It is important to note that, though abstinence and the double standard have been modified, they are still the dominant force in America today and are likely to remain powerful. The choice between the traditional standards and the new ways, in the end, is always a matter for personal conscience.

♕ December, 1960.

Did the older generation fail the young in this time of preoccupation with Depression, hot war and cold? Who is to blame and who can cure the unhappy aberration called juvenile delinquency? Bridging the gap between his own Studs Lonigan and today's ducktailed hoods, novelist James T. Farrell brings to the subject the wisdom of his memory and personal experience.

What Makes Them That Way?

BY JAMES T. FARRELL

AFTER A DODGER NIGHT BALL GAME AT EBBETS FIELD last year, my wife said that she would like to see some of New York's so-called tough East Side bars. While we were having a beer quietly at one, a rowdy group of adolescents, obviously a gang, burst in and began acting as though they owned the "joint."

The leader was a husky, rather handsome blond boy who demonstrated his authority by egging his followers into a raucous show of horseplay patently, though unconsciously, designed to antagonize. I got to talking with him and in the course of the conversation remarked that nobody in the bar disliked him, and that no one wanted to hurt *him*.

He turned immediately hostile.

I took him by the shoulders, and looking directly into his eyes I said (and I said it deliberately): "Listen, boy, I'm an old football end and don't want monkey business. To you I may seem to be just an old man of fifty-two. But I am wiser than you."

His followers crowded around us.

"Get away," he said. "We're talking man-to-man."

"You don't have to act this way in order to be respected," I went on. "You and your boys are looking for trouble, and if you keep on drinking you may find it. And it will be rougher than you think. I'm giving it to you straight. Go home and think about it."

He considered this a moment, then gave his cohorts a large wave of the hand and they quickly followed him out of the tavern.

I was lucky enough to catch that boy at a doubtful moment when he was at a turning point. And I am certain that many of the teenagers who prowl our cities are at that turning point, when they need quiet but firm and judicious authority—*not necessarily police*—applied to them. But they need to know that it is being applied without vindictiveness and without any feeling of guilt, for they can sense both as an animal can catch a scent. I was in no danger in the performance of a seemingly rash act for I felt neither, and the blond boy sensed it.

And that gets to the root of the matter—that today's teenagers want to be *men* and *women* rather than *big boys* and *big girls*. They are play-acting their own horrible, mixed-up concept of maturity. In this acting, they are making of themselves grotesque caricatures of men and women, while they are still children.

Many things over the years have brought this about. For the fact is—and it is a crucial one in the highly complicated over-all picture of delinquency—the fact is, that times have changed, and with them the teenagers *and* their parents.

The condition of youth today is different from what it was in my own time, the late 1910's and early '20's. There were boy gangs then as now. In the tough Chicago neighborhoods near my own, there were two rough ones, the Cornell Hamburgs, and the Regans or Regan Colts. But relatively few carried weapons. Boys in the Black Belt were rumored to carry razors. Possibly some did.

In my own Fifty-eighth Street neighborhood, the background for my "Studs Lonigan" trilogy, I knew of only one boy who ever carried a gun. There were gang fights, but these were with fists, and there was general contempt for anyone who would use brass knuckles.

Many people have regarded "Studs Lonigan" as a study of juvenile delinquency, and Studs as a delinquent. In no serious sense of the word would I

185

consider Studs to have been a delinquent. He merely wanted to appear in the eyes of the adolescents with whom he associated as "strong and tough and the real stuff."

There were crap or dice games under the Fifty-eighth Street elevated station and in the lavatory of a fairly tough dance hall at Sixty-third and Stony Island. But few of Studs' or my peers ever were in court or went to jail. A couple snatched a pocket-book, were caught and one of the local police sergeants handled the case in a way to save the boys; they never did this again. Ice boxes, which used to be on back porches, were sometimes raided, or candy was stolen from stores.

My first experience with "juvenile delinquency" came in 1927. I was attendant at a Standard Oil Company filling station in what was called the Central Manufacturing District. A group of boys ranging in age from eight to fourteen used to rob the cash registers of restaurants, or break into gasoline stations, rip off the telephone cash box, break it open and divide the nickels.

Several times, they broke into my station and went off with the telephone cash box. One night when I had forgotten to lock the safe they broke a window and climbed into my station. They found the unlocked safe. But they were afraid to take the bills inside—about $75. Instead, they ripped the telephone cash box off the wall, and stole only the change. Teenage crime was still small time.

Meanwhile, with Prohibition had come another development: gangsterism, a big and rather efficient business. And the gangster became a cultural hero. The positive values which we had gained in honesty, frankness and the respect for truth were partially negated by a species of contempt for the law which helped to weaken civic spirit.

And with the emergence of the gangster as hero, respect for honest work declined. The principle of the dignity of work, and that work is what makes our culture possible—this was more seriously weakened than many Americans have come fully to realize.

The rising wave of prosperity further complicated the situation. Teenagers could now buy cheap cars, or steal them. With automobiles, boy gangs and prowling groups had greater mobility. On country roads, delinquent driving became a grave problem. Adult drivers who protested risked a serious beating.

Since the end of World War II, guns have become more easily procurable, and some kids have learned to make their own. With increased opportunities for antisocial behavior, with prosperity and loose money, destruction and violence have increased among those whose antisocial conduct tends toward the extreme.

Any idea that delinquency and extreme behavior are mainly products of slums and poverty is furthermore disproved by the fact that many families of delinquents dwell in well-to-do neighborhoods and the suburbs. These problems, in fact, have spread through many layers of our society and many of its subcultures.

Television, as had radio, has contributed indirectly

to this rising tide of delinquency. Dr. Bruno Bettelheim, an authority on disturbed children, has pointed out how family-situation serials often confuse children. The father is derogated. He is a dope, manipulated by mother. The only form of work revealed is housework, that of the mother. The idea of the father performing his major role, that of bread winner, is often not treated. Father is a bumbling adjunct to mother. The association of the father with work and authority is thus weakened in the minds of children. The children sense this. For children are more honest and aware than they have the vocabulary to articulate.

These then are the background factors which have contributed to today's problem. Essentially, it boils down to a question of values—the values by which we have lived, are living and by which we are going to live tomorrow.

I have discussed this problem with psychiatrists, social workers, judges, teachers, policemen, parents. I have sat with magistrates in adolescent courts and watched the parade of emotionally immature teenagers, both boy and girls, who have been acting out in their daily lives a distorted script spawned in the dark recesses of their minds.

Before the court comes a well-to-do boy charged with disorderly conduct, for instance. His father is overworked, and gives him little attention. His mother is busy with her social life and is cold and dominant. The father at home is passive and under the mother's thumb. They have two automobiles. The boy drives, recklessly. He imitates his mother and dominates other boys. He becomes a gang leader.

The home has not been a source of directing values; the parents have been a bad example. The boy is really finding his own means of imitating his mother.

A Negro boy is charged with felonious assault. He lives in a crowded home. His parents come from a poor rural area of the South. They are uneducated to city life. The father and mother work. The father drinks. Because of poverty and color, the boy's family seems worthless in society. There is no incentive to study. In school, he gets in with other boys whose circumstances of life are parallel. Excitement, release, expression of pent-up feeling and frustration all come through violence. The boy is imitating the destructiveness and aggressiveness his father shows while drunk.

A girl of thirteen, in high-heeled shoes, her face grotesquely made-up, is charged with prostitution. She is a little girl play-acting the role of a woman, even of a vampire. Neglected, knowing her family would like to be rid of her, she runs away and is caught with a boys' gang.

In her case, as in that of many young girls who are brought into court today, sex is incidental. The girls are confused about sex and love. But sex is all they have to give. It is the only asset which will give them worth, make them valued and wanted.

Among girls, one of the decisive factors contributing to delinquency is the desire of parents to get the

girls off their hands. This is the case even among "nondelinquent" girls. Girls are a danger to many parents. The girls might go wrong, or have an illegitimate baby. The girls feel unwanted.

One girl's father drinks and is trying to turn her over to the care of the state. Another has been raised strictly. She revolts, steals, runs away and has affairs with four or five boys. The parents go to the police. The girl is caught. The parents take the daughter to court. They do not know why their girl has acted as she did. If the court takes custody of the girl, the parents are relieved.

One of the terrifying aspects of the growing problem of our delinquent, wayward, destructive teenage youth is that these half-children, half-adults do not know. They do not know why they are against society while they are within it. They do not know that, if they increase in number, they can become the barbarians within the gates of our cities. They know that they are rebels, but they do not know that, at the heart of their rebellious sickness, one of their motives is revenge. A second, and this is of overwhelming significance, is their virtual instinct in sensing the guilt toward youth which many adults feel. As I sat in court I could not miss this fact. This is one of the sources of delinquency which is to be found more in the home than in society at large. In many instances it is more obvious in the case of fathers and mothers with girls.

Concerning the blond boy in the tavern, one of the reasons why I was in no danger with him was that I conveyed no sense of guilt to him. This is standard knowledge to trained workers with emotionally sick and troubled children.

More important, however, is the factor of neglect. By and large, it is the neglected children who become delinquent and end up in the courts, the reformatories or in jail.

Generally speaking, such kids have never known love—love in the more general sense, and focusing principally in the mother. They have not, in what little—and futile—education they have received, either found or been sufficiently helped to find the avenue to the development of self-insight.

I have watched many of them brought into court on criminal charges, surly, their fear and fright repressed. One boy of eighteen had, in the space of about two years, established a record of felonious assault and burglary. His career in crime began, significantly, at the time that his divorced mother remarried.

He had become a lone wolf in our society. To him, the city was a jungle. He had not seen his mother but once in a year. He had not seen his father in many years.

Day after day, such boys go through the mill of the courts. A number of them have fathers who have vanished from their lives. They have known neither the restraint of authority, nor love. And in consequence, the values of society have not been fixed in their minds.

In many cases, talking to them is almost like speaking to a stone wall. They will rob and destroy, attack and eventually even kill, because they know no other way of proving themselves. At the same time, some of the toughest of such boys were, in court, whistling to keep up their courage.

The human nature of children is frail. It snaps because of mistreatment and of glaring inconsistencies in home and society. And if this human nature is mangled at an early age, and steadily, then you get the young killers, the incorrigibles. Today, also, authority has partly broken down in home and school. The children have more freedom than they can command. Case after case of boys brought to court on serious charges reveals a total intolerance to any authority.

Also, violence, sadism, cruelty are coming more to the fore than sex. This fact stands out in the crimes of teenage gangs. Some are senselessly brutal.

Also, there is growing destructiveness. It was rare in my day for teenagers to wreck a school, a library or a theatre. A few broken windows through which rocks had been thrown was big stuff. This was the pattern. There were exceptions, but fewer than now if considered in the gross.

Sheriff Joseph Lohman of Cook County states that today there are probably four thousand to five thousand gangs in Chicago alone. Many of these are destructive. Less than a year ago, fifteen boys of a gang assaulted and killed a Negro boy who was waiting for a bus on a South Side street corner.

During one week in New York City, three youngsters were brutally murdered and two others critically injured in purposeless flare-ups of teenage violence. A street gang called "the Diplomats" calmly displayed a .45-caliber Thompson submachine gun —loaded and in good working order—with the warning: "Don't start any trouble with us."

Today's gangs don't fool, which is the frightening fact about them.

The problems posed by these delinquent, emotionally disturbed and sick children cannot be overlooked. Society must, if it would meet them, develop methods of preventive delinquency. This calls for more effort and more expenditure of time and energy, as well as money, than society is apparently now prepared to make. This is not only foolish; it is dangerous. For not only are the Presidents of tomorrow growing up among our children today; so are the criminals. It takes many years to make healthy and normal little babies into criminals and monsters.

Today we perhaps do not know too much about how to cope with the problem of juvenile delinquency. But *something* is known, some techniques have been developed. The application of what is known and of what techniques have been and are being developed requires all the resources needed for this work.

There is no need for endless research which establishes the same conclusion, and for a staggering compilation of case histories. Already there are enough studies and enough case histories to fill entire libraries.

Trained people and more trained people are

needed, for one thing, and they must be paid sufficient salaries so that they will stick at this work. In New York City, for instance, much better rehabilitative work could be done if there were a larger and better-paid staff of probation officers.

But money is not enough. The child is a reflection of, and an anticipation of, the adult. The payment called for by all of us if we would do something to meet this problem is heavier—and it must be exacted by us and upon ourselves and our consciences. We must act upon ourselves and seriously try to check and correct *adult* delinquency.

And we must consider the morals, the manners, the goals of our society. We cannot have our birthday cake if we eat it. We cannot have a reduction of delinquency unless we work to develop a society which is improving and creating better conditions of growth.

The alarming growth of delinquency in America is a challenge and a criticism of our society. If a growing number of children become disturbed, emotionally sick, destructive, criminal, then we are failing to reach these children. This we must recognize.

We, individually and as we compose society, must prevent so many children from developing aberrantly or we will pay the consequences of their aberrations. For unloved and neglected children become unloving and neglectful parents.

From generation to generation, hates, guilts, dislikes, distortions are carried on. This, as much as love and growth, is part of the mystery of man. We cannot easily and by routine break these negative circles whereby conditions of destructiveness are perpetuated. Yet somehow we must.

Delinquency is a legal term, a mode of behavior. Also, it is an extreme, dramatic and tragic illustration of the problem of youth. And the problem of youth is one of the values current, not only in our society, but in others as well.

What legacy are we leaving to youth? Is it a good legacy? Will the values we cherish—the values which distinguish us from the brute animal kingdom and the jungle—inspire future mankind to make its best effort to complete with success the experiment which we call civilization?

♕ January, 1958.

In the darkest hours of the Depression the light of unquenchable human goodness—faith, hope and charity—shone the brightest, as the author of **The Cardinal** recalls in this tender memorial.

The Trusting Heart

BY HENRY MORTON ROBINSON

ON THE WALL OF MY STUDIO, CAREFULLY FRAMED between plates of glass, hangs a narrow slip of paper, thumb-smudged and peppered with spindleholes. It is a promissory note for $200, bearing my signature and payable to one Frank B. Happy.

To all appearances, it is an ordinary commercial instrument, a trifle on the dingy side perhaps. Yet to me it is a bright memento of the tradesman-saint who "trusted" for me for bread and meat during the most critical period of my life.

Frank B. Happy (does the name make you smile?) ran the only grocery store in Woodstock, New York, a Catskill town inhabited by painters, writers and musicians.

If Frank Happy had been a connoisseur of the arts or a patron of literature, there'd be no point to my story. Actually, he was a simple storekeeper who didn't know the difference between a Picasso and a Rube Goldberg cartoon. He merely knew that food was man's only defense against hunger—and on the strength of this he had become provisioner-at-large to a community of always-hungry, often-penniless customers.

My first transaction with Frank Happy took place on a blustery March evening in 1929. A stranger, I had just arrived in Woodstock with the fixed intention of putting a crimp in Tolstoy's reputation as a novelist.

The village was dark, save for a dim-wicked lamp in a shop window. As I opened the shop door, mingled odors of coffee beans, dried fish, cider and horse feed told me I was in an old-time general store. All the traditional props were in place; by the murky lamplight I saw the cracker barrel, pickle jar and coffee grinder of legend. Behind the counter a stoop-shouldered man was taking off an alpaca apron.

"Is there any place around here where I can get something to eat?" I asked.

He paused in the act of hanging up his apron. "Folks 'round here eat mostly to home," he said. "But if you're hungry, guess we can fix you up."

From his shelves he selected a can of salmon, a loaf of bread and a jar of raspberry jam. He took a bottle of milk from a wooden icebox, stowed the lot in a brown paper bag, then as an afterthought tossed in a can opener and a wooden fork.

"Eat hearty," he said, handing me change from a dollar bill.

I "ate hearty" that night—and for twenty years thereafter—on provisions from Frank B. Happy's shelves. I set up as a free-lance writer, got married, started a family and promptly ran into financial difficulties.

My charge account at Frank Happy's store climbed at the prodigious rate of thirty dollars a month until I was three months behind. Then, deep in the fearful winter of 1930, I had a heart-to-heart talk with my friend in the alpaca apron.

He wasn't much to look at, this man who out of sheer trustingness had kept food on my table. His features were molded from a pallid, rubbery-looking substance that must have begun to sag when he was quite young. Years of pushing groceries across a counter, of bending over molasses barrels and peering at labels, had given him a certain blinkered look.

As he listened to my plea for an extension of credit, his watery blue eyes took on the patient expression of a willing horse whose fate it was to pull an ever-increasing load up an always-steepening hill.

He seemed unalarmed, however, either for me or himself, as he prepared to take on my burden. "Let's see what you've been buying," he said, gazing through his bifocals at my itemized slips in his McCaskey System rack. "H—mm—two pounds store cheese, three pecks potatoes, five gallons kerosene." From other slips he sought further evidence: "Coffee, bacon, cornmeal, sugar."

He put the slips back and said: "I don't see anything out of line here. All solid staples." Then he continued: "It's only when a man goes in for fancy items like anchovies and chutney sauce that I get worried. But when he asks me for family necessities in reasonable amounts—why then I'll see him through."

He did. He carried me all winter and far into the spring, always greeting me as though I were his best customer instead of a man who was virtually living off his bounty.

When I finally received a check from an editor, two-thirds of it went toward clearing up my account with Frank B. Happy. He gave me a fatherly smile with my receipted bill. "Knew you'd make it, Henry." He seemed very proud that one of his boys had come through.

But the oddest part of the whole affair was this: in trusting me for groceries, he had somehow instilled in me a new trust in myself. I left his shop brimming with fresh confidence. With Frank Happy behind me, I knew I couldn't fail.

As I came to know Frank better, I realized that he had a high, almost sacerdotal regard for his calling as grocer. He was dealing in the daily bread that men pray and sweat for; from his shelves came the stuff of life itself. Naturally he hoped to collect what was owed him, but steadfastly refused to demean himself in the process.

I once watched a salesman for a bill-collecting service try to sell his "system" to my grocer friend. The system was a series of increasingly severe letters threatening legal action if the bill went unpaid.

The final letter, truly terrifying, bore a red seal with the words WRIT OF ATTACHMENT in bold capitals. Reading it, even Mr. Happy quailed.

"Why, this would *scare* a man," he remarked gravely.

"That's just what it's supposed to do."

The salesman thought this was the clincher, but Frank held otherwise. "A man oughtn't be scared about his food," he said slowly, then went back to measuring sugar into five-pound bags.

For many years my writing career was a touch-and-go affair. The free-lance life is precarious, at best, and my incurable addiction to gambling with words made me a dubious risk for any tradesman. Some refused to do business with me except on a cash basis—until Frank Happy dropped a reassuring word in their ear.

I remember him coming into my studio one bitter January morning as I sat wrapped in a quilt at my typewriter. My single-burner oil stove was dead for the very good reason that my oil tank was empty.

Frank Happy did not deal in fuel oil and was certainly under no obligation to keep my tank filled. Still, he made it his business to do so.

That very afternoon the oilman stopped at my place (he had been in the habit of *not* stopping) and gave me fifty gallons of warmth—on credit. Now do you begin to understand why I bless the memory of Frank B. Happy?

As the Depression deepened, there was a long period when my sources of income ran dry. Of course Frank carried me. He was sick and ailing now; his stoop became more pronounced as some internal malady sapped his strength without embittering his gentle spirit.

Because there seemed to be no immediate prospect of my paying his bill, I suggested that I give him a promissory note in lieu of cash. He balked at my proposal. "I don't need any note from you. Your character's always been good enough for me."

"But suppose something should happen to either of us? If I give you a note, the record of my debt would still stand."

For the first time I heard a muted note of tragedy in Frank Happy's voice. "Nothing's going to happen —leastwise, nothing that a note can prevent. But if you want it that way, why all right."

I made out the note—a non-interest-bearing promise to pay for food that had sustained me and my growing family. Frank stuck it on his spindle, and took it off again whenever I came in to make small installments—ten dollars, five dollars, fifteen dollars, whatever it was. On the back of the note he scrupulously wrote down the amount and date, deducting my payment from the total.

During this prolonged bookkeeping process, the note became smudged by molasses, kerosene, peanut butter. And because the grocer's eyesight was failing, he could never quite find the same spindle-hole when he put it back.

The whole record stands before me now as I look at the besmudged, much perforated note that hangs framed on my studio wall. The date on its face recalls the grimmest period of my life. Turning the note over I can see the penciled notations that Frank made on its back. Progressively, the handwriting becomes weaker, more wavering. Then it stops entirely. . . . Frank B. Happy died before I could pay him the last thirty-five dollars I owed him.

Notations in the bold new hand of his successor show that I finally paid off the note. The legal debt was discharged, but my real obligation to Frank Happy can never be paid.

That debt has nothing to do with cornmeal, bacon or any of the other staples that he trustingly pushed across his counter into my anxious hands. Rather, it is concerned with trust in the largest sense, with one man's charity toward his fellow man, with personal remembrances of kindness and sympathy too deep, too complex for any known mode of reckoning.

The debt that I shall always owe Frank Happy is the *self*-trust that he nourished in me—literally and figuratively—at a time when I needed it most.

👑 March, 1955.

Money, "easy money," was the symbol of a materialism that was the sordid side of the postwar boom years. "Never dreamed that livin' could be so nice," exulted the hillbilly Orpheus, Hank Williams. But on New Year's Day, 1953, he died in his gilded limousine, a tragic victim of the "success" syndrome.

The Life and Death of a Country Singer

BY ELI WALDRON

WHEN HANK WILLIAMS, PERHAPS THE GREATEST hillbilly singer of all time, died on New Year's Day, 1953, the coroner turned up traces of alcohol in his veins. He also found a refillable prescription for chloral hydrate (knockout drops) in his pocket and noticed an unanswered question that seemed to linger in the sad, puzzled expression on the dead singer's face: *What does it all mean?*

The Oak Hill, West Virginia, coroner might well have asked himself the same question. At the age of twenty-nine, Williams was earning more than $200,000 a year; he had fifteen million adoring fans, ten million in this country and another five million abroad; as a poet, composer and entertainer he quite literally had the world at his feet.

In Nashville, Tennessee, which today competes with New York and Las Vegas as a high-priced and rather fabulous entertainment center, Williams had reigned as undisputed king. His Cadillacs, his elegant suburban home, his $300 suits and sterling-silver-toed cowboy boots—all these were evidence of a tremendously successful career.

For four years that career had been unrivaled in its brilliance. Yet this very brilliance had seemed to drive him toward self-annihilation—as though success meant nothing to him at all and destruction everything.

Williams had died early that New Year's morning in the back seat of a limousine en route to an engagement in Canton, Ohio. His plane had been forced down by bad weather in Knoxville the previous evening and he had checked into a hotel there to get some rest. A painfully thin, tired-looking figure, tortured by sleeplessness, he had called a physician who had given him an easeful injection of morphine.

For a few hours he slept, and then he rose and continued his fateful journey. For exactly a year now he had been fighting the old familiar battle—driving himself with alcohol and drugs to a task of which his spirit had long since wearied.

In Canton that afternoon, when the news of his death was given to the audience that had come to hear Hank Williams sing, there was a moment of shocked silence. Then the spotlight was turned on the empty stage and the audience rose to its feet and sang "I Saw the Light," one of Williams' best-loved religious songs.

This was their boy who had come to them out of nowhere—out of a poverty-stricken Alabama background—bringing songs as few singers had brought them to the people before. "Kawliga," "Your Cheatin' Heart," "Hey, Good Lookin'," "Jambalaya," "Cold, Cold Heart," "Settin' the Woods on Fire," to name but a very few. They were shocked and unbelieving when they learned of his death.

There was a story behind "I Saw the Light" that might have shocked them even more. A few months earlier, Williams had appeared in Los Angeles with Minnie Pearl, the well-known Grand Ole Opry comedienne.

He was in a bad way, his nerves raw with exhaustion, his spirit deeply troubled. In an effort to keep him away from the bottle, the comedienne and another friend had driven him around the city the afternoon of the engagement. "Well let's sing!" Williams said, trying hard to co-operate with them. They began to sing "I Saw the Light" when suddenly Williams shuddered, buried his face in his hands and cried out in real agony, "But they ain't no light! They ain't no light!"

He was a pitiable figure at that moment, the comedienne later recalled—a man who had been sustained in his early years by a simple faith in the goodness of life, and who was now torn and shattered by doubt. And yet his personal doubt had not destroyed his gift. *That* remained intact to the very end.

His gift had carried Williams swiftly from obscurity into the national spotlight on Nashville's Station WSM and the Grand Ole Opry, all in the space of a few years. From 1950 on, his name rose steadily until he finally found himself at the very top of the glittering hillbilly heap.

"It fair took my breath away," Williams used to say, with a grin, of those first years. "Never dreamed livin' could be so nice."

Williams had begun his public career in Georgiana, Alabama, as a child, selling peanuts, shining shoes and doing whatever odd jobs he could to earn a

little money. It was in Georgiana that he had made the acquaintance of a Negro street-singer named Teetot who began to teach him how to play the guitar. At the age of twelve he won an amateur-night prize at the Empire Theatre in Montgomery with a song called "The WPA Blues."

The same year, at twelve, he began playing the honky-tonks. At thirteen he had his own string band, "The Drifting Cowboys." At fourteen he was playing over Montgomery's Station WSFA. In the South, during the depression years, the responsibilities of adulthood tended to arrive very early in life.

From fourteen to seventeen, Williams played honky-tonks, dances, hoedowns and medicine shows, beginning to travel now and learning to love the land and the people in it. Love, in another sense, took him very neatly and abruptly at seventeen. Playing a medicine show in Banks, Alabama, he met and married a pretty, cool-eyed blonde named Audrey Shepherd.

In a biographical sketch written after his death, Hank Williams' mother spoke of his early marriage. "I must admit I was a little jealous at times," she said. "Not really. I'm joking. Hank's mother was always his first girl and he never forgot it."

At nineteen, despairing of ever making a living out of music, Williams gave up playing altogether. But his mother had unquenchable faith in him, and an indomitable will.

Using the last of her money, she rented a car and went to every night club in the Montgomery area. She booked Hank solid for sixty days. "When Hank saw the datebook for those shows," she wrote later, "he gave me the sweetest smile I've ever seen and said, 'Thank God, Mother. You've made me the happiest boy in the world.'"

Success was waiting for him now. Joking with his wife Audrey one day, she asked him what he'd do if he came home too late and she locked him out. He thought about this for a moment and said, "I'd go out and tell that little old dog to move it on over in the doghouse." And then he thought about *this* for a while and took his guitar and picked out a fast-moving, happy little tune called "Move It on Over."

Hank liked "Move It on Over" so well he decided to send it to Acuff-Rose, one of the top publishers in the hillbilly music field. The Rose half of the firm liked "Move It on Over" so well that he promptly summoned the composer to Nashville.

Fred Rose was an old-timer in show business and a cautious man. He said to Williams, "It's good, but how do I know you wrote it? Here, I'll give you a test. Take this situation: There's a girl who marries a rich boy instead of the poor boy who lives in a cabin. Go in the room there and see if you can make a song out of *that*." Hank emerged thirty minutes later, singing "A Mansion on the Hill." This made two hits on his first day with the firm.

With this brace of hits on his hands, Williams had no difficulty getting bookings from that moment on. Leaving Nashville, he quickly established himself on the well-known Louisiana Hayride over Shreveport's station KWKH. From there he moved up to Nash-

ville and WSM's Grand Ole Opry and his fortune was made, for the top hillbilly singers earn as much as our top brokers and bankers.

But it wasn't "easy" money that he was making. Williams soon discovered that country entertainers work hard, impossibly hard, for their wages. A typical week might find him singing in the broiling sun in a Dallas fairground one day, in a Los Angeles auditorium the following day, in San Francisco's Cow Palace that same night—in Denver, Seattle, Toronto, in baseball parks, picnic grounds, indoors and outdoors. Finally, the typical week turned into Saturday and it was time to high-tail it back home to Nashville and the Grand Ole Opry. It was a merciless program.

While exhausted from this grind one day in 1951, Williams somehow made the acquaintance of a certain "Doc" Marshall, a quack and a first-rate con man. Marshall knew a good "patient" when he saw one and he hinted at a "pleasant" way to handle the problems of exhaustion, depression, insomnia and all the other assorted ills that tend to beset a harried man, always on the go.

The "pleasant way," of course, was the vicious benzedrine-barbiturate cycle, the "wake 'em up, put 'em to sleep" routine, plus, perhaps, the use of even stronger drugs.

Marshall was soon made Williams' personal physician at a fee of $300 a week. Now the country singer had entered, as it were, into a pact with the Devil.

"It's impossible to describe what happened," one of Hank's friends said later about Williams' swift descent. "It happened so fast. It was 'Doc' Marshall, it was money, it was whiskey, it was some sickness or sadness he had carried around with him ever since he was a kid."

Whatever it was, the pendulum was soon swinging in wider and wider arcs. Williams became quixotic, crazily unpredictable, drinking wildly now, throwing great gouts of money on the floor wherever he might be and stamping on it and screaming with rage. The money bothered him, there was no doubt of that.

But his audiences stuck by. Even when, toward the last, he took to weaving onstage, telling his fans to go to hell, they *applauded*. It was just further evidence of his greatness.

It was evidence, however, of something else to bookers, agents, house owners and managers. Broken engagements could mean financial disaster. And when Williams took to packing a pistol in the back of his belt and shooting up hotel rooms and even his own home on at least one occasion, it was plain that something had to be done.

In September they booted him out of the Grand Ole Opry and sent him into that limbo from which they say hillbilly singers never return. Four months later, struggling now to keep alive, he embarked on a plane from Shreveport to keep his New Year's Day engagement in Canton, Ohio. The next day he was dead.

👑 January, 1956.

The story of one book is the story of the great transformation of public and official attitudes toward sex, censorship and the arts. The furor over Constance Chatterley and Oliver Mellors spanned the quarter-century and was resolved in a manner to set precedent for years to come.

Lady Chatterley's Lover

BY BERGEN EVANS

ONE OF THE MOST IMPORTANT BOOKS PUBLISHED IN the U.S. in 1959 was written and first published in Italy in 1928, set in type by compositors who couldn't understand a word of it, and had, for thirty-one years, been confiscated by our customs officers and banned from our mails: D. H. Lawrence's *Lady Chatterley's Lover*.

Like water pressure that has slowly built up behind a cracked dam, the suppressed book suddenly burst upon us, challenging the power of our Postmaster General, demanding reinterpretation of our Constitution by the U.S. Supreme Court and, in its movie version—produced in France—dealing U.S. film censorship a vital blow.

On opening the book at random, the casual reader might chance on passages that would make his hair stand on end. Most female readers have probably never seen—many never even heard—some of the words that would be spread before them. Most men are familiar with all of them but have probably never seen so many in print.

President Eisenhower, when Postmaster General Arthur E. Summerfield showed him a copy of the book in which these words were marked, exclaimed "Dreadful. . . . We can't have it!"

But Judge Frederick van Pelt Bryan, of the U.S. District Court, said that we can have it and that the Post Office must bring it to us if we send for it. And the U.S. Supreme Court said that we could see it represented on the screen; and that the banning of the picture by New York State was a denial of our Constitutional right to be exposed to ideas that do not necessarily support the conventions of our society.

Few works by established authors have had as much difficulty getting published in full, unexpurgated form as has the "shocking" version of *Lady Chatterley's Lover*. Since D. H. Lawrence wrote the book in three versions, of which the "shocking" version is the third, it has been one of the most controversial books of all time.

Upon the private printing of this version in a limited edition of one thousand copies, in Florence in 1928, the book was promptly pirated, parodied, confiscated, expurgated and bootlegged—all to the accompaniment of a violent attack in the press. The Manchester (England) *Sunday Chronicle* typically had no "hesitation in describing (it) as one of the most filthy and abominable (books) ever written," an outrage on decency "reeking with obscenity and lewdness." *John Bull*, an English magazine, found it "shameful . . . a landmark" in obscenity, "the most evil outpouring that has ever besmirched the literature of our country."

A few voices were raised in the novel's defense, but were scarcely heard in the uproar of condemnations. The customs and mails of Great Britain and the U.S. were at once closed to the book. This, of course, established a lively trade in smuggling, which couldn't meet the demand that the vociferous disapproval had created. Within a few years there were several pirated European editions which could be bought in France and elsewhere. For about thirty years, intellectuals were practically compelled to sneak copies past the customs inspectors in the U.S. or England exactly as a good hostess had to serve bootleg whisky during Prohibition.

When in the spring of 1959, a book club mailed circulars advertising an unexpurgated edition of this notorious work, and Grove Press of New York mailed out copies of the book, a challenge was hurled which Postmaster General Summerfield (charged by Congress with the duty of excluding obscenity from the mails) could hardly ignore.

Not that Summerfield was inclined to do so. He found the book "obscene" and denied it the mails.

The publisher—who could have been ruined by this edict for, aside from financial loss, he would also be subject to criminal penalties—immediately sued in Federal District Court to have the ruling set aside. He called as witnesses some of this country's foremost literary critics. They insisted the book was "one of the most important works of fiction of the century" marked by "intense nobility of purpose." They even went so far as to stress its high "religious quality" and "consecrated vein."

Judge Bryan, after hearing both sides, decided that *Lady Chatterley's Lover* was "an honest and sincere novel of literary merit." The scenes which affronted the Postmaster General he found "relevant to the plot and the development of the characters" and the language which Mr. Eisenhower regarded as "dreadful" seemed to him "not inconsistent with character, situation or theme." He therefore overruled the Postmaster General and ordered that the uncensored book be allowed the privileges of the mails. This ruling stands as of the present writing.

The publicity leading up to the decision gave the book an enormous sale. Not only did the Grove Press edition sell briskly (@ $6 a copy) but rival editions sprang up like mushrooms. Some were of the earlier (less spicy) versions and some were expurgated, so that many a reader must have been frustrated if he was searching for salacity.

The attitude of the public was one of puzzlement. People wondered, If the Postmaster General is ordered to exclude obscenity from the mails, must he not decide what is obscene? Or if not he, who is to decide? And most important of all, does such exclusion do any good? Before we can attempt to answer these questions we must examine the message of *Lady Chatterley's Lover*.

Constance, Lady Chatterley, is married to Sir Clifford Chatterley, who has been severely wounded in World War I and is paralyzed from the waist down and sexually impotent. He has become a successful writer and his house, in the coal district of the English Midlands, has become a meeting place for a group of intellectuals. Sir Clifford and his guests talk interminably (*Chatterley* is not without significance). Constance is their equal but she finds them utterly sterile. She has an unsatisfactory affair with one of the guests. The emptiness of her husband's world frightens and depresses her.

Sir Clifford is aware of her depression. He casually suggests that she have a child by some other man, a child he will treat as his heir. She is shocked more by the casualness of the suggestion than by the suggestion itself. His arrogant disregard of her as a person with dignity and feelings makes her resolve to leave her husband, rather than commit any mere breach of their marriage oath.

At this point she is drawn to Oliver Mellors, Sir Clifford's gamekeeper, a working man who had become an army officer (a much rarer occurrence in the British Army of World War I than it would be today). He has no intention of "creeping up into the middle classes." But he cannot return to his own class and prefers to live alone in the woods, occupied with his guns, his dog and game birds.

Mellors, so different from her husband, fascinates Lady Chatterley. After several chance meetings they become lovers. He does not seduce her. But, once involved, his love is passionate and tender.

Their encounters are described in great detail. In each of his two revisions of the novel, Lawrence elaborated the particulars of their love meetings. He felt the intimate details to be essential.

To Sir Clifford, the body was a repulsive nuisance which he felt would be eliminated in time ("by whatever God there is") as the race evolved into "a higher, more spiritual being." Constance, awakened by Mellors' intense love, has come to believe that the body can be spiritual. "I feel," she defiantly answers, "that whatever God there is has at last wakened up in my guts . . . and is rippling happily there."

The thought that God inhabits the guts, as well as the heart and brain, will be offensive to many people —as it was to Sir Clifford. But contempt for such a reaction was the very thing Lawrence was seeking to express; and his torrent of four-letter words was intended to defy his own generation just as Lady Chatterley defied Sir Clifford.

As Constance is drawn into love for Mellors, Sir Clifford sinks into an infantile sexual dependence on his nurse. In suggesting this relationship, Lawrence employs none of the four-letter words because to the author it isn't basically a healthy, four-letter relationship but a sick and complicated business. As Sir Clifford descends into perversion, he becomes a hard-driving and successful business man.

This is not intended as a coincidence. Lawrence, who believed passionately that the modern industrial, mechanized world was sterilizing and stultifying, leaves no doubt that in his mind there was some connection between business success and arrested sexual development.

At the end, Constance is pregnant and is planning to obtain a divorce and marry the gamekeeper.

That such ideas about love, marriage and success would be startling and repugnant to many people goes without saying. But the book would not have been forbidden had it not been for Lawrence's profuse use of six of the so-called "Anglo-Saxon four-letter words." (Actually, one of the six is debased Latin.)

Malcolm Cowley, in the *Lady Chatterley* Federal court hearing, called them "the secret language of men" and said that with the general decline of male superiority they had been appropriated by women. But this is not accurate. Most educated men still use them very little and most women not at all.

Up to and through the time of Shakespeare and the King James Bible, the four-letter words were not secret. But their suppression in the seventeenth century by the Puritans, who hated the body, created a linguistic problem not only for authors who write in English but for the hundreds of millions of people who read and speak it. We must face the extraordinary fact that, alone among the languages of the world, ours simply has *no* decent, respectable words to express the daily acts of excretion and procreation upon which all life rests. In France, one sees *"Defenser de pisser ici"* on official public signs but the equivalent in English would be unprintable.

In our everyday lives we have two sets of terms for sex and excretion, one scientific, the other vulgar. Most people, in desperation, develop a private family language to meet the necessities of communication. But that doesn't help the writer who must speak to a general audience.

To have employed the scientific terms would have defeated the central purpose of *Lady Chatterley's Lover*. Lawrence regarded them as dishonest evasions that endorsed the belief that sex is a dirty secret. And so he chose the common words which, he felt, had retained in the mouths and minds of the working class a sturdy, earthy reality and a noble frankness.

That, of course, was romantic nonsense. The modern reader is embarrassed by these words, and not so much by their indecency. They just don't ring true. The four-letter words (despite Lawrence's own belief) have little to do with the basic idea of the novel—that men and women allow their animal and emotional selves to save them from dehumanization in an industrial world.

And the theme of the book is not, as the Postmaster General saw it, "an approval of promiscuous sexual relationship. . . ." It is rather that sex without love is a sin against humanity.

This may or may not be so, but it is about as far from dirt for dirt's sake as one can get.

As a teacher and a student, I believe that the censoring of books is an affront to every adult in the nation. It is the control of learning by ignorance, of wisdom by stupidity. "As good almost kill a man as kill a good book," John Milton wrote more than three hundred years ago. "Who kills a man kills a reasonable creature . . . but he who destroys a good book kills reason itself."

Censorship always professes, of course, to be for our own good. Though scores of censors have insisted, in the past thirty years, that *Lady Chatterley's Lover* will corrupt anyone allowed to read it, no censor has ever admitted that *he* was corrupted by it. Today, in particular, it is the juvenile who will become delinquent if these self-appointed guardians do not intervene. But juvenile delinquents spend very little time with books, obscene or otherwise; they do not live in the world of the printed word.

In the realm of sexual customs—the field in which censors are most industrious—the effect of books is very slight. Raping is a much older activity than reading and men are rarely incited to it by the printed page. If those who insist on censoring books are sincere, they should regulate all diversions—music and dancing and, above all, conversation; even advertising and beauty parlors; and no clothing but gunny sacks must be permitted to women. But these restrictions won't work. Some civilizations have tried almost all of them and, strangely, have been most distinguished for their sexual excesses.

Today, many people sincerely believe that our society has a right to suppress the expression of repugnant ideas. But the men who established the United States of America thought otherwise.

Knowing that their own morality had recently been heresy and their own political ideals high treason, our forefathers wrote into the First Amendment to the Constitution, a guarantee of the citizen's right to advocate ideas—any ideas.

This has never been more forcefully stated than in the Supreme Court decision which set aside the New York State ban on the movie of *Lady Chatterley's Lover*, a picture made in France and exhibited here with English subtitles, but without offensive language.

"It is contended," wrote Justice Potter Stewart, in the majority opinion, "that the State's action was justified because the motion picture attractively portrays a relationship contrary to the moral standards, the religious precepts and the legal code of its citizenry. This argument misconceives what it is that the Constitution protects. Its guarantee is not confined to the expression of ideas that are con-

ventional or shared by a majority. It protects advocacy of the opinion that adultery may sometimes be proper, no less than advocacy of socialism or the single tax."

It is my personal belief that those who are bewildered by this principle are somewhat bewildered about the real meaning of America.

♛ December, 1959.

The struggle between good and evil is as old as time, and is always present in the thoughts of men of high purpose and noble accomplishment. Our times are no exception, as this moving correspondence between two great Americans confirms.

Our "Rigged" Morality

BY ADLAI E. STEVENSON AND JOHN STEINBECK

On a hot June day last summer I visited John Steinbeck and his wife in an ancient cottage in Somerset. He was hard at work on a book about King Arthur and the Round Table, a legend that has fascinated him since childhood. After lunch—a fine fresh salmon!—he took me to see "the true Camelot"—the site of King Arthur's court. A narrow sunken roadway passed straight up the side of a conical wooded hill through ridges and wide ditches, the remains of the outer and middle fortification that then circled the hill. Pausing to rest in the shade of the great beech trees, the sound of bells from the village church in the valley suddenly filled the glade with medieval magic. With John's help it wasn't long before I saw a Knight of the Round Table on his great charger, his lance erect and armor flashing in the dappled sunlight, ride slowly past up the steep ascent to Camelot and the King.

On the broad, uneven summit listening to Steinbeck I could see a castle rise out of the mossy stone and shimmering heat. Was it Camelot? Who knows? There are six "true" Camelots in England. But long before King Arthur, it was clearly a Roman fortress and signal hill. To the west lay Cornwall and the ancient tin mines; to the east rose the ridge where Alfred stopped the Danes; to the north lay the Bristol Channel, and the Vale of Avalon, and Glastonbury, in whose ruined abbey legend has it that King Arthur and Queen Guinevere were buried side by side, how long ago no one knows.

Here surrounded by all the ghosts—Druid, Saxon, Roman, Norman, English—John Steinback talked about the Arthurian legend and its symbolism of the recurrent need in times of confusion and doubt for moral authority and direction. He talked of its meaning for us today, of the everlasting struggle between simple goodness and clever evil, and the hunger for purity and ennobling purposes after intervals of corruption of the spirit of man. So when

many months later he came back home to our wealth, moral flabbiness, uncertainty and TV scandals, it is easy to understand why he wrote me this letter.

ADLAI STEVENSON

Dear Adlai:

Back from Camelot, and, reading the papers not at all sure it was wise. Two first impressions. First, a creeping, all pervading, nerve-gas of immorality which starts in the nursery and does not stop before it reaches the highest offices, both corporate and governmental. Two, a nervous restlessness, a hunger, a thirst, a yearning for something unknown—perhaps morality. Then there's the violence, cruelty and a hypocrisy symptomatic of a people which has too much, and last, the surly, ill temper which only shows up in humans when they are frightened.

Adlai, do you remember two kinds of Christmases? There is one kind in a house where there is little and a present represents not only love but sacrifice. The one single package is opened with a kind of slow wonder, almost reverence. Once I gave my youngest boy, who loves all living things, a dwarf, peach-faced parrot for Christmas. He removed the paper and then retreated a little shyly and looked at the little bird for a long time. And finally he said in a whisper, "Now who would have ever thought that I would have a peach-faced parrot?" Then there is the other kind of Christmas with presents piled high, the gifts of guilty parents as bribes because they have nothing else to give. The wrappings are ripped off and the presents thrown down and at the end the child says—"Is that all?" Well, it seems to me that America now is like that second kind of Christmas. Having too many THINGS they spend their hours and money on the couch searching for a soul. A strange species we are. We can stand anything God and Nature can throw at us save only plenty. . . . If I wanted to destroy a nation, I would give it too much and I would have it on its knees, miserable, greedy and sick. . . . And then I think of our "Daily" in Somerset, who served your lunch. She made a teddy bear with her own hands for our grandchild. Made it out of an old bath towel dyed brown and it is beautiful. She said, "Sometimes when I have a bit of rabbit fur, they come out lovelier." Now there is a *present*. And that obviously male teddy bear is going to be called for all time MIZ Hicks.

When I left Bruton, I checked out with Officer 'Arris, the lone policeman who kept the peace in five villages, unarmed and on a bicycle. He had been very kind to us and I took him a bottle of bourbon whiskey. But I felt it necessary to say—"It's a touch of cheer, officer, and you can't consider it a bribe because I don't want anything and I am going away. . . ." He blushed and said, "Thank you, sir, but there was no need." To which I replied—"If there had been, I would not have brought it."

Mainly, Adlai, I am troubled by the cynical immorality of my country. I do not think it can survive on this basis and unless some kind of catastrophe strikes us, we are lost. But by our very attitudes we are drawing catastrophe to ourselves. What we have beaten in nature, we cannot conquer in ourselves.

Someone has to reinspect our system and that soon. We can't expect to raise our children to be good and honorable men when the city, the state, the government, the corporations all offer higher rewards for chicanery and deceit than for probity and truth. On all levels it is rigged, Adlai. Maybe nothing can be done about it, but I am stupid enough and naïvely hopeful enough to want to try. How about you?

JOHN
♛ March, 1960.

Just as the mended broken bone is often stronger than the undamaged limb, so a marriage that has survived confrontation with reality is the stronger for the test. A gifted novelist, employing the restless analytical probing so characteristic of our Freudian era, reveals the aching truths about the two out of three marriages that don't end in divorce.

The Invisible Divorce in Every Marriage

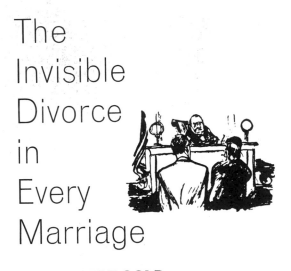

BY HERBERT GOLD

WRITTEN IN EVERY MARRIAGE, SOONER OR LATER, there is a chapter of trespass and regret. In any given year, there is one divorce for every three marriages in America. The history of a love stops. The book is closed.

But, happily, for two out of three marriages annually—for four out of six people—the story goes on. It goes on despite passages of intense distress, found in every love, during which the relationship seems strained to the breaking point. Reviewing such times, the couple asks in wonderment, "How did we weather that storm? By what magic did we survive? What happened to save us?"

During the crisis, the man and wife retreated from the other, but for the sake of appearances or the children or for religious reasons, or simply because of lack of money or energy, neither dared cut the legal tie. Instead, the marriage is crudely cemented.

They are still together. Yet these are divorces-in-spirit, every bit as real and painful as most tragic legal divorces.

In the beginning, when legal divorce seemed inescapable, perhaps the two actually parted. The husband folded his favorite ties into his overnight bag and left, slamming the door "forever." But the mocking loneliness of the hotel room quickly became more than he could bear. And the wife's world, without her husband, became suddenly ringed with terror. They reunited. They resolved: We have built something together; we must not tear it down.

So the show goes on. It may be *only* a show, but at least each has finally given up the romantic dream of heavenly perfection in love. With the abandonment of that dream, they are that much ahead. They have learned that marriage is not a movie fadeout into carefree, sheltering arms. It is a struggle and achievement in which two people decide: We will make the best of a real world. It is all we have—the daily rhythm of work, joy, disappointment and renewed hope—and it is all we can expect.

Because of this new pact with reality, because of habit and loneliness, guilt and hope, children and convenience—often because of passion heightened by separation—they come together again.

Once again they try to wave away disagreements —about relatives, about money, about television programs, about nothing. They forget all the issues, comic and serious, that drove them apart. They sit together, and court almost shyly. They promise.

But, are the promises kept?

No, of course not. They will quarrel again; there will be more small, invisible divorces within their marriage. But they have learned something about need and desire despite resentment and anger; they have made up their minds: *We stand together.*

This is probably the greatest balm after reconciliation—the knowledge that no other solution can work. The show must go on, "for better, for worse."

First efforts to resolve differences frequently end poorly. The husband suggests a compromise: "I can go my way, and she can go *my* way." The wife purrs sweetly, "I'll let him decide the big things if he lets me decide the small matters. Isn't that fair? But I'll decide what is big and what is small."

Or the quarrel may be more serious. The wife may think: "I married *that?* What can I do about it? Often a period of hopeless fury follows, leading to absolute stalemate. The husband thinks, "Well,

perhaps I am selfish, inconsiderate, unsuccessful in my work, a liar, complaining, cold, rude, uninterested in the children, impatient, critical, lazy, stingy, argumentative, and jealous, as she says. Maybe I have no backbone, no respect for others and no business marrying a paragon of virtue like her. But these minor flaws are as nothing compared with her crime—*she nags.*"

Within the comedy of marriage, we can recognize all the little deaths, the invisible divorces—and reconciliations—which enter into every lasting union.

It is impossible to estimate the number of marriages that have been saved by these periods of estrangement. While the couple is separated, the imagination which once labored overtime to dream of liberty now dreams of the perfection of the conjugal past. The wife, who had fantasies of dining by candlelight with some fine figure with heroic sideburns, now dreams of picnicking in the sun with her balding husband. She may remember that Sir Galahad didn't bathe the whole winter long; the husband recalls that Carole Lombard sometimes had temper tantrums.

As he and she once falsified the possibilities of the future, they may in a time of temporary estrangement glamorize the happier moments of their past life together. The investment a couple has made in each other is usually the heaviest they have made in life. To destroy this investment risks emotional bankruptcy. Before this danger, all else can be forgotten and forgiven—even the secret and invisible issues clustered about sexual harmony.

In a series of family studies presently being conducted by a large Midwestern university, researchers are getting some surprising answers to some old questions. "Are you happy in your intimate relations?" they ask. In many cases, the wife's reply has been, "No, but my husband is satisfied." And her husband is answering the same question in another room: "No, but my wife is satisfied."

Oddly enough, this failure of communication may lead to a high degree of compatibility in marriage. Each partner, despairing of "perfection," has at least the gratification of pleasing someone else. On this illusion may be founded the reality of contentment and stability. To be sure, any hidden tension is a sleeping dog; a breakdown of communication, an isolation from the vital interchange of love, may lead to despair and a new dispute. But—and this is a very large but—the marriages on which the above study is based have already endured over twenty years! As long as each partner avoids complaint and keeps up the pretense, they go on, and they seem to continue with a sense of pride and creative achievement. Many of the disputes which lead to the total war of divorce are like that ancient story about the little boy who came home black and blue and with his clothes torn. What happened? "Well," he says, "it all started when he hit me back."

Perhaps it is time to recall that to avoid striking back—and particularly to avoid striking back before you are struck!—seems to be one of the realistic solutions to conflict in marriage. Discussion is of value when the issues are defined and the solution can be realistically imagined. "Talking it out" has become a great fetish in America. But to talk in order to impress your partner with your suffering is a sure way of ending the discussion emotionally black and blue.

The language of marriage counseling has changed entirely since the seventeenth century when John Milton wrote that in marriage we have "a duty to God to be happy." Today we are more likely to be told that marriage is "a continuous pleasure-yielding relationship." The *right to be happy* has steadily become more important than any other element, and "to communicate" is considered the key to such happiness.

Implied in the frequent complaint about "failure to communicate, failure to adjust" is this threat to contemporary marriage: *I will communicate elsewhere; I will adjust without you.* The emphasis on sex has placed this thought at the very center of marriage. The easygoing separation of pleasure from the many other functions of a marriage is almost unknown in contemporary America.

We long for strong feeling. When we have fallen away from the ability to feel, the suffering of a break and reappraisal of the marriage may freshen a couple. They have quarreled exactly because of the pleasure of beginning courtship anew.

What advice to give a couple after their time of trouble? Probably the worst thing would be blot out the memory of separation. Return to passionate hope, yes; resolve not to let it happen again, yes; but hold to your history and remember the occasions of solitude and resolution so that you can learn from the disaster. Perhaps the small divorce, the weight of hurt and disappointment, is the ballast needed to prevent the ship of marriage from capsizing.

A crisis overcome is a step toward strengthening the marriage, a step of understanding and recognition. The difference between conflict and tension is that conflict is recognized and can be dealt with; tension may cause unhappiness without being understood. Very often, for example, tension about money is actually tension about unhappy sexual relations. It requires intelligence, good will, and real courage to transform a tension into a conflict which can be recognized for what it is and then be resolved.

A temporary separation or withdrawal may offer the respite within which conflicts can be reshaped into solvable form. The painful, necessary separation can be seen then as a mere extension of the normal privacy which even two people very much in love must learn to protect. A separation may give time for the gathering unto itself of a personality, making a more firm relationship with the partner possible. Of course, in the loneliness of separation, the issues which have divided a couple may become exaggerated. That is the risk that must be taken.

Very often, however, a more mature understanding of marriage follows. The ideal of absolute perfection is abandoned. We learn to accept the fact that the largest things we love cannot ever be completely known, as we cannot ever completely comprehend a great work of art, or the movements of the stars. The romantic desire to possess the beloved one utterly is a childish, hopeless and dangerous desire. If the lover succeeds, he despises his loved one for being so predictable. Occasional periods of quiet and isolation, even the brutal isolation of estrangement, may well serve to preserve the vital mystery of the other person.

The necessary divorce in every marriage is that essential privacy which is often forgotten in our contemporary American relish for shared experience. To be too much together is to forget the joy of being together. One of the most dramatic incidents in the disastrous history of absolute idealism in marriage concerns the great Russian writer Tolstoy and his wife.

They decided to hide nothing from each other. They began their marriage with a resolution to keep journals in which they would report every vagrant thought, quibble and objection. They would then read each other's diaries. "She makes noises when she eats. Sometimes I think she has no sense of humor. I remember that peasant girl who used to laugh so. . . . He believes he is smarter than anyone. His feet smell in bed. He . . ."

Naturally, instead of being perfectly united, they were quickly at each other's throats. The author of *War and Peace* wanted to cease this terrible truth-trumpeting, but his wife had caught a severe case of the disease. Her effort to invade his privacy— and his angry exclusions of her—provide one of the tragic examples of unhappy marriage.

As Kahlil Gibran's *The Prophet* says,

Let there be spaces in your togetherness. . . .
And stand together yet not too near together:
For the pillars of the temple stand apart. . . .

The temple of marriage needs spaced pillars for good support. Otherwise the slightest trembling may topple it. Let us be reconciled to the space between the pillars. Marriage is a social entity, requiring two separate human beings, not a variety of four-legged animals. The separateness may generate estrangement; it also produces strength.

Despite trouble, the bonds of love can fill the spaces between two human beings in the same way that the sky gives dignity to the stars, which make sense only because they are related by space within the broad expanse of sky. The black mystery of isolation gives the stars their brave clarity and brightness. In marriage, too, coherence may be gained by sometimes standing apart in a small, necessary divorce.

♛ March, 1959.

The cult of personality

Do challenging times produce great men? Or do men of great and original genius shape the times? The argument, pondered by Carlyle, Nietzsche and others down to Winston Churchill, remains open, but from the beginning of this generation the "hero" concept swept into vogue and remains in fashion.

To the sudden speed-up of communications must be attributed much of the responsibility for it. In the late Thirties the power of radio reached its zenith; into the living room, the restaurant, the garage, the bedroom and the automobile the chattering little box insinuated itself. The sound of "the man"—whether it be the orators at a political convention, the F.D.R. fireside chats, Fiorello La Guardia's recitation of the funnies or, from Yankee Stadium, Babe Ruth's hoarse, emotion-filled farewell as he prepared to die—supplemented the written word and heightened the closeness of hero to public. Then came television with its overwhelming capacity to create intimacy; the public not only read about and listened to its hero, it now confronted him, vis-à-vis, observing his every nuance, looking him over from the comfort of the living room.

The power of these media encouraged the development of a new approach to what its entrepreneurs called "image projection." What the advertising industry had achieved for the corporation, the publicity merchants began to do for the personal client. This thus became an age of the press agent, the ghost writer, the public relations consultant, a corps of experts whose job it was "to get their man across." These operators moved into national elections, teaching candidates how to make up, when to kiss babies, what to do with their hands on the platform and when and to which side to slant the profile for the camera. Most students of such doings concede that a couple of elections were certainly swayed by these methods. And almost everyone agrees that the "personality contest" on TV between Nixon and Kennedy swung the election to the latter.

Altogether these devices sat us almost onto the laps of our self-created gods. Everything became personified: Hitler was evil itself, Churchill indomitable courage. When Joe DiMaggio married Marilyn Monroe, it was the union of the All-American Boy and the All-American Sex Symbol. When she married Arthur Miller, it became a union of The Beauty and The Brain. Toscanini was classical music; Jimmy Dean, teen-age rebellion.

Yet of the whole fascinating cast of characters, those who stamped their personality marks on the period were also those who would outlive it, in effect if not in years, and give impetus to the drama of the generations to come.

Fast-paced, with brassy overtones and blue notes underneath, here was the tempo and the leitmotiv of the era; sometimes lyric, sometimes discordant, but always American and contemporary. Gershwin was all of this in his own person, as in his music.

Portrait in Our Time

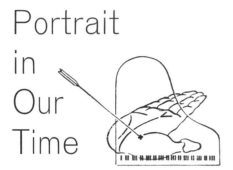

BY NANETTE KUTNER

UNCLE DAVE SAID IT. HE SAID, "I'D RATHER OWN ONE rich relative who doesn't look at me than six poor ones who hang on my neck!"

Right after this, as if it were a sign, Minnie, our rich cousin looked at us, indirectly of course, but she looked, reaching through the mails with a pair of tickets to a concert. "Perhaps you can use these," her secretary wrote.

Perhaps we could. At first we tried to give them away. Nobody wanted to go. The intellectuals scoffed at jazz. The others said they preferred The Palais Royale where you could *dance* to Paul Whiteman.

So we went, Uncle Dave who loves to get things for nothing, and I, who have no ear for music.

Sometime during the performance, it might have been toward the end of the first half, a man walked across the platform, and, even from where we were sitting, you could tell he was very young.

He paused at the piano which stood in the center. We heard a metallic clink, like the sound of a coin shooting through a slot. He smiled, sat down and gave an imitation of a player piano in a honky-tonk restaurant.

I don't remember whether the audience cared for this. More than likely they were surprised. I do remember his hurried walk, the long-legged, hasty stride of one unaccustomed to parading in front of a crowd.

Later, probably near the end of the second half, Mr. Whiteman made an announcement. They would present, he said, a jazz composition which this young man had written for the occasion.

Then the orchestra played, accompanied by the composer, so new, so well-groomed, so politely seated at the piano.

I remember how that performance vested him with a kind of glamor. And I repeated his name.

And the name of his piece. George Gershwin. The *Rhapsody in Blue.*

Meeting him proved a shock.

Here was no art pose, but a blatant earthiness. God be praised . . . he was alive; lusty, suntanned, athletic; wearing blue shirts, smoking black cigars. Musically he could re-create the tempo of our day because he naturally spoke its crude cards-on-the-table lingo.

We met in the white house on One Hundred and Third Street, a neighborhood too far up and too far west to be rated good New York.

You rang the front door bell, a terrier yelped, a maid, neither prompt nor neat, answered, or his mother or his sister Frances.

Framed above his desk were two autographed pictures, one of Charles Chaplin, the other, the face and signature of the Duke of Kent, "To George from George."

It was still new to him, celebrities, success. His rich voice excitedly described a party he had just given. "They had the run of the house. They did stunts! Everyone was here! Like Marc Connelly!"

He was busy with the *Oh, Kay* score. He had letters to write. And no one to write them. Autograph demands multiplied. The letters lay unanswered. It did not occur to him to have a secretary.

He finally purchased a portable typewriter, for a while playing with the keys, entranced.

Then we started on the letters. First, those in the chest of drawers near the bed. A note from Lady Diana Manners.

A letter from Adele Astaire, who puzzled him; her lovable, outspoken breeziness remaining a mystery to his nature, self-conscious and studied.

With the autographs he was painstaking. To W. H. Handy went a copy of the *Rhapsody*, signed, "For the Father of the Blues."

Mornings, Bill Dailey often present, he worked at the piano. As he played he sang wordless strains over and over again. He said, "I do it until I get it right."

He thought in a straight line, showing me a thin book, declaring, "Someday I'll make an opera out of it." The book, just published, was titled *Porgy.*

Pictures come forward, like quick shots on the screen. When, exuberant, he danced the "Black Bottom" to see if its steps fitted his rhythms, the times he argued, "But everybody's got an ear!" refusing to credit my inherent lack; the rainy afternoon he thought was "a swell day to work if I had an idea"; the morning his greeting exploded, "I woke up at three with a tune, even the title! I got right up and wrote it, like you read about! But now . . . it's not so hot!"

So he worked, in quiet, but for interruptions illuminating the family life buzzing below us. Once his sister hollered up the stairs, "I've got to have that money for my dancing lessons!" Once his brother Ira's fiancée reported on the patient's progress, Ira having lost an appendix.

On his twenty-seventh birthday his photograph appeared in the *New York Times.* He telephoned,

"You wouldn't believe it, but everyone saw that picture and congratulated me!"

The next summer he appeared with the Philharmonic Symphony Orchestra as soloist in an all-Gershwin program at the Lewisohn Stadium, drawing a record crowd of about eighteen thousand listeners.

The following day I met him on the street. He was rushing from a rehearsal of *Strike Up the Band*.

He shouted, "Look what I've got here!" Pushing me into a cab, he dropped a pile of clippings on my lap. "The write-ups about last night!"

My mind wandered back to that scared young man at his first concert, then jumped to this one whom I had seen the night before, running down a flight of steps toward his audience, as if he was glad and couldn't wait to meet them.

He had come far in such a short time. He kept going too, the pulse of his career as fast as Colonel Lindbergh's airplane that had just flown across the Atlantic, as fast as the taxi that was hurtling us uptown or the radio waves that had already carried news of his success, news bubbling from his lips while he sat there, boyish, marveling at everything. And I held my breath and I hoped it would continue. His life was so wonderful.

He leased an apartment, glaringly modern, a penthouse on Riverside Drive, away from the bulk of his family. There was a silver piano, and a bedroom that seemed all bed, the cover of light tan fur. Nothing out of place here, a punching bag in the room meant for games, a man wearing a white coat who answered the door.

He still ran to the telephone himself. Any summons could mean another miracle.

His moods changed. Losing his temper at Ira: "Why don't you attend to things for me!" Awed at the prospect of study with Ravel. Thirsty hero-worshiping of those who knew more musically than he, Ernest Newman, Stravinsky. Hurt surprise over a failure. Pacing the floor about it, shouting, "They forget everything you've done when you make one mistake!"

Incredulous anger at Ziegfeld, who held back royalties because *Show Girl* wasn't a hit. Dignified, dependable, he expected others to be the same. George Gershwin was probably the only man on Broadway who didn't have a lawyer.

His discipline superb, he could not understand Vincent Youmans being sidetracked into producing plays. For he had one objective. Through the years his greeting to me, "Haven't you written your *Rhapsody* yet?" revealed what that first ambitious work had grown to mean.

It was a treacherous light, dividing him, making him, now well accustomed to privileges, drill at his gusher of popular tunes, while forcing a humble, steady studying, a learning day by day, as he tried living up to an artistic dream created by adulation.

Thorough, he could not tolerate carelessness. Shaking his head, he told me of the night Rudy Vallee broadcast the *Concerto*. "We had to mark the pages so he could get the beats."

On his part he puzzled others. Vincent Youmans grumbled, "Doesn't he know society only invites us if we bring along a piano?"

He knew, and relished that piano and the playing of his songs in the center of a smart crowd.

He was big enough to have dragged his family on up with him, some of this goodheartedness a sop to fate, a bargaining with a life that had generously catapulted him beyond his sphere.

He was not unique. Others traced that pattern. Who knows? In every profession, each, at the top, for all the hard work and God-given talents, might have been looking at his fellow man, not really believing he belonged, trying to outdo that last effort, dreading the one mistake, waiting for the day his gift would disappear as unreasonably as it came, each, a little boy, knowing rewards were out of proportion, feeling he didn't deserve quite so much, scared to death of his nightmare overtaking him.

He moved again, to a duplex apartment on the East Side. The enormous high-ceilinged living room fitting background for his newly acquired art collection, a modern and expensive assortment, wherein Gershwin's impression of his father audaciously stared steadily across at a Rousseau.

He loved that room. "Done by one of our best decorators," he said, oblivious to the naked shelves, deserted but for an occasional unread book.

He painted now. At one end of the dining room hung a self-portrait, the shade of the skin browner, the face longer, leaner than the model's. Upstairs, in an easel-scattered studio stood his proudest study, a colored girl from Catfish Row. This second talent, amazing, not only for its own qualities, but because he found the time and energy to develop it.

He planned touring with an orchestra. At the end of rehearsals, as he stood upon the podium, his well-cut suit was a contrast to those baggy pants of the musicians who surrounded him.

They were leaving the next week.

"What do you want us to wear?" was asked.

The answer, his order, unhesitating: "Morning coats, pin-striped trousers."

A silence then, broken by one speaking, low-toned, timid. "But I haven't got them."

He appeared surprised. He had forgotten that these men, fine musicians, went weeks, months, without work, that they continually faced the bread-robbing horror of mechanical sound. And he must have felt ashamed as he stood before them, so embarrassingly successful. For a look of compassion crossed his face. "Wear what you have," he said, his voice gentle.

He grew thoughtless. Once, after having me wait two hours, he walked into the dining room saying that I could watch him eat. The following day he was sorry, running everywhere, showing me the new bar, the English den, the ink-spattered studio on the second floor.

He was indignant when people criticized him for allowing a cathartic company to be his radio sponsors. "They forget it gives me enough money to spend months on an opera."

Porgy and Bess was his triumph. No Ferde Grofé,

no Bill Dailey to help here. "Look," as he handed me the thick score, "I orchestrated the whole business— every note myself!"

These days, a difference, he was very nervous. Glimpses of his old enthusiasm would shine through it all, but most of the time he seemed worried. "I can't sleep. I'm being psyched. I can't fall in love."

And I remember thinking that here was a man who didn't have much fun.

Then Winchell reported he was seriously ill. I read this aloud on the roof of a Broadway hotel, over-heard by Frances Williams, the blues singer, by a crooner with Ben Bernie's band, a saxophonist who worked for Guy Lombardo.

In a night club Frances Williams had once sung a lyric to the *Rhapsody*. She said, "When he heard it, Gershwin kissed me."

Throwing back her blond head, she sang it again, shouted it to the smoky city skies while the crooner and the saxophonist hummed a swinging accompaniment and from down below in the pit of the streets the variegated honks of traffic horns rose to join them.

As the melody floated off the roof, floated one block eastward to the Carnegie he loved so much, I could not help thinking that although Bill Dailey, the faithful, had long since died, and little Hannah Williams was a matron named Mrs. Jack Dempsey, there would, no matter what happened, always be people to keep Gershwin's songs alive.

I was wrong. I reckoned without death.

As long as the abrupt stopping of a life was news to be teletyped, printed, photographed, broadcast, they were interested. He could keep pace.

A radio concert the night after, time and distance shot. California, Fred Astaire speaks; Texas, White-man plays; we hear Jolson from New York.

In spite of the heat and the rain, the funeral, in the heavy bronze-doored temple had standing room only. Thirty rows down front reserved for his family and for the first night, first-rate elite, men-about-town, society, politics, the arts. "There's Bennet Cerf, Cobina Wright. . . ." Necks stretched, heads turned, shoulders pushed, voices whispered, rising, "There's the mayor." "There's George M. Cohan." "There's Jimmy Walker!"

It seemed as if he were there, putting on another show, making his relatives proud of him in his final performance.

In the back balcony, far from the reserved section, the man seated next to me smelled badly. He smelled from subway sweat, from Second Avenue, from the terrific distance he journeyed in all that heat. Who-ever he was, butcher, barber, tailor, neighbor, he sobbed with a cry that had retched its way past throats of many cantors, echoing itself in the melodic

wails of the boy he loved. For he must have loved him and the songs he made, this man with the gasping sobs, the wringing hands and the Hebrew paper, honest label, sticking from his pocket.

Dead. Stopped. Finished. Not so fast. True, the radio was tapering off, but the Stadium planned a concert. The rich are buying their tables two weeks in advance; the poor carry their suppers as they wait; the ones who knew him can't believe, still hear his deep voice ringing in their ears.

Stretching, whispering. "There's the governor." "There's the mayor." My cousin Minnie. "Ethel Merman's gonna sing." Cig-ar-ettes, Coca-Cola, pop, root beer.

With the first note a heavenly conductor plants a star. It twinkles high above a Gothic tower. His songs begin.

Sweltering, they listen, attentive, sentimental for the moment. The second half, they rise in silent prayer. It's thrilling, doing what the governor and mayor are doing, the thing to do.

Impressed they sit again, but now it is as if a secret signal told each one the drama part was through, this man done for; a restlessness com-mences, a constant murmuring, a feeling of things over.

From the back: "Ethel Merman had fur on her dress." "Those colored singers sure were fine." "We'd better go, avoid the rush."

What matter the *Rhapsody* to be played, an elo-quent finale, the *Rhapsody* that shaped his soul, his life and plans.

From the center: "You heard the *Rhapsody* be-fore . . . come on."

From a table: "I can't forget dear Gawge in Lon-don, his hair and shoes just too, too shiny. But my dear, where *did* you get that dress?"

This a Greek chorus up to date.

The first note of the *Rhapsody* tears torrid atmos-phere. The mass disintegrates without a beg-your-pardon. Snakelike it weaves its fickle way toward every exit, so as the last chord strikes they who feel no honest love for gentleness, for peaceful void, will have no more. Steadfastness takes minute upon minute, days and years, is not for those who rush, not for the tough, the speedy, the live, well on their way to autos that can race them home, to subways that can travel fast.

Then I knew. We find no time for last month's death, nor for its aftermath, the patient stationary quiet, no time to cry out, even to him who knew, feared, felt our modern hearts, pace-setting, whip-cracking.

So I pause, give credit, bow and say, "Oh, George, you made your one mistake! It was to die."

♔ February, 1938.

Neither the Thirties, the Forties nor the Fifties quite knew how to take Frank Lloyd Wright. His individualistic, irreverent genius never "fit" any time, yet gave impetus to new ideas in dozens of different directions. Too modern for the modernistic, too simple for the sophisticated, his was a spirit for all ages.

Master Builder

BY MEYER LEVIN

FRANK LLOYD WRIGHT, WHO HAS MORE REASON FOR bitterness than any living American artist, seems to be pouring forth a stream of energy refined through a life of vicissitudes that must have burned out everything but the pure gold.

Eight new buildings, scattered over the country, and each with a strikingly original solution of a tough architectural problem, are growing up created by him and under his supervision. For a Wright building does not "go up," it grows. One house is slung across a waterfall. There is an office building, without conventional windows or doors. And for that building he has tossed off an invention in architectural engineering which leaves the skeptics as flabbergasted as they were when his "crazy" floating foundation held the Imperial Hotel of Tokyo upright through two earthquakes. Even the company whose cement he used declared that his startling new type of pencil-line mushroom pillars would not support the required load. So the master builder showed them—but of that, later.

An upright, active figure, garbed in dark-blue loose trousers tied around the ankles, a storm shirt, his face at once kindly and wry under the blazing white arc of his hair, if Frank Lloyd Wright plays the prophet and patriarch at Taliesin it is with a singularly American touch of humor, candor.

Some thirty apprentices, all volunteers, have surrounded him, forming the Taliesin Fellowship. Mr. Wright has designed a life with them that is constructive action. If it seems superficially to have a touch of cultism, this vanishes when one realizes everyone in the place has a sense of humor, in other words a sense of proportion, and when one sees what is being accomplished.

Wright's Taliesin today is noted not only as the residence of America's master-architect; his home happens to be a master's masterpiece. The name, in Wright's ancestral Welsh, means "shining brow." Perhaps the tragic scourgings and burnings that have taken place on that hill were a crucible for the beautiful form that has emerged; sculptures plucked fire-hot from the ashes of the second burning are imbedded in the walls today; and the entire edifice, with its transcending note of firm calm, seems to sing the triumph of a young-spirited Job.

It is a masterpiece well worked-over. Before the building of Taliesin III, Wright made a series of forty designs to educate himself. The workmen never saw them. There is nothing tricky, nothing spectacular about the place. One scarcely notices it from the road at the bottom of the hill, as Taliesin is a perfect example of Wright's thesis of harmony between buildings and terrain. The form of the construction becomes part of the landscape.

The five hills of his home place were farmed by his grandsire and uncles; "man-sized hills," he calls them, for they are in man's proportion, no mild hills, yet hills man can "do something with." In places one sees the red-yellow stone bared, and it is from such a quarry, a mile distant, that Taliesin stone came. The masonry courses suggest the natural strata of stone in the hillside.

Any minor architect would have stuck the group of buildings smack on top of the hill. That's what they do around the hills of Hollywood, Wright remarks. His place curls snugly to the ground just below the hilltop; one cannot help comparing it to a wreath upon a brow.

In one wing of the U-group are workshops, kitchens, dining halls and rooms for the apprentices. Each apprentice room is a little masterpiece of built-shelving, built-in furniture, fireplace, an expansive drawing board, a couch. Natural-colored woods, bright walls.

The open part of the U is a garden courtyard, with its little pools in which a grandchild's blue-sailed toyboats float. The courtyard mounts to a viewplace on the hill, the stone so skillfully used here that one can't tell whether it was placed there or grew there. On a great circular stone bench of a warm afternoon, Mrs. Wright, who leads the fellowship with her husband, and a group of apprentices, I found sitting, shelling home-grown lima beans. The base of the U, seen below, connecting apprentice wing with master wing, consists of studio and drafting rooms.

The creation of the fellowship is as important to Mr. Wright and Mrs. Wright as the creation of buildings. For here they are designing an entire way of life. The first impression is of a life drenched in music. Upon entering the Taliesin courtyard, one fancies himself in some wilderness conservatory: pianos on the left, a cello in the workrooms, sounds of a harpsichord from the master's house. Oratories, concertos, symphony recordings pouring from loudspeakers within the buildings and one mounted on the tower overlooking the hill-garden.

In every room there seems to be a grand piano; one even stumbles onto a grand piano in a tiny balcony over the drafting room; an apprentice remarks, with a twinkle, "Oh, yes, we may have them in the bathrooms too."

This master builder avows the affinity of the arts. "That is ear-music," he says, "and this—" waving his hand toward all Taliesin, "is eye-music." Music, architecture and all the arts are interchangeable to him. "I could have been a composer, or a painter, or a writer, for that matter. An artist is simply someone with unusual sense and objectivity." There can be no such thing, he contends, as genius for one art alone, though "a man may be so foolish as to train himself in only one."

And there he reveals his passion for the fully rounded life; his hatred of specialization. Taliesin is to remove the curse of specialization from today's education. Frank Lloyd Wright is constantly preaching "the thing as a whole." His favorite word next to "integral" is "organic." "Nothing is of value except as it is naturally related to the whole in the direction of some living purpose." This goes for the building of a house or of a human character. It is the leitmotif of Broadacre City, a design for civilization. And how do his apprentices go about developing the "sense of the whole"?

First, they do all kinds of work. They farm the two hundred acres of Taliesin, raise wheat and corn, make wine from the hillside grapes, fill the root cellar with vegetables, preserve fruits; they take turns in cooking, in baking bread and cake for the fellowship; they build roads, plant trees, between their whiles making designs, tracing plans, superintending buildings. They bolster the trusses, they lay the stone flooring of the new drafting room. Construction is never ended at Taliesin.

In the drafting room, lettered in red and black, hangs Frank Lloyd Wright's "Work Song," written in his youth. The first verse of four reads:

> I'll work
> As I'll think
> As I am!
> No thought of Fashion or Sham
> Nor for Fortune that Jade
> Serve vile Gods-of-Trade
> My Thought as beseemeth a Man
> My Thought
> Thought that beseemeth the Man

Evenings there is music, talk, often a gathering in the master's living room. Distinguished artists, designers, musicians from all over the world make the pilgrimage to Taliesin. Sunday has a special routine. At eleven, Taliesin goes on a picnic. This, Mr. Wright offers as a fair substitute for church services. The fleet of deep Indian-red cars and trucks rolls out over the hills, winding up on some promontory from which one views ravines and farm lands. Like clockwork, campfires are built, steaks for forty people broiled, consumed. For an hour, folks loll around, talk.

Sprawled picturesquely over the rocks, some in shorts, some in corduroys, the women in brilliant reds, yellows, blues, daughter Svetlana in a billowy peasant skirt, Olgivanna, his wife, in delicate summery prints, Iovanna, child in pigtails, climbing the cliff—they make an idyllic picture, altogether.

The "sense of space" is one of the master's pet phrases, and the key to his architecture. For he strives to get rid of the oppression of enclosing walls. The house must be one with outdoors. Even in his first residence, built in Oak Park, there was the elimination of the little rooms, all of the useless partitions that cluttered homes of the period. Sewing rooms, living rooms, music rooms, dining rooms, sitting rooms were thrown into one large living room. Windows ceased to be holes in the wall, walls rather became connectives to window spaces. The cornerwise, or wrap-around, window so popular in "modernist" architecture was first used by him in 1903!

Taliesin may seem to be a little Utopia, a Shangri-la, with its rhythmed life, but it has been achieved only through astounding hardship. Frank Lloyd Wright's career is the most certain contradiction of the adage about the mousetrap. He could build practically anything better than his neighbor, but the world of yesterday seemed intent only upon nailing up his door. Practically seventeen years of the maturity of the master builder was unutilized by the society of his own country. There was a period of seven years, at the peak of his creative power, when he was not given a single building to build, although he kept on building up Taliesin.

It would seem that his American common-sense approach to architecture would have been readily accepted, and it was to a remarkable extent. Yet his life is one long story of battle with contractors and doubting engineers. Doubly strange, for as a boy he had gone through an experience which made it certain he would never put up a building of whose safety he wasn't positive. He had seen the State capitol in Madison collapse, seen people crushed to death in the debris. He studied engineering before architecture.

Yet the struggle began with a windmill tower. For thirty-five years, Wright's doubting uncles came out after every thunder storm to see whether it had fallen. It has outlived them all. Then came Unity Temple, the church in Oak Park which was the first monolithic use of concrete. Church committees were skeptical. Contractors refused to bid on the job. Wright got it built.

He had a fairly successful period in Oak Park; has put up nearly two hundred buildings, some of them great ones known around the world. Immersed in work, he had become a stranger to his family. Probably he had, by then, grown far ahead of his child-love wife. Domestic troubles began. He wanted a divorce, was refused, went into exile abroad. Returning, he went back to his people in Wisconsin, built Taliesin in the ancestral valley for his second mate. They were never married. One night while he was in Chicago building Midway Gardens, a servant ran amok, hacked seven people to death, set fire to the place. This was "God's punishment," in the yellow press.

The living quarters had burned down. The work-

shop stood. That saved the architect and the man. He set to work, rebuilt. While he was still numb, emotionally, another woman came to him—the exotic Miriam Noel. They went to Japan, where he was to build the Imperial Hotel.

Again, the unbelievers. Wright planned to float the building on short pin piers reaching into the sixty feet of mud bed, to build it light and flexible, so that it would ride an earthquake. The government waived the rules and put the affair up to the owners should the building collapse. It stood, the only safe place in Tokyo, through the worst quake in history. Still the world would not let him go on building. The design of his private life, as unconventional as his architectural design, was just as firmly based on the necessity of principle. Only, the human materials were faultier than concrete and steel. He had received a divorce, at last, from his first wife, and married Miriam Noel. Then it appeared that Miriam Noel was psychopathic.

He was again in Taliesin when the second fire came. Once more the working half was saved. And while building Taliesin III, he was with his present wife, Olgivanna. There were years of the most fantastic persecutions aided by publicity and Miriam Noel. She had him arrested for the Mann act even after a divorce had apparently been granted; deportation of Olgivanna was attempted; there were lurid flights, nights in jail—and in the end, Miriam Noel sold him a final decree in return for the last scraps of his fortune and died.

Then Taliesin was taken by the bank. During all this time, what projects he had designed! The depression stopped most of the jobs. He pioneered air conditioning, metal furnishing and fireproofing in the Larkin building thirty years ago. Today he is pioneering a new heating system, eliminating radiators, letting heated floors distribute warmth evenly through the rooms of his new houses.

Meantime, the banks had found no one else could make use of Taliesin, so they called him back some years ago. Arrangement was made to "incorporate" Frank Lloyd Wright for $70,000. This corporation faded away about 1930. Then he started the fellowship in 1932.

Slowly commissions again began to trickle in. Among the many misapprehensions regarding Frank Lloyd Wright is the idea that his buildings are fabulous in cost. Yet here is the Herbert Jacobs house, built for a reporter in Madison, total cost, $5,500. Here are models for prefabricated houses, from $1,800 up. Frank Wright, apostle of individualism, designing prefabricated houses! He sees no contradiction. It is his job to individualize even such houses, and forty different combinations of these prefabricated sections are possible.

This prefabricated model is only one of the hundreds of inventive features in his Broadacre City, where every dwelling has at least an acre of ground, where auto roads are concave, low-lighted, center-drained where there are no poles, wires or ditches, where there is "no private ownership of public prop-erty, no public ownership of private property," where nine sectarian temples are built around a central temple of universal worship. Broadacre City may never be built. Yet, like many of Wright's unbuilt projects, it has already led to advances in housing and new ideas in city planning.

In Mill Run, Pennsylvania, he is completing a house over a waterfall for Mr. Edgar Kaufmann, who loved the tinkle and splash of the stream that ran through his woods. "Why not build your house over it?" the architect suggested. In Racine, Wisconsin, he is building both home and office for Herbert Johnson, the floor-wax magnate. It is in the office building that Wright has let himself go. A carport, with employees' sport courts on the roof, leads into the main structure. Rows of glass tubing band the windowless building, providing more light area than conventional sets of windows. Two huge ventilator stacks, Wright calls them nostrils, reach up like giant ship funnels, sucking air down into the conditioning plant and breathing it out again.

The vast main office is studded with slender, tapered columns. Here is Wright's latest invention, the source of his latest battle. Until now, this type of support has been regarded much as a plate balanced on a stick. There was a rule-of-thumb formula for measuring the stress—a simple right-angle stress. When Wright turned in his plans, the state building department was aghast. According to their computation his slender pillars could be allowed a safety load of only two tons. The estimated load was twelve tons.

Building permission was refused. So Frank Lloyd Wright offered to make a test. He set up a sample pillar and invited building department, cement company and all comers to observe. They began hauling sandbags and pig iron onto the table top of the pillar. Twelve tons—the estimated heaviest load for the building—were on. More bags and pig iron. Twenty tons, thirty—the afternoon was waning. Finally, sixty tons lay on the pillar; night had fallen, and anyway there was no room to pile on more. So they let it go at sixty tons. The only way they could crash the sample pillar was to tip it over.

Where was the secret? Had Frank Lloyd Wright violated mathematical fact? Architects, engineers began to study the pillar. The secret was in its curving expansion; the formula could no longer be a simple matter of right-angled stress, but of diagonal stresses, one against the other. It had simply taken the mind of a genius to make the leap; for in Wright's mind the whole thing existed as one element; he "knew" the combination of concrete and steel and curving shape.

An engineer comes to Taliesin, with another famous German architect. They marvel over Wright's new pillar. "Yes, you could figure it out mathematically," the engineer says. The engineer looks around the place, as does the designer, as does the visiting architect. "You know, I feel like I could stay here for a while and do some work."

ᵂ December, 1937.

Not really of the era, but very much in it,
The Great Profile brought something of the
Rabelaisian robustness of a lustier day to
the tense Depression and grim wartime period—
and gave even more than he got.

Why
Barrymore
Will
Marry
More

BY JOHN BARRYMORE

AT LAST INVENTORY, THE SUM TOTAL OF MY MARRIAGES
was four. All four have been dissolved, as every
newspaper reader who devotes some attention to
pages other than the comic section must know.

This may lead the casual observer to believe that
I am through with love, matrimony and its closely
related institution, alimony, with all of which I have
had more than a nodding acquaintance.

The casual observer and other interested persons
can now take time out to banish that thought. I may
have more annual rings than a redwood. I may not
be able to play Romeo without close co-operation
from both corset and girdle. But with my increasing
girth, I have lost none of my mirth.

But the point around which I am unintentionally
digressing is this: I am still not the cynic who believes love is a disease curable only by marriage.
Nay. Let cynics celibate in their cells or partake of
a hemlock cocktail. I shall continue to celebrate with
belles and partake of the cup of love—again and
again—and again.

Solomon, renowned for his sagacity, married many
times. So why not Barrymore? And I do not take
this stand for the sake of being able to notch my
belt with every "I do."

I have never married without being in love. Unfortunately, this thing called love cannot endure
like Gibraltar or the Rockies, as composers of popular ditties, inspired by a nagging wife or a sheaf of
bills, would have us believe. Unfortunately, I might
add, love does not enjoy my longevity.

Ever since the incident in Eden when Adam met
his Evil, laymen and philosophers have developed
acute insomnia in attempting to define the word

"love." Not entirely satisfied or dissatisfied with reducing it to what some may consider its lowest terms
in the definition—"a biological urge"—I am offering
a few definitions of my own which will probably
never be adopted by Mr. Webster.

At times I feel love is an intermittent—or, in
some cases—a continuous form of hypnosis. At this
moment I am inclined to subscribe to the feeling that
it is a form of insanity cured only by association.

Allow me to repeat for emphasis. I have never
married without being in love. I might go further
and admit that I have never wedded a single woman.
They have all wedded me. There is not room enough
here, of course, to recount the circumstances of each
marriage nor to reveal in each instance the weakness in my armor.

In my last joust with the fair sex which culmi-
nated in my marriage to Elaine Barrie in 1936, I
learned that a strong offense is the best defense. I
was recuperating in a New York hospital when
Elaine stormed the doors, supposedly on an interview assignment for the Hunter College newspaper.

I was in no condition to resist. But I held ground
temporarily. A week or so later, I fled like a thief
in the night. I fled west. But she came. She saw. She
conquered. It was at that time that I evolved this
little philosophical nugget: one must not flee *from*
the inevitable but *toward* it. We were married and
lived turbulently ever after—for five years.

Some time after a verbose press agent discovered
that I had a profile—and shared his discovery un-
selfishly with millions of readers—I was labeled the
world's greatest lover.

I did not consider him or other gentlemen of the
Fourth Estate who put my profile on paper for public
consumption Brutuses in the strict sense of the
word. It was they who helped women discover me.
And it was they who helped me discover that there
are far less pleasant annoyances.

And so, my profile was exalted to unheard-of
heights by the printed word and word of mouth. It
was exalted only to plunge to earth again years later
—to be dunked in cement at Grauman's Theatre for
posterity. But like truth crushed to earth, it rose
again—a slightly used profile, true, but nevertheless
a profile.

Great lover or nay, the women operated against
me. However, I have never developed delusions of
persecution because a fair damsel in Hoboken sent
to my theatre dressing rooms a carton containing a
rag, a bone and a hank of hair. I did not feel persecuted because a hotel detective, as a routine precaution, searched every corner of my bedchamber to
uncover old maids who might be lurking there.

I've always been plagued by writers and reporters
as to whether I am the world's greatest lover.

The question has even been propounded before
large public gatherings. It came up one night while
I was doing *My Dear Children* in Chicago.

It was a practice of mine to make comments to
latecomers to performances, comments that livened
up the show. A duchess of a lady, such as you see in

Esquire cartoons, came bouncing down the center aisle. I think I shouted, "Why in hell are *you* late?"

In one glance she penetrated my make-up, made the astute observation that I was no longer in my teens and answered to the delight of even deaf customers in the last row of the second balcony:

"Is this the world's greatest lover? Excuse me if I laugh!"

There was nothing left to do but arch my Mephistophelian eyebrows and ask pointedly—

"Madame, just when did I spend the night with you?"

To those who to this day are curious as to whether Barrymore is the world's greatest lover, I can only issue this formal statement: "That is something every woman must find out for herself."

For some unfathomable reason, I am regarded an authority on women and questioned constantly, to wit: Who are the five most beautiful women in the world? Would Venus de Milo suit me as a marital companion? How does one tame a shrew? Etcetera.

I cannot name the five most beautiful women in the world, but John Decker, my close colleague and one of America's foremost artists, can and does.

"They are Hedy Lamarr," he says.

Why anyone should wish Venus de Milo upon me as a hypothetical bride, I cannot say, but I shall go on record saying that while I would not be cad enough to make reference to her inability to embrace because of an arm shortage, I have often reflected that in her present form she would be far too cold to embrace.

In regard to how to tame a shrew, I cannot offer advice freely. Every man must learn for himself. Each shrew is an individual problem insoluble with mathematical formulae, but perhaps understanding and consideration may contribute in this taming process.

For instance, review the facts of a certain film director and a luscious bit of femininity who is his protégé and whom I know only from ogling distance. Neither the director nor the lassie hides the fact that they're smitten with love pangs.

Recently an extra girl on the movie set made the fatal error of accidentally bumping into our aforementioned lassie, who, in a rage, delivered a vicious kick to the proper kicking area of the extra girl.

Excitedly, the director rushed over. "Did you hurt your foot, dear?" he asked solicitously.

Such things do not serve to disillusion me about women. Women are a necessary and enjoyable evil. They are so necessary that I cannot offer even two reasons why I should be through, even temporarily, with love.

That, in brief, is why I, John Barrymore, sane of mind and sound of body, intend to search as if inspired for a fifth and final wife—a perfect mate! I don't care whether she be blind, deaf, or dumb—which she will probably have to be—so long as she has excellent manners—if you follow me.

♛ *July, 1941.*

The informal, get-things-done-and-to-hell-with-red-tape atmosphere of the New Deal's beginnings was carried to its highest point by the ebullient "Little Flower." The lethargy of the Depression could not withstand such energy, such warmth and such fearless impudence.

"I Remember Fiorello"

BY ERNEST CUNEO

WHEN I STARTED WORKING FOR FIORELLO LA GUARDIA, I was a law student awaiting admission to the Bar. Fiorello held an enviable position at the time: He controlled the balance of power in the Seventy-seventh Congress. His bewildering footwork was beyond the comprehension of President Hoover—and some of his pronouncements were a mystery to me.

Money meant absolutely nothing to him. "Do you know who the wealthiest man in the world is?" he asked me. "Gandhi. The only thing he owns is a sheet. And nobody would think of depriving him of it."

Fiorello had very little use for bookmakers because they battened on a human weakness. He had a scheme for ruining bookmaking once and for all: Everybody should bet. Those who won would insist on being paid off, and those who lost would refuse to pay up.

"That'd fix 'em," he said.

La Guardia sometimes patronized a modest upstairs speak-easy after a particularly hard day's work. He was a violent opponent of Prohibition and made no bones about it.

When he first invited me to accompany him, his words on entering were, "I'll have a license up on that mirror again in a year." This grumbled promise seemed to ease a slight twinge of conscience.

Before ordering, he said, "Ernest, what do you drink when you drink with your father?"

"My father doesn't drink."

"That settles it," he said. And to the bartender: "Give this boy a ginger ale, and me an Old Fashioned."

Though I very seldom drank, I told Fiorello heatedly that I often had a drink, and an Old Fashioned at that, and if it was all the same to him I'd have one right now.

He looked at me quizzically for a moment and apparently something in my rebellious face made him change his mind. He gave the bartender the slightest nod of acquiescence.

The drinks arrived. We drank in silence and I felt pretty good about things until he turned to me and said sternly, "Now, I'm going to have another one and you're *not*."

When we left, Fiorello said, "Good night, Ernest. And behave yourself, or I'll tell your father."

We laughed and parted.

In his public life, Fiorello never lost the common touch. As 1932 groaned in, with bread lines multiplying daily, many people came to his office for help. One cold winter night a big man in blue overalls appeared. He had walked down from Harlem to see Mr. La Guardia, he said, because his kids were freezing; the gas had been turned off and he needed a quarter.

At the mention of the cold kids, Fiorello's hand was on his wallet. But, abruptly, he started to give the man hell. He said that even if the kids were warm they would still be hungry. It was a strange performance. I think Fiorello had been torn inside by the story, and got mad so he would not cry.

He handed the man some bills and told him to get home fast. Then he suddenly asked if the gas company had given him any notice.

The man said no, none.

Fiorello took down his name and address and curtly motioned him out.

As soon as the man was gone, disregarding the lateness of the hour, Fiorello called the Public Service Commissioner in Albany. Miles of insulation must have peeled off the telephone wires from the blast that went over them.

Within an hour, an emergency crew turned on the man's gas and he telephoned to express in a heavy, inarticulate way, his gratitude.

Fiorello listened impatiently for a moment, then snapped: "Now make sure those kids get fed. If you can't . . . come and see me again." And he slammed down the receiver.

One afternoon a young man asked to see Congressman La Guardia, refusing to state his business or name or to speak with anyone else. He was still there, waiting, when the office closed.

As we went out the door, he dropped into step beside us. "Mr. La Guardia," he said solemnly as we walked, "a dog bit me."

"He did?" said Fiorello incredulously. "Did you get his name?"

"No," said the young man, "I didn't."

"Well," said Fiorello, "how can I do anything for you if you don't know the dog's name?"

"I guess you're right," the young man said soberly. "I should have gotten his name."

La Guardia nodded vigorously and the young man walked away deep in thought.

La Guardia's lifetime devotion to aviation began when he was counsel for an airplane company. Within a couple of years he had learned to fly. When World War I came he was appointed Commanding Officer of the U. S. Air Branch on the Italian-Austrian front.

After the war, he heatedly supported Billy

Mitchell's thesis that the air age was not only here to stay but that air power was the country's chief military weapon of offense and defense.

In 1925, he somehow contrived to appear before Mitchell's court-martialing board to deliver a fiery tirade. A senior general questioned the propriety of statements Fiorello had made to the press. "Are you quoted correctly in the newspapers, sir," he growled, "in calling me nothing but a beribboned dog robber?"

"No, sir," snapped Fiorello, glaring back. "I was not aware you had any ribbons."

At exactly midnight on January 1, 1934, Fiorello H. La Guardia took the oath of office as Mayor of New York City. At exactly one minute after midnight, he ordered the arrest of the most notorious gangster in town—Lucky Luciano. This jet-propelled momentum never let up during the next twelve years.

Girl laundry workers went on strike because they were badly underpaid and their working conditions were very poor. Fiorello became their vigorous champion. Under the guise of keeping order, he practically blockaded the laundries with squads of police.

The laundry owners came to City Hall to protest that he was interfering in a labor dispute, and that the city was supposed to be neutral. Fiorello heartily agreed. The labor-union leader tried to say something, but Fiorello told him to shut up.

The laundry owners then produced a written request that the city withdraw all support from either side. Almost instantly, Fiorello announced that the application was granted; the city henceforth would be absolutely neutral. Thereupon he picked up the telephone and blandly ordered the Water Commissioner to turn off the water in all laundries, since the city was neutral in the fight.

The laundry owners gave up on the spot.

As mayor, La Guardia insisted on City Hall support for honest cops. Early in his administration, a physician who was a casual personal acquaintance got a ticket for illegal parking. The doctor forcefully told the young patrolman that the ticket was unacceptable, whereupon the boy arrested him and brought him to the station house.

The physician reported this grievous act to Fiorello, who called the station house and asked to speak to the young patrolman. The captain of the precinct came on, all apologies, instead. He explained that the rookie just hadn't known any better.

Fiorello hit the ceiling. "He's a better cop than you are," he stormed, "and I called up to tell him I am sending him a box of cigars. He's the kind of cop I want—and you're not!"

The rookie got his cigars, delivered significantly by the mayor's car, and Fiorello very nearly broke the captain.

The mayor's office gave La Guardia plenty of opportunity to indulge his fondness for the spotlight. Conducting the combined Police and Sanitation departments' bands for a capacity Carnegie Hall audience was meat and drink to him.

Before this stupendous spectacle got under way, the stage manager asked Fiorello how he wanted the spotlights used. "Shall I play them on you as you come down the aisle, and follow you right up to the podium, Mr. Mayor?"

"Hell, no!" said Fiorello. "Just treat me like Toscanini!"

Colonel David "Mickey" Marcus, who served as Fiorello's Commissioner of Correction, discovered when World War II came along that he couldn't really get away from La Guardia anywhere. Mark Clark had just taken over Naples and Marcus was made military governor. He received a cablegram from Fiorello reading: "Reliably informed 150,000 women and children without shoes Naples area. Demand explanation."

Mickey cabled back: "We took over this city only twenty-four hours ago and we sure as hell didn't steal them."

He received this tart reply: "I want a good explanation, not a poor excuse."

As head of UNRRA, La Guardia's slapdash ebullience saved precious weeks and miles of red tape. In a critical situation, cotton was needed—a very substantial quantity of it. Peru, he was told, had cotton for sale.

Negotiations through the usual channels was too slow a procedure for Fiorello; he wanted the cotton at once. He got it, too—horse trading via long distance with the President of Peru, Manuel Pradoy Ugarteche. He threw diplomatic protocol out the window by beginning the conversation: "Hello, Manny. Listen—"

The last time I saw Fiorello was in Paris in the summer of 1946—a little over a year before he died. When I walked into his characteristically plain office at UNRRA, I didn't like the way he looked. I had often seen him tired, but some of the old resilience seemed to have gone.

On the surface, though, nothing had changed. He had heard how I had come to Paris, and before I could say hello he wanted to know where I got off grabbing an Army plane for myself, and who did I think I was, anyway?

We talked about his work with UNRRA, and the political scene back home. When I stood up to go, he paused at the door and said, "Do you know where you are?"

"Well, sure," I said, completely at sea.

"I'll tell you where you are. You are in Paris. In *Paris*," he growled, gripping my arm. "So you behave yourself, Ernest. Or I'll tell your father!"

♛ January, 1956.

The country was desperately ready to listen to any proposed solution to the Depression, and not all the proposers were honest. "Kingfish" Huey Long took Louisiana for a ride while he made hay, and though an assassin cut him down before our generation began, Long left his legacy of fear, false promise and acrimony for the future. **It Can't Happen Here,** Sinclair Lewis' novel read; Long's career proved that it almost did—as indicated by this story, written by a Federal official who pursued him relentlessly.

The End of the Kingfish

by Elmer L. Irey and William J. Slocum

HUEY LONG LIES BURIED BENEATH EIGHT FEET OF STEEL and concrete in front of the Louisiana State Capitol at Baton Rouge. Each day fresh flowers are set before the mausoleum. Thus Louisiana pays tribute to the memory of the greatest "confidence" man of our century.

Huey Pierce Long was a "con" man, just like any gold-brick peddler. A successful "con" operator must have the trust of his victims. Huey's victims, the people of Louisiana, loved him. Another absolute requirement is cruelty, because bankers won't buy gold bricks but widows will. Huey was extremely gifted in that direction. And, of course, the gift of gab is essential to any swindler. Huey's gab was the finest ever produced in a section of the country where political spellbinders grow like weeds.

Huey became a lawyer at twenty-one, after preparing for only eight months. Although he seldom practiced, his explanation was typical of his unusual frankness: "I studied law because I wanted to be a politician, and I came from the bar examination running for office."

At twenty-four, Huey ran for the job of Railroad Commissioner and won with the help of $500 loaned by a friend, O. K. Allen, whom Long later rewarded with the governorship of Louisiana. Huey's brother, Earl, neatly described Allen's talents as a governor when he said:

"A leaf once blew in the window of Allen's office and fell on his desk. He signed it."

In 1923, Huey reached the age of thirty and celebrated his birthday by announcing himself as a candidate for governor. He was beaten—but in 1928 he won, with the campaign slogan, "Every Man a King but No Man Wears a Crown," and a promise of free bridges, paved roads and free textbooks.

Huey promised these things, and he delivered them. He also promised that the people of Louisiana would not have to pay, since the "corporation high muckety-mucks" would bear the cost. But the people paid and paid. The "muckety-mucks" paid too, but they quickly learned that Huey reacted to arguments based on cash.

As governor, Huey ruthlessly fulfilled his political credo that "everybody who ain't with us is against us," and literally fired every officeholder or charwoman over whom he had control and replaced them with his own people. Huey floated a $30,000,000 bond issue for state improvements, and when cement companies naïvely suggested that they present bids to the Highway Department, he bellowed: "Hell, I am the Highway Department!"

He roamed the legislature floor during debate, giving orders to his "elected" underlings and freely admitting, "I deal with the legislature like a deck of cards."

The representatives of the people made one attempt to escape Huey's yoke. The lower house impeached Long on nineteen charges, including fixing state courts, bribing legislators, misappropriating funds, gross personal misconduct, blackmail and attempting to bribe a bodyguard to kill a state legislator. The house voted impeachment and turned the case over to the senate for trial.

But the senate was blocked by the "Famous Fifteen." The "Famous Fifteen" episode is the blackest mark ever chalked up against American democracy. It consisted of a "round robin" signed by fifteen senators, stating that they would not vote to convict Huey, no matter what was proven against him. A two-thirds vote was necessary, and the fifteen senators were enough to block it. Huey was not convicted, the "Famous Fifteen" reaped political and business plums and "The Kingfish" began to fulfill his early promise as a despot and thief.

All America was intrigued by this loud-mouthed dictator. I read of his exploits with unusual interest, because in 1930 and 1931 my mail was heavy with anonymous letters from Louisiana, stating that Huey Long and his crowd were stealing $100,000,000 and what was the Treasury Department going to do about it?

In July 1932, I asked Archie Burford, our Dallas agent-in-charge, to make a preliminary survey of the Louisiana situation. He and a few men poked around, and then Archie walked into my Washington office.

"Chief," he said, "Long and his gang are stealing everything in the state—and they're not paying."

Promptly, I sent Burford and thirty-two agents into Louisiana and things began to hum, both there and in Washington. Long was now a U.S. Senator, having left his governorship in the perfectly disciplined hands of O. K. Allen. Huey heard of our investigation and called on my boss, David Burnet, Commissioner of Internal Revenue. Dave listened as Long lectured him on the dangers of investigating U.S. Senators. But Burnet did not halt the probe.

Long then sent a message to me through a mutual acquaintance. "Huey told me," the friend said, "that you're in his 'S.O.B. Book.' "

That "book" was getting quite a reputation in Washington. Huey actually kept it, under the pointed title above, and if he put your name there, you were politically dead in Louisiana and in danger of a ruined career in Washington.

Long, a Democrat, was pressuring the Hoover Administration to call me off. When Hoover was defeated in the 1932 election, his Secretary of the Treasury, Ogden Mills, summoned me.

"Have you developed enough evidence to indict Long before March 4 (Roosevelt's Inauguration Day)?" he asked.

"No, Mr. Secretary. We haven't had enough time."

"Very well, then. Suspend your investigation and write a report of what you have done and what you propose doing for my successor. After all, the Senator is one of their (the Democrats') babies. Let them decide what to do."

The report was almost a year old when Henry Morgenthau, Jr., sent for me, and I met the man who was to be my "boss" for thirteen years.

When I walked into Morgenthau's office, the secretary was brusque. "Why have you stopped investigating Huey Long, Mr. Irey?" he asked.

I told him that I had been ordered to stop by Ogden Mills and to turn in a report. Now I was "awaiting instructions."

Morgenthau said, "You put Capone in jail, didn't you?"

I replied, "My unit did."

"Very well, then. Proceed with the investigation of Long as though he were John Doe. And let the chips fall where they may!"

Burford and I then laid down the strategy that we were confident would clean up Louisiana and a portion of the U.S. Senate. We were riding for an awful fall, but our optimism was based on solid grounds. We knew that Long and his gang had collected millions in graft, and we knew that taxes had not been paid.

We set up headquarters in the Masonic Building in New Orleans, guarding it day and night. Here we examined bank statements, forged and unforged checks, questioned contractors who had paid bribes and generally went about the laborious job of putting thieves in jail with comptometers. We had knocked off Capone's assistants before getting the big man himself, and thus would we work on Huey. And, as in the Capone affair, we wanted to infiltrate one of our operatives into the Long gang.

This meant a call for Pat O'Rourke, the agent we had planted in Capone's hotel. Pat was told to find out about Long's right-hand man, Seymour Weiss.

O'Rourke moved into Weiss's hotel, posing as a radio executive determined to supply New Orleans with a good radio station. He visited local stations, including one in Weiss's hotel, and soon met the proprietor himself.

O'Rourke grumbled to Weiss about his difficulties in getting an FCC license, and Weiss suggested that he talk it over with Monte Hart, who was right behind Weiss in the Long hierarchy. Hart had hardly shaken O'Rourke's hand when he said, "I can get that radio permit fixed up for $5,000."

O'Rourke begged off, but became friendly with Hart, and soon was sitting in on card games with Hart, Weiss and occasionally the Kingfish himself.

Meanwhile, we had learned that practically every contract let in Louisiana under Long's governorship had been graft-ridden. We had investigated 232 individuals, 42 partnerships and 122 corporations covering 1,007 tax years. We were ready to indict, and early in 1935 we started looking for a fearless and honest lawyer to do the indicting. He had to be a Southerner, for we knew we wouldn't have a chance if we brought a "damnyankee" lawyer down.

I told this to Morgenthau and he said, "Come with me. I want you to tell it to somebody else."

Soon I found myself explaining the Long situation to Franklin D. Roosevelt. When I had finished, he said, "Henry, see that Mr. Irey gets the type of lawyer he wants."

Ex-Governor Dan Moody of Texas was exactly the kind I wanted, but he was reluctant to leave his private practice. Then Morgenthau took Moody and me to see the President. F.D.R. poured on the charm, and the Texan agreed to go along with us.

On September 7, 1935, I sat with Burford and Moody in the latter's office at Austin, Texas, when Burford set before us the evidence on Long as a tax defaulter on vast sums in graft.

"We'll never convict Long before a Louisiana jury by simply proving he cheated on his tax," Moody warned. "Nor because Yankee contractors paid his gang graft. Still, we want a conviction."

Burford and Special Agent Tom Reese had dug up something that might do the job—the story of the "Win or Lose Corporation." The people of Louisiana loved Huey because he "made them big corporations pay through the nose." He made them pay, all right, but he took it for Huey Pierce Long, which made him a tool of the vested interests. If we could prove he was friendly with the oil and gas people, we might induce a Louisiana jury to do its reluctant duty.

"Win or Lose" was formed in 1934. Long owned thirty-one shares, for which he paid not a penny. Seymour Weiss had twenty-four free shares and Governor Allen twelve; and Long's current and former secretary were written in for a free share each. It all totaled one hundred shares and no investment. And the company had earned $347,937.50 in 1935.

"Win or Lose" owned twenty locations in gas fields near Monroe, Louisiana, acquired in a bookkeeping transaction. The state rights were acquired for nothing from Governor Allen. Now the corporation offered two gas companies these locations for $25,000 each. The companies said no.

Immediately following this rude "no," Allen announced that Louisiana was going to increase the taxes on natural gas. "Them corporations" thereupon offered $16,000 for each of the twenty locations; "Win or Lose" accepted the $320,000, and the plan to increase taxes was never heard of again. "Win or Lose" promptly declared a dividend of $2,000 a share, giving Huey $62,000 in loot. We thought that little tale would rob Huey of his stature as the poor man's friend.

"I will go before the Grand Jury next month and ask for an indictment against Long," Moody told us.

Then fate intervened. Next day, Huey Long and Dr. Carl Weiss (not to be confused with Seymour Weiss) were killed in the State Capitol. Weiss is generally believed to have assassinated Long. He had a .22 pistol in his hand when Long's bodyguards mowed him down. But Huey Long was killed by a single .45 caliber slug. And, as yet, nobody has explained this mystery away.

The death of Long, however, did not stop our plans. In 1937 a special group from the U.S. Board of Tax Appeals heard the government's civil suits against the Long gang. And every person whose case was "too weak" for Justice prosecution admitted guilt and paid every penny the Treasury claimed they owed, plus penalties. Seymour Weiss paid, the estate of O. K. Allen paid, even the Long estate paid. In all, we collected more than $2,000,000 in taxes and penalties. Thus we won a battle but lost the war.

We jailed Weiss, Governor Don Leche, the president of Louisiana State University and others of the Long gang. Besides cleaning up Louisiana politics and convicting 149 individuals, we brought the Treasury $6,372,360.24 in additional taxes and penalties. Yet I doubt if the whole investigation cost the American people more than $250,000.

The number of thieves we jailed and the millions of dollars we recovered are not, however, the important thing about the Long gang's downfall. I hope this story will destroy for all time one of the blackest libels ever made against our American system of democracy: the libel that, had not Dr. Weiss (or somebody) assassinated Huey Long, our country might have been taken over by the Kingfish as a dictator. In other words, that our system was no match for Huey's genius and ruthlessness.

But let me say this: the bullet that killed Huey did not save us from a dictator. It saved Huey from going to jail. Huey had broken the law and was about to be indicted for it when he was killed. We had the proof, and when we took the proof to court, the estate of Huey P. Long offered no defense and paid every penny we demanded.

Isn't all this conclusive proof that our system had worked perfectly?

♛ January, 1948.

HOLLYWOOD AND FATHER

The bored man at the Movie is Father.

He paid fifty cents to be distracted.

Father is Hollywood's chief problem.

He wants to get his mind off things.

They gave him platinum blondes, happy marriages, amusing children.

They tried Dickens—then Shakespeare.

It takes a lot of money to keep Father's mind off things.

—OTTO S. MAYER

"As beautiful as the Aurora Borealis," she was called in a time when Hollywood was a set designer's dream of heaven-in-Technicolor, and stars were demi-goddesses. To judge how Hollywood has changed, compare Garbo to the current crop of would-be temptresses in blue jeans. For those who can never put beauty out of mind, her special star still shines as brightly as ever.

Greta Garbo: Sphinx Without a Secret

BY HELEN WORDEN

GRETA GARBO WAS ONCE CALLED THE WORLD'S GREATEST movie actress. Thousands of adoring fans trailed her wherever she went. At the height of her career some fifteen years ago, five thousand men, women and children waited six hours on the Stockholm docks to catch a glimpse of her walking down the gangplank. When she finally appeared, the mob surged forward and one hundred people were shoved into the water.

Here and abroad, police were called out again and again to protect her. Never in Hollywood history had any star aroused such frenzied interest. There are hundreds of clippings about her in the New York Public Library, including endless raves from critics.

Said Alistair Cooke: "Garbo manages, because she is a supremely beautiful woman, to make beauty look like a mark of religion." Jack Hitt wrote: "Garbo is poetry, sunrise and great music."

Despite all this acclaim, Greta has been in seclusion for nearly eight years, using another name, dropping her eyes when she meets people and doing all she can to blot out the person that was the famous Garbo.

Meanwhile, her friends ask: Is Garbo still determined to turn her back on a world without the man she loved, or is she caught in a web of indecision which has been gripping her since the failure, in 1941, of the last film she made, *Two-Faced Woman?*

What evidence is there to support the former theory? Arnold Genthe, famous photographer, told me in 1942 that Maurice Stiller, the Swedish film director who discovered Garbo, was the only man she ever loved. "After Stiller died, she began shutting people out of her life," he said.

She was twenty-five when Stiller died in 1930 in Stockholm. All that she wanted so desperately—money, fame, possessions—became meaningless without him.

"After he died I could not sleep, eat or work," she said. "I wanted to go back to Sweden but they said to me, 'You must be faithful to us and your work.' I told them, 'You will have something dead on the screen.'"

However, if she loved Stiller so deeply, how can anyone explain her friendship with Rouben Mamoulian, her director; the romance in Hollywood with the late John Gilbert, her leading man; her deep admiration for Leopold Stokowski, the symphony conductor or the subsequent rumors of her engagement to Gayelord Hauser, the Manhattan diet expert?

The answer may be the one she gave friends who were puzzling over Isadora Duncan's life. Garbo, who had been sitting inarticulate in a corner, suddenly spoke. "Perhaps," she said quietly, "she was forgetting for a little while the pain of being a human being."

More recently, she may have been striving to forget the Garbo of the intervening years. This might explain her actions when I saw her recently in the lobby of the Ritz Tower, her New York City home. She glided mysteriously out of an elevator, her head averted, her eyes downcast. Wisps of ash-blond hair straggled from beneath a spooky hat. A worn tan raincoat flapped about her thin body. Her black rubbers were scuffed. Her brown bag was battered. She looked as if she didn't have a cent in the world.

Yet, from 1925 to 1941 she was among Hollywood's highest-paid stars and today is rated as one of America's richest women. As she turned into the Fifty-seventh Street corridor, she collided with a chow dog.

"I'm sorry," she apologized to its owner, then leaned over to pat the dog's head. "What a beautiful animal!"

"I'm glad you like my dog, Miss Garbo," said its owner.

Garbo shrank back into the shadows. "I'm not Miss Garbo, I'm Harriet Brown." The next moment she was gone.

At the Fifty-seventh Street entrance, a flock of high-school boys and girls waited with open autograph books. Greer Garson was also stopping at the hotel. Garbo drew up her coat collar, yanked down her hat and hurried off in the rain.

"Who's that?" asked a girl.

"That's Greta Garbo," said the doorman.

"Who's Garbo?"

Today, a whole generation is growing up which has neither seen nor heard of this woman whom Cecil Beaton, the noted English photographer, once described as "being as beautiful as the Aurora Borealis." Yet her obscurity today is no less remarkable than that with which she began life.

Greta Garbo was born on September 18, 1905, in a Stockholm tenement. Her parents were Sven and Louvisa Gustaffson, and she was named Anna. Her father, a mechanic, died when she was fourteen. Poverty drove her to work.

Her first job was mixing lather and washing towels in a barbershop. Her second was as a milliner's apprentice in a department store, where her big blue eyes, yellow curls and cameo profile won her a job as hat model for illustrations in the store's catalogue.

A Captain Ring, who was making a commercial movie of the shop, noted that Anna Gustaffson photographed well, so he gave her a part. The following year, Ring used her in a propaganda film for the Orient. Then, at seventeen, she landed her first professional movie role—as a bathing beauty in a comedy called *Peter the Tramp.*

Anna wanted dramatic training but couldn't afford it. Frans Enwall, private theatrical coach, arranged a tryout for a Royal Dramatic Academy scholarship. She won. In 1922 and 1923, she concentrated on voice culture, fencing, dancing and dramatics. During vacation she acted in real plays at the Royal Theatre and drew a real salary—$10 a week.

In 1923 she met Stiller. Later, she described that eventful encounter to a friend: "On a streetcar in Sweden I saw a man. He was like a mountain—colossal. He looked as though he belonged to some other race of men that did not walk with us. I thought of him often.

"One day he came to the Royal Dramatic School in search of someone to play the part in a book which had taken the Nobel Prize. He was one of the great screen directors of the world. He gave me the woman in *Gösta Berling* to do—without my ever having acted before.

"'Do you understand her?' he asked me. I answered, 'I understand.' And it was well with us from the beginning."

Stiller had brooding gray eyes, black hair touched by gray and stood over six feet. He was twice Anna's age and Europe's top director. Realizing her potentialities, he changed her name to Greta Garbo and began training her.

In *Gösta Berling*, she was an instantaneous success. At the *première* in Berlin, they appeared on the stage hand in hand, and from that moment onward romantic rumors surrounded them. It was stated, then denied, that they had been married in Constantinople. Actually no one knew.

Stiller was a better director than a businessman. His company failed in Constantinople. He was not rich. Meanwhile, Garbo had become his religion, his life: all his plans pivoted around her. She must go

to Hollywood. But without money, how could he accomplish this?

Louis B. Mayer of Metro-Goldwyn-Mayer, then traveling in Europe, saw the film *Gösta Berling*. He wired Stiller, offering a contract. Stiller accepted on one condition—Greta must go with him. Mayer vaguely recalled her as an unknown young actress in *Gösta Berling*. After all, who was Garbo?

"The greatest actress in all Europe!" said Stiller.

Mayer agreed to give Garbo a screen test, so Stiller borrowed $6,500 and sailed with Garbo for America in July 1925. After weeks of interviews and tests in New York, Garbo signed a $350-a-week contract with M-G-M and left for Hollywood with Stiller.

He had become her world, she his. But now he impressed upon her the fact that she must learn to stand alone and, deliberately, he began to withdraw from her life. She was given the feminine lead in *The Torrent*. Monta Bell, not Stiller, directed. She agreed to make a second picture, *The Temptress*, if Stiller would direct it. Instead, he took *Hotel Imperial* with Pola Negri.

Shortly after Stiller completed this film, he returned to Sweden without Garbo. Friends believed that, having launched Greta on a great career, he purposely withdrew. She was numb for weeks, speaking to no one, seeing few outside those working with her on *The Temptress*. Then Stiller died in far-off Stockholm.

"In all the world there is no place for me," she mourned to a friend. "Not in Sweden, where my mother is, nor here, where my work is. I look everywhere—everywhere—and I do not understand. I am thinking that perhaps the world is not for people like myself."

Then she remembered Stiller's words: "Your work is all you can be sure of."

Between 1925 and 1941, Garbo starred in twenty-five films. Her first two movies—*The Torrent* and *The Temptress*—completely sold her to the public. Then she did a series with John Gilbert—*Flesh and the Devil, Love, Woman of Affairs, Queen Christina* and *Anna Karenina*.

After *Anna Karenina* she went into a decline, then came up with *Ninotchka*, which proved her real talents as a comedienne. Her best personal performance was given in *Grand Hotel*, but to most observers *Anna Christie*, her first talkie, is still her finest picture. During those years of harvest, her salary was variously estimated at from $7,500 a week to $500,000 a year.

As she continued up the ladder, each of her screen lovers was reputed to be genuinely in love with her. Clark Gable, Charles Boyer, Melvyn Douglas, Robert Montgomery, Conrad Nagel, John Gilbert and Ramon Novarro were among those mentioned.

Her only real screen failure was *Two-Faced Woman*. Strictly speaking, it was not a failure, for it played to packed houses; but it was condemned by the Legion of Decency, scored by the *Catholic Review* and blasted by Cardinal Spellman.

It was her last movie. Little has been heard of her since. What is she like at forty-three?

The once-familiar disdain has been superseded by a tolerant grandeur. Specifically, this means a balancing of two features—a gentling of the eyes and a hardening of the mouth. When she landed in America, she was nineteen and plump. Today she weighs 130 pounds and wears size twelve dresses.

Greta worships the sun. She likes rooms that face the sun, terraces where she can lie nude in the sun, barefoot walks on Malibu Beach in the sun. She washes her own straight, shoulder-length hair and dries it in the sun.

Under Hauser's influence, she has become a vegetarian. Every day when she is in New York, fresh vegetables and fruits are delivered to her hotel apartment. In the afternoon, she drops in at Kubie's Health Shop on East Fifty-seventh Street for a swig of carrot juice.

They call her the recluse of Hollywood. But even the most consistent recluse must have go-betweens with the outside world. Garbo has three: Leland Hayward is her professional agent. The second is George Schlee, husband of Valentina, the dressmaker. The third is Frey Brown, an ex-resident of Reno and a friend of Hauser's, who has been identified as Garbo's real-estate and business agent.

Frequently she window-shops on Manhattan's Third Avenue with Brown. Her blond hair blows in the wind and she strides along like a boy as they flit in and out of secondhand stores. New York picture dealers describe her as a pedestrian art connoisseur. She goes from gallery to gallery—questioning, studying trends and analyzing old and new masters. She owns four Renoirs, one Soutine, a Modigliani and a Rouault.

Her taste in furniture is rococo—her favorite period at the moment being Louis XV and Italian eighteenth century. Pieces in these periods are constantly being shipped from New York to her California home, in care of "Miss Harriet Brown."

In 1943, she bought the Beverly Hills house of singer Gladys Swarthout. As Hollywood homes go it is simple—having neither swimming pool nor tennis court. Within its confines, Garbo seems content with her lonely life. Her only companion for the past six years has been a housekeeper. During the war she let her chauffeur go. She is her own gardener. Her closest friends are Salka Viertel, widow of a German movie director, Constance Collier, Clifton Webb, Ina Claire, Schlee, Hauser and Brown.

While she occasionally goes on a clothes-buying spree at Valentina's, paying as much as $395 for a plain street dress, she much prefers old corduroys and tweeds. She hates perfume, loves diamonds, adores fancy lingerie and never wears slips.

Greta has never been heard to say an unkind word about anyone, and those who have worked with her find her just. Once, she read and liked a script, but when she saw it in rehearsal changed her mind. Instead of letting M-G-M meet the bill, she paid all costs.

Garbo is independent yet prefers to have a man

about to make decisions. Always she takes a man along when she shops. When neither Brown, Hauser nor Schlee can accompany her, she invites one of her many acquaintances among the dealers. To them she is Harriet Brown. Yet wherever they go, people exclaim: "There is Garbo!"

The more she shuns publicity, the more she attracts it. Does she seek seclusion because she wants to live with her memories of Stiller, or because, as some insist, she has been uncertain about her career since criticisms of *Two-Faced Woman?*

Ina Claire subscribes to the latter theory. "Garbo says she wants to return to the movies, but I don't think she does. She is still a great actress, but she does not wish to be connected with another failure."

How does George Schlee explain Garbo? I found him at his wife's luxurious dressmaking establishment on East Sixty-seventh Street.

"Garbo is not the rosebuds-and-ribbon type," he said. "She is what she is—honest, direct, unassuming, terribly shy and passionately concerned with doing whatever she does to the best of her ability.

"She reminds me of Duse, whom I first saw in St. Petersburg. She had been in retirement eleven years and returned to greater triumphs than ever. This will happen to Garbo."

Greta's last dealings with the press were characteristically unsatisfactory. When she returned from Sweden in 1946, Schlee arranged an interview on the ship's deck. Her face was expressionless and she winced as photographers' flashlights blazed. After answering a few obvious questions, she edged nervously toward the gangplank.

Her actions recalled a previous interview, when she said: "I hate to be stared at. I know how the animals in the zoo feel when people poke them with little sticks."

Hollywood directors are notoriously afraid of her. Yet when Woody Van Dyke took over a film she was to appear in, he got up courage to call on her to discuss it. He expected to meet an imperious, haughty and difficult woman. To his amazement Garbo greeted him with, "Come on, Turp! Let's have a few takes."

Clarence Brown, the M-G-M director, probably had as much as anybody to do with Greta's success in America. When I asked him how the Garbo of today compared with the Garbo he directed in *Flesh and the Devil, Anna Christie* and *Anna Karenina,* he replied: "I see very little change. For me, she could play any age required for the part."

Howard Dietz, dramatist and head publicity man for M-G-M, gave me the final word on Greta Garbo. "A lot of people think her snobbish," he said. "But she isn't. It's only natural reticence. Garbo is no mystery. She makes me think of Oscar Wilde's line, 'A sphinx without a secret.'"

☙ July, 1949.

In the brown-skinned hemisphere, the teeming millions stirred and shook themselves awake from the sleep of centuries. Soon the undeveloped countries became a battleground for men's minds, as Communist and Western ideologies strove for domination. Suddenly, Americans were made aware of how truly important men such as Vinoba Bhave may someday become.

The Story of a Saint

BY A. M. ROSENTHAL

POCHEMPELLI LAY BAKING IN THE SUN OF SOUTH India on April 18, 1951. Like thousands of other villages in the Telengana district it was sick with hunger, angry with landlessness, ready for the Communists.

But that day in Pochempelli a saint was born— at the age of fifty-six—and the strangest economic movement of modern times began.

The movement was based on the simple idea that the peasant must have land, his own land, to live. And that those who had more than enough should, just because it was right, give to those who had none. Its essential ingredient was something unashamedly called "love."

Since that day, thousands of Indians have sat on the ground listening to a frail little man with a pale goatee, slipping spectacles and a faraway look. When he has finished his message they have signed over part of their precious land for him to give to others. What's more, thousands who have never even seen this man have sent him slips of paper, legal in the courts, stating: "I give to Vinoba this much of my land."

The man who started all this was Vinoba Bhave. Until he came to Pochempelli, he was not much more than another religious intellectual—part hermit, part sage.

He believed in goodness and nonviolence but he

lived remote from men. Though he had his disciples, his name meant little to others.

Today, Vinoba Bhave is known in every corner of India. In the villages—and India is a country of 500,000 villages—they call him Saint Vinoba. He has walked 10,000 miles preaching a simple message.

To the landed, he says: "You who have land, give to the landless. If you have five sons, make me your sixth and give me my share and I will give it to those who have no land."

To those who will receive it, he says:

"The receiver of the land will have to work it, improve it, wet it with his sweat before he can get his bread from it."

This sixth son of India has collected almost four million acres of land from the rich *and* from the poor. He has distributed about seventy thousand acres of it so far. The rest is being parceled out by dedicated followers who work for thirty rupees a month (about six dollars) or for nothing.

Vinoba has set a target of fifty million acres— one-sixth of the farmable land in this country where every foot of decent soil is guarded as a family's most precious heritage and where men will fight in the courts for years over ownership of yards.

This is his solution to one of India's biggest problems—finding land for the landless farmer—and millions believe it will work.

It all began in April of 1951 when Vinoba was walking through the Telengana to attend a conference of the followers of Gandhi, now three years dead. At the time, the Telengana, in the state of Hyderabad, was the center for Communist activity.

The Communists already ruled many of the villages. They ruled by terror and through the despair of the hungry famers, and the still greater despair of the wandering or rent-gouged landless. Untouchables, these latter used to be called, until Gandhi renamed them Harijans, children of God.

Everywhere Vinoba went, the villagers, who saw him a disciple of the great Gandhi, came to him. They told him that they were afraid of the Communists, true, but were beginning to think—why not communism?

Vinoba talked peace and work to them, nonviolence to the marauding Communist bands. But he had no real answers; he and the peasants and the Communists knew it.

On the eighteenth, he entered the village of Pochempelli, a place much like all the villages of India. He held a prayer meeting. In the group squatting before him were many Harijans.

"We have no land," said one of their leaders. "The government is not helping us. The Communists say they will give us land."

More in despair than out of any other motive, Vinoba said to the other villagers: "What will you do for the families of the Harijans?"

In the group was a man wealthy, by the standards of Telengana. His name was Ram Chandra and he belonged to the caste of the Reddis, not high-born but hard-working and powerful. Like everybody

else, he was worried about the Communists, and the fact that some landlords had thought it the best part of bravery to fall in with them.

That day, when Vinoba asked what was to be done for the landless Harijans, the answer came quite simply to Ram Chandra. Suddenly he was on his feet, offering his own land.

Vinoba looked at Ram, shook his head slightly and said he did not believe him. Ram Chandra asked for a scrap of paper. On it he wrote a sentence signing away one hundred acres.

Vinoba, a man who almost never displayed emotion, clapped his hands with joy. For in that moment of elation he had decided that what Ram Chandra would do, others would do, and that this would be the mission of his life.

"A man does not find it difficult to part with money," he said later, "but to give away land in charity is felt like sharing one's body with others."

That was the beginning of the Bhoodan—land gift—movement. For fifty days, Vinoba walked through the rest of Hyderabad, talking and thinking out the idea. And during that time twelve thousand acres were given to him.

The Communist threat to Hyderabad is now dead. Vinoba did not kill it himself. Indian troops, new legislation, abolition of some of the rent-collecting middlemen who had been riding the back of the peasants—all helped make Hyderabad a place where men could walk without fear. But few will deny that Bhoodan took the edge off the bitterness in the unhappy state.

After Hyderabad, the big men of the government in New Delhi acclaimed Bhoodan. Gifts came in from all over the country, from places where Bhave had never set foot.

There were attempts to tie up Bhoodan with a political party, with other organizations. But Bhave turned away from them and started walking again, through Bihar, into Bengal, into Orissa and Andhra.

Everywhere people waited for him and cried: "Victory to Saint Vinoba!" And everywhere Vinoba prayed and talked.

The man whom India is calling the new Gandhi was born on September 11, 1895, the son of a Brahmin family in Maharashtra in Western India. He was of the highest caste.

From his earliest years, Vinoba knew his way was the way of asceticism. At twelve, he took the vow of chastity. Like most Hindus, he is a vegetarian. A friend said of him: "He ate books."

When he was sixteen, Vinoba left his family to seek a life of study, self-denial and striving for understanding. While at the university in the Holy City of Benares, his road met the road of Gandhi.

For about twenty years, Vinoba studied and prayed and followed Gandhi. Once he asked for a year's leave of absence and spent it studying to train his mind and scavenging in the villages to train his soul.

In 1940, he was chosen by Gandhi to offer himself for arrest as a protest against British edicts barring public speeches and assemblies. He spent most of the next five years in jail.

After independence came to India, Vinoba took no part in the political life of the country. When Gandhi died by an assassin's bullets, many looked to Vinoba for a renewal of the spiritual light they felt had gone out of their lives. But others considered him only a pale reflection of the Mahatma.

Now, of course, millions speak of him as the new Gandhi, though it is a comparison that does not fit in all details. Gandhi, essentially, was a political leader. Vinoba, essentially, is a man of religion. Gandhi moved men to mass action, Vinoba moves them to individual action.

There probably never has been a national movement conducted with more simple discipline than Bhoodan. The leader and the men and women who follow him rise about 3:20 in the morning. Outside the village hut that Vinoba has been using for the night, his disciples gather for prayer. An hour later, without a word of command or direction, Vinoba sets off down the road. The disciples fall in behind.

For the first half hour or so, nobody approaches the leader. This is his time for silent thinking. (Every moment in Vinoba's day is rationed—a pocket watch is one of the few gadgets he carries.)

When the sun comes up, there is a pause for Vinoba's morning bowl of curds. Curds and milk, and once in a while some lemon juice, are all he eats. For a long time he refused any medicine, but now he takes malaria-suppressives. He has that unsaintly malady, ulcers, but generally his physical condition is good.

Along the road, peasants try to touch their foreheads to his sandals in the ancient Indian gesture of filial piety. He keeps walking until he comes to the village for the day, where a hut has been prepared for him, a shed made clean for his followers.

When evening brings some faint relief from the merciless sun, a portable public-address system is

set up—incongruously modern in a village where men live as they did a thousand years ago—and Vinoba sits under a tree and begins his meeting.

Not long ago, speaking of the meaning of Bhoodan, Vinoba told his listeners: "The life of India must be built on the villages. For centuries her people have let others, living far away in the cities, think and rule for them. Now, since independence, the power is theirs, but they must feel it and experience it themselves.

"Bhoodan is a step toward the realization of the independence of the village.

"You have to share your land with the landless in the village. You then have to start village and home industries and resolve that none of you will ever use cloth which is not produced in your village.

"Then, if there are five hundred people in the village, there will be one thousand hands and one thousand feet and five hundred brains. But there will be one heart."

In almost every village, land is given for Bhoodan. A maharajah gave 100,000 acres; a rival maharajah 100,001.

The poor give most. One peasant gave Vinoba one-fortieth of his lone acre. Vinoba accepted, but he deeded it back to the peasant and told him to give its produce to the poor.

Those who think Bhoodan is a lot of foolishness point out that about 30 per cent of the land given is bad land. Vinoba admits this. He says, however, that almost any land can be used for communal buildings or goat pasture, if not for farming.

The Communists, who dare not attack Bhoodan openly, try to undermine it as a reformist sop supported by the big landowners in an effort to save their necks from the rope of the peasants.

Economists, objecting to Vinoba's way, contend that to give all the landless in India land would require about eighty years and take two-fifths of the sown area of the country. Because of the swift increase in population, in 180 years there will be more than twice as many landless as there are today, so Bhoodan will be farther from its goal than when it started.

Figures in India, as in other countries, are what you make them. Vinoba says that India has 300,000,000 acres of cultivable land and 60,000,000 farm families. Split the land among the families and you get five acres to the family, which is more than what 60 per cent of the people have now. When the population goes up, new land will be found, land now undeveloped.

In New Delhi once, Vinoba mentioned some of the objections to Bhoodan and then turned away from them. It happened, he reminded his listeners, that Lord Vishnu, the Hindu Lord of Preservation, came to earth in the forms of the gods Rama and Krishna.

"Nobody can resolve all the world affairs," he said. "We had Rama and we had Krishna. They did what they could for the world. But there was no end to problems. One can only do one's work."

ꚍ January, 1956.

Sometimes one figure so bestrides his field as to become its very personification. Toscanini was the maestro; his white hair, burning eyes, romantic mustache the face of a conductor; his style the definitive interpretation. His refusal to play in fascist countries or with collaborationist musicians, and his memorable wartime performances of Beethoven blended into his music the chords of freedom.

The Many Sides of Toscanini

BY GLENN D. KITTLER

FOR ALL HIS EIGHTY-FIVE YEARS, THE LIFE OF Arturo Toscanini as been filled with music. He became a conductor at the age of nineteen, when without notice he substituted for a man who had so riled the audience that he was booed off the stage. Since then, Toscanini's career has always been at its zenith.

The simplest melody is sacred to him. This respect has instilled in him a reverent humility toward music. To transmit this feeling to his musicians, he has often gone to demonstrative extremes.

During one rehearsal, the orchestra seemed unable to capture the particular lilt that Toscanini wanted in a certain passage. After several repetitions, the maestro stopped the musicians and took out his handkerchief.

Surprised, the men watched him toss the handkerchief into the air, then closely studied its graceful glide to the floor.

"There," said Toscanini. "Now, let us play this passage as beautifully as that."

On a similar occasion, he told the orchestra: "You don't get to heaven staccato. You float!"

Yet, when the musical instructions specify *fortissimo*, he demands that, too. At the height of a Beethoven crescendo, Toscanini startled his audience by shouting at the orchestra: "Explode!"

Again, during a rehearsal, he stopped his musicians after they had finished a short, violent passage of a symphony.

"Try it again," he instructed. This time, the men feverishly bore down on their instruments, until the music was like thunder. Then once again Toscanini stopped them.

"So you can play stronger!" he shouted. "Why didn't you play it that way the first time? Were you asleep?"

Then he began to beat his chest. "Look at me," he said. "I am an old man, but I give music my all—everything I have. You are all stupid! You are idiots! You have no feeling for music."

On that, he stamped out of the rehearsal hall, leaving behind a room of stunned musicians. Startled, the men kept their seats. He returned in a few moments, and—typical of his inability to sustain annoyance—he was calm and gentle, as if nothing had ever happened.

Guest soloists are frequently victims of the demands that Toscanini makes of his orchestra.

Once, a famous soprano insisted on arguing with him over the interpretation of her aria. When he remained adamant, she said, "We will do it my way. After all, I am the star!"

Toscanini glared at her. "Madame," he said, "the stars are in heaven. Here, we are all artists—good or bad. And you are a bad artist!"

With a heavyweight contralto who could not take his direction, he pointed to her head, saying: "If you had as much here as you have here"—he pointed to her bosom—"you would be a great singer."

Evidence of Toscanini's quest for perfection in music occurred one night in his New York home. With friends, he was listening to a recording made of a symphony he conducted. Suddenly he rushed across the room and turned off the machine.

"At this point," he declared vehemently, "I was betrayed!"

Despite his long career, Toscanini considers himself still a student. Though he knows most symphonies by memory, he approaches each as if it were a new composition, searching through it for a new expression he might have missed before, then changing his own interpretation upon discovering it.

After such an occasion, an old friend commented to the maestro that he seemed to conduct the last movement of a symphony faster than he had several years ago.

"Yes, I know," said Toscanini, "but I was stupid then."

Furthermore, he is the first to admit—and be miserably depressed—when his performance is the least bit inferior. After a New York concert that displeased him, some friends tried to console him by assuring that his reaction was wrong.

"So you think I don't know music!" he bellowed. "The trouble with you is that you have all been poisoned by me!"

This sensitivity to his work has made Toscanini respected and loved by his musicians. Aware of his devotion to music, they admire his painstaking efforts to achieve perfection for them and himself. Thus, apologizing to a musician he had berated, Toscanini admitted, "I have a bad character."

"No, Maestro," said the man. "Just a bad temper, sometimes."

One morning during a South American tour, the orchestra prepared itself for further evidence of that bad temper.

Weary from the constant traveling, the men groaned their complaints when they were called early from their beds.

"Why this rehearsal, Maestro?" they asked Toscanini as they took their places on stage. "Yesterday, you promised us the morning off."

"This is not a rehearsal," said Toscanini mildly. "It is a concert."

Surprised, the men glanced at their music and recognized the score of *The Star-Spangled Banner*. Toscanini poised his baton and the curtain rose.

"For America," whispered Toscanini. And the orchestra played with an inspired vigor. When they finished, they heard the applause of one person. Startled, the musicians looked at the lone man sitting in the vast theatre. Suddenly they understood. The special concert was played for a man who, like themselves, was a long way from home on this morning of Independence Day.

He was the United States Minister to Uruguay. Toscanini turned to him and bowed to his appreciative applause.

Toscanini has long been a towering obelisk against political oppression. For this reason, he has refused all invitations to conduct in Russia, nor would he perform in Germany or Italy during the Hitler-Mussolini era.

He rejected the friendship of musicians who played for the dictators, and he would not conduct abroad until all those with whom he worked were cleared of any hints of collaboration.

His reasons for this were expressed when, during a rehearsal of Beethoven's *Ninth Symphony*, he stopped the orchestra and frowned at the soloist.

"Do you know what you are singing about?" the maestro asked. The singer was puzzled. Toscanini walked to him, and pointing his baton, said: "You are singing about brotherhood, but your facial expression looks like you hate everybody. That will show in your music."

♔ September, 1952.

Coarsely scratching his belly, or mumbling
in search of the right word, actor Marlon Brando
personifies the new school of "Method"
acting that came into vogue during the postwar
era. Like the postwar generation which he
in many ways reflects, his introspection, his
brooding irreverences and his affected crudities
never really succeeded in disguising the
underlying qualities of the character—in
Brando's case, a special and gifted talent.

The
Many
Moods
of
Marlon
Brando

WHETHER HE'S CLOWNING IN APOLOGY FOR SCRAMBLING
his lines (left), or rotating his torso in "limbering-
up" exercises (right), "Method" actor Marlon Brando
is a volatile, impulsive personality—figuratively
thumbing his nose at convention. In 1959, while
filming the motion picture *One-Eyed Jacks*, which
he directed and starred in, Brando ran the gamut of
his explosively different moods. He indulged in wild
water-pistol fights with his young co-star, Pina
Pellicer. He slipped back into boyhood during lunch-
hour breaks, tossing a football—although his right
arm occasionally slips out of its socket due to an
old injury. And, when work stopped, he displayed a
remarkable ability to turn off his emotional valves
and, childlike, fell into a quiet cat nap, using a broom
to shield his eyes from the sun. The movie was shot
on location in Monterey and Death Valley, California.
In addition to his duties as director and star, Marlon
also labored as producer and part-time script writer.
Shooting continued for six months, because of his
insistence on careful characterization, and the budget
soared past $4,500,000, but Brando shrugged this
off. He often used mood music—the folk ballad
"Shenandoah," for example—and urged his actors to
improvise action and dialogue, hoping that spon-
taneity would intensify each scene's emotional impact. "The only tool an actor has is his feelings,"
Brando explained quietly. "An actor's brain is sometimes his arch-enemy!"
♕ October, 1959.

The war years did something even to those who were too young to fight. This "shook-up" generation, bubbling with rebellion, fascinated by violence, speed, raw sensations, took as its symbol a wild one who reflected its restless mood. Psychologists sought clues to adolescent behavior in their weird worship of a dead boy's memory.

The Strange James Dean Death Cult

BY HERBERT MITGANG

AS DUSK FELL ON SEPTEMBER 30, 1955, A LOW-SLUNG silver Porsche Spyder sports car, a large 130 painted on its side, was roaring along Highway 466 near Paso Robles, California. At the wheel of this $7,000 worth of gleaming metal and super-charged motor was James Dean, twenty-four, actor; beside him, Rolf Weutherich, German auto mechanic. They were headed for the races at Salinas.

At the intersection of Highway 41, a car driven by Donald Turnupseed, a college student, made a left turn and the two vehicles met head-on. The student and the mechanic survived. The actor, who owned the racing car, died on the way to a hospital in Paso Robles.

The State Highway Patrol, which had ticketed Dean for speeding near Bakersfield less than two hours before the crash, made the startling revelation that he must have driven his car all the way at an average speed of nearly seventy-five miles an hour.

And with that, the James Dean legend began.

Strange things have happened since the day this talented young actor lost his life. The number of his fans and the steady requests for photographs and other Dean memorabilia have gone far beyond normal expectations; the pictures in which he appeared are today considered hot properties; and he is idolized by thousands of teenagers.

This fall, what is supposed to be his greatest movie achievement, portraying the character Jett Rink, Texas oil tycoon, in Edna Ferber's *Giant*, will be released. And Warner Brothers, Dean's home studio, will not be too surprised if he receives the first posthumous Academy Award for acting.

These are credible things. But the fantastic climax of the Dean legend is the oft-repeated rumor, perpetuated by movie columnists, which calls for the resurrection of James Dean himself, in person, alive. According to this weird story, first given currency in a gossip column, when Dean crashed, his face was badly mutilated. Since then, he has been in hiding, undergoing facial repairs. Someone else supposedly was buried in his place.

The living Dean was complex enough without any such embellishments. To some, he seemed a less mumbling imitation of Marlon Brando—an honor graduate of the black leather jacket and motorcycle jackboots school of acting and living it up. To others, he was a lovable, albeit moody, young man who liked animals, his profession and young people. To those who judged him by his films and television appearances, he was the rebel without a cause, the misunderstood delinquent—but, in any case, an actor of talent.

The facts of his brief life perhaps cast light on his strange afterlife.

James Byron Dean was born in Marion, Indiana, on February 8, 1931. His father was a dental technician at a Veterans Administration Hospital. When his mother died in 1940, Jimmy was sent back to Fairmount, Indiana, to live on a farm with his aunt and uncle.

All through his high-school days he was respected as an athlete and character actor in a dramatic society. He left Indiana after high school to live with his father in Los Angeles.

There, Dean first enrolled at Santa Monica Junior College as a physical-education major, also participating in dramatics and announcing on the school's FM station. "Just for the hell of it," he said, "I signed up for a prelaw course at the University of California in Los Angeles." But he was kicked out of a fraternity for "busting a couple of guys in the nose," and this ended his brief college career.

Physically, Dean was of medium height and on the slim side. He had poor vision and usually looked in need of a barber.

Encouraged by actor James Whitmore, he obtained bit parts in a Hollywood television play and in two films, then with a few hundred dollars in his pockets embarked for Broadway by bus. There he got a few small parts on TV and patrolled the streets of midtown Manhattan West in the uniform of the day for the young actor: suntans, white sneakers, polo shirt and sports jacket, plus the hungry look. Aloneness and a resonant voice were the hallmarks of Jimmy and his friends.

When Dean went broke, he learned that the owner of a sloop had theatrical connections, and applied for the job of a sailor. This calculated

scheming—so unlike the simple farm boy he has been pictured—paid off. Dean was interviewed for a part in *See the Jaguar*, which opened on Broadway in December 1952. Although the play closed after a week, he had been noticed. A year later he was in a second Broadway play, *The Immoralist*, in the role of an unpleasant, blackmailing Arab boy.

Of his acting skill, there was no question. He won Broadway's Donaldson and Perry Awards as the most promising young actor. Then Warner Brothers gave him a screen test for *East of Eden* and he was on his way to stardom. His reputation was enhanced by his second picture, *Rebel Without a Cause*.

It was more for Dean's peculiar behavior than his one Broadway success that he is remembered in New York, where he seemed well on the way to becoming a character. Or an adolescent, depending on how one looked at his self-centered behavior.

"Jimmy was beautifully nuts," says a photographer friend of his. "He could make you dislike him and like him at the same sitting."

A young actress, fascinated by his antics, recalls, "He would do anything to attract attention. Yet he could be kind and attentive, if he was in the mood, or he could be sullen and enraged."

A veteran actress who worked with him took a less sympathetic view of Dean's antics. "He was thoroughly unprofessional and unreliable—a selfish little boy," she says. She admits that she disliked him but respected his acting ability.

Perhaps this attitude toward life which brought Dean mixed notices as a person and personality was best explained by Jimmy himself once: "Acting is to me the most logical way for people's neuroses to manifest themselves. Actors act so that they may express the fantasies in which they have involved themselves. The problem for this cat is not to get lost."

In Hollywood, Henry Ginsberg, co-producer of *Giant*, said of Dean: "In sixteen months of film acting he left a more lasting impression on the public than many stars do in thirty years. Jimmy was a perfectionist in everything he attempted. His manner of approach to the role of Jett Rink is an example. Jimmy learned to rope cattle, ride horseback and play a guitar. He didn't have to do any of these in the picture. Yet he felt he could obtain a deeper understanding this way."

The startling aspect of the Dean story is not so much the life as the afterlife. Even the professionals in the industry are surprised. Occasionally, some personality comes along whose proportions are so magnificent or whose magnetism is so compelling that he becomes the object of posthumous worship. Exactly thirty years ago, this happened with a man named Rudolph Valentino, the old sheik. It is happening again with Dean.

"A curious case of juvenile frustration, sex-substitution and hero-worship running like electrical lines into a centrally convenient fusebox" is the way a New York psychologist sums up the Dean phenomenon.

To most Dean cultists, it really doesn't matter by this time whether Dean is around. Indeed, many of his "new" fans do not know that he died in an accident while challenging the speed laws. People see his movies and conceive of him as alive.

His studio reports that he gets more fan mail and requests for photographs than such stalwarts as James Stewart, John Wayne and Spencer Tracy. At the time of his death he received a few hundred letters monthly; today they arrive at the rate of five thousand. The letters themselves attain rare levels of intimacy and desire.

A television program that ran a tribute to Dean received this letter from a club formed in his honor: "Everyone who joins the club is so happy. They write the club to tell how good it makes them feel inside, how it brings inner peace. We can't accomplish anything by it but his faith is spreading. It is just wonderful meeting people who love Jimmy so much and want to keep him alive in their hearts always."

There are other evidences of this strange afterlife. A souvenir shop in New York exhibits amateurish oil paintings of Dean that sell for from $40 to $200 apiece. Another store bills a long, wicked-looking knife as "The James Dean Special." On the West Coast, a couple bought the wreck of Dean's car and put it on display at fifty-cents admission.

Besides these macabre touches, there are serious efforts to perpetuate the Dean memory and legend. Pilgrimages are made to Fairmount, where the actor is buried. At the funeral, six hundred people crowded the Quaker Friends Church while three thousand stood outside.

On the thirtieth of each month, the day he crashed, flowers are put on his grave, anonymously. On his posthumous twenty-fifth birthday, forty baskets and bouquets were found there.

All this naturally leads to the question: What is the special appeal of this darkling youth whose star fell in a crashing twilight? To discover the answer, one must listen not so much to colleagues as to ordinary fans. For it is among them that the Dean of fact and fancy still lives.

Hear, then, the sixteen-year-old president of a James Dean fan club with nearly two hundred members ranging in age from fourteen to seventy. She is a high school student, and listening to her pleasing voice with its surprising levels of sensitivity, one learns about Dean's appeal—and the public to whom he appeals:

"I started out following Jimmy's career when I was fourteen—I was only a kid then. My girl friend and I would come to New York to see the TV stars. We'd go to the Cromwell Drugstore in the RCA Building where the actors would be sitting before the shows. We'd go up and get their autographs. My girl friend and I noticed Jimmy. He looked so nice. He was so sweet. He smiled at us. I never thought of him as a grownup, more as a friend, like us, but a boy. *He would talk to us even though we weren't anybody.*

"Oh, the disgusting things they've said about him.

That he was rude. But he was sweet and gentle. He was natural. I went to see all his pictures about twenty times.

"I don't like to talk about his accident. My girl friends and I were planning to come to see him when he came to New York. We wanted to see if he would recognize us because we were kids then, but we're big now. This other girl friend of mine, she can't speak a month after the accident, she can't concentrate in school. There's this other girl friend who hasn't done anything, and hardly eats or sleeps since Jimmy died. She dates an older man.

"Jimmy dated a lot of girls but he wasn't serious about any of them. Except Pierre Ann-jelly (Pier Angeli). She jilted Jimmy. I hate her. A girl friend of mine found out where she was staying in New York. My girl friend tripped her in the lobby for what she did to Jimmy.

"A lot of boys I know don't like Jimmy. But they respect him. He's so different from the boys in high school. He did what he wanted to do. *If he didn't want to do something, he didn't.* Nobody bossed him. At all those Hollywood parties, he didn't dress up. Nobody told him what to wear.

"I hate all boys compared to Jimmy. I keep looking for him in other boys. He was intelligent and smart. He spoke so softly. I don't know, he was just perfect, like in his pictures. He wasn't too tall or too short. He didn't talk like a hep cat. When you were with Jimmy you knew he was listening to you when you spoke. He was conscious you were there.

"I don't like to talk about the accident. I don't think he was going as fast as the papers say. Maybe he wasn't the one who was driving, I heard it was someone who was with him.

"Is Jimmy still alive? I've heard that, but I don't think so. I don't think he would want to make so many girls suffer as much as we still do pining for him."

♕ November, 1956.

Babies, babies, babies. That was the postwar's most significant product. And while the stork grew groggy, **Baby and Child Care** staked out a permanent lease on the best-seller lists of all time. As mobile America separated young wives from their mothers, the do-it-yourself baby book became another kind of a family bible.

The Uncommonly Sensible Dr. Spock

BY CALVIN KYTLE

DR. BENJAMIN SPOCK IS PROBABLY THE MOST FREquently consulted authority in America today, bar none. At last count his *Baby and Child Care*—sometimes known as the "Gospel according to Spock"—has been the nursery companion to more than eight million American mothers. New and prospective parents have been buying the thirty-five-cent paperback edition at the rate of nearly one million copies a year.

Since last October, moreover, the personality that

came through so engagingly in print has been confirmed and amplified by TV. His informal talks with mothers, on subjects they choose, are a Sunday afternoon feature on fifty-two NBC stations.

All told, it is reliably estimated that nowadays one out of every four American babies is being brought up by Spock-doting parents. His unrestrained admirers say that he has already been of greater influence on the future than Einstein.

Spock himself is always worried by such extreme statements, as he is by almost any effort which tends to set him up as *the* authority.

"Too many parents think it's only professional people who know the answers about everyday management of children," he says. "I want the mothers who look at us to identify themselves with the mothers on the show. I want them to understand that there can be a lot of different and satisfactory ways of dealing with the same problems, to understand that parents find their own solutions."

The TV program, sponsored by one of the largest manufacturers of baby-food products, is strictly extracurricular with Spock. Full-time, he is professor of child development at Western Reserve University in Cleveland.

His office at the medical center is an old white frame house distinguished by a sign on the porch reading CHILD THERAPY. He works in a room as neat, plain and nonclinical as he is. Near his desk stands an old-style floor lamp with a dime-store shade, a kitchen table holding a telephone and several tidy stacks of papers. There are no pictures of babies, his or anybody else's.

Spock, at fifty-three, is not quite old enough to look the part of the reassuring elder that so many young parents have cast him in. He dresses his trim, six-foot-four-inch frame conservatively. His graying hair is short, and thinning, his eyes bright and friendly behind dark-rimmed glasses.

He talks earnestly, yet in a tone of quiet good humor, smiling and occasionally breaking into a guffaw, like a man dedicated to his work but refusing to take himself too seriously. He emphasizes his points with a movement of his remarkably mobile brow, a sweep of his large hands, a shrug of his enormous shoulders.

"I wrote my book at a time when pediatrics generally was still bound by the doctrine of extreme regularity," he explains. "All the way through the book I was consciously pleading against things like too rigid feeding and too forceful toilet training. Now I find that some uncertain parents are interpreting me as an advocate of extreme permissiveness. So in the revisions I'm making in the book, I'm having to emphasize the limits of permissiveness.

"Actually, it's the spirit that counts. Strict discipline's no good when it's merely a way for the parent to work out his own harshness. Neither is permissiveness when it's only a reflection of the parent's uncertainty. But when administered with love and good sense, both methods can produce nice people."

Spock's own parents belonged to the strict-but-loving school. His father was a conservative, well-to-do New Haven lawyer, his mother a forceful, independent New Englander who took her responsibilities to heart.

"I was the oldest of six children," Spock says, grinning as at some private recollection. "Mother gave herself completely to us. Wouldn't have a nurse and allowed herself no frivolities. She waited until the last of us was in his teens before she took up bridge. She was afraid it might take her away from her duties.

"It was sometimes my job to feed bottles and change diapers. Like the first child in any big family, I loved playing parent. I grew up taking it for granted that kids were very important."

Young Spock attended a country day school in New Haven, then prep school at Andover. He was a long-legged gangling adolescent whose quick growth made him self-conscious. But self-confidence came when he made the track team. At Yale he was something of a campus hero—a member of Scroll and Key and an oarsman on the crew that swept the 1924 Olympics.

For several summers he had been a counselor at a camp maintained by the Newington Crippled Children's Home. Impressed by the work of the orthopedic surgeons on the staff, he decided to take some pre-med courses, "just in case." He entered Yale Medical School still wondering if he were not better suited for architecture.

Two years later he married Jane Cheney, of the famous silk family, and transferred to Columbia's

College of Physicians and Surgeons. He was graduated, at the top of his class, in 1929. Completing his medical internship in 1931, Dr. Spock became a resident in pediatrics at the New York Nursery and Child's Hospital. There he became increasingly aware of the need to understand children's emotional problems. That led to a residency in psychiatry at New York Hospital.

In 1933, he began private practice in Manhattan. For two years, he barely paid the rent.

"My first years of practice were complicated by my psychiatric training," he admits. "My head was full of theoretical causes and almost empty of practical advice.

"My psychiatric training, for example, taught me that a child's resentment could often be traced back to his having been weaned too early or toilet-trained too drastically. But it hadn't taught me what was the right age or the right method. I had to learn that for myself.

"It was six to eight years before I knew enough so that I could relax. And, like a new mother, I had to relax before I could do my job well."

But parents and children had learned to love him long before that. To mothers he seemed refreshingly like the old-fashioned family doctor. To their children he didn't seem like a doctor at all. He never wore a white coat, and usually made visits seem like fun. In time, he achieved a flourishing practice, mainly because he felt it was as important to relieve the mother's anxieties as it was to treat the child.

"Have fun with your children," he told them. "Don't feel guilty. You're doing the best you can. No parent is going to do a perfect job—and it isn't necessary." Most mothers left his office confident that they were doing all right in the world's most important job.

By 1943, Spock figured he was ready to write a book. In his own words he's a "natural do-gooder," and by then he thought he had learned enough to be helpful.

The book *Baby and Child Care* occupied him almost every night for the next three years. (Before the book was finished he was a lieutenant commander in the Navy, a psychiatrist in charge of severe disciplinary cases.)

It came out in 1946, a time when parents were younger than ever before, larger in number, and most of them far from home. Bewildered by the conflicting child-care advice they were getting, harried mothers picked up the Spock book and read:

"It may surprise you to hear that the more people have studied different methods of bringing up children, the more they have come to the conclusion that what good mothers and fathers instinctively feel like doing for their babies is usually best after all."

Spock was their man.

Today, besides carrying a full teaching load, Dr. Spock spends the equivalent of one day a week preparing for and filming his TV program. He writes a monthly magazine column and works on the re-

vised edition of his famous book.

On weekends and vacations, he still finds time to go sailing, fishing and swimming with Mrs. Spock and John, eleven. His older son, Michael, twenty-two, is married and a student at Antioch College.

Spock sometimes refers to mistakes he's made with his own children—an admission that some people find surprising. "That's all right," he explains. "Parents should be reminded that bringing up children is more a matter of feelings than knowledge.

"On this point, I think, if anything, that the kind of academic education we get *un*suits us for parenthood. Instead of learning about life by doing and feeling, students learn special subjects through words. If they don't learn the words, they flunk. Later, when they have babies—without technical training *or* experience—they tremble for fear they'll flunk."

It's this exaggerated respect for intellectual concepts, he believes that thirty years ago, when behaviorism was in vogue, kept some parents from cuddling their babies; and today, in the name of permissiveness, is causing others to cuddle them all evening when they should be asleep.

Fortunately, the excesses of theory have always been modified by stabilizing currents, Spock feels.

"The first is love," he says. "Good parental love will take care of nine-tenths of the problems. I don't mean love in the sense of undiluted adoration, but the kind that includes control, that can say both yes and no.

"The second is the child's own natural desire to conform. Until this century, the dominant theory was that the child was a barbarian who had to be forced to become civilized. Children, however, paid very little attention to this theory. They just kept right on trying to be grown-up anyway.

"And, third, no matter how much theory they may profess, in the dozens of minor crises every day, parents find themselves dealing with their children the way *they* were dealt with as children.

"This is a difficult century. Essentially, the job parents have on their hands is to develop stable individuals in an unstable world—to prepare children emotionally for the demands of a free and increasingly complicated society. Although I suppose the bring-'em-up-rough-for-a-rough-world school still finds it hard to believe, it was the men who'd lived in loving, stable families who made the best sailors and soldiers during the war."

He smiles. "We're in for a period of consolidation, I hope. We're beginning to settle down now and fit together the best of all our theories and experiences. At least most of us seem to have found there's a happy medium between adapting to the baby's individual needs and to maintaining a sensible control over him.

"Psychological theory and experience both teach that it's impossible to write something that means the same thing to everybody. But I go on thinking, *'This* time I'm going to say it so that everybody will understand.'"

◈ July, 1956.

Of all the entertainment figures who sparkled
during the generation, none was so many-faceted
as Charlie Chaplin. Almost alone he was
the clown of the era. Because tragedy feeds the
root of comedy he made us sharply aware of
tragedy in our time. In his own life as in
his work there was the blending of both.

Charles
Chaplin:
Clown
Without
a
Country

Al Jolson   Ronald Colman   Douglas Fairbanks   Joseph M. Schenck   Samuel Goldwyn
     Mary Pickford   Gloria Swanson   Charles Chaplin   Eddie Cantor

CHARLES CHAPLIN'S FATE HAS BEEN TINGED WITH DARK laughter. Almost everyone who ever worked with Chaplin calls him a genius. Mack Sennett, who discovered Chaplin playing in vaudeville in 1912, once said: "He's the greatest actor who ever lived." With a flick of his cane, a flirt of his coattails, a quick shuffle of his tiny feet—encased in oversized tramp's shoes—Charlie could steal a scene from any comedian.

But his political views have made Chaplin a paradox. In *The Great Dictator* (1940) he savagely lampooned the dictator Hitler. Yet in 1954 he played affable host to Red Chinese tyrant Chou En-lai. (However, when the Chinese offered him only $5,000 for Far Eastern rights to his old silent films, Charlie cracked, "What do you boys take me for, a Communist?") Chaplin calls himself an "anarchist"— and is certainly an individualist and a capitalist, with reputed assets of $20,000,000.

Women have also brought Chaplin woe. As the little tramp, Charlie rarely got the girl. Off the set, it's been a different story. He has been married to and divorced from three leading ladies—Mildred Harris, Lita Grey and Paulette Goddard. He also was successfully sued by Joan Barry in 1945 as the father of her illegitimate daughter, although blood tests proved he could not have fathered the baby. He still pays $100 a month toward the child's support. Chaplin cites the "impossible" paternity verdict as part of the "vilification" campaign that allegedly drove him from the U.S. and into exile in 1952. He's been happily married since 1943 to Oona O'Neill, daughter of playwright Eugene O'Neill. He married Oona when she was 18, and they now have seven children. Their last child was born in 1959, when Chaplin was 70. Charlie also has two grown sons by his second wife, Lita Grey. In all his moods, Charles Chaplin is still good copy, retaining his flair for the pungent, quotable phrase. "I'm known in Tibetan lamaseries where they never heard of Jesus Christ," he snapped to one reporter.

♕ June, 1960.

Today, Charlie Chaplin—
the little tramp—is
on the outside looking
in, as in this scene
from The Circus. Now,
after 20 years of play-
ing other roles, he is
planning to revive his
baggy-pants hero in
his 86th film.
From his home in Vevey,
Switzerland, Chaplin
has also been writing
his autobiography.
Assailed, admired,
hounded and desired,
the "Clown Without a Country"
turns a furrowed face
at a still-fascinated public.

As in all eras, they flash on stage, smiling and expectant—the adored, the glamorous, the beautiful. And then, in an almost inexorable compensation, the cost of their public posture is their individuality, their serenity, and eventually their fulfillment as anonymous human beings.

The Penalty of Beauty

SORAYA   The anguished woman at the right typifies them all. A queen in the traditional sense, selected by her king for her exotic beauty, she discovered how fleeting is even royalty. Because the same capricious nature which provided her with so much in appearance also denied her the capacity to bear a child, she was discarded by her husband and returned, whence she came, into the world of the commoner—an ex-wife and an ex-queen.

MARLENE DIETRICH   Of all the glamour ladies in this generation she is by far the most durable and the most elusive. Those who know her well insist that her bucolic origins make her in truth a warm and embracing friend. But Marlene, the glamour symbol, exists even more for the world than for her intimates. Committed to the aura of taunting remoteness, she plays the game as she finds shelter behind a smoky swirl of her special mystique.

TUESDAY WELD   An infant in a big girl's body with a big girl's posturing, she grows up far too fast, softening before she ripens. But the world of show business must market this kind of merchandise to accommodate a curious public. Far more than her competitors, Tuesday possesses a unique talent which she ambitiously provides while older observers speculate as to its eventual effect on the soul of this precocious provider.

ELIZABETH TAYLOR   What remained constant, from the moment of her birth, was her award of almost limitless beauty. But almost nothing else in her life did. For a while it seemed as though she would find the key in her marriage to Mike Todd, until death tore him from her. The public took out after her when she captured her good friend's husband. Then she fought and overcame almost fatal illness and now, as Mrs. Eddie Fisher, she struggles to find evenness in life which seems so cruelly to keep eluding her.

DEBBIE REYNOLDS   The teenager grown up made a fairy-princess marriage and suffered the anguish of a tawdry dissolution. She bit her lip and nervously fingered her baby's diaper pin as a relentless press corps pressed her for details of her own heartbreak. But she survived the worst and earned the cheers of all for her discipline and dignity and for her comeback into stability.

INGRID BERGMAN   She first came to America carrying her baby papoose-style on her back. The world adored her for her wholesomeness, her windblown cleanliness. As her marriages and affairs foundered, the same world passed harsh judgment on her but never permitted her the privacy of being shunned. And then it forgave her and loves her as she is now, a wiser woman, polished into greater beauty by the emery board of experience.

MARILYN MONROE   She has run the gantlet from poverty and fear to fame and fortune. But despite the adulation, the richness of her professional life, the elegant men of her marriages, fear will not abandon her and security never envelops her. And many wonder whether she has yet passed the worst in the long run of life's gantlet.

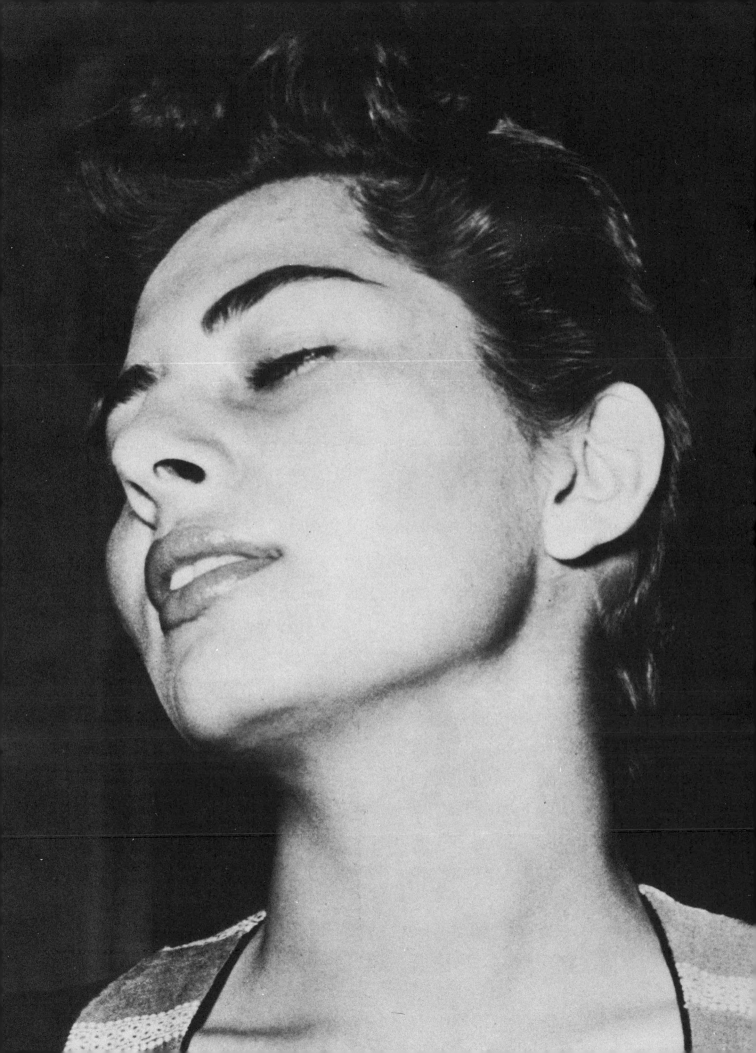

He was, in his own judgment, "a link with a very distant past . . . the last survivor of an epoch dead and gone." He wrote these words in his own obituary two decades ago, modestly assuming that by now he would be gone and almost forgotten. Yet he lives still, one of the century's greatest minds, not in luxurious, contemplative retirement, but in active, intellectual pursuit, issuing stern warnings about the dangers of nuclear experimentations and their effects on a generation he will never see.

Bertrand Russell's Own Obit

BY BERTRAND RUSSELL

BY THE DEATH OF THE THIRD EARL RUSSELL (OR Bertrand Russell, as he preferred to call himself) at the age of ninety, a link with a very distant past is severed. His grandfather Lord John Russell, the Victorian Prime Minister, visited Napoleon in Elba; his maternal grandmother was a friend of the Young Pretender's widow.

In his youth he did work of importance in mathematical logic, but his eccentric attitude during the First World War revealed a lack of balanced judgment which increasingly affected his later writings. Perhaps this is attributable, at least in part, to the fact that he did not enjoy the advantages of a public-school education; he was taught at home by tutors until the age of eighteen, when he entered Trinity College, Cambridge, becoming seventh Wrangler in 1893 and a Fellow in 1895.

During the fifteen years that followed, he produced the books upon which his reputation in the learned world was based: *The Foundations of Geometry, The Philosophy of Leibniz, The Principles of Mathematics* and (in collaboration with Dr. A. N. Whitehead), *Principia Mathematica.* This last work, which was of great importance in its day, doubtless owed much of its superiority to Dr. (afterward Professor) Whitehead, a man who, as his subsequent writings showed, was possessed of that insight and spiritual depth so notably absent in Russell; for

Russell's argumentation, ingenious and clever as it is, ignores always those higher considerations that transcend mere logic.

This lack of spiritual depth became painfully evident during the First World War, when Russell, although (to do him justice) he never minimized the wrong done to Belgium, perversely maintained that, war being an evil, the aim of statesmanship should have been to bring the war to an end as soon as possible, which would have been achieved by British neutrality and a German victory.

It must be supposed that mathematical studies had caused him to take a merely quantitative view, which ignored the questions of principle involved. Throughout the war, he continued to urge that it should be ended, on no matter what terms. Trinity College, very properly, deprived him of his lectureship, and for some months of 1918 he was in prison.

In the year 1930 he paid a brief visit to Russia, whose government did not impress him favorably, and a longer visit to China, where he enjoyed that rationalism of the traditional civilization, with its still surviving flavor of the eighteenth century.

In subsequent years his energies were dissipated in writings advocating socialism, educational reforms and a less rigid code of morals as regards marriage. At times, however, he returned to less topical subjects. His historical writings, by their style and their wit, conceal from careless readers the superficiality of his thought and are not without value as a *reductio ad absurdum* of the antiquated rationalism which he professed to the end.

In the Second World War he took no public part, having escaped to a neutral country just before its outbreak. In private conversation he was wont to say that homicidal lunatics were well employed in killing each other, but that sensible men would keep out of their way while they were doing it.

Fortunately, his outlook, which, reminiscent of Bentham and John Stuart Mill (who was his godfather), has become rare in this age, which recognizes that heroism has a value independent of its utility. True, much of what was once the civilized world lies in ruins; but no right-thinking person can admit that those who died for the right in the great struggle have died in vain.

His life, for all its waywardness, had a certain anachronistic consistency, reminiscent of that of the aristocratic rebels of the early nineteenth century. His principles were curious, but, such as they were, they served to govern his actions.

In private life he showed none of the acerbity which marred his writings, but was a genial conversationalist and not devoid of human sympathy. He had many friends, but had survived almost all.

Nevertheless, to those few friends who remained he appeared, even in extreme old age, full of enjoyment of life, no doubt owing, in large measure, to the happiness of his private circumstances, for politically, during his last years, he was as isolated as Milton after the Restoration.

He was the last survivor of an epoch dead and gone.

👑 September, 1941